MÉXICO BEYOND 1968

EDITED BY JAIME M. PENSADO
AND ENRIQUE C. OCHOA

MÉXICO
BEYOND 1968

*Revolutionaries, Radicals, and Repression During
the Global Sixties and Subversive Seventies*

THE UNIVERSITY OF
ARIZONA PRESS
TUCSON

The University of Arizona Press
www.uapress.arizona.edu

ISBN-13: 978-0-8165-3842-3 (paper)

Cover design by Leigh McDonald
Cover illustration: *Libertad de expresión* by Adolfo Mexiac, 1968

This book is made possible in part by support from the Institute for Scholarship in the Liberal Arts, College of Arts and Letters, University of Notre Dame.

Library of Congress Cataloging-in-Publication Data
Names: Pensado, Jaime M., 1972– editor. | Ochoa, Enrique, editor.
Title: México beyond 1968 : revolutionaries, radicals, and repression during the global sixties and subversive seventies / edited by Jaime M. Pensado and Enrique C. Ochoa.
Description: Tucson : The University of Arizona Press, 2018. | Includes bibliographical references and index.
Identifiers: LCCN 2018008709 | ISBN 9780816538423 (pbk. : alk. paper)
Subjects: LCSH: Mexico—Politics and government—20th century. | Mexico—Social conditions—20th century. | Social movements—Mexico—History—20th century. | Protest movements—Mexico—History—20th century. | Political culture—Mexico—History—20th century.
Classification: LCC F1236 M47166 2018 | DDC 972.08/2—dc23 LC record available at https://lccn.loc.gov/2018008709

Printed in the United States of America
♾ This paper meets the requirements of ANSI/NISO Z39.48-1992 (Permanence of Paper).

CONTENTS

PREFACE

Mexico Today

JAIME M. PENSADO AND ENRIQUE C. OCHOA

OVER THE PAST DECADE, well over 120,000 people have been killed in Mexico, 30,000 forcibly disappeared, and more than 250,000 driven from their homes.[1] While much of this violence is linked to drug wars, the governments of Felipe Calderón and Enrique Peña Nieto erroneously portray those killed or disappeared as criminals and imply that those deaths and disappearances are justified. However, the actual impact reaches well beyond the drug trade and the state's war against it. Neoliberal policies implemented since the 1980s have led to the expulsion of hundreds of thousands of campesinos from the countryside, forcing them to migrate throughout Mexico and to the United States, exacerbating internal dislocations. By attributing the deaths to "criminal elements," the state purposefully downplays the complex forces at work, its complicity in the widespread physical and structural violence, and the ways that crime, drugs, and economic policy are intimately related. At the heart of this is the militarization of society coupled with the devastating impact of neoliberal capitalism that has exacerbated the legacy of colonialism, racism, sexism, and overall inequality.

Mexico's devastating economic crisis in the 1980s and 1990s, coupled with the neoliberal response, led to the shredding of the nation's already tattering social fabric. Deep cuts to inadequate social programs spurred a series of popular movements. Throughout these years, grassroots movements in the countryside and the urban areas both challenged the hegemony of the ruling Partido Revolucionario Institucional (Institutional Revolutionary Party, or PRI) and led to major electoral challenges, although fraud led to the PRI's continuance in power until 2000. The 1994 Zapatista uprising and the emergence of other guerrilla movements shook the foundations of PRI rule. While there were political openings and more competitive elections, much of this has been a formality.

The opening of the economic system unleashed a massive wealth transfer, enriching a handful of Mexican millionaires and billionaires and making Mexico the second most unequal country in the world.[2] As many observers have pointed out, it is not coincidental that Mexico's increase in militarization and violence has occurred as social movements have proliferated.[3] Like financial aid, military aid is fungible. The massive U.S. aid to its neighbor in the south for military weaponry in the name of the Drug War during the administration of the Partido de Acción Nacional (National Action Party, PAN), from 2000 to 2012, and since the return of the PRI in 2012, has also been employed to stifle social movements. This violence occurs with impunity since over 98 percent of deaths go unsolved.[4] The recent state repression and state-sanctioned violence are linked to neoliberal policies and the resistance they engendered.

The disappearance of the forty-three students of the Escuela Normal Rural (Rural National Teachers' College) "Raúl Isidro Burgos" in Ayotzinapa, Guerrero, in 2014 demonstrates both how the state obscures its role in political violence and the complex forces at work. Award-winning Mexican journalist Anabel Hernández has recently drawn the connections between the student radicalism of the *normales rurales* and the state's efforts to silence these students. According to Hernández, "From the time that [Mexican President] Peña Nieto assumed power [in 2012], he and his cabinet considered the normal school students from Ayotzinapa a 'national security priority.'"[5] That controlling mobilizations of the Ayotzinapa students was deemed the number two top national security threat, while drug trafficking and criminal activity didn't even make the list, underscores the intimate relationship between militarization, state violence, and stifling popular dissent.[6] Hernández's exposé points to the complex forces at work in perpetuating and then obscuring state violence, all the while defaming, dehumanizing, and then erasing its victims.

The dissection of the origins and impunity of violence against members of social movements and everyday peoples shows that the case of the forty-three missing Ayotzinapa students is unfortunately not the exception. Since the 1990s, escalating rates of *feminicidio* (femicide), the murder of women in the context of misogynist and patriarchal systems of power, was met with alarm in Ciudad Juárez and led to the creation of a courageous popular movement that has

been increasingly visible while raising awareness about gender violence throughout Mexico. Nevertheless, these movements have been met by government
stonewalling and impunity.[7] Consequently, feminicidios and sexual assaults
continue to increase throughout Mexico, amidst official silence and impunity;
the number of women murdered daily has risen from approximately 6.3 in 2014
to at least 7 women killed each day in 2017.[8]

Organized crime has permeated multiple sectors of society, including universities. Most recently, at the Autonomous University of Tamaulipas (UAT),
Héctor Alejandro Villanueva García was arrested after being accused of "kidnapping and extortion." A leading figure of the Schools of Law and Political
Science, Villanueva García was allegedly a representative member of the Zetas,
one of Mexico's most notorious criminal organizations. As a school authority,
he was in charge of student affairs and, as a loyal supporter of Juan Fernando
"El Ferrari" Álvarez Cortez, he laundered money for the Zetas. According to
Proceso, Villanueva García also used his position at UAT to recruit *porros* as
drug traffickers and *sicarios* (hit men).[9] Porros have been employed as agents
provocateurs since the 1950s, but they had been historically contained within
the mechanisms of control facilitated by the state. In the 1970s porros began
trafficking drugs inside the schools and played an instrumental role as agent of
repression. But today, as the case of Villanueva García and others demonstrate,
the use of porros is no longer delimited to the apparatus of the state. As the
lines between the state and drug traffickers continue to blur, it is essential to
understand that its roots go back to Mexico's Dirty Wars of the 1960s and 1970s.

Press freedoms and access to information have also been under assault.
Since 2000 about 125 journalists have been murdered, about 25 disappeared,
and since 2010 nearly 800 have been severely harassed with threats and break-
ins to their homes and offices.[10] Few of the murders and crimes have been
solved, even when security footage exists. The chilling effect of this violence
is notable as Daniel Moreno, the editor of *Animal Político*, recently remarked,
"Freedom of expression here becomes a myth . . . [given] the fact that the
authorities have proven they are incapable of solving most crimes against journalists, and are often the perpetrators of this violence themselves, then we can
legitimately say that journalism is in a state of emergency in this country."[11]
In 2017 it was revealed that the Mexican government has been systematically
spying on human rights advocates, journalists, lawyers, consumer advocates, and
their families using sophisticated software that was meant to surveil criminals
and drug traffickers. The use of millions of dollars to spy on citizens exercising

their democratic rights has sparked outrage.[12] The increasing sophistication of surveillance builds on the surveillance state that was created during the 1960s and 1970s and adds to the traditional repertoires of state violence. These forms of censorship also extend to historical research, since with the return of the PRI to power in 2012, the documents related to recent Mexican history and state violence became more difficult to access, and in 2015, academic access to these sources was closed.[13]

The chapters in the book provide some of the historical context for understanding current violence and repression in "México"—a name we highlight in the title in reference to a vast and far from homogenous nation.[14] While some regions enjoyed greater political stability and economic prosperity during the 1960s and 1970s, others, including many of the regions and local communities examined in the book, did not. Through analyzing a number of struggles throughout rural and urban Mexico and divergent notions of radicalism and state repression during this period, the book rejects the Mexican state as "exceptional" and challenges the centrality of the 1968 movement. The 1968 student movement is treated here not as a watershed of the nation's history of democracy, as commonly stressed in the historiography of post-revolutionary Mexico, but as an important historical movement that is connected to a broader history of struggle and repression. It is during this period that the tools of state repression, including surveillance, co-optation, *porrismo* (the use of porros as agents of mediation and repression), disappearance, torture, and murder, were refined and employed to stifle popular, guerrilla, and social movements up until the present day.

México Beyond 1968: Revolutionaries, Radicals, and Repression During the Global Sixties and Subversive Seventies emerges from our long collaboration together. Since the late 1990s when Jaime was an undergraduate and graduate student at California State University, Los Angeles, we developed a close working relationship that was built on a mutual passion for learning, social justice, and the history of greater Mexico. Enrique was born and raised in Los Angeles, the largest metropolitan area of Mexicanas/os outside of Mexico City, and Jaime migrated to the same city in the mid-1980s. We connected in our belief in the importance of studying and teaching Mexican history in a society (the United States) with a significant Mexican and Latinx population that has been publicly denied a full understanding of the deep history of Mexico in the United States. The process of colonialism and coloniality as it plays out in the U.S. academy erases knowledge systems and the deep histories and ways of knowing that communities have. We see it as our goal to unlock the hidden histories of power to understand how power works, the structures of inequality, and the long history of resistance. For us, this must be done through a broad collaboration that challenges the conservative, elitist, and assimilationist structures of the academy. One important step in this process has been to work to foster the expansion of Mexican/Latinx scholars in the writing of history.

The study of Mexican history in the United States, like the field of Latin American studies, has its roots in U.S. hetero-patriarchal colonial and capitalist domination.[15] Therefore, it has been dominated by white scholars with little contact with Mexican or Latinx communities in the United States, and this has been reinforced by the nation-state focus of the study of history. When Enrique was a graduate student in the late 1980s and early 1990s in the United States, there was only one Mexican American historian of modern Mexico, Ramón Eduardo Ruíz (UC San Diego), teaching at a Research 1 university. While affirmative action and diversity programs have made some inroads since then, as this volume attests, such programs are still woefully inadequate. Instead, given the crisis in higher education funding, we argue that, using the logic of meritocracy and reduced funding, programs in the United States have been complicit in further restricting working-class students of color.

It is in this spirit that in October 2016 we brought together at the University of Notre Dame an intimate group of critical scholars who have been researching Mexican authoritarianism and state violence, as well as social and guerrilla movements, and who seek to intervene in political debate by engaging a broader public and by working with communities with long histories of resistance. Nearly all of the contributors have deep roots in broader Mexico, including communities in the United States. By centering the scholarship of Mexican, Chicanx, and Latinx scholars, we underscore that how we do history is just as important as what we do. We know that those who write history shape the narrative and that narrative has power. We have gathered together a passionate group of scholars for whom the production of knowledge is representative of power, and herein lies the second reason why we have employed the term "México" in the title. The authors bring to the center the work of Mexican scholars who have published in Spanish. All too often, the history of Mexico published in the United States and Europe marginalizes Mexican scholars or buries their arguments in the footnotes. Mexico, student movements, revolutionary organizing, and state repression are not just academic areas of interest for several of the authors here. For them, these topics and events are personal, and they have shaped their lives.

NOTES

1. While the figures are contested, there is a growing acceptance of the reports of human rights organizations. See Meade's introduction to Valdez Cárdenas's *The Taken*, 4; and Staudt and Méndez, *Courage, Resistance, and Women*, 1.
2. OECD, "Crisis Squeezed Income."
3. See Rochlin, *Redefining Mexican "Security"*; Gledhill, *La cara oculta*.
4. Azam Ahmed, "In Mexico, 'It's Easy to Kill a Journalist,'" *New York Times*, April 29, 2017.
5. Hernández, *La verdadera noche*, 51.
6. Ibid., 52; and Aviña, "Mexico's Long Dirty War."
7. See Staudt and Méndez, *Courage, Resistance, and Women*.
8. Nájar, "Feminicidio en México"; Larios, "El infierno cotidiano."
9. Cedillo, "Operador de los Zetas."
10. Ahmed, "In Mexico, 'It's Easy to Kill a Journalist'"; and Ureste, "La impunidad mata a periodistas."
11. Ahmed, "In Mexico, 'It's Easy to Kill a Journalist.'"
12. Nichole Pearlroth, "Spyware's Odd Targets: Backers of Mexican Soda Tax," *New York Times*, February 11, 2017; and Azam Ahmed and Nichole Pearlroth, "Using Texts as Lures, Government Spyware Targets Mexican Activists and their Families," *New York Times*, June 19, 2017.
13. Gornea and Noel, "Mexico Quietly Placed Archives."
14. As micro history has shown for decades, there is not one, but many Mexicos.
15. González, *Culture of Empire*; Soldatenko, *Chicano Studies*. See also Salvatore, *Disciplinary Conquest*.

BIBLIOGRAPHY

NEWSPAPERS

New York Times

OTHER SOURCES

Aviña, Alexander. "Mexico's Long Dirty War." *NACLA Report on the Americas* 48, no. 2, (Summer 2016): 144–49.
Cedillo, Juan Alberto. "Operador de los Zetas era jefe de área en la Universidad Autónoma de Tamaulipas." *Proceso*, October 18, 2017.
Gledhill, John. *La cara oculta de la inseguridad en México*. Mexico City: Paidós, 2017.

Gornea, Gabriela, and Andrea Noel. "Mexico Quietly Placed Archives Related to Its 'Dirty War' Under Lock and Key." *Vice News*, April 15, 2015.

González, Gilbert G. *Culture of Empire: American Writers, Mexico, and Mexican Immigrants, 1880–1930*. Austin: University of Texas Press, 2004.

Hernández, Anabel. *La verdadera noche de Iguala: La historia que el gobierno trató de ocultar*. New York: Vintage Español, 2016.

Larios, Manuel. "El infierno cotidiano de las mujeres en México," *Newsweek en Español*, November 17, 2017. http://nwnoticias.com/#!/noticias/el-infierno-cotidiano-de-las-mujeres-en-mexico.

Meade, Everard. Introduction to *The Taken: True Stories of the Sinaloa Drug War*, by Javier Valdez Cárdenas, 3–52. Translated by Everard Meade. Norman: University of Oklahoma Press, 2017.

Nájar, Alberto. "Feminicidio en México: Mara Castilla, el asesinato de una joven de 19 años en un taxi que indigna a un país violento." *BBC Mundo México*, September 17, 2017. http://www.bbc.com/mundo/noticias-america-latina-41303542.

OECD (Organization for Economic Cooperation and Development). "Crisis Squeezed Income and Puts Pressure on Inequality and Poverty." 2013. Accessed June 24, 2017. http://www.oecd.org/els/soc/OECD2013-Inequality-and-Poverty-8p.pdf.

Rochlin, James F. *Redefining Mexican "Security": Society, State, and Region Under NAFTA*. Boulder, Colo.: Lynne Rienner, 1997.

Salvatore, Ricardo D. *Disciplinary Conquest: U.S. Scholars in South America, 1900–1945*. Durham, N.C.: Duke University Press, 2016.

Soldatenko, Michael. *Chicano Studies: Genesis of a Discipline*. Tucson: University of Arizona Press, 2009.

Staudt, Kathleen, and Zulma Y. Méndez. *Courage, Resistance, and Women in Ciudad Juárez: Challenges to Militarization*. Austin: University of Texas Press, 2015.

Ureste, Manu. "La impunidad mata a periodistas: 4 homicidios en mes y medio; aún no hay culpables sentenciados." *Animal Político*, April 15, 2017.

ACKNOWLEDGMENTS

THE BOOK EMERGED FROM a conference organized by the Mexico Working Group at the University of Notre Dame. We are grateful for the generous support we received from various institutions affiliated with the university, including the Helen Kellogg Institute for International Studies, the Institute for Scholarship in the Liberal Arts, the History Department, and the Institute for Latino Studies. We thank all the participants of this conference for the vigorous discussion and debate. In addition to the authors published here, we would like to acknowledge the other participants, including Ted Beatty, Guillermo Trejo, Sandra Mendiola-García, Maria Muñoz, Lindsey Passenger Wieck, Ryne Clos, Robert Palermo, and Augusto Rocha Ramírez. We are particularly thankful to Therese Hanlon and to those from the Kellogg Institute who helped us organize the conference. We give special thanks to Carla Villanueva for her extraordinary help and enthusiasm in helping us organize the conference and playing a leading role with the Mexico Working Group.

We would like to thank the contributors of this book for their cooperation in transforming an exciting conference into *México Beyond 1968: Revolutionaries, Radicals, and Repression During the Global Sixties and Subversive Seventies*. Kristen Buckles and the staff at the University of Arizona Press, especially Stacey Wujcik, Amanda Krause, and copyeditor Joyce Parks, have been outstanding. We also thank the anonymous readers for their excellent recommendations and insightful questions.

Finally, we thank our families for their love and support with this project.

Jaime M. Pensado and Enrique C. Ochoa

MÉXICO BEYOND 1968

INTRODUCTION

MÉXICO BEYOND 1968

Revolutionaries, Radicals, and Repression

JAIME M. PENSADO AND ENRIQUE C. OCHOA

DURING THE 1960S AND 1970S, a series of popular, intellectual, artistic, and revolutionary movements sought to directly challenge the uneven capitalist growth and state repression that characterized Mexico's "economic miracle." These diverse movements envisioned a more democratic nation with a more equitable distribution of wealth. For some this meant a return to the Cardenismo of the 1930s, while for others it meant the creation of a mass-based socialist revolution that would be in the interest of the workers, campesinos, and other victims of colonialism and capitalism. Revolutionaries and radicals during this period drew on Marxist and other revolutionary theories and applied them to the deep histories and social conditions in Mexico's various regions.

These revolutionary movements emerged during the much-vaunted period of the Mexican Miracle. This period, from the 1940s to the 1960s, was characterized by a "stabilizing development" with high rates of economic growth that averaged 6 percent a year and low inflation rates. It was spurred by public investment in modernization programs that led to rapid urban industrialization, the expansion of capitalist agriculture and defunding of campesino agriculture with the "Green Revolution," the centralization of state power, and a more harmonious relationship of the state with the United States, the private sector, and the Catholic Church. Coupled with these material transformations was the construction of a Mexican nationalism that promoted national unity. Together the façades of economic modernization and cultural nationalism served to mask the deleterious impact that capitalist transformation, the rein-forcement of authoritarian political structures, the stifling of union democracy, internal government disputes and contested local elections, rural and popular uprisings, rampant income inequality, and political repression had on workers, campesinos/as, and indigenous communities.[1]

The social and revolutionary movements of the 1960s and 1970s examined in this book took a variety of forms, including militant strikes, land invasions, cross-country marches, independent forums, popular organizing, and urban and rural guerrilla uprisings. These were infused with a mix of Third World and Marxist revolutionary ideas coupled with new countercultural expressions. But above all, the divergent radicalisms that emerged during this period were most frequently framed in favor or in rejection of a long history of popular resistance and local legacies of struggle rooted, among others, in competing and often institutionalized notions of Zapatismo, Cardenismo, and Catholic traditions. Independently, for the most part, they challenged state power, the Partido Revolucionario Institucional (Institutional Revolutionary Party, PRI), and its alliances with local and regional power structures. In response, state-sanctioned violence led to the death of thousands of people and many more imprisoned, kidnapped, disappeared, and tortured.[2] These Dirty Wars included efforts to crush or co-opt popular organizing and youthful rebellions through social and cultural policy and coercion, coupled with innovative (and repressive) forms of espionage, the use of revolutionary and/or religious rhetoric, and the publication of apocryphal news coverage and government-sponsored literature that aimed to discredit those who joined the various radical movements that proliferated during this period.

As Mexico came to represent the first Third World and Latin American country to host the Olympics in 1968, a massive student movement exposed the nation's mechanisms of state control and repression.[3] The façade of political stability came to an end with the state's cold-blooded repression on October 2, 1968, as government soldiers fired upon a peaceful demonstration, killing more than a hundred people and wounding many more in Mexico City's historical plaza of Tlatelolco. An undetermined number of student organizers were then arrested and jailed, effectively driving the creatively organized student move-ment underground. The student movement had galvanized youth and various sectors of society to call attention to the contradictions of the Mexican miracle.

While much has been written on the 1968 student movement, these accounts have often minimized the importance of earlier and subsequent revolts and have tended to reduce '68 to the October 2 massacre in Tlatelolco.[4] This literature has portrayed the strike as a unified movement, has overemphasized the role of leftist male leaders in Mexico City, and has caricatured both the Right and the Left.[5] *México Beyond 1968: Revolutionaries, Radicals, and Repression During the Global Sixties and Subversive Seventies* complicates these traditional narratives of youth radicalism and places urban and rural rebellions within the political context of the nation's Dirty Wars during the 1960s and 1970s. In doing so, it pays attention to the lasting legacies of the Mexican Revolution (1910–17), the labor strikes of the 1950s, the Cuban Revolution, and the Tlatelolco massacre. But in doing so, the authors also point to additional influential moments that further shaped the radicalism of the era but have only received scant attention in the historiography: namely, the lasting effects of the Cristero Rebellion (1926–29) in the Cold War context; the defunding of popular education on the part of the state in the 1940s, '50s, and '60s; the various anticommunist campaigns launched by competing sectors of the Church in the 1960s; the dramatic, yet failed assault of the Madera barracks on September 23, 1965, in the state of Chihuahua; and the June 10, 1971, Corpus Christi student massacre when dozens of young people were killed in Mexico City at the hands of the government-sponsored paramilitary group Los Halcones (the Hawks).

The contributors to the book explore the multiple expressions of democracy that developed from the ground up in different regions of Mexico with particular attention on Chihuahua, Guerrero, Jalisco, Mexico City, Puebla, and Nuevo León, where state repression were most noticeable.[6] They also examine student movements and organizations that aimed at forging a broad national student movement that felt the brunt of state repression but have received little attention from historians, namely the Federación de Estudiantes Campesinos Socialistas de México (Mexican Federation of Campesino Socialist Students, FECSM), the Central Nacional de Estudiantes Democráticos (National Organization of Democratic Students, CNED), and Política Popular (Popular Politics).[7] In addition, the authors include voices from various parts of Mexico that remain marginalized in the literature, including those of young peasants from the *escuelas normales rurales*, conservative Catholic students, right-wing youth groups, post-1968 activists, young indigenous leaders, working-class barrio youth, and political prisoners. The result is a nuanced portrait that questions, among other concepts associated with radicalism, the rigid division one often finds in the literature between the "Old" and the "New" Left.[8] But the authors of *México Beyond 1968* also take into consideration the internal contradictions, disputes, and paradoxes that shaped the outcome of the various movements led by leftist and conservative actors, as well as the cross-class networking and unique relationships that young radicals developed as rural and/or urban activists. Similarly, as the authors blur the lines between rural and urban forms of radicalism, they also expand restricted definitions of both the Left and the Right by analyzing the various *izquierdas* and *derechas* that emerged across the country during the most turbulent years of the Cold War period.[9]

In situating their respective case studies within the local, national, and global contexts of the 1960s and '70s, the authors complicate our understanding of the *priista* government (the PRI), presenting it not simply as a monolithic, powerful, or weak representative of an "exceptional" state, as frequently depicted in the literature, but rather as an often-contradictory state party that modernized its legal and extralegal mechanisms of control to negotiate with and/or repress those who defied its authority during these years.[10] Political violence and co-optation, however, are not presented here exclusively in relation to a homogenous PRI. In complicating this constricted view, the authors examine the distinct "gray zones" of power that proliferated in various regions of Cold War Mexico in tandem with the multiple social movements that voiced their social and political discontent during this period. These, explains Pansters, are spaces "'where the deeds and networks of violent entrepreneurs, political actors and law enforcement officials secretly meet and mesh,' that is, where the boundaries between state and nonstate, violent and nonviolent actors become blurred."[11]

Specifically, the chapters elucidate important case studies ranging from analyses of competing powerbrokers within the government and leading institutions of the political opposition, the private sector, and the Church to detailed studies that point to the variety of "contact zones," or local spaces where the broader rhetoric, ideas, institutions, and instruments of coercion of the Cold War permeated with everyday practices, behavior, and experiences.[12] These include clandestine prisons, student newspapers, rural schools, street gangs, student organizations, school assemblies, provincial universities, and government-sponsored rural stores and theaters. Emphasis is also given to the myriad radicalisms of young people and the effects and consequences associated with their multiple interactions with divergent sectors of society, namely rural teaching communities, local institutions governed by powerful caciques (local bosses), leftist and right-wing intellectuals, religious and indigenous leaders, and progressive figures in the government.

México Beyond 1968 examines competing notions of democracy and political violence not entirely as isolated phenomena, strictly defined by local history, but rather—as Zolov argues in this volume—as a culture of the "Global Sixties" era (1960s, c. 1956–c. 1973) with shared language, myths, rituals, and behavior.[13] This period, which in the 1970s (c. 1965–c. 1980) took more "subversive" overtones, represented a unique moment in history, characterized, on one hand, by the emergence of a distinct spirit of utopia and revolution and, on the other, by a novel rhythm of despair and political violence.[14] Innovative notions of democracy emerged at the center of this tension across the world. These were often epitomized for a new generation of activists by the liberation movements in China, Africa, Cuba, and Vietnam. For many of them, the term *liberation* became the key word of the day.[15] Without question, its field of meanings was political and contested. For example, the term was centrally linked to an unprecedented awareness of international solidarity and an overwhelming rejection of imperialism and new forms of colonialism.[16] For many, including young activists in Mexico, it served as part of an innovative "language of dissent" and "egalitarian ethos" that young male and female student activists embraced to confront capitalism as well as the reformism, authoritarian structure, and corporatist apparatus of older Communist parties, labor movements, and intellectuals.[17] But similar to other parts of the world, liberation in Mexico meant something broadly cultural and religious as well.[18]

By contrast, for influential actors in competing positions of power in Mexico as well as for a new generation of conservative and right-wing students, the different radical expressions of "liberation" expressed during the 1960s and '70s denoted specific "threats" to the status quo. Allegedly, these threatened national unity, the nation's Catholic identity, and traditional notions of masculinity and femininity. For influential conservatives, including leading figures of the state, this period did not represent a moment ripe for revolution, but one of chaos and immorality in which the lines between the countercultural and the political were frequently blurred. Yet, as the most conservative activists of the Right rediscovered the writing of iconic Catholic and Hispanic figures during this period, they also drew from the examples and writings of leftist radicals, such as Ernesto "Ché" Guevara, and like their leftist counterparts, they too called for the creation of a "New Man."[19] Consequently, in this blossoming of youthful radicalism, competing voices within and outside the state demanded "law and order," and in so doing, they either justified or turned a blind eye to the expansion of the repressive apparatus of the government as spaces for democratic participation were being closed. Right-wing activists also launched their own disruptive movements with new conservative ideas, values, and specific projects that further polarized these turbulent years of the Cold War period.

The state as well as the various sectors of Mexico's conservative society accused young left-wing activists of adopting "foreign" ideologies. But as many of the authors demonstrate in their respective chapters, these activists were far from mere cannon fodder manipulated by *manos extrañas* (foreign elements), as the leading representatives of the state, the media, and the Catholic Church so readily insisted. The authors indeed demonstrate that leftist activists embraced a variety of socialist and communist ideas and often had links with the youth wing of the Mexican Communist Party, but these responses were overwhelmingly rooted in homegrown realities. Similarly, the radicalism of the far Right was also overwhelmingly expressed in what Herrán refers to as a "Post-Cristero" view of Cold War Mexico. Some of these conservative movements framed their activism in religious terms while others, such as Conciencia Joven (Conscious Youth) in Monterrey, understood their movement in relation to their entrepreneurial and local free-market identity. Both framed their activism in the global context of the 1960s and '70s.

México Beyond 1968 examines the repercussions of state repression as well as the various forms of symbolic and physical violence associated with the multiple Dirty Wars that took place during the López Mateos (1958–64) and especially the Díaz Ordaz (1964–70) and Echeverría Álvarez (1970–76) presidential administrations. In some of the cases examined by the authors, the repression that Mexicans experienced at the hands of the military, local caciques, paramilitary groups, and official government agents during these years rose to the level of state terrorism.[20] For those who felt the weight of the state the most, particularly in regions with large campesino and indigenous communities, the priísta system was not representative of a *dictablanda* but of a brutal regime that too frequently relied on force and coercion.[21] The emphasis on "soft authoritarianism," we argue, not only abates the magnitude of state repression that characterized the 1960s and '70s, but also supports the notion that Mexico was exceptional for not being as authoritarian as other countries in Latin America. Instead, this volume argues that much like its southern neighbors, the Mexican state modernized its mechanisms of political repression and intelligence surveillance during this period and with the collaboration of the United States embarked on its own Dirty War, not as a pawn of the imperialist North, but as a key global actor of the era.[22]

In stressing the repressive nature of the Mexican state, the book gives special attention to counterrevolutionary actions, but it also examines various forms of legal and extralegal mechanisms of control promoted by competing institutions of power that ranged from co-optation to *porrismo* (the use of agents provocateurs to negotiate with and/or repress student activists), imprisonment, disappearance, torture, and murder. The authors of *México Beyond 1968* explore a broad range of perspectives on youth radicalism hitherto overlooked in the literature, including those articulated by a press often sympathetic to the government, agencies of espionage that reached new levels of impunity, a business sector that did not always agree with the populist rhetoric of the government, rural local bosses who defended their autonomy, labor unions and intellectuals who embraced and/or rejected independence from the state, and a Catholic Church that had to deal with its own polarization. Collectively, the authors present those who engaged in militancy to contest state repression and demand a more democratic nation, including many who opted for armed struggle, not as "mindless dupes," "dogmatic conspirators," or "self-destructive avengers," as frequently depicted in the literature, but rather as thoughtful and hopeful rational actors who fought against state terror.[23]

México Beyond 1968 intervenes in two growing historiographic tendencies. In examining this history, some of the authors frame their respective studies within the rubric of the Global Sixties. Others see less value in adopting the term and instead explicitly examine their studies in the particular context of the '70s or the more "subversive" years of the *guerra sucia*, a period of Mexico's Dirty War that first intensified in the mid-1960s, as evident in the repressive campaigns that proliferated in rural communities in the aftermath of the 1965 barracks attack in Madera, Chihuahua, examined in this volume. For those who embraced the radicalism of the era, insurgent or subversive politics often meant a militant, even violent act of defiance that some came to believe was necessary to expose the brutality of the state. Yet, for those in power, the concept of "subversion" provided the legal and illegal mechanisms to amplify and justify state repression against anyone who challenged the authority of the state.[24] By including both of these conceptual frameworks in the title of the book—the "Global Sixties" and the "Subversive Seventies"—we hope to inspire debate about this broader period (c. 1956–c. 1980).

In sum, by not seeing the Mexican state during the 1960s and '70s as exceptional, and by challenging the myth of 1968, we are free to understand the important, complex, and brutal history of underground struggles and state repression in broader Mexico throughout this period. This multifaceted but interconnected history, we argue, blurs the lines between the rural and urban divide and highlights the limitations of the so-called moderate, soft, and/or inclusionary nature of the authoritarian priísta regime during the fading years of its "golden age."[25] Moreover, as we noted in our preface, it also sheds historical light on the nation's current situation of institutional racism (as a form of violence), land dispossession, organized crime, socioeconomic marginalization, coercion, insecurity, impunity, militarization, illegal espionage, and lack of accountability and rule of law.[26] Just as in the 1960s and '70s, these multiple forms of state violence have not equally affected the nation as a whole. The brunt of neoliberal repression has primarily taken place in working-class urban communities and in rural and indigenous regions of Mexico with long traditions of resistance.[27] Yet, as we reflect on the importance of the radicalisms of the 1960s and '70s on this fiftieth anniversary of 1968, we are reminded that Mexico has yet to reconcile with its violent past, evident not only in its lack of a truth commission but also in the closure of its archives on this period and in the assassination of those who write about and publicly expose the crimes of the state.

México Beyond 1968 is divided into three parts, followed by a selected chronology. The chronology (c. 1946–c. 1980) lists prominent national and international events and figures that shaped the radicalism of the 1960s and '70s, including influential cultural, economic, religious, and political moments, institutions, leaders, and publications noted in the chapters, as well as others that are not examined in the book but that also shaped the multiple forms of radicalisms and state repression of this period. The detailed chronology emerges from the scholarship cited by the authors, and it reveals the long history of Mexico's Dirty Wars. Their roots can be traced back to the 1940s, but as noted in both the chronology and the chapters in the book, these became more aggressive in the 1960s and '70s. Paradoxically, this period coincided with Luis Echeverría's "democratic opening" as well as the "modernization" of the institutions of espionage that included the enhancement of repressive and intelligence gathering techniques and the incorporation of new mechanisms of state violence. The consequence, as the authors further point out in their chapters, resulted in the killing, torturing, disappearing, kidnapping, co-opting, threatening, and imprisoning of thousands of young activists—all representative outcomes of a dicta*dura*.

Besides a rich, and often interdisciplinary, secondary literature, the contributors draw from myriad primary sources that include interviews; political manifestoes; national, local, and student newspapers; human rights reports; and Secretaría de Educación Pública (Ministry of Public Education, SEP) pamphlets. They also carefully draw from documents of espionage and repression representing the Dirección Federal de Seguridad (Federal Security Directorate, DFS), the Dirección General de Investigaciones Políticas y Sociales (General Directorate of Political and Social Investigations, DGIPS), and the Secretaría de la Defensa Nacional (Secretariat of National Defense, SDN). Declassified to the public after the historic defeat of the PRI by the conservative opposition led by the Partido de Acción Nacional (National Action Party, PAN) in 2000, these documents grew exponentially during the 1960s and '70s and so did the number of government agents who infiltrated and spied upon the countless groups and figures who questioned the authority of the state. More recently, since the return of the PRI to the presidential office in 2012, these documents have become more difficult to access, and in 2015, academic access to these sources was closed.[28]

The first part of the book is composed of two conceptual essays by Zolov and Pansters. Both essays serve as an introduction that helps to frame some of the larger issues that the authors grapple with throughout the volume. In his contribution, Zolov explains the centrality of the concept of the Global Sixties, a period documented in the chronology that has yet to be thoroughly historicized, and how Mexico is central to understanding this period in history. Similarly, Pansters reevaluates state repression during the broader period of the 1960s and '70s, employing key concepts of state-making, points to central themes for further research, and identifies the chapters in this volume as representative examples of a new "paradigm shift" in Mexican historiography.

The second part of the book, "Revolutionary Organizing and State Response," with chapters by Padilla, Villanueva, Cedillo, Dillingham, and Aviña, centers its attention in the countryside. Particular emphasis is given to young campesinos and indigenous activists, including the multiple interactions they had with urban students. Active throughout the twentieth century, these actors were participants of the global radicalism of the era, but they were primarily concerned with national issues, namely those related to land retribution and popular education policies, as guaranteed in the 1917 Constitution. For them, and especially for female activists, as Padilla argues in her chapter, political participation was an expression of empowerment. By and large, male and female militants opted for nonviolent forms of resistance, and despite their factionalism and numerous internal disputes and contradictions, they collectively succeeded in forming broad national alliances, including, as Villanueva details in her chapter, the influential Federación de Estudiantes Campesinos Socialistas de México (Federation of Socialist Campesino Students of Mexico, FECSM) and the Central Nacional de Estudiantes Democráticos (National Organization of Democratic Students, CNED). But these and other organizations explored in this part of the book were met with state repression and further government cuts in popular education. During the administration of Luis Echeverría (1970–76) the policy-oriented rhetoric of *tercermundismo* (Third-Worldism), examined in Dillingham's chapter, complemented state violence. As Cedillo and Aviña explain in their respective case studies, state repression reached atrocious consequences in northern Mexico and Guerrero—particularly in local communities with high concentration of campesinos and indigenous people. In these communities, the incipient War on Drugs overlapped with the government's antisubversive violence that characterized this period.

The third part of the book, "Youth Radicalisms and State Violence," with chapters by Herrera Calderón, Soldatenko, Herrán Avila, Santamaría, Oikión Solano, and McCormick, shifts the focus from rural to urban Mexico. While some of the authors situate the various leftist, Catholic, and ultra-right radicalisms in the local, national, and global contexts without losing sense of the internal contradictions and factionalisms that characterized the respective movements, others pay closer attention to political violence and state repression. Particular attention is also given to the impact of the Tlatelolco massacre when activists and state agents were forced to determine "what to do next?" The authors explore the difficulties and numerous challenges activists faced in an increasingly repressive nation that forced scores of young leftist and conservative people to opt for violent solutions. For some, this translated into armed struggle. For others, including hundreds of militants who remained active in Mexico City after the October 2 massacre, as Oikión and Soldatenko demonstrate, this took the shape of new alternative forms of democratic resistance. For Catholic and ultraconservative radicals in Puebla and Monterrey, as Herrán Avila and Santamaría examine in their respective chapters, the 1960s and 1970s also represented a period ripe for student militancy. These conservative radicalisms, as those from the Left, were influenced by local, national, and international figures that ranged from José Vasconcelos to Ché Guevara. For the state, the reality of the 1960s and 1970s meant a more aggressive form of repression that included illegal mechanisms of control in the cities (such as porrismo), paramilitary violence, various forms of popular co-optation in rural Mexico, and torture and killings of activists across the nation. In Guadalajara, as Herrera Calderón argues, state-sponsored shock brigades played an important yet unsuccessful role in deterring student radicalism in both schools and working-class barrios. When legal and illegal mechanisms of control ultimately failed in containing the radicalisms of the era, the state then opted for more repressive measures. As examined throughout the book and documented with chilling detail in McCormick's chapter, state repression in Mexico was far from "exceptional." Like its South American counterparts, the priísta state also identified its youth as a national problem and went to great lengths to eliminate it.

We finish the book with a short essay. In it we take a brief yet critical look at the historiographies of both the 1968 student movement and guerrilla uprisings in the 1970s. We highlight some of the major contributions made by the authors of the book, and to complement the chronology we list key questions that remain overlooked in the scholarship.

NOTES

1. Niblo, *Mexico in the 1940s*; Ochoa, *Feeding Mexico*; and Gillingham and Smith, *Dictablanda*.
2. Herrera Calderón and Cedillo, *Challenging Authoritarianism*, 8.
3. On the multiple contradictions that developed in 1968 between the Olympics and the student movement, see Witherspoon, *Before the Eyes of the World*.
4. For a recent discussion on the victims of Tlatelolco, see Allier-Montaño, "Memory and History."
5. These and additional critiques are further elaborated in our final remarks at the end of the book.
6. Morelia, Yucatán, Sinaloa, Sonora, and Oaxaca also experienced important student movements during the 1960s and '70s. For these and additional cases, see de la Garza, Ejea León, and Fernando Macias, *El otro movimiento estudiantil*; and some of the essays in Rivas Ontiveros, Sánchez Sáenz, and Tirado Villegas, *Historia y memoria*.
7. A notable exception is Oikión Solano, "La Central Nacional."
8. For a cautionary comment on the term, see Cedillo and Calderón, "Análisis de la producción."

9. See Carr, *Marxism and Communism*; Rodríguez Araujo, *Las izquierdas en México*; and Pani, *Conservadurismo y derechas*.
10. Padilla, *Rural Resistance*; and McCormick, *Logic of Compromise*.
11. See Pansters's essay in this volume. See also Auyero, *Routine Politics*.
12. Joseph, "What We Now Know and Should Know."
13. See also Zolov, "Introduction: Latin America in the Global Sixties."
14. For detailed discussions of these terms, see Sorensen, *A Turbulent Decade*, "Introduction."
15. Ibid.
16. Slobodian, *Foreign Front*; and Marchesi, *Latin America's Radical Left*.
17. Sorensen, *Turbulent Decade*, 1–14; and Suri, *Power and Protest*, 3.
18. See Zolov's contribution in this volume, and Zolov, "Expanding Our Conceptual Horizons."
19. See Herrán's chapter in this volume; Pensado, "'To Assault with the Truth'"; and Moreno González, "El movimiento anticomunista."
20. We share the conclusions in Oikión Solano and García Ugarte, *Movimientos armados*; Herrera Calderón and Cedillo, *Challenging Authoritarianism*; Aviña, *Specters of Revolution*; and Rangel Lozano and Sánchez Serrano, *México en los Setenta*.
21. In this sense, we do not see the benefit of using the term *dictablanda*, long referenced by Mexican scholars and recently defined by Gillingham and Smith in their otherwise excellent book as a "hybrid," "dynamic," and "complex" "regime that combines democratic and authoritarian elements." Gillingham and Smith, *Dictablanda*, vii.
22. See Collado Herrera, "La guerra fría, el movimiento estudiantil de 1968 y el gobierno de Gustavo Díaz Ordaz"; and Keller, *Mexico's Cold War*.
23. For examples depicting this sort of language, see our concluding chapter in this volume.
24. On the divergent meanings of both "insurgency" and "subversion"—real or imagined—during this period, see Sierra Guzmán, *El enemigo interno*.
25. For a discussion of the PRI's "golden age," see selected chapters in Joseph, Rubenstein, and Zolov, *Fragments of a Golden Age*.
26. Meade, "Introduction," 3–52.
27. See the articles in *NACLA Report on the Americas* 47, no. 1 (Spring 2014); and Trevizo, *Rural Protest*.
28. Padilla and Walker, "Dossier: Spy Reports"; and Olcott and Mannion, "Open Forum on Archives and Access."

BIBLIOGRAPHY

Allier-Montaño, Eugenia. "Memory and History of Mexico '68." *Revista Europea de Estudios Latinoamericanos y del Caribe*, no. 102 (October 2016): 7–25.

Aviña, Alexander. *Specters of Revolution: Peasant Guerrillas in the Cold War Mexican Countryside*. New York: Oxford University Press, 2014.

Auyero, Javier. *Routine Politics and Violence in Argentina: The Gray Zone of State Power*. Cambridge: Cambridge University Press, 2007.

Carr, Barry. *Marxism and Communism in Mexico*. Lincoln: University of Nebraska Press, 1992.

Cedillo, Adela, and Fernando H. Calderón. "Análisis de la producción historiográfica en torno a la 'guerra sucia' Mexicana." In *El estudio de las luchas revolucionarias en América Latina (1959–1996): Estado de la cuestión*, edited by Verónica Oikión Solano, Eduardo Rey Tristán, and Martín López Ávalos, 263–88. Zamora, Mexico: El Colegio de Michoacán, 2014.

Collado Herrera, María del Carmen. "La guerra fría, el movimiento estudiantil de 1968 y el gobierno de Gustavo Díaz Ordaz: La mirada de las agencias de seguridad de Estados Unidos." *Secuencia* 98 (May–August 2017): 158–203.

Garza de la, Enrique, Tomás Ejea León, and Luis Fernando Macias. *El otro movimiento estudiantil*. Mexico City: Extemporáneos, 1986.

Gillingham, Paul, and Benjamin T. Smith, eds. *Dictablanda: Politics, Work and Culture in Mexico, 1938–1968*. Durham, N.C.: Duke University Press, 2014.

Herrera Calderón, Fernando, and Adela Cedillo, eds. *Challenging Authoritarianism in Mexico: Revolutionary Struggles and the Dirty War, 1964–1982*. New York: Routledge, 2012.

Joseph, Gilbert M. "What We Now Know and Should Know: Bringing Latin America More Meaningfully into Cold War Studies." In *In from the Cold: Latin America's New Encounter with the Cold War*, edited by Gilbert M. Joseph and Daniela Spenser, 3–46. Durham, N.C.: Duke University Press, 2008.

Joseph, Gilbert M., Anne Rubenstein, and Eric Zolov, eds. *Fragments of a Golden Age: The Politics of Culture in Mexico Since 1940*. Durham, N.C.: Duke University Press, 2001.

Keller, Renata. *Mexico's Cold War: Cuba, the United States, and the Legacy of the Mexican Revolution*. Cambridge: Cambridge University Press, 2015.

Marchesi, Aldo. *Latin America's Radical Left: Rebellion and Cold War in the Global 1960s*. Cambridge: Cambridge University Press, 2017.

McCormick, Gladys I. *The Logic of Compromise in Mexico: How the Countryside Was Key to the Emergence of Authoritarianism*. Chapel Hill: University of North Carolina Press, 2016.

Meade, Everard. Introduction to *The Taken: True Stories of the Sinaloa Drug War*, by Javier Valdez Cárdenas, 3–52. Translated by Everard Meade. Norman: University of Oklahoma Press, 2017.

Moreno González, María Guadalupe. "El movimiento anticomunista en Jalisco durante los años Setenta." *Espiral: Estudios sobre Estado y Sociedad* 24, no. 68 (January–April 2017): 113–53.

Niblo, Stephen. *Mexico in the 1940s: Modernity, Politics, and Corruption*. Lanham, Md.: SR Books, 2000.

Ochoa, Enrique C. *Feeding Mexico: The Political Uses of Food Since 1910*. Wilmington, Del.: SR Books, 2000.

Oikión Solano, Verónica. "La Central Nacional de Estudiantes Democráticos, una historia de militancia juvenil." In *Historia y memoria de los movimientos estudiantiles: A 45 años del 68*, edited by José René Rivas Ontiveros, Ana María Sánchez Sáenz, and Gloria A. Tirado Villegas, 2 vols., 2:105–33. Mexico City: UNAM/Editions Gernika, 2017.

Oikión Solano, Verónica, and Marta García Ugarte, eds. *Movimientos armados en México, siglo XX*, 3 vols. Zamora, Mexico: El Colegio de Michoacán/CIESAS, 2006.

Olcott, Jocelyn, and Sean Mannion. "Open Forum on Archives and Access: The DFS Controversy." *Hispanic American Historical Review On-Line*, September 16, 2015. Accessed November 2, 2017. http://hahr-online.com/open-forum-on-archives-and-access-the-dfs-controversy/.

Padilla, Tanalís. *Rural Resistance in the Land of Zapata: The Jaramillista Movement and the Myth of the Pax Priísta, 1940–1962*. Durham, N.C.: Duke University Press, 2008.

Padilla, Tanalís, and Louise E. Walker, eds. "Dossier: Spy Reports: Content, Methodology, and Historiography in Mexico's Secret Police Archive." *Journal of Iberian and Latin American Research* 19, no. 1 (2013).

Pani, Erika, ed. *Conservadurismo y derechas en la historia de México*, 2 vols. Mexico City: Fondo de Cultura Económica, 2011.

Pensado, Jaime M. "'To Assault with the Truth': The Revitalization of Conservative Militancy in Mexico During the Global Sixties." *The Americas* 70, no. 3 (January 2014): 489–523.

Rangel Lozano, Claudia E. G., and Evangelina Sánchez Serrano, eds. *México en los Setenta. ¿Guerra sucia o terrorismo de Estado? Hacia una política de la memoria*. Chilpancingo, Mexico: Universidad Autónoma de Guerrero, 2015.

Rivas Ontiveros, José René, Ana María Sánchez Sáenz, and Gloria A. Tirado Villegas, eds. *Historia y memoria de los movimientos estudiantiles: A 45 años del 68*, vols. 1 and 2. Mexico City: UNAM/Editions Gernika, 2017.

Rodríguez Araujo, Octavio. *Las izquierdas en México*. Mexico City: Orfila, 2015.

Roman, Richard, and Edur Velasco. "Mexico: The State Against the Working Class." *NACLA Report on the Americas* 47, no. 1 (Spring 2014): 23–26.

Sierra Guzmán, Jorge Luis. *El enemigo interno: Contrainsurgencia y fuerzas armadas en México*. Mexico City: Plaza y Valdés, 2003.

Slobodian, Quinn. *Foreign Front: Third World Politics in Sixties West Germany*. Durham, N.C.: Duke University Press, 2012.

Sorensen, Diana. *A Turbulent Decade Remembered: Scenes from the Latin American Sixties*. Stanford, Calif.: Stanford University Press, 2007.

Suri, Jeremi. *Power and Protest: Global Revolution and the Rise of Détente*. Cambridge, Mass.: Harvard University Press, 2003.

Trevizo, Dolores. *Rural Protest and the Making of Democracy in Mexico, 1968–2000*. University Park: Penn State University Press, 2012.

Witherspoon, Kevin B. *Before the Eyes of the World: Mexico and the 1968 Olympic Games*. DeKalb: Northern Illinois University Press, 2014.

Zolov, Eric. "Expanding Our Conceptual Horizons: The Shift from an Old to a New Left in Latin America." *A Contracorriente* 5, no. 2 (Winter 2008): 47–73.

———. "Introduction: Latin America in the Global Sixties." *The Americas* 70, no. 3 (January 2014): 349–62.

PART I

INTRODUCTORY ESSAYS

1

INTEGRATING MEXICO INTO THE GLOBAL SIXTIES

ERIC ZOLOV

QUITE RECENTLY, a new historiographical paradigm has emerged that is pressing upon scholars of the Cold War period, and particularly of the mid–Cold War era (c. 1955–75). This paradigm looks to situate analyses of nation-state processes within a wider conceptual frame, one that encompasses a deeper awareness of geopolitics while adopting a transnational lens through which to interpret local cultural and ideological practices. The label "Global Sixties" has been increasingly attached to this new interpretative perspective, and its rapid spread, in particular among scholars who approach the period through analysis of the Third World, is a strong indicator of the paradigm's resonance.[1] In the brief essay that follows, I would like to outline the key defining elements of this paradigm and to make a case for how and why we, as scholars of Mexico, need to take into consideration the global context—beyond that of the U.S.-Mexican relationship—in our ongoing reconceptualization of the relationship between the state, youth movements, and political violence during this period.

A GLOBAL SIXTIES AGENDA

To invoke the term Global Sixties is to reference simultaneously a unique epistemological frame of analysis, one that takes as a given a deep embeddedness of transnational linkages, and a particular if loosely defined periodization. In my efforts to define the term, the Global Sixties represents "a new conceptual approach to understanding local change within a transnational framework, one constituted by multiple crosscurrents of geopolitical, ideological, cultural, and economic forces. Such forces produced a simultaneity of 'like' responses across disparate geographical contexts, suggesting interlocking causes."[2] For me, there are two intersecting axes to the Global Sixties (here, with an emphasis on Mexico) that define this new epistemological approach.

The first is that of geopolitics. Mexico was a major Cold War actor with internationalist aspirations throughout the 1960s and 1970s. Indeed, it is no longer possible to think about Mexico during this period without situating national and regional-level politics within a global framework. We must do so, moreover, not simply by incorporating these internationalist aspirations in anecdotal terms, as descriptive points of reference, but rather by considering the motivating forces behind those aspirations and locating their interrelationship with national and local-level politics and social history. By repositioning Mexico as a Cold War actor of consequence—shaped *by* and as an agent *of* the international Cold War—we will not only gain a deeper understanding of Mexico as a global state actor, but, crucially, we will also transcend a narrower framework that too frequently conflates "Cold War" with the United States and thus presupposes that Mexico had little agency (much less, motive) to act within a fluid geopolitical context.

The second axis that defines this new epistemological approach courses along what Mary Kay Vaughan has recently defined as "affective subjectivity." Using an innovative methodological approach in which she integrates biographical history with perceptive readings of mass cultural, individual artistic, and state-produced cultural texts and projects, Vaughan delineates and brings to life shifts in the structure of feeling that characterized succeeding generations of urban Mexico City youth—or, to be certain, a particular element of those youth—who came of age during the 1950s through the 1970s. By charting such shifts in affective subjectivity, Vaughan makes the case that newly emergent discourses and practices related to transforming conceptualizations of "youth" and "liberation" were inextricably embedded within transnational flows of cultural and ideological influence.[3] While the geopolitical axis that defines the idea of a Global Sixties thus urges us to situate Mexico within the fluid dynamics of Cold War diplomacy, the axis of "affective sentiment" exposes the "global" within local practices and discourse.

Efforts to reach consensus on how to "periodize" the Global Sixties inevitably conflict with competing interpretations of start and end points. This is how it should be, as disagreements over periodization help to reveal conflicting interpretations over what constitutes a critical juncture within particular national contexts. Thus Jaime Pensado, for instance, adopts a starting point of 1956 in his discussion of a Mexican "Long Sixties," adopting the year of the conflictive student strike at the Instituto Politécnico Nacional (National Polytechnic Institute, IPN) as the key event that set in motion a shift in the culture of student protest and public perceptions about youth more generally.[4] Others look outward for starting points, as does Renata Keller who regards the Cuban Revolution in 1959 as a starting point.[5] Similarly, establishing when the 1960s "ended" is also an important point to contemplate. Louise Walker points to 1973 as a "crisis year" that marked a shift toward new forms of political mobilization and state surveillance, a shift that heralded the endpoint of the "Mexican Miracle."[6] Walker situates this turning point within a global context and thereby underscores the centrality of the OPEC oil crisis to an interpretation of Mexican national and domestic politics. It is important that we have these debates over periodization, as they help us to clarify historical turning points and contribute to the important discussions about interlocking causes.

At the same time, I would argue that what is still missing from this discussion is a conversation about turning points *within* the Global Sixties historical framework. In continuing to discuss the Global Sixties—or "long 1960s"—as a single period, we risk the danger of perpetuating a nebulous conceptual category, one that may unintentionally conflate significant temporal shifts within this time frame. Equally important, we need to initiate a conversation about how the Global Sixties framework lays the basis for interpreting what comes next—in the 1970s and 1980s. As the essays in this collection reveal, there is both continuity and disjuncture between the "long 1960s" and the latter period. Yet there is no clearly emergent paradigm that might encompass the diverse investigations in the 1970s and 1980s. The original research included in this collection provides an excellent opportunity for us to begin a conceptualization of a succeeding historical era, one that builds upon, engages, and hopefully helps to redefine the Global Sixties paradigm.

In short, it is no longer possible to think about Mexico in the 1960s and '70s without situating the nation-state within a global framework. This has special bearing on how and when one deploys the term *guerra sucia*, a phrase that Mexicanists have eagerly embraced to define the period c. 1965–78, an expanded time frame, and one that encompasses many of the essays in this collection. Mexico's Dirty Wars were deeply permeated by geopolitical upheavals and transnational forces, from the oil crises induced by OPEC and the emergence of détente, to the impact of Maoism and rise of countercultural refusal. The insistence by the scholars in this collection to align Mexico's Dirty War within a broader Latin American trend is crucial to debunking long-standing notions of Mexican "exceptionalism." Mexico's "perfect dictatorship" masked dark episodes of violence and a prolonged strategy of low-intensity conflict, especially in the countryside. At the same time, however, we must situate Mexico's Dirty War within a global context as well, just as those studying the Southern Cone have done.[7] Only by doing so will we make our work increasingly relevant to non-Mexicanists. At the same time, this move to "globalize" Mexican history will push scholars to account for the embedded motivations, sentiment, and global parameters in which these otherwise "local" histories occur. The crucial challenge of such an approach is that we seek to identify the interconnections among geopolitics, regional identifications, state-level struggles to consolidate a "national form" and local contestations that reconfigure the discourse, signifiers, and practices of global dissent.

GEOPOLITICAL CONSIDERATIONS

In geopolitical terms, it is essential that we pivot away from the traditional bilateral axis of U.S.-Mexican relations and expand our investigative reach to grasp the complexities of a dynamic global landscape that defined the Cold War. Mexico's geopolitics clearly encompass far more than that country's relationship with the United States, a false premise that Tanya Harmer, Vanni Pettinà, and others have recently pushed historians to acknowledge.[8] The bilateral relationship was clearly central to Mexican national and international relations, but analytically it is overdetermined as well. It is striking, for instance, how references to Mexico's broader internationalist agenda—whether when addressing state-to-state politics or in examining left- or right-wing ideological currents—far too often become linked, almost tautologically, to U.S. strategic influence and decision-making. The wider geopolitical context mattered especially because actors across the political spectrum believed, at different moments, in the real potential for an assertive Mexican leadership in global affairs and thus in the possibilities of breaking free of U.S. dominance.

One important area of investigation is to revisit the relationship between the Communist world and Mexico, a relationship that far too often is presented simply in terms of a false dichotomy between the forces of "communism" versus "anticommunism." By the late 1950s and throughout the early 1960s, the Soviet model of economic development—with its emphasis on state-led growth and a push for heavy industrialization—coincided in important ways with the developmentalist outlook of Mexico as well as other Latin American governments. Indeed, the Soviet Union prepared an ambitious and calculated strategy to gain widespread diplomatic approval in Latin America. This was the high point of what Soviet international diplomacy labeled a policy of "peaceful coexistence," and, prior to the Cuban Missile Crisis at least, various governments across Latin America showed an eagerness to harness the possibilities of geopolitical "balancing" by engaging diplomatically and economically with the Soviet bloc. From the Soviet perspective, this approach entailed proffering favorable trade relations and support for critical industries, such as oil refineries, as well as a broader "cultural offensive" that included, for example, support for Soviet bloc film festivals, musical performances, and other cultural presentations.[9] Ironically, these efforts to normalize Soviet relations with Latin America were hindered by Khrushchev's increasingly strident support for revolutionary Cuba, a relationship that had more to do with Soviet competition with communist China for leadership within the emergent Third World than a genuine alignment of strategic interests with Cuba's own revolutionary goals.[10]

My point is that Soviet outreach to the Americas (leaving aside the Cuban Revolution) created an important opportunity for certain Latin American governments, Mexico included, to diversify their international relations and thereby gain bargaining power vis-à-vis the United States. The embrace, in other words, was mutual, even if the geopolitical motives mostly diverged. Much to U.S. State Department consternation, there was a respectful attitude expressed by a cross-section of Mexican society toward the seemingly spectacular Soviet advances in science, industry, and agriculture. Many Mexicans, moreover, pointed to shared historical trajectories between the Russian and Mexican revolutions, a trope that was reiterated in various ways when Soviet Vice-Premier Anastas Mikoyan visited Mexico in the fall of 1959—the highest-level Soviet official to travel to Latin America up to that moment—to inaugurate the Soviet Exhibition of Science, Technology, and Culture. Thus, the otherwise resolutely anticommunist newspaper *Excélsior* editorialized about the exhibition, "There is indeed much that we can learn from Soviet advances."[11]

Indeed, Mexican diplomatic, economic, and cultural relations with the Soviet Union remain woefully underexplored for the 1960s and 1970s. In the wake of Mikoyan's visit, for instance, there was a concerted yet ultimately frustrated series of efforts to establish meaningful economic ties, while at the same time diplomatic gestures prospered.[12] Although President López Mateos never traveled to the Soviet Union (despite an invitation from Khrushchev to do so), his foreign policy aspirations included direct engagement with various Eastern bloc nations, notably in an official state visit to Poland and Yugoslavia, and a level of diplomacy that elements on the Mexican Left viewed favorably as a proxy for the nation's defiance of U.S. Cold War expectations. Indeed, scattered throughout the 1960s one can locate intriguing glimmers into a relationship that was clearly far more complex, and quite likely of mutual benefit, than the prevailing "anticommunist" interpretation of Mexican state policies would otherwise lead us to believe. For instance, although President Díaz Ordaz retreated from the high-profile internationalism of his predecessor, and in 1968 cast blame on a communist conspiracy to undermine his presidency, his administration nevertheless promoted an elaborate mission of cultural diplomacy with Soviet bloc nations. These ties bore evident fruit in the widespread availability of Soviet films, books, performances, and other cultural manifestations to Mexican citizens from the 1960s through the 1980s.

Another dimension of the relationship between Mexico and the communist nations concerns diplomatic and cultural relations with China and the ways in which Maoism was disseminated and refracted through Mexican political discourse. Too often scholars conflate positions of "communism" and "anticommunism" with the Soviet Union alone, a perspective that detracts from our understanding of how the Chinese revolution was interpreted both by the general public as well as within left-wing intellectual and student circles. Outside of Cuba, China had no formal relationship with any government in Latin America until Salvador Allende breeched this de facto blockade and established diplomatic ties in late 1970. Mexico followed in quick succession (bucking the United States, which did not establish diplomatic relations until 1979), thus signaling an eagerness to explore the geopolitical opportunities created by détente. Curiously, Mexico's diplomatic opening to China coincided with the emergence of Maoist-influenced left-wing movements. Indeed, we need to learn much more about how the Cultural Revolution (c. 1966–71), on one hand, and Mexico's diplomatic opening to China, on the other, played a role in delaying (or inspiring) this turn toward Maoism. It is notable, for instance, that Maoism does not attain significant influence among Mexican youth nor is

Maoism transformed into revolutionary praxis until the early 1970s, practically a decade after the origins of the Sino-Soviet conflict.[13]

Similarly, there has been almost no discussion concerning the relationship between the Non-Aligned Movement (NAM) and Mexico.[14] In the summer of 1961, U.S. State Department officials breathed a sigh of relief when it became evident that Mexico would not in fact send an official representative to the founding meeting of NAM, held in Belgrade, Yugoslavia, that September. Nevertheless, throughout the early 1960s official state policy articulated an ideological affiliation with the political and economic objectives of NAM and Cold War "neutralism" more generally. Thus, while never formally joining NAM, President López Mateos paid official visits to key nonaligned countries, including Indonesia, India, and Yugoslavia, and reciprocated with elaborate state receptions for the principal statesmen identified with the NAM movement (Sukarno, Nehru, and Tito). Moreover, an outcrop of this early "flirtation" with nonalignment was Mexico's role in cofounding the Group of 77, a (mostly) Third World caucus that by the mid-1960s would push for a transformation in global economic trade relations and whose focus was central to the establishment of the United Nations Conference on Trade and Development (UNCTAD). The first international conference of UNCTAD, held in Geneva in 1964, was a watershed moment in the articulation of a critique of the global capitalist order, and Mexico's sustained engagement with UNCTAD throughout the 1960s helps to account for the subsequent proposal of a "New International Economic Order" by President Luis Echeverría in the 1970s. Indeed, a deeper appreciation of Mexico's ideological affinities with NAM during its founding period, coupled with Mexican activism within the Group of 77, helps to clarify Echeverría's internationalism and to pivot away from the overly simplistic argument that Echeverría's global travels and leadership within the United Nations merely reflected efforts to "co-opt" the Left. There is still much to disentangle in terms of how the logic of presidential internationalism intersected and conflicted with the logics of left-wing mobilization, collaboration, and confrontation, not only in the period of Echeverría, but also during the presidency of López Mateos and even, perhaps somewhat differently speaking, under Díaz Ordaz.

Finally, we need to move away from a geopolitical framework that elevates the relevancy of the Cuban Revolution as the primary focal point for interpreting left-wing mobilizations and countermobilizations during this period. As Renata Keller has amply demonstrated, the Cuban Revolution was deeply imbricated in the logic of U.S.-Mexican relations, as well as for political activism (on the Left as well as the Right).[15] Yet analogous to the distortions that singular attention to the 1968 student movement has had on the historiography, overly focusing on the centrality of the Cuban Revolution similarly distracts historians from grasping not only a more complex regional and international diplomacy but also the multitudinous influences (ideological and cultural) on Mexican youth's "affective sentiment." Indeed, the Cuban Revolution became an impediment to Mexico's regional (and international) leadership aspirations, even while also serving as a useful tool, as Keller argues, to help contain an explosion of revolutionary fervor.

COLD WAR TRANSNATIONALISMS

As we seek to come to a clearer understanding of the shifting aspirations and complexities of Mexico's geopolitical configuration, there is also the need to understand the motives and repercussions from the scores of individuals who made pilgrimages, mostly voluntarily, to centers of revolutionary activism. These travels began during the 1950s and accelerated into the 1960s and 1970s, when numerous Mexican youth went to the Soviet Union (including throughout the Eastern bloc) and Cuba, as well as to China, North Korea, and quite likely other sites of political fervor. Some pursued training in revolutionary methods, while many more traveled as part of international delegations that attended gatherings such as those hosted by the Soviet-backed World Peace Council or socialist youth festivals. As Patrick Iber explores in his recent book, regional and global solidarity conferences mobilized tens of thousands of participants, mostly youth, around appeals to world peace and, later, global socialist revolution.[16] These gatherings were important ideological and cultural contact zones as well as places of intersection, cross-pollination, and intellectual enthusiasm that would have an important impact on how youth interpreted and acted within their social networks.

Another example comes from youth who traveled to Communist bloc countries to study. One notable location in that regard was the Peoples' Friendship University in Moscow, which opened its doors in 1960 and shortly thereafter was renamed the Patrice Lumumba People's Friendship University in honor of the martyred Congolese independence leader. During the 1960s and 1970s, Mexicans joined with hundreds if not thousands of other Latin Americans, as well as those from other continents, who took up residency at the university and in turn helped transform the school and dormitories into a home away from home for university-age students from across the global south. To date, we know very little about their experiences there and how those experiences shaped their later political and social identities. For instance, in my own archival research I encountered brief references to Mexican students studying in the Soviet Union who complained of poor conditions and racial discrimination. These pilgrimages continued and likely even accelerated during the 1970s, when Mexican-Soviet relations became further normalized.[17]

Who were these young individuals and what were the social and ideological forces that motivated them to travel abroad, whether to participate in an international conference or youth festival, to enroll in university, or, in smaller numbers, to gain knowledge of guerrilla warfare? What kinds of friendships and romances were forged? How were ideas and differences regarding politics, the aesthetics and ethics of revolutionary praxis, and global knowledge of events transmitted? In what ways did interactions in these contact zones lay a foundation for future relationships—and disagreements—that spanned the global divide and thus helped to shape the intellectual and political dimensions of the Global Sixties?

There is also the underexplored realm of right-wing youth in Mexico and the ways in which their own travels mirrored in fundamental ways those of their left-wing counterparts. As Jaime Pensado has cogently documented, we must not conflate the categories of "youth" and "Left" during this period, as is too often the case.[18] Many youth were far less inclined to support the political activism and performative speech acts of their left-wing peers than most scholars have felt comfortable to presume. Moreover, as Luis Herrán documents, an emboldened right-wing conservative movement, with points of organizational contact spread across the globe, emerged in tandem with the left-wing frontist politics of the Soviet World Peace Council and Cuba's Casa de las Américas.[19] During the 1960s and '70s, organizations such as the World Anti-Communist League, with its multiple regional and local-level affiliate groups, grew in strength with its pledge to counter the perceived threat of a vast left-wing communist conspiracy. These organizations were deeply intertwined with religious politics, especially emanating from the Catholic Church. Yet Catholicism was shaped by the competing forces of liberation theology and social conservativism; like "youth," we cannot reduce Catholicism to a single category. These religious currents, too, were situated in constant dialogue with elements external to the nation-state. The Global Sixties framework allows us to encompass this far more complex notion of "youth politics" and thus to begin to recognize the deeper implications of ideological polarization.

We also need to delve more profoundly into the ways in which cultural practices were globally contextualized. Recent work on Latin America has brought
to light the numerous pathways by which the sounds, imagery, and aesthetic
sensibilities crisscrossed the Atlantic and, in doing so, enmeshed themselves
within local, national, and regional contexts of youth consumptive practices and
activism.[20] There is much, however, to explore for Mexico in this regard. This
is especially true for the 1970s, when we see a resurgence of state-sponsored
and underground artistic movements, as well as the explosion of new forms of
identity regarding what it meant to be young, defiant, and engaged in transforming the world as it was. One is struck, for instance, by the "dropping out" of
youth reflected in the spread of *jipismo* (the hippie movement) and communal
living options, concurrent with an increased ideological rigidity of a newfound
compromismo (political commitment) as many youth (on the Left and Right)
policed themselves and one another for ideologically suspect cultural practices
that might detract from commitment to revolutionary and counterrevolutionary
struggle. How did hair style, fashion, language, and musical tastes, among other
points of reference, speak *to* and *about* youth of different ideological positions?
In what ways did social class shape the response of youth to these consumptive
practices? What was the impact of market forces (national and transnational)
on establishing access to and thus defining the "value" of cultural consumption?
How were such points of reference mobilized by state agencies, by parental
authorities, by political parties, and in quotidian exchanges to define not only
"which side" one was on but what constituted the boundaries between "national"
and "foreign," "Right" and "Left" in an era when regional and global affinities
were in dramatic flux?

One of the concerns raised by participants in the conference that gave rise to
this volume was that the insertion of Mexico within a Global Sixties paradigm
risked subsuming local and regional histories into a wider narrative. As Michael
Soldatenko asked, what do we lose in terms of the "autonomy of local stories"
when we approach Mexico globally? This is an important question and one that
highlights the significance of research taking place at the regional level. For too
long, these narratives have been doubly "provincialized"—overshadowed by
the drama of social movements that occurred in Mexico City (the 1968 student
movement is the prime example here) and marginalized by a bias that has
tended to conflate the capital with the "nation." The excellent research taking
place outside of Mexico City will continue to push the historiography of Cold
War Mexico to acknowledge not only the significance of "local stories" on their

own terms, but to reenvision a dominant political narrative that is still over-whelmingly grounded by events that occurred in the capital.

At the same time, no story is wholly local. This is especially the case in an era charged by the crosscurrents of ideological and cultural intercourse. If we look for them, we will discover myriad evidence of these crosscurrents embedded in even the most local of stories. This is not to diminish the autonomy of local actors but rather to acknowledge how global events shaped local narratives. At the same time, the absence of democratic process and the direct experience of economic inequalities profoundly shaped how provincial youth perceived and responded to events and ideas emanating from beyond the nation-state. A deeper probe of local and/or provincial histories thus provides us with a more nuanced understanding of how to conceptualize the relationship between local and global in this period.

Finally, in the Global Sixties, the transnational flow of people, ideas, imagery, and capital was intertwined with a perception, both in official circles and at the grassroots level, that Mexico had an opportunity to leverage a fluid geo-political order to its advantage. We need to identify how this perception of opportunity—and the fears or aspirations of societal "collapse"—also shaped local stories and sentiment. Positioning Mexican political narratives within this global framework provides a new entry point into writing the history of modern Mexico, one that will help transcend the overbearing organizational structure dictated by the terms of changing presidential *sexenios* (six-year term presidential terms). A rich historiography is emerging that is reconceptualizing the significance of the Cold War from the perspective of the Global South. It is a propitious moment to squarely insert Mexico within this emergent dialogue.

NOTES

I wish to thank Jaime Pensado and Enrique Ochoa for organizing the conference that gave rise to this collection and for their comments on an earlier draft of this essay. I also wish to thank Mary Kay Vaughan and Terri Gordon-Zolov for their comments and close reading of an earlier draft.

1. See the articles and introduction to the special issue on "Latin America in the Global Sixties," *The Americas*. Recent volumes incorporating this label include Jian et al., *Routledge Handbook*; Chaplin and Pieper-Mooney, *Global 1960s*; Brown and Lison, *Global Sixties in Sound and Vision*; Christiansen and Scarlett, *Third World in the Global 1960s*.

2. Zolov, "Introduction: Latin America in the Global Sixties," 354.

3. Vaughan, *Portrait of a Young Painter*.

4.   Pensado, *Rebel Mexico*, 83–84.
5.   Keller, *Mexico's Cold War*.
6.   Walker, *Waking from the Dream*, 47.
7.   Armony, "Transnationalizing the Dirty War," 134–68; Brands, *Latin America's Cold War*; Langland, *Speaking of Flowers*.
8.   Pettinà, "Beyond U.S. Hegemony"; Harmer, *Allende's Chile*; Garrard-Burnett, Lawrence, and Moreno, *Beyond the Eagle's Shadow*.
9.   Rupprecht, *Soviet Internationalism After Stalin*.
10.   Friedman, *Shadow Cold War*.
11.   Editorial, "Realidad y Propaganda," *Excélsior*, November 19, 1959.
12.   Pettinà, "¡Bienvenido Mr. Mikoyán!"
13.   Cuba established diplomatic relations with communist China in September 1960 and Canada in October 1970. The next Latin America government after Chile to establish ties was Peru in November 1971; Mexico and Argentina both followed in February 1972. Although a diplomatic opening was achieved under President Nixon, formal ties were not established by the United States until January 1979. For a recent scholarly overview of relations between key Latin American countries, including Mexico and communist China, see Rothwell, *Transpacific Revolutionaries*.
14.   See Pettinà, "Global Horizons." For a parallel discussion from the Brazilian perspective, see Hershberg, "'High Spirited Confusion.'"
15.   Keller, *Mexico's Cold War*.
16.   Iber, *Neither Peace nor Freedom*.
17.   A useful starting point can be found in Rupprecht, "From Russia with a Diploma: Latin American Students in the Soviet Union," chap. 4 in *Soviet Internationalism After Stalin*.
18.   Pensado, "'To Assault with the Truth.'"
19.   Herrán, "Anticommunism, the Extreme Right, and the Politics of Enmity."
20.   Barr-Melej, *Psychedelic Chile*; Dunn, *Contracultura*; Markarian, *Uruguay, 1968*; and Manzano, *The Age of Youth in Argentina*.

BIBLIOGRAPHY

NEWSPAPERS

Excélsior

OTHER SOURCES

Armony, Ariel. "Transnationalizing the Dirty War: Argentina in Central America." In *In from the Cold: Latin America's New Encounter with the Cold War*, edited by Gilbert Joseph and Daniela Spenser, 134–68. Durham, N.C.: Duke University Press, 2008.
Barr-Melej, Patrick. *Psychedelic Chile: Youth, Counterculture, and Politics on the Road to Socialism and Dictatorship*. Chapel Hill: University of North Carolina Press, 2017.

Brands, Hal. *Latin America's Cold War*. Cambridge, Mass.: Harvard University Press, 2010.

Brown, Timothy Scott, and Andrew Lison, eds. *The Global Sixties in Sound and Vision: Media, Counterculture, Revolt*. New York: Palgrave Macmillan, 2014.

Chaplin, Tamara, and Jadwiga Pieper-Mooney, eds. *The Global 1960s: Convention, Contest, and Counterculture*. New York: Routledge, 2017.

Christiansen, Samantha, and Zachary A. Scarlett, eds. *The Third World in the Global 1960s*. New York: Berghahn Books, 2013.

Dunn, Christopher. *Contracultura: Alternative Arts and Social Transformation in Authoritarian Brazil*. Chapel Hill: University of North Carolina Press, 2016.

Friedman, Jeremy. *Shadow Cold War: The Sino-Soviet Competition for the Third World*. Chapel Hill: University of North Carolina Press, 2015.

Garrard-Burnett, Virginia, Mark A. Lawrence, and Julio E. Moreno, eds. *Beyond the Eagle's Shadow: New Histories of Latin America's Cold War*. Albuquerque: University of New Mexico Press, 2013.

Harmer, Tanya. *Allende's Chile and the Inter-American Cold War*. Chapel Hill: University of North Carolina Press, 2014.

Herrán, Luis. "Anticommunism, the Extreme Right, and the Politics of Enmity in Argentina, Colombia, and Mexico, 1946–1972." PhD diss., The New School for Social Research, 2016.

Hershberg, James. "'High Spirited Confusion': Brazil, the 1961 Belgrade Non-Aligned Conference, and the Limits of an 'Independent' Foreign Policy During the High Cold War." *Cold War History* 7, no. 3 (August 2007): 373–88.

Iber, Patrick. *Neither Peace nor Freedom: The Cultural Cold War in Latin America*. Cambridge, Mass.: Harvard University Press, 2015.

Jian, Chen, Martin Klimke, Masha Kirasirova, Mary Nolan, Marilyn Young, and Joanna Waley-Cohen, eds. *The Routledge Handbook of the Global Sixties: Between Protest and Nation-Building*. New York: Routledge, 2018.

Keller, Renata. *Mexico's Cold War: Cuba, the United States, and the Legacy of the Mexican Revolution*. New York: Cambridge University Press, 2015.

Langland, Victoria. *Speaking of Flowers: Student Movements and the Making and Remembering of 1968 in Military Brazil*. Durham, N.C.: Duke University Press, 2013.

"Latin America in the Global Sixties." *The Americas* 70, no. 3 (January 2014).

Manzano, Valeria. *The Age of Youth in Argentina: Culture, Politics, and Sexuality from Perón to Videla*. Chapel Hill: University of North Carolina Press, 2014.

Markarian, Vania. *Uruguay, 1968: Student Activism from Global Counterculture to Molotov Cocktails*. Berkeley: University of California Press, 2016.

Pensado, Jaime M. *Rebel Mexico: Student Unrest and Authoritarian Political Culture During the Long Sixties*. Stanford, Calif.: Stanford University Press, 2013.

———. "'To Assault with the Truth': The Revitalization of Conservative Militancy in Mexico During the Global Sixties." *The Americas* 70, no. 3 (January 2014): 489–523.

Pettinà, Vanni. "Beyond U.S. Hegemony: The Shaping of the Cold War in Latin America," *Culture and History Digital Journal* 4, no. 1 (June 2015): 1–4.

————. "¡Bienvenido Mr. Mikoyán!: Tacos y tractores a la sombra del acercamiento soviético-mexicano, 1958–1964." *Historia Mexicana* 66, no. 2 (2016): 793–852.

————. "Global Horizons: Mexico, the Third World, and the Non-Aligned Movement at the Time of the 1961 Belgrade Conference." *The International History Review* 38, no. 4 (2015): 741–64.

Puma, Jorge. "Los maoístas del norte de México: Breve historia de Política Popular-Línea Proletaria, 1969–1979." *Revista Izquierdas* (April 2016): 200–29.

Rothwell, Matthew. *Transpacific Revolutionaries: The Chinese Revolution in Latin America.* New York: Routledge, 2013.

Rupprecht, Tobias. *Soviet Internationalism After Stalin: Interaction and Exchange Between the USSR and Latin America During the Cold War.* New York: Cambridge University Press, 2015.

Vaughan, Mary Kay. *Portrait of a Young Painter: Pepe Zúñiga and Mexico City's Rebel Generation.* Durham, N.C.: Duke University Press, 2014.

Walker, Louise E. *Waking from the Dream: Mexico's Middle Classes After 1968.* Stanford, Calif.: Stanford University Press, 2013.

Zolov, Eric. "Introduction: Latin America in the Global Sixties." *The Americas* 70, no. 3 (January 2014).

2

ZONES AND LANGUAGES OF STATE-MAKING

From Pax Priísta to Dirty War

WIL G. PANSTERS

A LETTER FROM DURANGO

ON MAY 5, 1979, rural teacher Raul Ortíz López from Topia, Durango, wrote a letter to president José López Portillo. In it he complained about the arbitrary behavior of three unknown platoons that entered the villages of Galancita, Palmarejo, and Platanar. The letter claims that soldiers attacked the local population with unnecessary force, raped women, stole from the poor, detained and physically punished entire families, and even arrested children. After appealing to the state discourse of revolutionary nationalism, Ortíz López lectures the president on the constitutional articles allegedly violated by the military, and then asks rhetorically, "Or is it that soldiers are subject to another Constitution? Is there is a special Constitution for the poor?"[1] He closes with an ironic appeal to the president's flagship political reform initiative: "I hope that justice is done and that under the course of your Political Reform you haven't created spaces for the Army to impose its 'loving' brutality."[2] In a postscript, he subtly insinuates that with the president's prompt intervention, "the people of the area don't have to violate Article 17 of the Constitution," which states that citizens are not allowed to take justice into their own hands and use violence to claim rights.

The army denied the charges, pointed to Special Task Force Condor, and suggested that the allegations were most likely untrue since the people in the area were involved in drug trafficking and hence could not be trusted. The commander of Task Force Condor IV, based in Badiraguato, Sinaloa, confirmed that his troops had engaged in "the localization and destruction of poppy and marihuana, as well as the arrest and indictment of those responsible."[3] In one of their operations children were initially captured as they were caring for poppy fields, but they were subsequently released. The commander concluded that the army's operations caused resentment.

The letter from the Durango schoolteacher and the response make clear some key features of state-society relations. First, the documents demonstrate how the language of Mexican state-making was appropriated by ordinary people. The reference to constitutional protections and the remarkable boldness with which they were penned appear to suggest the negotiation of rule. On the other hand, the Condor commander invokes the duties of the drug trafficking campaign and refers to popular attempts to smear "the work of the Army." The allegations are said to lack veracity and "it is deemed suitable to file the incident."[4] The documents bear witness to concrete state-society encounters, in which citizens and authorities appear to share and employ the formal language of the state. Is this a microcosm of negotiation of rule, or just a formalistic charade?

Second, the letter voiced popular protest against state violence. Peasants and teachers long represented the identity and morality of the revolutionary project, but during the 1960s and 1970s they embodied popular resistance against the postrevolutionary state, often in conjunction with students. Since the late 1950s, popular resistance and protests revealed Mexico's increasingly pronounced socioeconomic and political contradictions. This volume contributes significantly to understanding the origins of the social, political, and ideological makeup of (radical) popular organization and mobilization during the 1960s and 1970s, as they interacted with particular state actions and responses, effectuating changing modalities of state-making.

Third, this particular case anticipates what over time became a major source of contention and violence between state and nonstate actors. Topia lies in the Golden Triangle, a region with an established tradition of drug cultivation and trafficking. The area was a target for military interventions from the early stages of the War on Drugs. The evolving relationships between state agents and local and regional drug trafficking networks and organizations profoundly shaped the dynamics of state-making.

Fourth, the letter explicitly refers to López Portillo's "political reform," which raises the question of if and how the latter should be understood as political accountability, a response to the grievances raised by (radical) popular movements since the late 1950s. This speaks to the changing nature of Mexican authoritarianism, more in particular the shifting relations between coercion, repression, and violence on the one hand, and co-optation, incorporation, and accountability on the other.

In sum, the encounter between an angered local community and state agents provides insights into particular languages and narratives of the state; practices of coercion, abuse, and violence; and contentious citizen-state relations. How to make sense of this conceptually? What does it tell us about state-making during this particular historical conjuncture? I will propose a workable approach to state-making, and then reflect on debates about the Mexican case. I then look briefly at key societal transformations during the third quarter of the twentieth century. This provides the background for an assessment of how these changes affected political conflict and state-making, and for a discussion of some promising lines of scholarly inquiry into these processes. My aim is to present some conceptual and historiographical components of a "paradigm shift" in the study of twentieth-century Mexican state-making.

LANGUAGES AND ZONES OF STATE-MAKING

Observers of Mexican affairs will easily recognize a paradox noted by anthropologists Hansen and Stepputat about state-making and state-society relations: while the authority and performance of the state are constantly questioned and undermined, there are also incessant demands on the state to confer rights and entitlements to its citizens, effectively address problems of development, and promote the rule of law.[5] While people shout, "¡Fue el estado!" (It was the State!), they also call upon the state to fix things. This paradox is related to the "persistence of the imagination of the state as an embodiment of sovereignty . . . ; as the representation of the volonté générale . . . ; a source of social order and stability; and as an agency capable of creating a definite and authorized nation-space."[6] These normatively laden imaginations of the state are called upon in quotidian encounters with violent, ineffective, or corrupt practices of governance and state-making. The state is key to our understanding and imagination of society. Always in construction, state-making occurs through the invocation of registers of governance and authority that Hansen and Stepputat called "languages of stateness." The study of state-making explores these languages, their localized meanings, and historical trajectories. It invites anthropologists and historians alike to study "how the state tries to make itself real and tangible through symbols, texts, and iconography . . . [and] how the state appears in everyday and localized forms."[7]

State-making is about talk about the state (representation) and about daily encounters between citizens and the state. With good reason historians of state-making in Mexico have paid considerable attention to narratives of the state. Narrating the 1930s reformist Cardenista state, with its strong nationalistic overtones, differed significantly from the narratives of the law-and-order Cold War state during the 1960s, and both differ from the militarized and securitized state of the 2010s. Such narratives matter to ordinary people, as they serve to hold the state accountable. Hundreds of thousands of letters to presidents and other authorities in the nation's archives form a rich repository of sedimented narratives of state-making. There is, however, also a tradition of research caught up in the gaze of state or presidential narratives. One study conceived the president during the heydays of the Partido Revolucionario Institucional (Institutional Revolutionary Party, PRI) rule as "the interpreter, guardian, and representative of Mexicanness in the exercise of political and cultural power."[8] Such a focus on federal presidential power may lose sight of the practices of governance and daily encounters between local state institutions and citizens far removed from Los Pinos. Was this perhaps why Echeverría was such a "preacher" who talked so much to divert attention from what was happening in peripheral places but central to ordinary people's lives?[9]

Viewing an actual state as a historically specific configuration of languages of stateness, Hansen and Stepputat distinguish between practical and symbolic languages. Three practical languages of governance are concerned with the assertion of territorial sovereignty by the continued attempts to monopolize violence, the gathering and control of knowledge of the population, and the generation of resources, development, and the economy. State-making also involves three symbolic languages of authority: the institutionalization of law and legal discourse as the authoritative language of the state; the materialization of the state in signs, rituals, monuments, buildings, uniforms, and the like; and the nationalization of territory and institutions through symbolic links between history, community, and territory. These symbolic languages aim to imagine the state as the authoritative center of society, an authority capable of social and political ordering. Specific trajectories of languages of stateness depend on time and place, but modern states exist when the practical and symbolic languages of governance and authority coexist.[10]

What about the changing historical configuration of state-making in postrevolutionary Mexico? What are the terms of the debate? Elsewhere I proposed the analytical but historically framed distinction between hegemonic and coercive zones of state-making.[11] Certain practical languages of governance and symbolic languages of authority substantiate the zone of hegemonic state-making, while others substantiate the zone of coercive state-making. The study of these zones focuses on distinctive dimensions of state-making and on particular social and institutional actors and processes. In addition, a gray zone between the hegemonic and coercive zones of state-making can be identified. Typically, this is one of messy articulations between state and nonstate actors and institutions.

The zone of hegemony features processes of state-making and power relations through negotiation and incorporation, oriented toward establishing a common moral and political project between rulers and ruled, giving rise to a consensual and inclusionary model of state-society relations.[12] In contrast, the zone of coercion highlights force and violence in state-making and social control. It features the practices of the army, the police, paramilitaries, and security apparatuses as well as criminal organizations, guerrillas, and their multiple interactions. The gray zone is "where the deeds and networks of violent entrepreneurs, political actors, and law enforcement officials secretly meet and mesh"—that is, where the boundaries between state and nonstate actors become blurred.[13]

Some years ago, Knight argued that the Weberian monopoly [on violence] has been compromised by illegitimate covert state violence or privatized nonstate violence.[14] The key question is how this condition changes over time. Mexico's political-economic and sociocultural diversity also raises questions about diverse historical patterns across the national territory. Time and place are key to grasping the workings of zones of state-making in twentieth-century Mexico, their changing modalities, and their relative weight. Which conditions determine their changes in form, function, and weight? Have zones expanded or narrowed over time, and why? The languages of stateness can serve as optics into these developments.

A new generation of scholars has started to investigate these matters against the background of a debate about the historiography of Mexico's post–World War II state-making. A long-term emphasis on nonviolent forms of conflict resolution and institutionalized mediation (a.k.a. *pax priísta*) has privileged research about hegemonic state-making and neglected coercion, violence, repression, and criminal networks in Mexican state-making. Many recent publications frame their research findings in terms of "war" (Cold or Dirty, or both), which hints at an exciting paradigm shift. Moreover, the functional connections between hegemonic and coercive zones of state-making, and between state-making zones and levels of government require attention: "the successful elimination of violence at the *national* level involved its *displacement* to the *provinces*," or more emphatically, *grassroots* violence and repression complemented and facilitated "the more ostensibly peaceful conduct of *national* politics."[15] This point is crucial and I will return to it later. I will further elaborate on the new paradigm in the last section.

ECONOMY AND SOCIETY IN THE 1960S AND 1970S

Economic, demographic, social, and cultural transformations shape state-making and politics as much as languages of stateness shape the former. Mexican society underwent profound transformations between the 1950s and the mid-1970s. Population growth was impressive: from almost 26 million in 1950, to nearly 35 million in 1960, 48 million in 1970, and almost 67 million in 1980![16] Internal migration contributed to rapid urbanization. Metropolitan Mexico City grew from 3.1 million (1950) to almost 9 million (1970), and Guadalajara from 380 thousand (1950) to 1.2 million (1970).[17]

This demographic dynamic was in part absorbed by economic growth. During the 1950s and 1960s, a period known as stabilizing development, Mexico's economy grew an average of 6 percent a year, while inflation remained low. The main motor of the national economy was import substitution industrialization.[18] A huge transfer of resources took place from the agricultural sector to the rest of the economy.[19] With this shifting economic weight, people moved to the cities en masse. Despite economic growth, population increase and internal migration laid the basis for an expanding informal economy. Also, inequality increased as income distribution worsened, and the real income of many dropped in the 1960s and early 1970s.[20] Certain sectors of Mexico's industrial working classes benefited from the social pact and *charro* (corrupt, government-sponsored) unions, but large parts of the population continued to live in poverty.[21] By 1975, Mexico differed deeply from what it had been in 1950. This had important consequences for state-making and the politics of social control.

When Echeverría assumed the presidency in 1970, the government addressed the problems of inequality and agricultural development. The goal was to distribute the benefits of economic growth more evenly in a "shared development." Initially successful, a series of domestic and international factors soon undermined macroeconomic stability, causing a severe financial crisis. At the beginning of the 1970s, GDP growth was above 8 percent, and during the entire presidential term real wages increased by 40 percent, leading, among other things, to a decline of income inequality.[22] Shared development increased public investment in agriculture, launched a new industrial policy, protected industrial wages, expanded welfare provisions, and attempted to reform a "weak and inequitable tax system."[23] But tax reform failed, while federal expenditures increased from nearly 12 percent (1970) to over 20 percent of GDP (1976). The number of public sector enterprises rose spectacularly. Sustaining an ever more obese state, Echeverría oversaw an increase of foreign public debt from 4 to 22 billion dollars.[24] Inflation reached 24 percent in 1974. Adverse international economic circumstances further undermined Mexico's monetary position. The government's increasingly tense relations with the national business elite led to capital flight and disinvestment. In August 1976, Mexico abandoned the exchange rate (fixed since 1956) and devalued the peso from 12.5 to 20 to the dollar.

Population growth and socioeconomic development had consequences for the state's social service capacity. As state planners conceived their projects for social services and infrastructure, they must have felt overtaken by new demographic and social realities every sexennial planning cycle. In addition, the state was chronically strapped for cash. In 1965, Mexico ranked lowest in Latin America in terms of tax collected as percentage of GDP.[25] The practices of governance concerning population and development were stretched to the limit. Higher education constitutes a spectacular example. In 1950, there were around 32,500 students in institutions of higher education; there were already 76,000 in 1960, an impressive 250,000 in 1970, and 853,000 in 1980![26] This came with an increased involvement of students in politics and the public domain.[27]

POLITICS, STATE, AND SOCIETY

While no one doubts the profound changes in Mexican society, there are two basic approaches to how they affected the authority and capacity of political and state institutions to rule. First, there is the thesis of the increasing divergence between society and state/political regime. Stability and maintaining the status quo were the core objectives of the Díaz Ordaz government (1964–70).[28] Economic development, population growth, urbanization, and education changed class relations and generated new social groups and interests. Increasing social complexity and diversification contributed to the disruption of the "cultural, symbolic, and discursive unity . . . that was the ideological and cultural base upon which the presidential regime of the Mexican Revolution was built."[29] Societal change transformed what Pozas Horcasitas calls the strong vertical power of presidential hegemony into a more complex horizontal playing field. The accumulated effects of these trends culminated in the 1960s and 1970s. As the Díaz Ordaz presidency attempted to conceal the depths of social tensions and conflicts, the world of appearances of harmony and continuity collapsed by a "revenge of facts."[30] To manage the disjunction the state increasingly relied on violence.[31] There is much truth to this approach, but the argument is also rather general in contrasting societal complexity with state entrenchment. It tends to reproduce the thesis of powerful presidential authoritarianism and the methodological focus on the federal state.

The second approach instead focuses on the consequences of specific modes of state-making and regime-building, which were partially sustained by coercive and violent practices of governance at local and regional levels as well as inside corporatist institutions. The displacement of violence and repression to the provinces, combined with the particular development model pushed forward by the Mexican state, generated multiple points of contention and resistance that subsequently worked their way up the administrative hierarchy, eventually resulting in a new (and radicalized) politics of articulation between different social and political subjects. Foucault has famously used the image of the capillary basis of (state) power. We should concentrate not so much on state power in its "central locations," say presidential dominance, but in societal extremities, "where it becomes capillary, that is, in its more regional and local forms and institutions."[32] If state power is sustained by its capillary foundations, it can also be disputed and eroded from there.

Capillary sources of contradiction, contestation, and resistance accumulated over time and across the country. Unionized industrial workers had fared relatively well during the "golden age of charrismo," but as the latter became more corrupt, it unravelled by the mid-1970s and "sparked a worker insurgency."[33] Others trace labor militancy and activist networks to previous decades.[34] The growth of the urban informal economy bred new contradictions about livelihood, citizen rights, public space, and the place of new political subjects in the state order. Soon, street vendors became targets of repression, perhaps above all because they engaged in cross-sectoral alliances, which threatened the vertical logic of authoritarianism.[35] In rural Mexico sources of discontent and conflict multiplied as the state basically left its management in the hands of caciques, corrupt state officials, and agribusinesses. Meanwhile, electoral channels clogged. In the late 1940s and early 1950s, state and PRI elites imposed restrictions on electoral competition, most importantly ending primary elections. It caused a wave of protests.[36] Although a degree of popular input of PRI candidate selection in rural municipalities existed in the 1960s, political authoritarianism was the rule.[37] During the early 1960s, the reintroduction of primaries was controversial and short-lived. Hence, during the third quarter of the twentieth century, elections resulted in "victories for the PRI and . . . the requisite supermajorities, rooted in formal and informal electoral manipulation, to block all but glacially incremental institutional change."[38] All the while, social contradictions multiplied, while the Cold War, especially the Cuban Revolution, provided a language of polarization and radicalization to discontented opposition groups and entrenched state and party elites alike. The rigid closure of the state, its blindness to the social causes of discontent, and its fixation to see communist conspiracies everywhere put the vicious circle of the Dirty War in motion.[39] From this perspective, the Tlatelolco massacre in 1968 was the "last explosion of a critical fault of the political system."[40] Armed conflicts and guerrilla movements emerged, and the Mexican state unleashed a wave of repression. Moreover, a campaign against drug cultivation and trafficking became an additional source of violence in the second half of the 1970s.[41] In most military counterinsurgency operations, the distinction between combating guerrillas, social mobilization, and drug trafficking was impossible to make. In sum, during the 1960s and 1970s, the Mexican state was overwhelmed by the accumulation and mutual reinforcement of large national conflicts and myriad capillary sources of contestation and resistance.

OPENING UP NEW RESEARCH FIELDS

Gillingham and Smith's use of the purposefully contradictory term *dictablanda* conveys a messy and ambiguous reality, characterized by "the combination of . . . a monopoly of national political office, carefully cultivated but thin cultural hegemony, and . . . hidden repressive violence, competitive if unequal elections, and salient popular bargaining and veto power."[42] By its very nature, the notion of dictablanda accommodates the simultaneous operation of hegemonic and coercive zones of state-making. To understand the conformation, features, and significance of the zone of coercion and violence, the broader forces that shape it, and the dynamic interplay of different (armed) actors,

I examine recent scholarship and identify three promising lines of inquiry and argumentation. The first line of inquiry concerns the coercive institutions of the state, the second is about the interconnections between state violence and (radical) popular movements, and the third speaks about the gray zone. This body of work and the contributions to this volume substantiate the paradigm shift identified before and appear to push the dictablanda more toward its harsher side.

VIOLENCE AND COERCION IN STATE-MAKING

Recent scholarly work has considerably advanced our understanding of the quintessentially coercive institutions of state-making.[43] During the 1940s and much of the 1950s, provincial Mexico remained a violent place, casting doubt upon the received wisdom of post-Cardenista pacification and stability during the time of an emerging party machinery.[44] Apart from *pistoleros* (gunmen) and *defensas rurales* (rural defenses), local violence involved, most importantly, the army. Despite civilian domination of national politics, the army and individual generals remained powerful and heavily involved in policing a disorderly countryside. They played a key role in "enforcing crude stability" in the service of political and economic domination.[45] Some excessively zealous military officers engaged in outright terror.[46] Others were more self-serving and able to turn their coercive power in provincial Mexico into political and economic interests and wealth.[47] Military force was essential for enhancing civilian (federal) political and social control and for building business empires. Mexico's political stability was not so much the product of the elimination of military strongmen, but of their regimentation. The Mexican military became less a national power contender but remained deeply involved in the everyday life of local societies. McCormick's study of rural Morelos has confirmed these findings.[48] Mexican demilitarization had a "partial, pacted, Faustian quality" to it.[49] Rath concluded that "the Mexican army's basic internal orientation had been decisively confirmed by the early 1950s," which means that there was little need to "import wholesale a new doctrine of domestic repression . . . that included both brutal and exemplary violence, or the more subtle cultivation of pistoleros and paramilitaries." This was part of military practice, and it provided "the hard edge of coercion the PRI required to rule."[50]

During the 1960s and 1970s, the military returned to the provinces to hunt down peasant activists, guerrilla forces, and drug traffickers. McCormick's political history of sugar cooperatives from the mid-1930s to the mid-1960s shows how Cardenista reforms gave way to disenchantment and anger about enduring poverty, corruption, and violence. The countryside became a laboratory for social control and repression later applied in urban centers and nationally.[51] From this follows an alternative periodization of Mexico's authoritarian state-making: the country's Dirty War did not start in the second half of the 1960s with the emergence of guerrilla groups or the 1968 student conflict, but "almost two decades earlier, in those places far away from the public eye of the national and international media."[52] Although no single categories account for negotiation and repression across Mexico, "political violence was key to understanding the governing regime's longevity."[53] The key role of coercive state-making should not mean losing sight of the state's capacity to generate acceptance, hope, and resignation. State-society relations are not black-and-white but permit multiple engagements.

STATE-MAKING AND POPULAR PROTEST

The second line of inquiry concerns the dialectic of state, popular resistance, and violence. Political scientists have examined this question in the context of debates about how state-centered views of Mexican authoritarianism can account for the remarkable record of popular mobilization, and state responsiveness.[54] Several years ago a study examined the main features of 207 social protests between 1946 and 1994 and their interaction with the state.[55] It found that the closed institutional structure of the regime exerted an influence over protest movements and government responses. Demanding civil and political rights questioned the restrictive system. With narrow institutional channels, protest movements realized that electoral politics, lobbying, or legal procedures would remain ineffective. Movements were therefore pushed to use contentious means to attract support and increase the state's costs for disregarding their demands. If regime structure and state repression determined the radicalization of demands and protest strategies, the study also found that the state pursued policy changes to appease social protest and reinforce authoritarianism. In sum, this large N study identified two regularities in the state-social movements interactions: radicalization of collective action and, paradoxically, repressive as well as reformist state responses. There is a family resemblance between the intrinsic ambiguity of the dictablanda state and the simultaneity of coercive and hegemonic zones of state-making.

However, sociological regularities cannot account for temporal and spatial specificities. How are languages of stateness shaped by subnational socioeconomic and political histories during the 1960s and 1970s? Historians have started to address these issues. Padilla's study of peasant resistance in Morelos during the 1940s and 1950s is particularly instructive in this respect.[56] Different moments of peasant activism to obtain a fair share of postwar economic and political modernization were met with state violence. This set in motion processes of radicalization, whereby peasants took up arms with Rubén Jaramillo. Padilla put forward the notion of the "escalating dialogue": "it was only when the state responded with repression that these groups became radicalized" and were pushed toward rebellion.[57] Echoing Knight's argument about how local level violence connects to national civilian rule, Padilla unequivocally demonstrates that "state terror undergirded Mexico's 'perfect dictatorship.'"[58]

When Jaramillo was assassinated in 1962, a cycle of resistance and repression initiated in neighbouring Guerrero. Again, "1968" was not the cataclysmic event that ended the PRI's golden period, which substantiates the idea of distinct historical cycles at national, subnational, and local levels. The radicalization of peasant resistance in Guerrero was above all the outcome of regional histories of protest and mobilization, and the state's violent response: "state terror made guerrillas and guerrilla supporters."[59] The case of Guerrero (then and now) occupies a position on the darkest side of coercive state-making, but it is not an exception.[60]

STATE-MAKING IN THE GRAY ZONE

The third line of inquiry concerns the gray zone between the hegemonic and coercive zones of state-making, and between state and nonstate actors and institutions. Recasting the interpretative framework that accentuated hegemonic and civilian state-making shouldn't mean replacing it with the opposite view that focuses exclusively on violence, coercion, and surveillance by a shady coalition of corrupt politicians, security and intelligence forces, and local elites. What characterizes much of Mexican state-making is messiness, ambiguity, contradiction, and diversity. It is here that the concept of the gray zone acquires its meaning. New scholarship provides evidence that the gray zone results from two mutually reinforcing processes: one refers to the tendency of the state to become more hesitant to openly employ coercive institutions particularly in certain institutional domains or territories; instead it conceals it by resorting to "deniable" actors. After 1950, the state actively created deniable actors. As a consequence, and secondly, overlaps and networks between public and private armed actors can be observed. To diminish the visibility and increase the deniability of direct involvement by the army in repression, the state started to farm out the dirty work to (semi-) private militia or intelligence agencies.[61] In the countryside and urban popular neighborhoods, the infrastructure was available in informal (and coercion-wielding) authorities such as caciques. With the rise to prominence of urban politicians, violence and killings became less evident, more suspicious (car accidents, suicides?), less explicit, and more covert, pushing state violence into the gray zone.

A telling example in urban Mexico of the informalization of state violence is the development of *porrismo*, "an extralegal tool of repression and conciliation to crush and negotiate with 'radical' student political forces."[62] The emergence of porrismo facilitated moving away from overt uses of force. It appears that during the "long 1960s," an important strategy in urban Mexico was that of taking different coercive mechanisms "underground," or into the "gray zone" of state-making. The preference for extralegal methods to ward off threats to political stability was motivated by the fact that recourse to legal tools of coercion was "tantamount to admission that the government is unable to control the perceived threat by any other means."[63] Extralegal methods were, however, also distinct from root-and-branch repression and state terror. Covert violence also fits the regime's concern to live up, at least partially, to its official credo of national unity, social justice, and civilian rule. It also enabled the government to protect the image of the army.[64] These findings signal the historical development and significance of the gray zone in state-making. Although understanding the historical evolution of the different zones of state-making, and their relative weight, requires more research, it is clear that the political functions of the army, the police, and other law enforcement agencies formed the groundwork for their de facto autonomy, corruption, and impunity. Out of these conditions, and the political expediency to conceal state violence, a gray zone arose that eventually became the natural habitat for the collusion of political, coercive, and criminal actors. Is it farfetched to suggest that in some parts of current Mexico the phantom-like violence of the gray zone has become the normality?

NOTES

I appreciate the comments by Benjamin Smith on an earlier version of this chapter.

1. Archivo General de la Nación, Secretaría de la Defensa Nacional, Exp. 1298–1979, caja 300, file Topia, Durango, 1979 (hereafter AGN SEDENA).

2. Ibid.

3.   Ibid.
4.   Ibid.
5.   Hansen and Stepputat, "States of Imagination," 1–38.
6.   Ibid., 2. The term *volonté générale* refers to a political philosophy, made famous by Jean-Jacques Rousseau, of the will of the people as a whole.
7.   Hansen and Stepputat, "States of Imagination," 5.
8.   Pozas Horcasitas, *Los límites del presidencialismo en las sociedades complejas*, 21.
9.   Cosío Villegas, *El sistema político mexicano*, 99.
10. Hansen and Stepputat, "States of Imagination," 8. This distinction broadly corresponds with Knight's approach in terms of state capacity and state legitimacy and authority, which speaks to its "affective" foundations. Knight views nation- and state-building as "related but distinct operations." This enables him to make the interesting point about the 1970s that while state capacity greatly increased, its affective foundations (legitimacy) markedly decreased. See Knight, "The Weight of the State in Modern Mexico," 215–16, 243.
11. Pansters, "Zones of State-Making," 26–32.
12. Knight, "Weight of the State in Modern Mexico," 226.
13. Auyero, *Routine Politics and Violence in Argentina*, 26.
14. Knight, "The Modern Mexican State," 190.
15. Knight, "Political Violence in Post-revolutionary Mexico," 107, my emphasis.
16. See INEGI, *Estadísticas Históricas de México 2014*.
17. Aguayo Quezada, *El almanaque mexicano*, 65–66.
18. Martínez de Campo, *Industrialización en México*, 77–91.
19. Gollás, "Breve relato," 232–33.
20. Ibid., 236. See also Levy and Székely, *Estabilidad y Cambio*, 174.
21. Levy and Székely, *Estabilidad y Cambio*, 171; Snodgrass, "The Golden Age of Charrismo," 175–95.
22. Moreno-Brid and Ros, *Development and Growth*, 128.
23. Ibid., 125.
24. Knight, "Cárdenas and Echeverría," 30–32.
25. Smith, "Building a State on the Cheap," 255–61.
26. ANUIES, *La educación superior en el siglo XXI*.
27. Pensado, *Rebel Mexico*.
28. Loaeza, "Gustavo Díaz Ordaz," 118–19.
29. Pozas Horcasitas, *Los límites del presidencialismo*, 18.
30. Loaeza, "Gustavo Díaz Ordaz," 121.
31. Ibid.
32. Foucault, *Power/Knowledge*, 96. For Mexico, see Rubin, *Decentering the Regime*.
33. Snodgrass, "The Golden Age," 191.
34. Alegre, *Railroad Radicals in Cold War Mexico*.
35. Mendiola García, *Street Democracy*, 119–38.
36. Gillingham, "'We Don't Have Arms,'" 162–64.
37. Smith, "Who Governed?," 227–71.

38. Gillingham, "'We Don't Have Arms,'" 166.
39. Keller, *Mexico's Cold War*; Alegre, *Railroad Radicals*; and Loaeza, "Gustavo Díaz Ordaz," 122–26.
40. Loaeza, "Gustavo Díaz Ordaz," 118.
41. Craig, "La Campaña Permanente."
42. Gillingham and Smith, "The Paradoxes of Revolution," 27.
43. For intelligence services, see Navarro, *Political Intelligence*; and Aguayo Quesada, *La charola*.
44. Smith, *Pistoleros and Popular Movements*.
45. Rath, *Myths of Demilitarization*, 201.
46. Ibid., 102.
47. See Gillingham, "Military Caciquismo in the PRIísta State," 210–37.
48. McCormick, *Logic of Compromise*.
49. Gillingham, "Military Caciquismo," 229.
50. Rath, *Myths of Demilitarization*, 171, 168.
51. McCormick, *Logic of Compromise*, 134.
52. McCormick suggests the notion of "low-intensity dirty war" in "The Last Door."
53. McCormick, *Logic of Compromise*, 210.
54. See, for example, Brachet-Márquez, *Dynamics of Domination*.
55. Favela Gavia, "Popular Protest and Policy Reform."
56. Padilla, *Rural Resistance*.
57. Ibid., 14.
58. Ibid., 7.
59. Aviña, *Specters of Revolution*, 112.
60. Oikión and García Ugarte, *Movimientos armados en México*.
61. Rath, "Camouflaging the State."
62. Pensado, *Rebel Mexico*, 3–4.
63. Stevens, "Legality and Extra-legality in Mexico."
64. Rath, *Myths of Demilitarization*, 172.

BIBLIOGRAPHY

ARCHIVES

Archivo General de la Nación, Secretaria de la Defensa Nacional

PUBLISHED SOURCES

Aguayo Quesada, Sergio. *La charola: Una historia de los servicios de inteligencia en México.* Mexico City: Grijalbo, 2001.
———, ed. *El almanaque mexicano.* Mexico City: Grijalbo/Proceso/Hechos Confiables, 2000.
Alegre, Robert F. *Railroad Radicals in Cold War Mexico: Gender, Class, and Memory.* Lincoln: University of Nebraska Press, 2013.

ANUIES (Asociación de Universidades y Instituciones de Educación Superior). *La educación superior en el siglo XXI: Líneas estratégicas de desarrollo*. Mexico City: ANUIES, 2000.

Auyero, Javier. *Routine Politics and Violence in Argentina: The Gray Zone of State Power*. Cambridge: Cambridge University Press, 2007.

Aviña, Alexander. *Specters of Revolution: Peasant Guerrillas in the Cold War Mexican Countryside*. Oxford: Oxford University Press, 2014.

Brachet-Márquez, Viviane. *The Dynamics of Domination: State, Class, and Social Reform in Mexico, 1910–1990*. Pittsburgh, Pa.: University of Pittsburgh Press, 1994.

Cosío Villegas, Daniel. *El sistema político mexicano*. 8th ed. Mexico City: Joaquín Mortiz, 1975.

Craig, Richard B. "La Campaña Permanente: Mexico's Antidrug Campaign." *Journal of Interamerican Studies and World Affairs* 20, no. 2 (May 1978): 107–31.

Favela Gavia, Diana Margarita. "Popular Protest and Policy Reform in Mexico, 1946–1994: The Dynamics of State and Society in an Authoritarian Regime." PhD diss., Tulane University, 2000.

Foucault, Michel. *Power/Knowledge*. New York: Pantheon Books, 1980.

Gillingham, Paul. "Military Caciquismo in the PRIísta State: General Mange's Command in Veracruz." In *Forced Marches: Soldiers and Military Caciques in Modern Mexico*, edited by Ben Fallaw and Terry Rugeley, 210–37. Tucson: University of Arizona Press, 2012.

———. "'We Don't Have Arms, but We Do Have Balls': Fraud, Violence, and Popular Agency in Elections." In *Dictablanda: Politics, Work, and Culture in Mexico, 1938–1968*, edited by Paul Gillingham and Benjamin T. Smith, 149–72. Durham, N.C.: Duke University Press, 2014.

Gillingham, Paul, and Benjamin T. Smith. "Introduction: The Paradoxes of Revolution." In *Dictablanda: Politics, Work, and Culture in Mexico, 1938–1968*, edited by Paul Gillingham and Benjamin T. Smith, 1–44. Durham, N.C.: Duke University Press, 2014.

Gollás, Manuel. "Breve relato de cincuenta años de política económica." In *Una historia contemporánea de México*. Vol. 1, *Transformaciones y permanencies*, edited by Ilán Bizberg and Lorenzo Meyer. Mexico City: Océano, 2003.

Hansen, Thomas Blom, and Finn Stepputat. "Introduction: States of Imagination." In *States of Imagination: Ethnographic Explorations of the Postcolonial State*, edited by Thomas Blom Hansen and Finn Stepputat. Durham, N.C.: Duke University Press, 2001.

INEGI (Instituto Nacional de Estadística y Geografía). *Estadísticas históricas de México 2014*. Accessed November 14, 2017. http://www.beta.inegi.org.mx/app/biblioteca/ficha.html?upc=702825058203.

Keller, Renata. *Mexico's Cold War: Cuba, the United States, and the Legacy of the Mexican Revolution*. Cambridge: Cambridge University Press, 2015.

Knight, Alan. "Cárdenas and Echeverría: Two 'Populist' Presidents Compared." In *Populism in Twentieth Century Mexico: The Presidencies of Lázaro Cárdenas and Luis Echeverría*, edited by Amalia M. Kiddle and María L. O. Muñoz, 15–37. Tucson: University of Arizona Press, 2010.

———. "The Modern Mexican State: Theory and Practice." In *The Other Mirror: Grand Theory Through the Lens of Latin America*, edited by Miguel Angel Centeno and Fernando López-Alves. 177–218. Princeton, N.J.: Princeton University Press, 2001.

———. "Political Violence in Post-revolutionary Mexico." In *Societies of Fear: The Legacy of Civil War, Violence, and Terror in Latin America*, edited by Kees Koonings and Dirk Kruijt, 105–24. London, New York: Zed Books, 1999.

———. "The Weight of the State in Modern Mexico." In *Studies in the Formation of the Nation-State in Latin America*, edited by James Dunkerley, 212–53. London: Institute of Latin American Studies, 2002.

Levy, Daniel, and Gabriel Székely. *Estabilidad y Cambio: Paradojas del sistema politico mexicano*. Mexico City: El Colegio de México, 1985.

Loaeza, Soledad. "Gustavo Díaz Ordaz: el colapso del milagro mexicano." In *Una historia contemporánea de México*. Vol. 2, *Actores*, edited by Ilán Bizberg and Lorenzo Meyer. Mexico City: Océano, 2005.

Martínez de Campo, Manuel. *Industrialización en México: Hacía un análisis crítico*. Mexico City: El Colegio de México, 1985.

McCormick, Gladys I. "The Last Door: Political Prisoners and the Use of Torture in Mexico's Dirty War." *The Americas* 74, no. 1 (January 2017): 57–81.

———. *The Logic of Compromise in Mexico: How the Countryside Was Key to the Emergence of Authoritarianism*. Chapel Hill: University of North Carolina Press, 2016.

Mendiola García, Sandra C. *Street Democracy: Vendors, Violence, and Public Space in Late Twentieth-Century Mexico*. Lincoln: University of Nebraska Press, 2017.

Moreno-Brid, Juan Carlos, and Jaime Ros. *Development and Growth in the Mexican Economy: A Historical Perspective*. Oxford: Oxford University Press, 2009.

Navarro, Aaron. *Political Intelligence and the Creation of Modern Mexico, 1938–1952*. University Park: Penn State University Press, 2010.

Oikión, Verónica, and Marta Eugenia García Ugarte, eds. *Movimientos armados en México, siglo XX*. Zamora, Mexico: El Colegio de Michoacán/CIESAS, 2006.

Padilla, Tanalís. *Rural Resistance in the Land of Zapata: The Jaramillista Movement and the Myth of the Pax Priísta, 1940–1962*. Durham, N.C.: Duke University Press, 2008.

Pansters, Wil G. "Zones of State-Making: Violence, Coercion, and Hegemony in Twentieth-Century Mexico." In *Violence, Coercion, and State-Making in Twentieth-Century Mexico: The Other Half of the Centaur*, edited by Wil G. Pansters, 3–42. Stanford, Calif.: Stanford University Press, 2012.

Pensado, Jaime M. *Rebel Mexico: Student Unrest and Authoritarian Political Culture During the Long Sixties*. Stanford, Calif.: Stanford University Press, 2013.

Pozas Horcasitas, Ricardo. *Los límites del presidencialismo en las sociedades complejas: México en los años sesenta*. Mexico City: Siglo XXI, 2014.

Rath, Thomas. "Camouflaging the State: The Army and the Limits of Hegemony in Priísta Mexico, 1940–1960." In *Dictablanda. Politics, Work, and Culture in Mexico, 1938–1968*, edited by Paul Gillingham and Benjamin T. Smith, 89–107. Durham, N.C.: Duke University Press, 2014.

———. *Myths of Demilitarization in Postrevolutionary Mexico, 1920–1960*. Chapel Hill: University of North Carolina Press, 2013.

Rubin, Jeffrey W. *Decentering the Regime: Ethnicity, Radicalism, and Democracy in Juchitán, Mexico*. Durham, N.C.: Duke University Press, 1997.

Smith, Benjamin T. "Building a State on the Cheap: Taxation, Social Movements, and Politics." In *Dictablanda: Politics, Work, and Culture in Mexico, 1938–1968*, edited by Paul Gillingham and Benjamin T. Smith, 255–76. Durham, N.C.: Duke University Press, 2014.

———. *Pistoleros and Popular Movements: The Politics of State Formation in Postrevolutionary Oaxaca*. Lincoln: University of Nebraska Press, 2009.

———. "Who Governed? Grassroots Politics in Mexico Under the Partido Revolucionario Institucional, 1958–1970." *Past and Present* 225, no.1 (November 2014): 227–71.

Snodgrass, Michael. "The Golden Age of Charrismo: Workers, Braceros, and the Political Machinery of Postrevolutionary Mexico." In *Dictablanda: Politics, Work, and Culture in Mexico, 1938–1968*, edited by Paul Gillingham and Benjamin T. Smith, 175–95. Durham, N.C.: Duke University Press, 2014.

Stevens, Evelyn P. "Legality and Extra-legality in Mexico." *Journal of Interamerican Studies and World Affairs* 12, no. 1 (January 1970): 62–75.

PART II

REVOLUTIONARY ORGANIZING AND STATE RESPONSE

3

"LATENT SITES OF AGITATION"

Normalistas Rurales and Chihuahua's
Agrarian Struggle in the 1960s

TANALÍS PADILLA

IN OCTOBER 1965, Francisco Chávez Orozco, director of federal education in the state of Chihuahua, received urgent orders from the Secretaría de Educación Pública (Ministry of Public Education, SEP) to visit the *normales rurales* (teacher-training schools) of Salaices and Saucillo. Founded as boarding schools for the sons and daughters of campesinos, officials argued that their constant demonstrations "created complete chaos, a situation that made them latent sites of agitation."[1] Chihuahua was indeed ripe with protest. In a state whose postrevolutionary land tenure system evoked Porfirian times, rural teachers and *normalistas* (student teachers) joined campesinos demanding meaningful agrarian reform. Together, they invaded latifundios, staged demonstrations, and organized constant marches. Triggered by cacique violence and government intransigence, the unrest was particularly intense during the first half of the 1960s and reached a critical juncture when a small teacher-campesino contingency—convinced the time for armed struggle had arrived—attacked the military barracks of Ciudad Madera on September 23, 1965. "Not everyone will give themselves to the revolution," stated Pablo Gómez, a teacher at the normal rural of Saucillo who died in the operation, "but someone has to start it."[2]

As in other parts of the world, Mexico witnessed major student mobilizations during the long 1960s. Amid a state with increasingly hollow revolutionary rhetoric and an ever-greater propensity for repression, Mexico's youth took to the streets. In Chihuahua, an important movement emerged when student

teachers joined the state's long-brewing agrarian unrest. Occupying an intermediary position between the campesino families from whence they came and the
socially conscious professionals they were to become, normalistas—especially
those from the federal normales rurales—drew on common sense notions of
agrarian resistance to formulate a repertoire of struggle. While a rural origin
was not exceptional for Mexican students, those from the normales rurales
were distinct because they preserved their campesino identity as a constituting
marker of their profession. They thus appealed to two politically rich categories:
that of campesino, with its deep roots in the Mexican Revolution (1910–20),
and that of student, which during the 1960s acquired such charged meaning.

The 1968 student movement in Mexico City has been the most prominent
signifier of Mexico's place within the global 1960s. Taking shape as the country
prepared to host the Olympics, the mobilizations called attention to the state's
authoritarianism, the nature of which the army revealed when it massacred
protesters on October 2, 1968. Long considered a watershed moment, recent
scholarship shows the extent to which widescale protest and repression predated
1968 and manifested itself outside the capital.[3] The causes of popular protest
varied. Students, for their part, sought university autonomy and self-governance,
fought to oust corrupt school administrators, and demanded greater educational
resources. But the ideological frameworks with which they engaged entailed a
battle over larger political projects, including the course of Mexico's revolution,
anti-imperialism, and the specter of socialism. Normalista struggles in 1960s
Chihuahua represent a cross-section of these elements, provide a glimpse of
state repression, and foreshadow paths of radicalization.

"THE YOUTH CANNOT ALLOW THEIR TEACHERS TO BE MURDERED"

Chihuahua's two normales rurales—one in Salaices and the other in Saucillo—
constituted part of a federal network of teacher-training schools that dated
back to the 1920s. Meant to prepare socially conscious educators for the countryside, normalista graduates would teach in Mexico's remote areas and facilitate the revolutionary state's projects. At their height during the presidency
of Lázaro Cárdenas (1934–40), normales rurales (then known as Escuelas
Regionales Campesinas, or Regional Peasant Schools) numbered thirty-five.
In the 1940s President Manuel Ávila Camacho's (1940–46) more conservative
administrations eliminated co-education, mandated a uniform curriculum with

urban normales, and reduced funding, leading some of these schools to close. His administration also eliminated Marxists from the SEP and overturned the socialist education framework the ministry adopted for the general curriculum during the 1930s. Nonetheless, the normales rurales preserved a distinct identity characterized by their boarding school structure, students' agricultural activities, and the presence of the Federación de Estudiantes Campesinos Socialistas de México (Mexican Federation of Campesino Socialist Students, FECSM).[4] Formed in 1935, and still in existence today, the FECSM has long politicized the student body of the normales rurales. With committees in each school, it has fought for campus resources, sought a voice in institutional matters, and participated in wider student and popular struggles.[5] Its militant advocacy has long contributed to the radical reputation rural normalistas still enjoy.

But this reputation also stems from the schools' association with emblematic guerrilla figures like Lucio Cabañas—a 1963 graduate of the normal rural of Ayotzinapa—or visible normalista participation in agrarian struggles such as those that shook northern Mexico during the 1960s. In each case, the militant teachers, and the armed strategy some eventually undertook, seemed to confirm the subversive quality of normales rurales. And yet, participation in armed struggle was the notable exception. A greater threat, from the point of view of the state, stemmed from the alliance normalistas rurales might forge with other popular sectors, precisely as they did in northern Mexico during the 1960s when teachers, students, and campesinos fought against the region's severe land concentration.

The ranks of the Partido Popular Socialista (Popular Socialist Party, PPS) and the Union General de Obreros y Campesinos de México (General Union of Mexican Workers and Peasants, UGOCM) spearheaded many of northern Mexico's 1950s and 1960s agrarian struggles. Local leadership included a strong presence of rural teachers who epitomized the socially conscious educators and community leaders SEP officials once envisioned.[6] The UGOCM participated in local and federal elections, defended collective land rights, and demanded the breakup and distribution of latifundios.[7] The party and union structure provided activists with networks that crisscrossed Mexico's northern states and frequently passed through Mexico City. Educational centers serving Chihuahua's poor rural sectors became important hubs of party support.[8] Indeed, normalistas from Salaices and Saucillo held demonstrations alongside students from schools under state jurisdiction. These included the Chihuahua State Normal, several normal night schools, the Arts and Trade School, and the Ladies' Industrial School.[9] The fact that the poorer students from the state normal and trade schools, whose families did not reside in the state capital, lived in the same dormitories facilitated cross-campus political organizing.[10]

During the 1960s, as in other parts of the world, students in Chihuahua engaged in active political participation. They protested Governor Práxedes Giner's (1962–68) authoritarianism as well as the United States' aggression against Cuba. But it was the state's latifundismo that produced the visible alliances with the campesino sector. Here the company Bosques de Chihuahua symbolized the unjust nature of the new postrevolutionary order and the persistence of the old. Founded in 1946 by Eloy Vallina and Carlos Trouyet, who acquired a Porfirian-era railway company and its land, Bosques de Chihuahua owed much of its success to President Miguel Alemán (1946–52). Aside from selling Vallina and Trouyet state railway land on favorable terms, Alemán (who would become a silent partner in the venture) also granted Bosques de Chihuahua a fifty-year, half-million-acre concession to supply raw materials to three major paper and lumber businesses.[11] As the company took possession of the land, it proceeded to enclose, partition, and sell plots that small-scale ranchers had inhabited for generations.[12] Arguing that Bosques de Chihuahua illegally constituted a latifundio, residents petitioned for ownership rights. Thus began a years-long struggle against a company whose investing partners, in addition to former president Alemán, included Chihuahua's most powerful men: Antonio Guerrero, a former military commander; Teófilo Borunda, state governor from 1956 to 1962; Tomás Valle, a businessman and state senator; and descendants of Terrazas and Almeidas, Porfirian-era dynasties.[13]

If Bosques de Chihuahua exemplified the crony capitalism that enabled mid-twentieth-century fortunes, the Ibarras, a family that bought portions of the land and forcibly removed its occupants, epitomized the violence undergirding the system. Chihuahua police allowed the Ibarras to carry guns even as newspapers and federal agents identified them as being responsible for numerous rapes and murders. José Ibarra, who often accompanied state police, had an especially damning reputation.[14] When, in 1959, an unknown assailant murdered the rural teacher Francisco Luján, community members blamed an Ibarra henchman. Luján had long aided campesinos in their land petitions and denounced cacique aggression. With his murder, "Bosques de Chihuahua, Assassins," became a rallying cry and protests spread to the state capital.[15]

Students, especially normalistas, held rallies in support of the sierra's rural poor, articulating a direct connection to the agrarian struggle: normalistas were sons and daughters of campesinos, who were the land's "legitimate owners."[16]

Arturo Gámiz, then a student at Chihuahua's state normal, delivered a moving speech that ended with an impassioned plea: "The youth cannot allow their teachers to be murdered. On the contrary, [we] must actively fight against injustice. Even though we are young, we worry about the fatherland's problems. We are poor students; we are the children of campesinos and workers. That's why we are here, asking the people to raise their voice in protest."[17] In claiming their family's campesino origin and asserting their status as youth invested in the country's future, Chihuahua's students attached the fate of the rural poor to that of the nation. This connection became a persistent rallying cry and foregrounded an agrarian reality that tore at the seams of Mexico's purported modernity.

ARTURO GÁMIZ AND PABLO GÓMEZ

While themselves schooled in Chihuahua's state normal rather than the federal normales rurales, few figures personify the essence of the committed rural teacher better than Arturo Gámiz and Pablo Gómez. It was partly because of their charismatic leadership that hundreds of normalistas joined Chihuahua's agrarian struggle. Their legacy, like that of Genaro Vázquez and Lucio Cabañas in Guerrero—1960s teachers turned *guerrilleros*—would become intimately linked to the narratives of the normales rurales. Gámiz and Gómez's personal histories and political leadership gave them a strong presence among a cross-section of Chihuahua's aggrieved population. Both came from humble backgrounds in northern Mexico, both studied for a time in Mexico City, both became involved in the PPS, and both returned to Chihuahua where they delivered themselves heart and soul to agrarian justice. Each life is a measure of the dynamics that produce movement leaders in the context of migration, urbanization, and access to education.

Born in Durango in 1940, Gámiz's extended family included several rural teachers and a tradition of political involvement.[18] Gámiz spent his early years in Mexico City, where his family had moved in 1950. There, he attended the Instituto Politécnico Nacional (National Polytechnic Institute, IPN) and was active in the youth section of the left-of-center Partido Popular (Popular Party, PP). In 1956 Polytechnic students went on strike demanding greater participation in the school's governance, the resignation of its corrupt director, and increased funding for scholarships and school infrastructure. The movement reverberated nationally as schools across Mexico—including the normales rurales—joined their strike.[19] As a student at the IPN, Gámiz participated in the mobilizations, distinguishing himself as a skilled orator and sophisticated thinker.[20] The government responded to this strike with repression, using the army to dislodge students on September 23, 1956.

Soon after, Gámiz moved to Chihuahua and worked as a teacher in the municipality of Guerrero. He remained there for two years and in 1959 applied to Chihuahua's state normal where he studied for two additional years.[21] At the normal, Gámiz participated in student mobilizations, especially those in support of campesino struggles. Gámiz's charisma, his political activism, and his passion for agrarian justice quickly made him an important avenue by which other students joined campesino mobilizations. Tellingly, a local agrarian leader referred to him as "the young man who always brings a lot of students to the campesino marches."[22] In 1962 Gámiz moved to Mineral de Dolores, a community that had not had a teacher in twenty-eight years. Because caciques used the school as a stable, Gámiz set up a makeshift classroom in the town plaza where he taught sixty-five kids.[23]

Fourteen years older than Gámiz, Pablo Gómez was another important protagonist in Chihuahua's mobilization. Born in 1926 "to an agrarista campesino family," as his daughter Alma Gómez describes it, his early life was one of poverty. In a region where temperatures reach freezing levels during winter months, with no heating at home and few warm clothes, Gómez would take refuge in local cantinas where he'd sleep huddled atop a billiards table "until the bar closed." Like Gámiz, Gómez studied for a career in teaching at Chihuahua's state normal, where he met his wife, Alma Caballero. But Gómez dreamed of becoming a doctor, a profession he pursued in the early 1950s in Mexico City at the Universidad Nacional Autónoma de México (National Autonomous University of Mexico, UNAM). Three of his five children were born during that time. To support his family, Gómez taught elementary school by day and attended medical school by night. After obtaining his medical degree, he practiced medicine in Flores Magón, a town in the northwestern part of Chihuahua where he knew several teachers at the normal rural. Unable to sustain a medical practice because he consistently treated poor patients for free, he supported his family by teaching at the normal rural.[24] In Flores Magón and later in Saucillo, where the school relocated in 1962, Gómez participated in local campesino struggles and became a member of the PPS and an UGOCM delegate.[25] For this work he faced constant harassment. Alma noticed new wounds on her father's body as his involvement deepened: "He had a scar from an attack with a glass bottle; his nose was broken; he had a stab wound on his back. He was detained several times. It was an environment of both generalized and selective repression."[26] Aside from the physical aggression he incurred as state and federal forces dislodged him and other campesinos from land takeovers, Governor Giner, and eventually SEP authorities, sought his transfer outside the state. Accused of inciting Saucillo's normalistas to participate in land invasions, the SEP reassigned him to Atequiza, Jalisco, in 1964.[27] Gómez quit before accepting this change. He sought instead to live in Cuba with his family, a move reportedly blocked by the upper echelons of the PPS.[28]

Gámiz and Gómez's humble beginnings, travel to urbanized centers, social mobility through education, struggle for an elusive agrarian justice, and state persecution exemplify the broader social experience of many mid-century normalistas rurales. That students from Salaices and Saucillo became important protagonists in the struggles they led intertwined these teachers' legacies with that of the normales rurales. In the pantheon of Mexico's unofficial heroes, Gómez and Gámiz stand alongside Rubén Jaramillo, Valentín Campa, Demetrio Vallejo, Othón Salazar, Lucio Cabañas, and Genaro Vázquez—popular figures who fought the PRI's authoritarianism and paid a heavy price. Gómez and Gámiz are ignored by official history—except as examples that normales rurales have a subversive tradition. From below, however, they signify a dignified resistance to a long history of injustice.

"WE COULDN'T BE DETACHED FROM SUCH CAUSES"

In the normales rurales, where the FECSM helped preserve the politicized rural teacher identity that dated back to the Cardenista years, agrarian leaders like Gómez and Gámiz found fertile organizing terrain. Chihuahua's normalistas rurales of the late 1950s and early 1960s recall their experience of political participation through two main frameworks: their own campesino background and the effervescence caused by the Cuban Revolution. If the Mexican Revolution had entitled campesinos to agrarian rights, Cuba's guerrillas heightened the sense of possibility. And these possibilities Gómez and Gámiz constantly invoked. Tracking the revolution's accomplishments and protesting U.S. aggression, moreover, created ample opportunities for popular organizing. So aside from providing ideological inspiration, Cuba, as a topic, drew diverse sectors. Silvina Rodríguez, a student from the normal rural of Saucillo, recalls, "We'd have meetings on Fridays where Prof. Pablo Gómez would bring a map and explain how the Cuban Revolution was going, who had advanced in what moment and on what day."[29] Likewise, Alma Gómez speaks of another teacher, Gonzalo Aguilera, "who made a map of Cuba which my father used to explain the Bay of Pigs invasion during the normal's cultural activities, ones involving the entire community."[30]

The SEP may have no longer advocated for an activist teacher, but the milieu of the 1960s did. Those who heeded such calls understood the struggle ideologically as much as through their personal background. To hear normalistas rurales' family histories is to follow an experience of decades-long poverty, bouts of resistance, and the sense that justice was within reach. While a poor rural background would not in itself spur political involvement, the normales rurales' own history, the political effervescence of the 1960s, and the inspiration of the Cuban Revolution created a propitious context for normalistas rurales to act on their institution's long proclaimed ideals. "We were educated to give ourselves wholeheartedly to the campesino causes," recalls José Ángel Aguirre, who studied at the normal rural of Salaices in the 1950s, "and in that time, there was a lot of caciquismo in the state, there were huge latifundios here. One of them, Bosques de Chihuahua, comprised almost the entire state. So land-petition groups began to emerge and we couldn't be detached from such causes."[31]

When relating his personal story, Aguirre begins with the founding of Nuevas Delicias, the hamlet where he was born. First populated in 1923, fourteen years before his birth, to hear Aguirre tell it, one would think he witnessed it himself. Those who originally came to Nuevas Delicias, states Aguirre, had been sharecroppers on a nearby hacienda. "They didn't own the land, they had to share everything they farmed with the boss and generally they didn't have enough to survive, not even to eat. They lived in crowded rooms, shacks, on top of one another." After the revolution, they petitioned the government and received their own land. "Men, women and children walked; they walked and walked, for three days until they got to a prairie, an inhospitable place. Life in the new setting was still hard, maybe even harder than on the hacienda," affirmed Aguirre.[32]

The strong sense of place in a broader revolutionary narrative with which Aguirre framed his family and community's origins reflected the social possibilities the new order created. The second of eight siblings, when he was six years old, Aguirre began to work the land alongside his father. "For two years that's what I did, until my father was practically forced to send me to school"—a blessing, as Aguirre tells it, for he quickly understood education as his path out of generations of poverty. Thanks to a teacher who arranged Aguirre's part-time attendance (he'd farm with his father the rest of the week), he finished elementary school and in 1952 gained a spot at the normal rural of Salaices. There, Aguirre went on to become head of the FECSM, an experience that no doubt reinforced and politicized the memories of his family history.

Younger than Aguirre, José Luis Aguayo, who studied at Salaices during the 1960s, relates a similar story: "My grandparents were agraristas at the end of the nineteenth century. They were also slaves in the southern haciendas. I learned of the subhuman conditions in which they lived and worked. That was the environment in which I grew up. My uncles had long waged agrarian battles. When I was young, they taught me about that struggle. And I listened: I had breakfast, lunch and dinner with the agrarian code." Aguayo, who also became head of Salaices' FECSM in 1965, recalls his early political awakening: "Our family was very poor . . . early on I perceived the social division, we were not all the same. And since my uncles were agraristas active in the struggle, they emphasized to us, to their kids, that one had to commit to the people."[33] Such personal memories grew deep roots at the normales rurales, institutions whose founding logic was to improve the campesino condition. That this generation's family history trove included memories of Porfirian-era exploitation enhanced the notion that popular struggle could bring about change.

While persistent, the idea of the politicized teacher was not without its contradictions. There was an inherent tension in the prospects of upward mobility that a teaching career afforded and the charge to serve the people. As with any politicized sector, normalistas rurales were often divided and there were many who were indifferent to the struggle altogether.[34] As Manuel Arias, a 1960s normalista from Salaices, explained: "We had everything, from the honest radicals, to the demagogues. . . . And there were also the indifferent ones: 'I came to study, and when I graduate, I'll be a teacher, locked inside my little school. I'll have my family, and the world will turn as it may.' Within those points, there was a broad spectrum of different character profiles."[35]

For those who did feel compelled to act, divisions manifested themselves in two ways: first, between students who thought that, at the normal rural, their responsibility was to complete their teaching careers, *then*, degree in hand, aid campesinos, and those who thought political participation *while* students should take priority. The form that political participation should take itself constituted a second source of contention. Some advocated peaceful and legal mobilizations while others sought more dramatic actions, ones capable of precipitating a revolutionary uprising.[36] Gámiz addressed the matter and rebuked the notion that normalistas best served the cause by first obtaining their degree. "If the goal is to serve the people," he wrote, "it is necessary to participate in their struggle and here a degree has no relevance. One does not serve the people as a professional, one serves them as a revolutionary and no university provides a degree for this cause."[37]

Such debates give a glimpse into how political ideologies interacted with family narratives, leading normalistas rurales to understand their educational opportunities as measures of justice brought about by the revolution.[38] But the persistent rural poverty and their schools' besieged conditions revealed the need for a vigilant defense. The 1960s, a decade of worldwide mobilizations, moreover, beckoned them to do more. Participating in land invasions alongside campesinos represented compelling political acts while evoking two basic principles of Mexico's revolutionary reforms: land and education.

"RURAL PROFESORCILLOS RILING UP THE HENHOUSE"

For authorities, normalista participation in northern Mexico's land invasions constituted proof that social unrest was the work of agitators rather than the result of unfulfilled or betrayed revolutionary promises. Reacting to the ubiquity of normalistas rurales in land takeovers, the assistant director of teacher education personally visited Saucillo, urging students to leave behind their "agitating and disorienting actions" and advising teachers to use "moral suasion and take advantage of students' affection as a means of guidance and control."[39] Mario Aguilera Dorantes, a top SEP official, also instructed all normal rural directors to threaten sanctions to those engaged in political actions.[40] At Saucillo teachers seemed resigned. Students had been duly warned, and "while they listen respectfully, they . . . were intractably committed [to the campesino cause]."[41] It was difficult to dissuade them, stated their teachers, since they "have an ideology that leads them to act in favor of the humble classes."[42]

It was in FECSM assemblies, recalls Silvina Rodríguez, that students decided how to support campesinos. If they did not receive permission to leave the school, she said, "We'd take off anyway." School authorities notified their parents, often in vain. In Rodríguez's case, for example, her father ignored the first such notice, but when he received the second one, he began to worry. "So he came to the normal, to the director's office, to talk to him. Then my father came to me, I don't think the director had really convinced him of anything. My father was a campesino and operated under a different logic. In his mind, what I was doing was magnificent."[43] The reaction of Rodríguez's father provides an example of how student-campesino alliances could stretch traditional gender constraints. Rather than order his daughter to remain under the school's guard, he was heartened by her defense of her family's class interests. But young women's actions had important gender implications, a fact captured by intelligence agents who, despite their generally dry reporting, could not help but condemn gender transgressions. One agent, for example, wrote that when students from Saucillo participated in land invasions, they "slept in the fields alongside campesinos with no regard to the honor they should preserve."[44]

Most female students were quite matter-of-fact about their actions, often conceiving them in terms of their future roles as teachers. Herminia Gómez, who participated in a land invasion, recalls, "Those of us from Saucillo, Salaices, and Aguilera [a normal rural in Durango] were in solidarity with the campesinos. We'd act as if the land was already theirs; it would be farmed and distributed. But what we [from the normales] did in that invasion was to start a school . . . I don't remember how long it lasted, until the very end in May, when one day we woke up surrounded by the army."[45] The state thus added a dose of repression to the experience of struggle, a process that in some cases produced seasoned activists and even guerrilleras.[46]

The state's heavy hand gave further cause for action. An especially tumultuous year in Chihuahua, 1964 saw the countryside dotted with land invasions, and protests erupted in several towns and urban centers. In mid-February, for example, normalistas rurales congregated outside the municipal jail in Saucillo, where authorities had detained several UGOCM leaders. The students remained there until the late hours of the night and the following day organized a demonstration of 1,500 people in the town plaza.[47] A few days later protests extended to the state capital where students from several normales and one junior high school gathered in Chihuahua City's central plaza demanding the freedom of jailed UGOCM leaders and the resolution of the state's agrarian problems.[48] As the event unfolded, a group of between two hundred and three hundred students headed to the agrarian office where fifty pushed their way in. Once inside, they demanded the officer phone national headquarters. The agent called the authorities instead. When the students refused to vacate the building, a SWAT team forced them out with tear gas. Authorities detained thirty-five students and hauled them off for processing to a nearby government building.[49] Amid a city center now guarded by municipal police, the secret service, and SWAT teams, students gathered outside that office demanding the release of their peers.[50] By then, their numbers had swelled, perhaps, noted one newspaper, the result of reinforcements from "outside normales." Refusing to heed the military general's orders to disperse, the police fired some thirty tear gas canisters, leading to a prolonged skirmish.[51]

As authorities hauled them off many students shouted, "We are sons and daughters of campesinos and won't remain indifferent to the injustices in the countryside."[52] Among the five people charged with forced entry, attack on the general communication lines, injury, and armed assault was Carlos Herrera, a teacher from Ciudad Juárez and a former student of the normal rural of Salaices.[53] Herrera declared that "he defended the interest of the campesino class, who, with no real advocates, had in desperation, turned to the student youth."[54] The student-campesino link was thus not only familial, but a product of students' social responsibility, one invoked to emphasize the extent to which the revolution had failed the countryside.

Blind to this reality, Governor Giner declared the increasing unrest work of "rural profesorcillos [no-good teachers] riling up the henhouse."[55] Accordingly, he moved to treat the symptom and ignore the disease: he requested the SEP shut down Chihuahua's normales rurales "because they are veritable serpents' nests, complete communist nests." If their closure was approved, boasted Giner, he'd "turn them into pig farms and oust all the lazy students; those who want to work can raise pigs."[56] Mendoza Domínguez, an army general close to Giner, declared about the female students who participated in the movement: "They are like those lowlife women from the streets. . . . What are those girls doing with campesinos out in the hamlets? . . . What are they doing far from home at night, at dawn?"[57] Not to be outdone, the governor himself mocked the female students when they protested his attempts to close their normal: "Why do they want boarding schools if they like to sleep with campesinos in the field?" he stated in response to student protests over the closing of dormitories.[58] So pervasive were these attacks on female normalistas' moral stature that the UGOCM felt compelled to protest—if paternalistically—against the numerous allegations. "Regarding the female students who have supported us," read an UGOCM statement, "we see them not as soldaderas, but as our daughters and as such have offered them what is at our disposal: our sincerity and, above all else, our profound respect and admiration."[59]

For women normalistas, their political participation was a source of empowerment. Few thought of themselves in feminist terms though the authorities' misogynist reaction reveals the extent to which their actions challenged patri-archy. The course of the struggle, along with the sense that they were part of a greater global shift, emboldened many young women. As Alma Gómez put it, "To see women do things that were traditionally meant for men influenced me. Of course, those were the years in which the Soviet Union sent Valentina Tereshkova to space, when women like [Celia] Sánchez, and Aleida [March] enter Havana with the bearded [revolutionaries]. Women were transforming society."[60] Gómez's words provide a clear sense of how local dynamics interacted with the changing global mores of the 1960s. In practice, female normalistas challenged much more than Chihuahua's land concentration; they upset norms of female domesticity. While the UGOCM denied them agency by referring to them "not as soldaderas but as daughters," images of guerrilleras toppling dicta-tors and conquering space animated female normalista visions of the possible.

The government's understanding of such unrest—as conveyed through intel-ligence sources—was simplistic at best. Reports dwell on what figures, political organizations, or subversive ideologies led teachers, students, and campesinos to protest. Some memos pointed to José Santos Valdés, the supervisor of Mexico's northern normales rurales, as the one pulling the strings. A longtime defender of the socialist education program of the 1930s and director of the normal rural of San Marcos, Zacatecas, from 1948 to 1955, Santos Valdés was also a strong proponent of student self-government. Such sympathies made him suspect to government agents who in one report proclaimed his control over the directors of Saucillo and Salaices and teachers like Pablo Gómez.[61] Since Santos Valdés oversaw student stipends in the amount of 1.5 to 2 million pesos, he used this money, implied one agent, to support political activity.[62] Normal rural directors and their teachers, the majority of whom, according to another report, sympa-thized with the PPS, influenced the ideology of students, inciting or allowing them to participate in land invasions.[63]

As the circle of blame homed in on the normales rurales, tensions mounted and rumors circulated that incoming president Díaz Ordaz would close twenty of the twenty-nine then in existence. As it turned out, these accounts were not that far off: his administration closed fourteen in 1969. At the time, however, the SEP feared that shutting down these institutions would provoke wide-spread unrest.[64] Governor Giner was less apprehensive and eliminated normales and dormitories under his jurisdiction. In the cities of Ojinaga, Parral, Juárez, Saucillo, and Chihuahua, the governor closed the normales' night schools, arguing they had served their purpose.[65] Charging they constituted sites of promiscuity and homosexuality, the governor also closed the dormitories hous-ing students from the State Normal School, the Arts and Trade School, and the Ladies' Industrial School.[66]

Students pointed out the political motivation behind the governor's actions. They proclaimed that Giner's real fear was cross-campus unity and their soli-darity with campesinos.[67] From jail, one teacher protested, "The problem is not moral, nor economic, nor pedagogical, but only and exclusively political. In their active, energetic and decided defense of their own rights and those of rural and urban laborers, the students have shown their combative nature."[68] Normalistas did not accept these measures without a fight, and the state normal quickly declared a strike.[69] Seeking to prevent the normales rurales from joining, local authorities postponed the start of classes, arguing that buildings needed repair, a lie students did not let slide.[70] Once classes did start, SEP officials again travelled to Saucillo and Salaices urging students not to support the strike, declaring that its leaders merely created "a climate of agitation that would harm their studies."[71] When the normal rural of Saucillo planned consecutive work stoppages and invited the region's campesinos to attend their demonstrations, the police intercepted vehicles transporting them to Saucillo.[72]

By year's end, the state of Chihuahua faced a critical situation. In the sierra, a teacher-campesino contingency had taken justice into their own hands against caciques, killing one of the despised Ibarra brothers; the state capital was the scene of persistent demonstrations—some with violent outcomes; normales were continuously on strike or under military occupation. While the federal government investigated the situation in Chihuahua, little came of it. On Sep-tember 23, 1965, Gómez and Gámiz, together with eleven teachers and campes-inos, attacked the military barracks in Ciudad Madera, a failed action in which eight of the thirteen participants died. Gómez and Gámiz revealed the length to which the discontent might resort, but they did not spark the revolution they hoped for.

CONCLUSION

The layered dimension of normalistas rurales' identity—one that blurred the lines between campesinos, students, and professionals—points to an expansive repertoire of struggle and the radical possibilities created by alliances between different popular sectors. The structural transformations taking place during the 1960s facilitated these groups' convergence. Mexico's urbanization, amid the rural poor's hunger for land, made evident the unjust nature of the process. If 1968 signaled the exhaustion of Mexico's economic miracle, Chihuahua—and the many agrarian conflicts that preceded and paralleled it—exposed the acute inequality that fueled it all along.[73] This is why the state relied on repression, to contain those protesting the unjust spoils of progress. Campesinos had lived this before, when they endured the harsh order of Porfirian progress. But a revolution taught them it could be different, and subsequent generations would not easily renounce that lesson. Nor would they forgo its possibilities.

The campesino family histories that the FECSM so deliberately harnessed became political fodder for teachers like Gómez and Gámiz, whose ideological message linked local, national, and global repertoires of struggle. That these teachers-turned-guerrillas experienced important educational opportunities in the nation's capital and returned to northern Mexico to forge common cause with campesinos is indicative of the limitations they saw in the country's economic project. And here the Cuban Revolution provided an alternative model. Socialism, after all, was not a foreign concept to rural teachers; Cárdenas had made it a constituting element of rural education during the 1930s. In stubbornly holding to an identity rooted in campesinos' experience of exploitation and struggle, the normales rurales served as an evocative reminder of the revolution's causes and promises, a dynamic that today continues to produce unruly subjects.

NOTES

I'd like to thank Enrique Ochoa and Jaime Pensado for their insightful comments on this piece.

1. "Estado de Chihuahua," October 26, 1965, Archivo General de la Nación, Dirección Federal de Seguridad (hereafter AGN-DFS) 100-5-1-65/L 14/H 401–402. All translations are my own.

2. Cited in Santos Valdés, *Madera*, 169.

3. For example, McCormick, *Logic of Compromise*; Alegre, *Railroad Radicals*; Pensado, *Rebel Mexico*; Aviña, *Specters of Revolution*; Herrera Calderón and Cedillo, *Challenging Authoritarianism*; and Padilla, *Rural Resistance*.

4. This distinct identity and the twentieth-century history of Mexico's normales rurales are the subject of my book manuscript, "Unintended Lessons of Revolution: Teachers and the Mexican Countryside, 1940–1980."

5. For the FECSM's interaction with other national student organizations, see Carla Villanueva's article in this volume.

6. Created in 1949 by organizations disenchanted with the government-controlled National Peasant Confederation, the UGOCM channeled that unrest into direct action. Affiliated with Vicente Lombardo Toledano's Partido Popular (Popular Party, or PP, formed in 1948), members of the union's executive council also

belonged to the party's national board. On the SEP's early conception of teachers, see Vaughan, *Cultural Politics*, chap. 2.

7. Grammont, "La Unión General," 225–28.
8. "Memorandum," September 18, 1964, AGN-DFS-100-5-1-964/L 10/H 56–58.
9. The normal night schools provided accreditation courses for educators who already worked as teachers but did not have the proper credentials. The Arts and Trade School and Ladies' Industrial School educated students in a variety of trades and technical skills.
10. García Aguirre, *La revolución que llegaría*, 54.
11. "Estado de Chihuahua," September 1965, AGN/Dirección General de Investigaciones Políticas y Sociales (hereafter DGIPS) c.1025/Exp. 22; Boyer, *Political Landscapes*, 145–46; and Vargas Valdés, *Madera rebelde*, 81–88.
12. Henson, "Madera 1965," 70; and García Aguirre, *La revolución que llegaría*, 69–70.
13. Henson, "Madera 1965," 70–71.
14. Ibid., 71–73.
15. "Bosques de Chihuahua, S.A. Asesinos," *Índice*, February 27, 1960; "'Bosques Asesinos S.A.' condenados en México por Renato Leduc en Siempre," *Índice*, April 21, 1960; and Vargas Valdés, *Madera rebelde*, 96.
16. "Eliminación total de Cacicazgos piden los jóvenes," *Norte*, March 7, 1960.
17. Arturo Gámiz, "Ritmo de libertad y de progreso que ha sido detenido," *Norte*, March 7, 1960.
18. Vargas Valdés, *Madera rebelde*, 184; López Rosas, "El pensamiento y estrategia política," 39–43.
19. Pensado, *Rebel Mexico*, 85–89.
20. Vargas Valdés, *Madera rebelde*, 186–87.
21. Henson, "Madera 1965," 96.
22. López Rosas, interview with Salvador Gaytán, June 30, 2007, Mexico City. Cited in López Rosas, "El pensamiento," 54.
23. Santos Valdés, *Madera*, 82; and López Rosas, "El pensamiento," 67.
24. Alma Gómez, author's interview, Mexico City, February 3, 2008.
25. Santos Valdés, *Madera*, 166.
26. Alma Gómez, author's interview.
27. "Memorandum," June 5, 1963, AGN-DFS/100-5-1-63/L 6/H 307; "Información sobre el estado de Chihuahua," June 6, 1963, AGN-DFS/100-5-1-963/L 6/H 310; and "Un Mentís a los Detractores Gratuitos del Dr. y Profr. Pablo Gómez Ramírez," *Índice*, October 21, 1964.
28. Alma Gómez, author's interview; and Santos Valdés, *Madera*, 167.
29. Rodríguez, author's interview.
30. Alma Gómez, author's interview.
31. Aguirre, author's interview. Bosques controlled slightly over a million hectares, which was not the state's total land extension. For Aguirre to express that Bosques encompassed almost the entire state is a measure of how large the company loomed. "Estado de Chihuahua," September 1964, AGN/DGIPS/1025/Exp. 22.
32. Aguirre, author's interview.

33. Aguayo Álvarez, author's interview.
34. One manifestation of these political divisions was a split in the FECSM itself, which from 1961 to 1964 had two factions.
35. Arias, author's interview.
36. While such ideologically divergent views often produced bitter divisions, as Adela Cedillos' contribution to this volume notes, strategically, reformist and armed struggle could be mutually reinforcing.
37. "La Participación de los Estudiantes."
38. See Padilla, "Memories of Justice."
39. "Torres Bodet decidirá la situación del grupo estudiantil de Saucillo," *El Heraldo*, February 23, 1964.
40. "Se informa en relación al magisterio," February 25, 1964, AGN-DFS/63–19/Exp. 1/H 277.
41. "Tratarán de disuadir a estudiantes de Saucillo de participar en las Asonadas," *El Heraldo*, February 23, 1964.
42. Ibid.
43. Rodríguez, author's interview.
44. "Memorandum," April 15, 1964, AGN-DFS/100-5-1-64/L8/H52–54.
45. Herminia Gómez, author's interview.
46. Alma and Herminia Gómez, for example, both later joined the Revolutionary Armed Movement (Movimiento Armado Revolucionario, MAR), a guerrilla group that operated throughout México during the 1960s and 1970s.
47. "Memorandum," February 19, 1964, AGN-DFS/100-5-3-64/L 1/406–407; "Memorandum," February 20, 1964, AGN-DFS 100-5-3-64/L1/H424–425.
48. "Última hora: Tres estudiantes y dos profesores detenidos y consignados," *El Norte*, February 23, 1964; and "Motín de estudiantes normalistas disuelto con bombas lacrimógenas," *El Norte*, February 23, 1964.
49. "La intervención enérgica de las autoridades se hizo necesaria," *El Heraldo*, February 23, 1964.
50. "Memorandum," February 22, 1964, AGN-DFS/100-5-3-64/L1/H441–444; "Motín de estudiantes," *El Norte*, 23 February 1964; "Última hora," *El Norte*, February 23, 1964; "El mitin por la tarde abundó en amenazas," *El Heraldo*, February 23, 1964.
51. "Actúan agitadores profesionales," *El Heraldo*, February 23, 1964.
52. "Última hora," *El Norte*, February 23, 1964. Normalistas rurales were not the only ones claiming a more expansive definition of student identity. As Fernando Herrera Calderón shows, in Guadalajara, the Federación Estudiantil Revolucionaria invoked a barrio identity rooted in students' working-class background. See his contribution to the present volume.
53. Ibid.
54. "La intervención enérgica de las autoridades se hizo necesaria," *El Heraldo*, February 23, 1964.
55. Toro Rosales, *Testimonios*, 29.
56. Ibid., 30.

57. Ibid., 27.

58. Guillermo Gallardo, "Carta Abierta al Sr. Presidente de la República Lic. Gustavo Diaz Ordaz desde la Penitenciaria del Estado," *Índice*, September 27, 1965.

59. "La UGOCM Cumplió y Cumplirá Mientras Exista con el Papel Histórico q'le Corresponde," *Índice*, November 7, 1963.

60. Alma Gómez, author's interview.

61. "Memorandum," April 15, 1964, AGN-DFS/100-5-1-64/L 8/H 52–54; and September 2, 1964, AGN-DFS/100-5-3-964/L 2/H 125.

62. September 2, 1964, AGN-DFS/100-5-3-964/L 2/H125.

63. August 24, 1964, AGN-DFS/100-5-1-964/L 2/H110–111.

64. "Se informa en relación con el magisterio," October 8, 1964, AGN-DFS/40-1-64/L 38/H1; and "Información sobre el estado de Aguascalientes," November 3, 1964; AGN-DFS/100-1-1-64/L 3/H147–184.

65. Prof. Gmo. Rodríguez Ford, "El Cierre de Internados y de las Escuelas Normales," *Índice*, September 12, 1964; "Clausuran las Normales Nocturnas de Chihuahua, Juárez, Ojinaga y Parral," *El Heraldo*, August 25, 1964; "Memorandum," November 11, 1964, AGN-DFS/100-5-1-64/L11/H80–83.

66. "Memorandum," September 12, 1964, AGN-DFS100-5-1-64/L10/H2–3; "Memorandum," November 8, 1964, AGN-DFS/100-5-1-64/L11/H 37–40; "Memorandum," November 11, 1964, DFS/AGN/100-5-1-64/L11/H80–83; "Memorandum," October 29, 1964, DFS/AGN100-5-1-64/Exp.10/H345–347.

67. "Memorandum," September 12, 1964, AGN-DFS100-5-1-64/L10/H2–3.

68. Rodríguez Ford, "El Cierre."

69. "Memorandum," October 29, 1964, AGN-DFS/100-5-1-64/Exp10/L345–347.

70. August 24, 1964, AGN-DFS100-5-1-964/L 2/H110–111; and "Memorandum," September 18, 1964, AGN-DFS/100-5-1-964/L10/H 56–58.

71. "Memorandum," October 29, 1964, AGN-DFS-AGN/100-5-1-64/Exp. 10/H345–347.

72. "Huelga en 16 escuelas Normales Rurales," *Índice*, November 21, 1964; "Memorandum," November 27, 1964, AGN-DFS100-5-1-964/L11/H258–260.

73. For various measures of México's inequality during this period, see Gillingham and Smith, "Paradoxes of Revolution," 3–4.

BIBLIOGRAPHY

ARCHIVES

Archivo General de la Nación, Ramo, Dirección Federal de Seguridad
Heméroteca Nacional de México

INTERVIEWS

Aguayo Álvarez, José Luis. Author's interview. Chihuahua, February 10, 2008.
Aguirre, José Ángel. Author's interview. Chihuahua, February 12, 2008.

Arias, Manuel. Author's interview. Chihuahua, February 13, 2008.

Gómez, Alma. Author's interview. Mexico City, February 3, 2008.

Gómez, Herminia. Author's interview. Chihuahua, February 13, 2008.

Rodríguez, Silvina. Author's interview. Chihuahua, February 11, 2008.

NEWSPAPERS

El Heraldo

El Norte

Índice

Norte

OTHER PUBLISHED SOURCES

Alegre, Robert. *Railroad Radicals in Cold War Mexico: Gender, Class, and Memory*. Lincoln: University of Nebraska Press, 2014.

Aviña, Alexander. *Specters of Revolution: Peasant Guerrillas in the Cold War Mexican Countryside*. Oxford: Oxford University Press, 2014.

Boyer, Christopher. *Political Landscapes: Forests, Conservation, and Community in Mexico*, Durham, N.C.: Duke University Press, 2015.

Gámiz, Arturo. "Participación de los estudiantes en el movimiento revolucionario." Ediciones Linea Revolucionaria, Resoluciones 6. Accessed July 24, 2016. http://www.madera1965.com.mx/res6.html.

García Aguirre, Aleida. *La revolución que llegaría: Experiencias de solidaridad y redes de maestros y normalistas en el movimiento campesino y la guerrilla moderna en Chihuahua, 1960–1968*. Mexico City: Aleida García Aguirre, 2015.

Gillingham, Paul, and Benjamin T. Smith, "Introduction: The Paradoxes of Revolution." In *Dictablanda: Politics, Work, and Culture in Mexico, 1938–1968*, edited by Paul Gillingham and Benjamin T. Smith, 1–44. Durham, N.C.: Duke University Press, 2014.

Grammont, Hubert C. de. "La unión general de obreros y campesinos de México." In *Historia de la cuestión agrarian mexicana*. Vol. 8, *Política estatal y conflictos agrarios, 1950–1970*, 222–60. Mexico City: Siglo XXI, 1989.

Henson, Elizabeth. "Madera 1965: Obsessive Simplicity, the Agrarian Dream, and Che." PhD diss., University of Arizona, 2015.

Herrera Calderón, Fernando, and Adela Cedillo, eds. *Challenging Authoritarianism in Mexico: Revolutionary Struggles and the Dirty War, 1964–1982*. New York: Routledge, 2012.

López Rosas, Abel. "El pensamiento y estrategia política del profesor Arturo Gámiz García en las luchas campesinas y estudiantiles de Chihuahua (1962–1965)." Bachelor's thesis, Universidad Nacional Autónoma de México, 2008.

McCormick, Gladys I. *The Logic of Compromise in Mexico: How the Countryside Was Key to the Emergence of Authoritarianism*. Chapel Hill: University of North Carolina Press, 2016.

Padilla, Tanalís. "Memories of Justice: Rural Normales and the Cardenista Legacy." *Estudios Mexicanos/Mexican Studies* 32, no. 1 (Winter 2016): 111–43.

————. *Rural Resistance in the Land of Zapata: The Jaramillista Movement and the Myth of the Pax-Priísta, 1940–1962*. Durham, N.C.: Duke University Press, 2008.

Pensado, Jaime M. *Rebel Mexico: Student Unrest and Authoritarian Political Culture During the Long Sixties*. Stanford, Calif.: Stanford University Press, 2013.

Santos Valdés, José. *Madera: Razón de un martirologio*. Mexico: Laura, 1968.

Toro Rosales, Salvador del. *Testimonios*. Monterrey: Universidad Autónoma de Nuevo León, 1996.

Vargas Valdés, Jesús. *Madera rebelde: Movimiento agrario y guerrilla (1959–1965)*. Chihuahua, Mexico: Self-published, 2015.

Vaughan, Mary Kay. *Cultural Politics in Revolution: Teachers, Peasants, and Schools in Mexico, 1930–1940*. Tucson: University of Arizona Press, 1997.

4

"FOR THE LIBERATION OF EXPLOITED YOUTH"

Campesino-Students, the FECSM, and
Mexican Student Politics in the 1960s

CARLA IRINA VILLANUEVA

IN FEBRUARY 1968, students from Mexico's *escuelas normales rurales* (rural teacher-training colleges) participated in a multi-day student march that began in the state of Guanajuato and was set to end in Morelia, Michoacán, where numerous political prisoners were being held. While students from various school systems participated, most of those at the Marcha por la Ruta de la Libertad (March through the Path of Liberty) were students who attended the normales rurales, or *normalistas rurales*. On the first day, the students were attacked by a group of campesinos who threw rocks and tomatoes at them. For them—the majority from rural communities—the fact that their attackers were campesinos was an important detail not to be overlooked. As one normalista rural recalled, "they could have been our fathers."[1]

In the 1960s, the national student council that united these schools, the Federación de Estudiantes Campesinos Socialistas de México (Federation of Socialist Campesino Students of Mexico, FECSM), established itself as one of the most influential student organizations in Mexico. Normalistas rurales participated not in solidarity with other students, but rather fully incorporated themselves into the waves of national actions, which echoed the international movements of the decade. The Marcha por la Ruta de la Libertad was one such manifestation. Unlike other students, however, the attacks they experienced by campesinos signified an ambiguous position that normalistas rurales held as both students and campesinos. While not all normalistas rurales were children of campesinos, the FECSM fostered a collective political identity of "campesino-students," both as a way to distinguish itself and as a way to build solidarity with other low-income students.

Historians have alluded to the central role of the FECSM in the social formation and politicization within the normales rurales.[2] In their testimonies, former normalistas rurales have also stressed this point. Some have commented, for example, on the advanced political analysis of the FECSM leaders, who traveled to different schools bringing with them reading materials, including Marxist propaganda from China and the Soviet Union, and leftist newspapers from Mexico City such as *Política*.[3] Furthermore, scholars have begun to explore the political activism of normalistas rurales outside of their campuses, especially their work and solidarity within campesino movements in northern Mexico.[4] Yet, despite the growing recognition of the importance of the FECSM, the organization is often portrayed as disconnected from Mexico's other students or merely present in solidarity. But the normales rurales were not isolated from what occurred in urban universities. Placing the FECSM within the context of student politics, I argue, challenges the urban-centric narrative of the 1960s that overly emphasizes the student actions of this era as the result of an expanding middle class. In particular, I examine in this chapter the relationship of the FECSM with Mexican student politics and give specific attention to the alliance members of the FECSM created with the Central Nacional de Estudiantes Democráticos (National Organization of Democratic Students, CNED), a broad student coalition, as Oikión notes in her chapter, that sought to unite young activists under the banners of democracy, popular education, and student politics independent of government coalitions. The FECSM, I contend, used the campesino-student collective identity as a way to defend the normales rurales and as a way to align itself with other popular students.

THE FECSM: "POR LA LIBERACIÓN DE LAS JUVENTUDES EXPLOTADAS"

The escuelas normales rurales were created through a series of education reforms in the 1920s and 1930s aimed at training rural teachers. The reforms supported the idea that in order to be effective educators, those who taught in rural areas required a different set of skills and know-how from that of their urban counterparts. These schools were part of a larger rural education and agricultural development project in which other, similar institutions existed.[5] For example, created in 1925, the Escuelas Regionales Campesinas (Regional Peasant Schools) were envisioned as key to modernizing rural Mexico, a project targeted at both campesinos and agricultural practices. The curriculum therefore included literacy and hygiene programs as well as agricultural development training.

The ostensible purpose of these institutions varied to reflect the political and economic policies of the government. Under President Lázaro Cárdenas (1934–40), the government supported socialist education and the expansion of agrarian reform. For the institutions of rural education, this meant that students received an education that encouraged them to prioritize social justice and popular education and envision a society in which campesinos were not exploited but rather formed the backbone of a strong rural economy. Faced with the uncertainty created by World War II and the adoption of a more capitalist agrarian model, the governments of Manuel Ávila Camacho (1940–46) and Miguel Alemán (1946–52) abandoned socialist education, which they believed created social "agitators" and national disharmony. The educational pedagogy instead prioritized national unity, capitalist modernization, and cultural nationalism. Other changes included an end to co-education, funding cuts, and a joint curriculum with urban teacher-training schools. By the 1940s, there were incidents of both teachers and students being targeted for being communist or for engaging in activities that were perceived to threaten national unity.[6] Despite the various reforms, the critique of social injustice and the importance of providing education to rural Mexico became defining features of the normales rurales.

The FECSM was founded in 1935 at the Escuela Regional Campesina of Roque, Guanajuato. It was a national student-run organization that united the students from the different rural teacher-training institutions. The FECSM contained a central directive and various changing committees in which students from the different campuses participated. In addition to the national structure, each normal rural campus also had its own *sociedad de alumnos*, or student council. Although the sociedades de alumnos worked closely with the FECSM, they remained largely autonomous. The normales rurales were boarding schools, which meant that the student organization influenced the political, cultural, and social makeup of the schools. Older students were responsible for incorporating younger generations into the FECSM and teaching them the political analysis adopted in the schools. The FECSM therefore became a source of institutional memory for the normalistas rurales. From the beginning, the organization adopted a black flag with a red star in the middle, and their correspondence always read, "Por la liberación de las juventudes explotadas" ("for the liberation of exploited youth").[7]

When it first began, the FECSM adopted a mixed political ideology, somewhere between the Mexican revolutionary nationalism of the 1930s associated with President Cárdenas and communism. In the first edition of its newspaper in 1935, the FECSM described its purpose: "Its tendencies will be the propagation of Marxist-Leninist ideas . . . All of the campesino-students hold an indestructible desire to complete the difficult task of transforming into a beautiful reality all that has been written about the Revolution; strong is its desire to destroy the structure of the bourgeoisie world in which we live."[8]

Achieving the goals of the Mexican Revolution (1910–17), as the FECSM understood them, was linked to destroying the bourgeoisie. The students had a responsibility to help make the goals of the revolution reality, and what united them was their position as campesino-students. One article implied that being a campesino was equivalent to a social class, further linking the revolution with class analysis. Although not all students who attended the schools were campesinos, the FECSM promoted a collective "campesino-student" identity.[9] By specifying that they were campesino-students, as opposed to just students, they identified themselves as aligned with, or part of, a specific, low social and economic group in Mexico. Furthermore, because the campesino image was central to Mexico's postrevolutionary nationalism, the FECSM was able to legitimize the defense of the normales rurales as part of the revolutionary promise to improve rural Mexico.

In 1950, after significant governmental efforts to reform the education system along the lines of a capitalist economic model, the FECSM updated its constitution. While it maintained its adherence to the Mexican Revolution, it also adopted new language that reflected the national and international politics of the postwar years. The doctrine of the organization was to fight for both "economic and political independence of the country." It stressed the need for national unity, which they felt was threatened by a list of various internal and external right-wing forces, including "the Partido Acción Popular, Sinarquismo, los Dorados, Francoism, fascism, international imperialism, the Truman Plan, Plan Clayton, and the Marshall Plan."[10] The FECSM also asserted that it aligned itself with international youth who during World War II fought for "peace, justice, and liberty." Furthermore, it reaffirmed its anti-imperialist position and membership in the International Student Union and the World Federation of Democratic Youth.[11]

Whereas in the 1930s the FECSM was excited by the prospect of bringing about the changes promised by the Mexican Revolution, its 1950 constitution focused more on stating its opposition to what the organization perceived as threats to national independence, including right-wing groups and the lack of resources allotted to their schools. Irrespective of these changes, the determination of the FECSM to unite campesino-students in order to bring about social change for rural Mexico remained.

STUDENT POLITICS AND FACTIONALISM

In the 1960s the FECSM was shaped by the radicalization of the era, which for the organization translated into increased political strength and activity. These years were, paradoxically, also filled with significant internal factions. In 1962, half of the normales rurales left the FECSM and created a separate group they called the Consejo Nacional Permanente (Permanent National Council, CNP). Vicente Rodríguez Quiroz, one of the student leaders of the splinter group described the disagreement as a fight between the "north," sympathizers of the CNP, and the "south," those who remained loyal to the FECSM.[12] While the split was not so geographically precise, the campuses in central and northern Mexico did lead the new group.

There exists no consensus over what led some normalistas rurales to create the CNP or what the different groups represented.[13] Many testimonials, however, focus on the disputes within the Confederación de Jóvenes Mexicanos (Confederation of Mexican Youth, CJM). Born from the corporatist political strategy of the Partido Revolucionario Institucional (Institutional Revolutionary Party, PRI) in the 1930s, the CJM coalition united the major popular student organizations in Mexico, including the FECSM. In the late 1950s, sectors mainly of Mexico's working class challenged the corporatist coalitions, a central component of Mexican politics. The CJM was no exception, and in 1962 members of the youth coalition who no longer found the CJM a viable means through which to demand change began to leave.[14] Though the FECSM did not leave until 1964, as members of the coalition, normalistas rurales participated in the discussions about the CJM. Those who supported leaving the FECSM and who helped create the new normalista rural student group (the CNP) were those who wanted to leave the CJM coalition. The FECSM's split was the reverberation of a fractured Left and the hard political lines created by the radicalization and polarization of the 1960s.

The infighting among normalistas rurales drew the attention of the Dirección Federal de Seguridad (Federal Security Directorate, DFS), and in 1963 the DFS reports on the FECSM significantly increased. While trying to grasp the internal workings of the normales rurales, including the external political spaces in which its students participated, DFS agents paid particular attention to possibilities of a "national student movement." In July 1963, one agent reported that, for the normales rurales, there was "no rational basis" to rumors of such a movement.[15] Days later, an eight-page report focused on explaining the role of the FECSM and the sociedades de alumnos in the administrative decision-making processes in the schools.[16] One agent reported that the infighting between students was actually about who controlled the scholarship funds and student admissions into their schools.

The divisions within the FECSM reflected the various leftist groups that were present in Mexico in the early 1960s.[17] And while the normales rurales were unique in their ability to maintain and foster leftist support within the student body, normalistas rurales participated in a range of political processes and spaces. What were not matters for debate were the continued importance of the schools, the need to defend popular education, and the use of a collective campesino-student identity to defend their schools. It still remains unclear how the local and/or regional politics of Mexico influenced the various campuses. A better understanding of the relationships that the sociedades de alumnos built with local campesino organizations, neighboring schools, the Partido Comunista Mexicano (Mexican Communist Party, PCM), or teachers' unions would contextualize the divergent positions taken at the different campuses.

AN INDEPENDENT NATIONAL STUDENT MOVEMENT

In 1963, the university students and the normalistas rurales that left the CJM organized the first national meeting of the CNED. The meeting was held in Morelia, Michoacán, at the Melchor Ocampo Casa del Estudiante. Approximately 250 delegates attended this important meeting that claimed to represent as many as one hundred thousand students from across Mexico. Due to the split within the normales rurales, the FECSM as an organization was not present at this meeting. The normalistas rurales who attended, rather, came from the group of campuses that supported the creation of the splinter group, the CNP. For example, CNP leader Eusebio Mata Mejia from the normal rural in El Roque, Guanajuato, was on the CNED's first coordinating committee.[18] Mejia was one of a handful of normalistas rurales who became leaders within the CNED.

It was at the Melchor Ocampo meeting that students produced the now famous "Declaración de Morelia" (Morelia Declaration). In this critical document, students called for the creation of a new national, independent, democratic, and "popular class" movement. Using populist language, the authors stressed the potential leading role of popular class institutions and, in doing so, highlighted the importance of the Escuela Nacional de Agricultura (National School of Agriculture), the Instituto Politécnico Nacional (National Polytechnic Institute, IPN), the Escuelas Normales Rurales, and the Universidad Michoacana de San Nicolás de Hidalgo (Michoacan University of St. Nicholas of Hidalgo). The declaration claimed that students organized in direct response to the "profound economic crisis in education." For them, the education reforms that limited assistance services were a "contradiction" to the needs of the popular classes. The authors of the declaration saw entrance exams and the attacks on assistance programs as a way to limit the access that popular classes had to universities—that is, to those youth from "sectors in need." Furthermore, the document exalted a number of "popular leaders" whom the authors believed truly represented their struggle. These included campesino and labor leaders such as Rubén Jaramillo, Román Guerra Montemayor, and Demetrio Vallejo, as well as student leaders Enrique Cabrera and Efrén Capiz. Their collective memory of past movements and leaders was framed as outside of Mexico's urban middle class. These ideas were not new to normalistas rurales. Rather these concepts, such as the need to protect access to education for poor youth, were already part of their collective politics. The influence of normalistas rurales is seen in the inclusion of campesino leaders and schools in the CNED's declaration and the creation of the "secretary of campesino issues" within their organizing structure. In the future, the CNED also participated in solidarity work with the Central Campesina Independiente (Independent Peasant Organization, CCI), the campesino union that formed in 1963.

The CNED declaration also called for a student, worker, and campesino alliance. This form of popular front politics was mostly likely an influence of the Juventud Comunista de México (Communist Youth of Mexico, JCM), whose members helped create the CNED. The direct relationship between the CNED and the PCM or the youth wing of the party is not clear, however, and questions still remain regarding the power relations between students and the party.[19] While still uncertain for historians, these ties were a cause for critique for students who argued that the CNED was not truly democratic and was rather a continuation of Old Left politics.[20]

The CNED meetings were, nonetheless, important places where student leaders of Mexico's universities and technical and rural schools met together to discuss the problems they faced and to build solidarity with each other.[21] In the meetings organized from 1963 to 1968, students shared their experiences, mainly similar stories depicting a growth of harassment from school and state authorities and an unprecedented presence of police forces inside their schools. They also demanded freedom for all political prisoners—a call that would intensify throughout the decade and would reach a boiling point in the aftermath of the 1968 student movement. During these meetings students frequently linked their struggles with broader international events. Some representatives of the CNED gave reports on international student movements in Europe and Latin America with particular focus on the war in Vietnam.

The CNED helped create a national network of students from various education systems, geographic locations, and socioeconomic situations. The significance of the coalition is commonly addressed in the student literature on Mexico City, but its role in student politics outside the capital are not as apparent. Rafael Aguilar Talamantes, one of the CNED's "[primary leaders from] la provincia (the providence)," as DFS agents called him, best explained the relationship that developed between normalistas rurales and the CNED when he called the escuelas normales rurales the *columna vertebral* (backbone) of the CNED, a phrase commonly repeated by other students.[22] Some students in Mexico City, such as the 1968 student leader Gilberto Guevara Niebla, claimed that the success of the CNED outside of the capital was due to the different type of student movements.[23] Liberal urban students, such as those who attended the Universidad Nacional Autónoma de México (National Autonomous University of Mexico, UNAM), conceived of themselves as the "vanguard" responsible for transforming the politics of the country, whereas they felt that students from the popular classes were constrained to government assistance and therefore did not challenge the state.[24] Though liberal students may have made this distinction in a disparaging way, by focusing on their socioeconomic position as a way to create a united front, popular students similarly created distinctions between themselves and others. Both the focus on "popular education" within the CNED and the concept of the "campesino-student" within the FECSM were forms of legitimizing their politics through their socioeconomic positions. The continued demand for popular education, at a time when students felt that these government services were at risk, continued to be an important component to student politics outside of Mexico City. It was through their work to maintain government assistance programs that students critiqued government corruption and authoritarian politics. By raising awareness about the underfunding of their institutions, the students highlighted the contradictions between government actions and government rhetoric, which claimed to prioritize education and rural Mexico.

1965 STRIKE IN DEFENSE OF THE NORMALES RURALES

In November 1964, all of the normales rurales reunited under the FECSM. Then in 1966, the FECSM became an official member of the CNED coalition.[25] Because of the ties between the CNED and the PCM, some scholars have framed this change in alliance, from the CJM to the CNED, as a moment in which the PCM increased its influence in the normales rurales.[26] While students no doubt participated in various political spaces, including the youth section of the PCM, to define these mixed political spaces as communist control over the schools seems to reinforce Cold War rhetoric of outside communist threats and overlooks the other forces that pulled normalistas rurales together. It was more than simply political rhetoric that motivated normalistas rurales; their campuses dealt with real increased violence and aggression from authorities and continued to lack basic resources. In other words, the threat to popular education, their daily living conditions, and what they understood as reasonable resource requests were issues under which normalistas rurales could unite, even at the height of political factionalism during the Cold War.

To this end, in 1965, the normales rurales went on strike for about five weeks after the Secretaría de Educación Pública (Ministry of Public Education, SEP) refused to meet the demands of the FECSM's petition. Among other things, normalistas rurales demanded an increase in the student food per diems, funds for medication, vehicles for transportation, materials for science courses, sports equipment, and school uniforms. The strike was part of an extensive campaign

organized by the FECSM and the sociedades de alumnos that included escalating actions, a letter-writing campaign directed at the president, and local
meetings.

Access to adequate resources was a constant struggle, and in their battles
to maintain their schools' functionality, the FECSM became the recognized
intermediary between normalistas rurales and the SEP. In the 1950s many of
the normales rurales lacked basic necessities such as water, food, and beds.[27]
A 1960 federal education reform that set out to expand basic education, commonly referred to as the Plan de Once Años or the Eleven Year Plan, resulted
in increased funds to the normales rurales. The changes were insufficient and
resources remained at the center of student actions within the schools.[28] During
the 1965 strike, the PCM's *La Voz de México* quoted the sociedad de alumnos of
the normal rural of Palmira as having said, "we do not know what your concept
of the word 'severity' is, but when you live in our circumstances there are plenty
of other words to express and demonstrate the realities."[29] This was directed at
the SEP's dismissive response to their petition. Students also pointed to past
government cuts of other services, including the closure of the dorms of the
Politécnico and the closure of the dining services in the Nacional de Maestros
(National Teachers College) in order to emphasize the real threats institutions
of popular education faced.[30]

The strike began with three escalating actions: a twelve-hour work stoppage
on March 26, a twenty-four-hour stop on March 29, and a forty-eight-hour
stop that began on March 31.[31] Long strikes were particularly difficult for normalistas rurales because administrators would stop the dining hall services and
food rations. These were boarding schools, so the dining halls were the primary
source of food for the students. Suspending school activities for weeks on end
therefore meant that students from the twenty-nine different campuses, about
eleven thousand students, depended significantly on local communities for food
and resources. In order to request help, normalistas rurales used their collective
identity of campesino-students; the fight for their schools was framed as a
fight of rural and poor communities. The FECSM's ability to coordinate such
a national strike underscores the level of organization and also lends itself to
consider the national presence of these students. From this perspective, both
the consequences and the success of the strike extended beyond the boundaries
of the school campuses.

The 1965 strike also included a letter-writing campaign directed at President Gustavo Díaz Ordaz (1964–70). Hundreds of letters were sent to his

office from across the country in support of the students. Campesino collectives, individuals, and ex–normalistas rurales then working as schoolteachers asked the president to comply with the student demands. Dozens of letters followed templates presumably formulated by the students themselves. Others, however, were more personalized, with longer explanations as to why they supported the students. Many stressed the important work normalistas rurales did in their communities. One letter read, "It is an embarrassment" that the government can "distribute thousands of breakfasts and millions of books" but it cannot "feed the future teachers."[32] The comment concerning books was a reference to the 1960 education reform, which included standardization and distribution of free textbooks. This letter therefore pointed out the contradiction in the government's education reform that claimed to expand basic education while simultaneously ignoring the needs of the future teachers of basic education in rural Mexico.

The image of normalistas rurales as both students and campesinos is further highlighted in the media coverage of the strike. While reports of the normales rurales were generally sparse, especially when compared to the newspaper coverage of student actions in Mexico City, the 1965 strike drew significant attention. Articles sympathetic to normalistas rurales detailed the poor conditions of the schools and the importance of the students' future work as teachers. For example, *Sucesos Para Todos* author Mario Menéndez Rodríguez listed the daily food ration that these students received in Yucatán. The three meals basically consisted of different amounts of beans and tortillas. He claimed that the food was not enough to "replenish the calories they burn[ed]." He went on to ask the readers to imagine what it meant "to work in the mountain, burn brush, cut wood, etc., under the Sirius sun of the land of the Mayas."[33] It was common for media to reproduce this overly romanticized image of students' poverty, but in doing so, they also reiterated the dual position normalistas rurales held as both students and campesinos.

While the internal division of the early 1960s presumably did not disappear, normalistas rurales were able to organize together and present a united front during the 1965 strike. Students continued to align themselves with conflicting ideologies and groups, but the increased harassment and the need to defend popular education brought normalistas together under the FECSM. Through their various campaign actions such as the letters to the president, their requests for support from surrounding communities, and even the urban-left media coverage, the 1965 strike highlighted the FECSM's continued use of the collective campesino-student identity to build their politics within the normales rurales.

MARCHA POR LA RUTA DE LA LIBERTAD

By 1966, the CNED faced significant criticisms in Mexico City, especially when the president of the coalition, Enrique Rojas Bernal, was accused of stealing money and working with the PRI. Some normalistas rurales also critiqued the CNED because they believed the coalition leaders were too involved in the internal workings of the FECSM.[34] Despite these challenges, the two groups continued to work closely together. The relationship was further solidified in 1966, when Matías Rodríguez, the general secretary of the FECSM became the secretary of campesino issues for the CNED.

· The connection was also evident by their joint organizing of the Marcha por la Ruta de la Libertad (the March Along the Route of Freedom) in 1968. The march was organized to demand the release of political prisoners, many of them student activists, who were being held in Morelia. The five-day march was a symbolic re-creation of the route Miguel Hidalgo took during the initial struggle for Mexican Independence in 1810. It started in Dolores Hidalgo in the state of Guanajuato and included stops in Guanajuato, Salamanca, and the Valle de Santiago. It was also presented as an opportunity to celebrate the national student movement, which, as they understood it, had begun with the creation of the CNED in 1963. It was billed as a "great civic party for Mexican youth and students" and an opportunity to "test the organizational and leadership capacities of all of the participants."[35] They organized various events that included speeches, poetry, and music. The march began at the normal rural in Roque, Guanajuato, and was accompanied by the marching band from that same school. Delegations from across the country arrived and joined the march at various points along the route.

The march faced significant opposition from several groups. In the weeks leading up to the march, DFS agents attempted to track how many students and organizations had registered to participate. They believed that the majority of the participants would be the "militant" normalistas rurales.[36] Newspaper articles warned readers about the march and suggested that the PCM was financing it.[37] In Guanajuato, some opposed the march because they disagreed with the use of national symbolism—that is, Miguel Hidalgo and the route of the Mexican Independence. Furthermore, students from the law school of the University of Guanajuato declared their opposition to the CNED and helped organize a counterprotest to condemn the march and the use of Miguel Hidalgo's image.[38] Finally, on the day that students from across the country traveled to Guanajuato, one of the trains did not stop at its designated location and students had to find alternative transportation back to the march. Students rightfully interpreted this as a clear attempt by authorities to limit their participation.[39]

It was at the onset of the march in Dolores Hidalgo where they were attacked by campesinos from the PRI's Confederación Nacional Campesina (National Campesino Confederation, CNC). Students left the town with head injuries and the windows of their buses broken.[40] This confrontation would not be the last between the CNC and normalistas rurales. A few weeks after the march, the CNC published a letter in national newspapers in which they told the FECSM that the administration of Díaz Ordaz was reasonable and open to dialogue, and that the students needed to find a way to work with them, especially since their demands had been met.[41] The use of the CNC to oppose the normalistas rurales further emphasizes the ambiguous position that these students held as both students and campesinos. This division also created a distinction between bad and good campesino groups, or those loyal to the government. Solidarity between campesinos was not a natural preposition of such identity.

The final obstacle that the marchers experienced was in the Valle de Santiago where the military stopped them before they were able to reach Morelia. The officers presented the students with a clear choice. The students could willingly get on the twenty-three buses provided by the military, or they could defy the military request and instead be forced onto the buses, dragged over the bodies of those who chose to disobey orders.[42] Student leaders opened the decision to the group and participants spent hours debating how they should proceed. Should they get on the buses? Would the military really shoot them if they chose to continue? The situation was symbolic of the decision many youths made during the Cold War: to confront the state head-on or choose a route of peaceful reform. Students eventually decided to obey the military orders.

In the following months authorities used the FECSM's participation in the march as a way to discredit the organization. For example, the general secretary of the SEP, Agustín Yáñez, dismissed a petition and a subsequent strike of nor-malistas rurales as merely a reaction to their "failed" march.[43] Normalistas rurales were quick to point out, however, that the FECSM petition in question was actually sent to the SEP on January 27, 1968, about one week prior to the march. In addition to their demands, the FECSM petition stated that students believed their requests could be resolved through "sincere dialogue" with the authorities. However, they also made it clear that if faced with any severe changes, students were prepared to resist if they had to: "We proudly maintain the combative tra-dition of our schools in struggles that have tested our profound preoccupation for the future of the Normales Rurales."[44] In February, after the SEP did not address their concerns, the normales rurales once again went on strike.

CAMPUS CLOSURES AND STUDENT RADICALIZATION

The February 1968 strike was the first of many confrontations between normalistas rurales and authorities over the next two years. In 1969, the SEP implemented drastic education reforms, which resulted in the closure of fifteen of the twenty-nine schools.[45] The FECSM's public written responses to these reforms highlighted the radicalization that the organization had undergone; open dialogue with the SEP was no longer a realistic option.

In August 1969, the FECSM organized the Primer Seminario de Estudios por la Reforma Democrática a la Educación Normal Rural (First Conference for the Democratic Reform of Normal Rural Education), a student conference held at the normal rural in Atequiza, Jalisco. The event was the first time normalistas rurales organized their own conference on education, independent of the SEP.[46] From this conference students produced the Declaración de Atequiza (Atequiza Declaration) and two subsequent public declarations in which they expressed their rage with the government reforms.

By closing half of the normales rurales, the government of Díaz Ordaz had crossed a line, which no other previous administration had ever dared to do. For normalistas rurales, this marked a clear attack not only against their schools and their political activism, but also, more generally, against popular education. The students were outraged by the violent use of military and police forces and accused the government of using members of the CNC, which they considered pawns of Mexican government, to infiltrate their schools and divide the FECSM. They understood the school closures as a continuation of student repression experienced in 1968 in Mexico City. Similar to the language of the CNED, the FECSM positioned its fight for popular education, including the need to keep all of the campuses open, as part of both a national independent student movement and an independent campesino movement.[47]

Finally, their declarations were signed off with the line, "hasta la victoria siempre" (ever onward to victory), a manifestation of the influence of the Cuban Revolution. The students also made direct references to the Cuban literacy reforms as an example of a successful education program implemented by a revolutionary government. They argued that the teaching profession was not something to be "discovered," rather they understood teaching as necessary to build a "revolutionary space for a new society."[48] The successful revolution, as it related to education reform for rural communities, was the Cuban Revolution, not the Mexican Revolution.

Despite its efforts, the FECSM lost half of its membership with the school closures. The process was violent; both military and police were used to either transfer students to different schools or to kick them off of campuses where young activists had occupied the schools in an attempt to save them. Furthermore, authorities prohibited the FECSM from organizing within the normales rurales for a few years. This process, in addition to the general increase in repression against both campesinos and students, pushed many toward more radical political paths, including both urban and rural guerrilla groups. When the FECSM reemerged in the early 1970s, its members had strong ties to the newly formed armed movements and other radical spaces, which impacted both the FECSM's internal politics and the repressive measures taken by authorities in the 1970s.

While the history of the FECSM eclipses the individual experiences of normalistas rurales and the local politics of the different campuses, it nonetheless provides an important framework from which to understand the normales rurales in the 1960s and offers an example of student politics outside Mexico City where normalistas interacted with both campesinos and middle-class students. The postrevolution education reforms created a group of students whose access to education was contingent on their modest economic position. The belief that education for rural communities was a victory of the Mexican Revolution, along with their use of a collective campesino-student identity, allowed for these same students to legitimize the defense of their schools. In the context of the sixties, the FECSM used these ideas to strengthen its ties with national student politics in Mexico.

Unlike other student organizations from this time, the FECSM still exists today and continues to represent the students from the remaining normales rurales. The most recent strike organized by normalistas rurales took place in June 2017 at the normal rural in Aguascalientes. The students protested against proposed government reforms that would have changed the all-women campus to a co-ed system and lowered the number of allotted admissions. In their fight to keep the school accessible to female youth from surrounding poor communities, the activists of the FECSM helped by participating in the marches and roadblocks near the campus.[49]

NOTES

I would like to thank both Enrique Ochoa and Jaime Pensado for their valuable feedback and support.

The first paragraph heading, "The FECSM: 'Por la Liberación de las Juventudes Explotadas,'" uses a phrase from the FECSM in their correspondence and means "for the liberation of exploited youth."

1. Paco, author's interview, January 20, 2013.
2. Civera Cercedo, *La escuela como opción de vida*, 207–48; Tanalís Padilla, "Rural Education, Political Radicalism, and Normalista Identity in Mexico After 1940," in Gillingham and Smith, *La Dictablanda*, 349.
3. Aguayo Álvarez, *Escuela Normal Rural Salaices*, 11; Hernández Santo, *Tiempos de reforma*, 304.
4. See, for example García Aguirre, *La revolución que llegaría*; and Tanalís Padilla's chapter in this volume.
5. For a complete history of the escuelas normales rurales and their relationship with these other institutions from 1921 to 1945, see Civera Cercedo, *La escuela como opción de vida*.
6. Ibid.
7. Ibid., 230.
8. Editorial, *FECS*, November 1, 1935, in AGN-Secretaría de Educación Pública, Departamento de Enseñanza Agricola y Normal Rural, box 33269, ref. x/200(04) (x-5)727.13/1.
9. Formed mainly after the revolution, campesino was "a distinct social group united by a shared set of political and economic interests as well as by a collective history of oppression." Boyer, *Becoming Campesino*, 3.
10. Archivo General de la Nación–Dirección Federal de Seguridad (hereafter AGN, DFS), public version, L1.
11. Ibid.
12. Rodríguez Quiroz, "Apunte autobiográfico."
13. For a detailed explanation of these contradictions, see García Aguirre, "Estudiantes normalistas rurales," 9.
14. Cuevas Díaz, *El Partido Comunista Mexicano*, 66; and Pensado, *Rebel Mexico*, 83–99.
15. AGN, DFS, public version, L1, Exp. 63–19–63.
16. Ibid.
17. On the various Lefts, see Keller, *Mexico's Cold War*.
18. "Hacia la Central Estudiantil Independiente," *La Voz de México* (June 15, 1963); AGN, DFS-FECSM public version, L1, 40–1-64.
19. The PCM newspaper, *La Voz de México*, hints at this relationship.
20. See, for example, Movimiento Juvenil Socialista, "El Sectrarismo y el oportunismo de la II Conferencia de Estudiantes Democráticos," September 13, 1964, in Cuevas Díaz, *El Partido Comunista Mexicano*, 161.

21. For an example of one meeting that involved students from the CNED, the Consejo Nacional Permanente, and students from Saucillo and Salaices in Chihuahua, see AGN, DFS-CNED public version, 11–142–64; AGN, Dirección General de Investigaciones Políticas y Sociales (hereafter DGIPS), box 458 exp. 1, 319–321.
22. See, for example, Martínez Nateras, *La flor del tiempo*, 37; AGN, DFS-FECSM public version L1, 63–19–65.
23. See Gilberto Guevara Niebla in Cuevas Díaz, *El Partido Comunista Mexicano*.
24. Gómez Nashiki, "El movimiento estudiantil mexicano," 204.
25. There are conflicting dates, but according to Sergio Briano Ortiz, this happened in 1964 at a meeting in the Escuela Normal Rural de Cañada Honda. See Ortiz Briano, *Entre la nostalgia*, 221.
26. Cuevas Díaz, *El Partido Comunista Mexicano*, 82; Calderon López-Velarde, "La Escuela Normal Rural."
27. Aguayo Alvarez, *Escuela Normal Rural Salaices*, 11.
28. Testimonials from the 1950s commonly describe the lack of access to clean water, electricity, and housing. See, for example, Bustos García, *Ximonco*; Aguayo Álvarez, *Escuela Normal Rural Salaices*, 137, 145; and Hernández Grajales, *El normalismo rural en Chiapas*.
29. "Huelga Nacional en las normales rurales," *La Voz de México*, March 28, 1965.
30. "Huelga en las normales," *Política*, May 1, 1965.
31. Ibid.
32. Becerra Sandoval Santos, Amatlán de Cañas, Nayarit, AGN, Fondo Gustavo Díaz Ordaz (hereafter FGDO), V117, C185, April 27, 1965.
33. Mario Menéndez Rodríguez, "La terrible verdad de Yucatán," *Sucesos Para Todos*, May 7, 1965.
34. AGN, DFS-FECSM public version L2, January 11, 1968, 301.
35. "Objetivos, contenido y significado de la marcha por la ruta de la libertad," *La Voz de México*, January 21, 1968.
36. AGN-DGIPS, Caja 471, 1, exp. 171.
37. "¿La libertad?" *Mañana*, March 17, 1968.
38. Ibid.
39. "Investigación del descarrilamiento; no se procede contra los 'hippies,'" *El Informador*, February 9, 1968; Martínez Nateras, *La flor del tiempo*, 54; Aguayo Álvarez, *Escuela Normal Rural Salaices*.
40. Paco, interview with author, 2013.
41. "Confederación Nacional Campesina: A los estudiantes de las escuelas normales rurales," *El Nacional*, March 2, 1968.
42. Martínez Nateras, *La flor del tiempo*, 22; "Por la ruta de la libertad," *La Voz de México*, February 11, 1968; Paco, interview with author.
43. "Represalia por la fallada 'Marcha,' las huelgas en las Normales Rurales," *El Informador*, March 1, 1968.
44. "Pliego general de peticiones," AGN, DFS-FECSM public version, L3, January 27, 1968.

45. Before 1969, the normales rurales included both secondary-level education and teacher training, which meant there was a big age range of students. The 1969 reform removed the secondary-level education from the teacher-training aspect of the schools. The "closed" normales rurales were either transformed into technical secondary schools or incorporated into other existing technical schools.
46. Hernández Santos, *Tiempos de reforma*, 282; and AGN, DFS-FECSM public version, L2, July 1967, 225.
47. "Llamamiento a la solidaridad con la lucha de los estudiantes normalistas rurales," AGN, DFS-FECSM public version, L6, September 3, 1969.
48. "En defensa de las Normales Rurales contra la reforma antipopular y reacionaria," AGN, DFS-FECSM public version, L8, August 8, 1969.
49. Luis Hernández Navarro, "Cañada honda: La dignidad de las normalistas," *La Jornada*, June 6, 2017.

BIBLIOGRAPHY
ARCHIVES

Archivo General de la Nación
  Dirección Federal de Seguridad (public versions only)
  Dirección General de Investigaciones Políticas y Sociales
  Fondo Gustavo Díaz Ordaz
  Secretaría de Educación Publica
Centro de Estudios del Movimiento Obrero y Socialista
Hemeroteca Nacional Digital de México

INTERVIEWS

Paco (pseudonym). Author's interview. January 20, 2013.

NEWSPAPERS

El Informador
El Nacional
La Jornada
La Voz de México
Mañana
Política
Sucesos Para Todos

OTHER PUBLISHED SOURCES

Aguayo Álvarez, José Luís. *Escuela Normal Rural Salaices: Formadora de maestros*. Mexico: Self-published, 2012.
Boyer, Christopher. *Becoming Campesino: Politics, Identity, and Agrarian Struggle in Post-revolutionary Michoacán, 1920–1935*. Stanford, Calif.: Stanford University Press, 2003.

Bustos García, Felipe. *Ximonco: La Escuela Normal Rural de Perote: Su historia*. Mexico: Self-published, 1995.

Calderon Lopez-Velarde, Jaime Rogelio. "La Escuela Normal Rural: Crisis y papel politico (1940–1980)." BA thesis, Escuela Nacional de Antropología e Historia, 1982.

Civera Cercedo, Alicia. *La escuela como opción de vida: La formación de maestros normalistas rurales en México, 1921–1945*. Estado de México: El Colegio Mexiquense, 2008.

Cuevas Díaz, J. Aurelio. *El Partido Comunista Mexicano 1963–1973: La ruptura entre las clases medias y el Estado fuerte en México*. Mexico: Universidad Autónoma de Guerrero y Universidad Autónoma de Zacatecas: Editorial Línea, 1984.

García Aguirre, Aleida. "Estudiantes normalistas rurales en la vida pública: De la defensa de sus escuelas a la crítica del sistema político, 1961–1965." *Memoria electrónica de XIV Encuentro Internacional de Historia de la Educación*, 2016.

Gillingham, Paul, and Benjamin T. Smith, eds., *Dictablanda: Politics, Work, and Culture in Mexico, 1938–1968*. Durham, N.C.: Duke University Press, 2014.

Gómez Nashiki, Antonio. "El movimiento estudiantil mexicano: Notas históricas de las organizaciones políticas, 1910–1971." *Revista Mexicana de Investigación Educativas* 9, no. 17 (2003): 187–220.

Hernández Grajales, Greogorio de Jesús. *El Normalismo Rural en Chiapas: Origen, desarrollo y crisis*. Mexico: Self-published, 2004.

Hernández Santos, Marcelo. *Tiempos de reforma: Estudiantes, profesores y autoridades de la Escuela Normal Rural de San Marcos frente a las reformas educativas, 1926–1984*. Zacatecas, Mexico: Universidad Autónoma de Zacatecas, 2003.

Keller, Renata. *Mexico's Cold War: Cuba, the United States, and the Legacy of the Mexican Revolution*. Cambridge: Cambridge University Press, 2015.

Martínez Nateras, Arturo. *La flor del tiempo*. Mexico: Universidad Nacional Autónoma de México y Universidad Autónoma de Sinaloa, 1988.

Ortiz Briano, Sergio. *Entre la nostalgia y la incertidumbre: Movimiento estudiantil en el normalismo rural mexicano*. Zacatecas, Mexico: Universidad Autónoma de Zacatecas, 2012.

Pensado, Jaime M. *Rebel Mexico: Student Unrest and Authoritarian Political Culture During the Long Sixties*. Stanford, Calif.: Stanford University Press, 2013.

UNPUBLISHED SOURCES

Rodríguez Quiroz, Vicente. "Apunte Autobiográfico." Unpublished memoir, 2013. Accessed October 19, 2017. http://www.seducoahuila.gob.mx/archivo/documentos /biografias/VICENTE%20RODRIGUEZ%20QUIROZ.pdf.

5

THE 23RD OF SEPTEMBER COMMUNIST LEAGUE'S *FOCO* EXPERIMENT IN THE SIERRA BAJA TARAHUMARA (1973–1975)

ADELA CEDILLO

ACCORDING TO HISTORIANS Gilbert Joseph and Jürgen Buchenau, the Mexican Revolution is unique among twentieth-century upheavals, since both opposition forces and the state drew from its traditions and symbols to legitimize their actions.[1] But a closer look at the 1960s and 1970s complicates this argument. I suggest that the guerrillas who emerged across Mexico during this period broke with this pattern and instead followed a path taken by the Latin American radical Left. Although Mexican guerrillas admired revolutionary heroes like Emiliano Zapata and Francisco Villa, they no longer believed in the 1910 Revolution as a source of legitimacy and claimed to be able to make a genuine revolution by way of Marxist-Leninist scientific principles.[2]

During the Cold War, peasant communities across Mexico also repudiated the legacy of the 1910 Revolution. For many of them, receiving an ejido (a communal land grant) from the government did not necessarily mean improvement in their living conditions, and in some cases they did not even benefit from land distribution. For the same reasons, these communities became allies of the guerrilla movements, primarily in the states of Chihuahua, Sonora, Guerrero, Oaxaca, and Chiapas. However, not all peasants disavowed the political principles of the Mexican Revolution and many of them took inspiration from a variety of sources that included agrarianism, Cardenismo, and Jaramillismo.[3] From the beginning of the socialist armed movement in Chihuahua in 1964, a tension existed in these various uprisings between radical peasants and middle-class guerrillas. Although both agreed on the need for armed struggle, their goals differed. These differences proved to be a recurring issue within rural guerrilla organizations, often resulting in the formation of splinter groups.

Scholarship on the Mexican Dirty War has analyzed the formation of guerrilla groups, but seldom has it compared the differences between groups or the conflicting views of members of the same organization.[4] This chapter looks at the overlap between ideology, class, and the struggle for hegemony to explain the clashes among some of the groups that made up the Liga Comunista 23 de Septiembre (23rd of September Communist League, or LC23S, hereinafter, the Liga)—the largest guerrilla coalition in Mexico. In 1973, the Liga launched a *foco* experiment, a small rural armed force, called the Comité Politico-Militar "Arturo Gámiz" ("Arturo Gámiz" Political-Military Committee, CPMAG) in the Golden Quadrilateral of the Sierra Madre Occidental, a region bordering the states of Chihuahua, Sonora, Sinaloa, and Durango. I analyze the political goals of the middle-class cadres who advocated communist tenets and the peasants from the Guarijío and Rarámuri communities of the Sierra who upheld agrarian goals, and how the alliance of these classes had contradictory outcomes.

The guerrillas' ideological and military foundations not only were distant from the 1910 Revolution, they neglected the culture and struggles of indigenous peoples. I argue that while indigenous peasants were responsive to communist ideas and often embraced the Liga's war, they also preserved their own agenda, which was dictated by their land demands and their specific history. The state eradicated the CPMAG after several counterinsurgency campaigns. However, the Echeverría administration distributed land for the first time among the Guarijíos in 1976 and launched civic action programs in the Sierra. Thus, while peasant rebels achieved their goals, guerrillas criticized themselves for having failed to bring about a socialist revolution.

The scholarship on the Mexican Dirty War has generally focused on the origins and failure of the socialist armed movement and the gross human rights violations committed by security forces, especially in the Guerrero countryside.[5] Sergio Aguayo and Verónica Oikión have broadened this perspective by claiming that the emergence of the human rights movement, the Political Reform of 1977, and the Amnesty Law of 1978 were collateral and unintended victories of the armed struggle.[6] However, scholars have tended to downplay other reforms that guerrilla struggles won because they have interpreted the government's civic action programs as mere expressions of a counterinsurgency policy designed to win the "hearts and minds" of people.[7] While there is compelling evidence that the reforms were part of a counterinsurgency plan, it is also beyond doubt that they met popular demands. The history of the Liga in the Golden Quadrilateral demonstrates how indigenous people took advantage of the upheaval to seek their emancipation on their own political terms. It also shows how the armed struggle benefited groups that lacked both political representation and a place in the public sphere and forced the state to recognize them as citizens.

Isolated highlander communities needed external support to fulfill their dreams of accessing land as a means of subsistence, social mobility, and cultural identity, while urban revolutionaries needed peasant participation to take state power and build a socialist regime. Ultimately both projects were incompatible, yet the peasant-student alliance demonstrated that guerrilla struggle was more than merely a failed attempt to start a new revolution: it was a path to change the balance of power from the bottom up and promote major transformations in the regime of the institutionalized revolution.

ENDEMIC VIOLENCE IN THE NORTHWEST

The states of Sonora, Chihuahua, Sinaloa, and Durango have significant regional differences. Nevertheless, in their overlapping region of the Sierra Madre Occidental, with its combination of deserts and valleys and common history, these states have a cohesive identity. One of the long-lasting processes of the region has been the complex relationship between indigenous peoples and colonizers that began with the Spanish conquest in the sixteenth century. Some indigenous communities built relationships of cooperation and coexistence with the Spanish settlers, while others maintained an armed resistance to preserve their territory and independence.[8] During the nineteenth century, indigenous peoples endured a number of extermination campaigns and fled to the Sierra, but groups like the Yaqui remained at war against the Mexican state until the 1920s.

During the Porfiriato the Northwest became one of the most dynamic regions for capitalist development through export-oriented mining, logging, railroads, and modern agriculture. When the revolution broke out in 1910, different political forces, including those representing elites, campesinos, workers, and indigenous peoples, disputed the hegemony in the region.[9] In the aftermath of the revolution, the so-called Sonoran Dynasty held the presidency for three consecutive terms from 1920 to 1928 and continued to dominate national politics until 1934, during a period that was crucial for state-building. State formation in the Northwest, however, occurred at a slow pace, as local governments favored the intermingling of private and public sectors.

The Cárdenas administration (1934–40) oversaw the largest period of land reform in the region, but the sharp division between ejidos and private agriculture led to the emergence of a new agrarian elite. The lack of change was most evident in the Sierra, where agrarian reforms made little headway and cattlemen controlled substantial grazing land.[10] In the post-Cárdenas era, the state subsidized private landholders, allowing for the formation of new large estates and neglecting the ejido. From the 1940s to the 1960s, the Northwest benefited from its connection to the U.S. Southwest's economy, and the Yaqui Valley became the birthplace of the worldwide Green Revolution, which yielded an accelerated expansion of agribusiness and the conversion of Sonora and Sinaloa into leading agricultural states.[11] Nevertheless, indigenous communities remained excluded from this revolution. By the 1960s, the high costs of private agriculture led to the crisis of this model, while the ejido system also failed. Rapid urbanization, industrialization, and population growth created a massive imbalance between rural and urban areas. Peasants and laborers faced the decision of either migrating—to towns or even to the United States—or fighting for land. The agrarian movement had to deal with the worst features of the authoritarian rule of the Partido Revolucionario Institucional (Institutional Revolutionary Party, PRI), including its protection of private economic interests over social needs and its lack of political will to negotiate with opponents. Recurring state violence created the conditions for an array of political responses from below.

From the 1950s through the 1970s, in the Northwest there were a series of protest cycles by ejidatarios, laborers, and landless peasants. In Chihuahua, the encroachment of ejidos and communal lands by landowners reached similar proportions to the prerevolutionary times. During the 1950s, the Partido Popular Socialista (Popular Socialist Party, PPS) through its Unión General de Obreros y Campesinos de México (General Union of Mexican Workers and Peasants, UGOCM) organized several rallies, land invasions, strikes, sit-ins, and cross-country marches. As the state repressed the movement and disregarded its demands, some leaders opted for the socialist armed struggle to foster a regime change. In 1963, an alliance of students, teachers, and peasants resulted in the formation of the Grupo Popular Guerrillero (Popular Guerrilla Group, GPG) in the municipality of Madera, in the Alta Sierra Tarahumara. A combination of guerrillas' strategic mistakes and counterinsurgency campaigns thwarted both the armed struggle and the peasant movement in late 1965. Nevertheless, the unrest prompted President Luis Echeverría's 1971 expropriation of land from some of the most powerful large estate owners in Madera to create the largest ejido in Mexico, El Largo.[12] This outcome did not prevent the guerilla movement from reemerging in Chihuahua, Sonora, and Sinaloa during the 1970s.

Since the 1940s, the region intersecting Sinaloa, Durango, and Chihuahua has been known as the Golden Triangle, a primary zone for marijuana and poppy crops. This illegal economy resulted from the lack of federal institutions in the Sierra, the unprofitability of ejidos, and the international demand for illegal drugs. With roots in the 1960s, the War on Drugs officially began in the 1970s, when the demand for Mexican drugs grew exponentially in the United States.[13] As Alexander Aviña demonstrates in his chapter, the War on Drugs overlapped with the Dirty War.

This brief review of the Northwest's long history serves to show how the region has been at the vanguard of some of the most critical processes of the Mexican twentieth century. It also reveals the extent to which violence has mediated the relationships between society and the state. Violence has been used to create a parallel order to the rule of law, where different forces have disputed hegemony through military means without reaching a lasting political pact. In the Golden Quadrilateral, this violent rule has prevailed over the state until the present day.

THE ALLIANCE OF INDIAN REBELS AND MIDDLE-CLASS REVOLUTIONARIES

In recent years, scholars have reassessed the GPG's assault on the army barracks in the town of Madera, Chihuahua, on September 23, 1965, as a key episode in Cold War Mexico.[14] They have focused on how a small faction of a peasant movement transformed into the first socialist guerrilla organization.[15] The story of the GPG in the aftermath of the assault is less known. Although post-Madera guerrillas lost their connection with the peasant movement in Chihuahua and were unrelated to international guerrilla organizations or socialist governments, they carried on and became a key actor to spread the armed struggle.

One of the most questionable interpretations of the origins of the socialist armed movement is the belief that it resulted from a combination of enthusiasm for the Cuban Revolution and indignation at the 1968 Tlatelolco massacre.[16] In fact, the armed struggle in Chihuahua was one of the events that contributed to the rise of radicalism within the national student movement in the late 1960s. While the Cuban Revolution had a significant impact on the Mexican Left, as several of the chapters in this volume demonstrate, it would be reductionist to argue that it caused the emergence of armed movements.[17] Nor was the assault on the Madera barracks an imitation of the attack on the Moncada barracks in 1953, as Hodges and Gandy claim.[18] Two survivors of the Madera assault, Florencio Hernández and Francisco Ornelas, have rejected the claim that they were merely mimicking the Cubans, since this tactic was common among armed conflicts.[19]

As some scholars have demonstrated, the multifarious causes of the armed struggle were related to the authoritarian regime, structural political violence in the countryside, the reception of global revolutionary ideologies—not only Castro-Guevarism but also Maoism, Vietnamese-Marxism, and liberation theology—and the generalized wave of change that marked the global 1960s and the more radical 1970s.[20] The guerrilla movement of the Sierra Tarahumara also had deep local roots, since peasants and indigenous communities were unsuccessful at obtaining land through legal means. Students and teachers became involved in social struggles after concluding that the PRI's developmental model would never bring social justice. They were morally shocked by systematic repression and believed that the channels to engage in traditional politics were closed; thus, the armed struggle was the only solution left.[21]

In October 1965, the survivors and sympathizers of the GPG formed the Movimiento 23 de Septiembre (23rd of September Movement, M23S), which shortly after its creation split into two factions due to ideological differences. The peasant wing, led by Oscar González Eguiarte, founded the Grupo Popular Guerrillero "Arturo Gámiz" (Popular Guerrilla Group "Arturo Gámiz," GPGAG), named after a revolutionary leader killed in Madera. The GPGAG sought to create a guerrilla foco in the Sierra Tarahumara to organize the peasantry for a revolution. The student wing, which kept the name M23S, proposed moving into urban areas to organize and launch guerrilla focos on a national scale. In 1967, the police discovered and dismantled the M23S, and in 1968, a counterinsurgency campaign wiped out the GPGAG in the Sierra Baja.[22]

In 1968, survivors of the GPGAG and the M23S merged under a new name, the Grupo 23 de Septiembre (23rd of September Group, G23S), led by Manuel Gámez Rascón.[23] In 1971, the G23S merged with the Movimiento Armado Revolucionario (Revolutionary Action Movement, MAR) and changed its name to MAR-23.[24] By 1971, there were so many guerrilla commandos dispersed throughout the country that their leaders discussed the need to build a national guerrilla organization. Thus, they formed the Organización Partidaria (Pro-Party Organization, OP).[25] The MAR-23 and Los Procesos (the "Processes"—a guerrilla group from Monterrey, Nuevo León) led the fusion of eight revolutionary groups.[26] The OP would eventually serve as the nucleus for the Liga, founded on March 15, 1973, in Guadalajara, Jalisco. Its political principles were outlined in a series of documents called Madera—also the name of the Liga's press.[27] By choosing these symbols, the Liga consolidated the vision of the 1965 assault as the foundation for a new revolution and the only source of political legitimacy.

The Liga sought the destruction of the bourgeois state, the establishment of the dictatorship of the proletariat, and the construction of socialism, and it maintained that the proletariat was the only revolutionary class. The peasantry was doomed to disappear, but in the meantime, it had to join the ranks of the revolutionary army against the oppressors.[28] The Liga aimed to promote the general insurrection of the masses through agitation and armed propaganda, while in the countryside it sought to build a popular army capable of creating liberated zones, using the strategy of the protracted people's war inspired by the revolutionary experiences of China and Vietnam.[29] Liberated zones were intended to serve as the rearguard for revolutionaries persecuted in the urban areas. The short-term objective was the "harassment and wearing down" of the bourgeoisie and its repressive apparatus through guerrilla warfare tactics, which would eventually evolve into a war of position.

The organizations that founded the Liga embodied the most radical faction of the student movement in each state, but only the MAR-23 and Los Enfermos (the Sick Ones) from Sinaloa had organic connections to popular movements.[30] The Liga consisted of a Coordinadora Nacional (National Direction, CONAL), whose ruling bodies were the Political Bureau and the Military Bureau. The CONAL divided the country into five Political-Military Regional Committees: Central, Northwest, Northeast, West, and South, and it established guerrilla focos by seizing on the sharp socioeconomic and political contradictions in the Golden Quadrilateral, Guerrero, Oaxaca, and the Southeast.[31] Despite the Liga's complex national structure, security forces had already attacked and weakened its coalescing groups. Consequently, the Liga was born as a weak organization, enabling the secret police to uncover it just a couple of months after its founding.[32]

The Liga's Northwestern Political-Military Regional Committee had a general coordinator as well as coordinators of urban brigades in Sinaloa, Sonora, Chihuahua, Durango, and Baja California. Leopoldo Angulo Luken was appointed the military chief of the guerrilla foco in the Sierra Tarahumara.[33] In April 1973, the CONAL chose guerrillas who were familiar with the region or with a peasant lifestyle to set up the Political-Military Committee "Arturo Gámiz" (CPMAG). That name implied a continuation of the struggle of the GPG and the GPGAG. The CPMAG planned to set up guerrilla camps in both the Alta and the Baja Tarahumara, where the former G23S had sympathizers. Salvador Gaytán, a peasant leader from Madera, announced to his followers in the zone: "Comrades, the 23rd of September Movement already has a League!"[34] This statement suggests that Gaytán probably disagreed with the Liga's stance on the subordination of the peasantry to the proletariat. However, Gaytán was pragmatic and did not contest this position, given that he had found an irreplaceable core of allies in the Liga for his fight against the government.

Gaytán was the oldest militant in the socialist armed movement, having lived underground since 1965. His mere presence seemed to legitimize the Liga above other guerrilla organizations, which might explain why the Liga's most dogmatic leaders initially tolerated his agrarian position. Furthermore, Gaytán had a thorough knowledge of the Sierra and served as an intermediary between urban cadres and peasants.[35] Yet the CPMAG continued to reproduce old divisions between students and peasants.

GUERRILLA WARFARE IN
THE GOLDEN QUADRILATERAL

In his testimony, Miguel Topete, an urban cadre who became a rural guerrilla, regretted that the CPMAG was active only in Sonora (Quiriego, Álamos, and the Mayo and Yaqui Valleys), Chihuahua (Chínipas and Urique), and Sinaloa (Choix and the valleys of El Fuerte and Mochis), but not in Durango.[36] In fact, the intersectional area of Durango belonged to the Golden Triangle and was controlled by drug traffickers, making it virtually impossible for the Liga to establish itself there. In their accounts, guerrillas acknowledged the existence of drug growers in the Sierra but did not consider them a security problem. For their part, *narcos* either were indifferent to guerrillas or sided with the security forces to reveal the fighters' whereabouts, given that some drug lords were in good standing with the police. However, at that moment, guerrillas did not represent a threat to drug interests.[37]

The CPMAG included not only the guerrilla foco but also the brigades in the valleys next to the Sierra that were intended to build supply lines. The foco's military actions were also projected as a distraction to draw the security forces to the Sierra instead of the valley. However, the foco lost contact with the brigades, and its military activities did not prevent repression in the valley.[38] For instance, in 1974, the security forces tortured and killed Liga members from Hermosillo, Sonora, who were unfamiliar with the foco.[39]

In the Guarijío community of El Frijol, Quiriego, Enrique Mendoza Beltrán and his wife, Micaela Bacasehua, leaders of the local peasant movement, became guerrilla supporters. The secret service discovered that the guerrillas had penetrated the region, and both the Federal Judicial Police and the military launched a counterinsurgency campaign commanded by Lieutenant Colonel Francisco Arellano Noblecía, chief of the State Judicial Police.[40] Although they attempted to eradicate the guerrilla camp in the Cerro El Frijol, the group escaped and dispersed through the region. Before the surprise attack, part of the group had abandoned the zone and made their way to Chínipas to set up another guerrilla camp, led by Salvador Gaytán and supported by Rarámuri communities from San Rafael de Orivo.[41]

Later on, militants from the dispersed group headed to Chínipas to join the new camp, although they suffered a couple of accidents during the journey. Given that two members required medical attention, the group decided to set up a temporary camp in the Quiriego zone with the help of the Guarijío people. Led by Gabriel Domínguez, they named themselves the Comando Guerrillero "Oscar González" (Guerrilla Commando "Oscar González," CGOG), comprised around six urban cadres and local peasants.[42] Although the CGOG was part of the CPMAG, it remained isolated.

Despite its low organizational capacity, the CPMAG established a third guerrilla camp in Urique, led by Eleazar Gámez, who had done political work in the zone's mills as a member of the G23S. Rarámuris called them "the students." Given its military experience, the Urique commando orchestrated several successful ambushes against security forces and suffered only a few casualties. It maintained fluid communications with the valley, but its politics were oriented toward gaining the leadership of the CPMAG. According to Angulo Luken, Chínipas and Quiriego resembled a backward Porfirian society, but Urique had greater capitalist development and offered better conditions for guerrilla warfare.[43]

The three camps operated as three separated focos. They displayed a high level of improvisation and disorganization, lack of structure, poor administration of resources, and lax recruitment policy. Nevertheless, the focos were able to survive for more than one year because of the support from indigenous communities. Angulo Luken argued that the creation of three focos stemmed from class divisions. Regarding the agrarian position of the Chínipas commando, Angulo stated:

> The quarrel that the poor peasant has against the cacique does not pose a revolutionary movement; it is a desperate radicalization due to poverty, the government's demagogic offers, and a remnant of the agrarian movement of the 1930s. That was the central difference between the Chínipas' group and us. We could say that they won their war, given that the government distributed land in the zone; we lost or have not won yet because class divisions and poverty continue.[44]

The Chínipas commando had several clashes with the security forces that resulted in a significant number of casualties among peasants. Angulo implied that the extermination of this foco was due to its agrarian politics. Gaytán behaved as if he stood above the CONAL and Angulo expelled him from the Liga without warning, thus provoking the isolation of Chínipas. Unlike urban cadres who had experience in guerrilla tactics and security measures, peasants lacked combat experience and acted more spontaneously, becoming an easy counterinsurgency target. Angulo also dismissed the politics of the Chínipas commando by claiming that it was parochial and an extension of domestic bourgeois programs, while the CGOG formed part of the revolutionary movement by the international proletariat.[45]

The Urique commando disagreed with Gaytán's agrarian positions, but it was dissatisfied with Angulo's leadership, too. Eleazar's brother, Manuel Gámez ("Julio") was the most important member of the CONAL after Ignacio Salas ("Oseas"). The struggle for power between both leaders came to an end in the spring of 1974, when Oseas convinced the CONAL to execute Julio, accusing him of betrayal.[46] Months later, when Eleazar Gámez realized that his brother was missing, the Urique commando made one last attempt to take over the Liga but ultimately left the organization.

The CGOG followed the Liga's orthodoxy, but it stayed out of internecine strife throughout 1974, given its geographical isolation. This enabled the commando to explore the area around Quiriego and San Bernardo, establishing close-knit relationships with Guarijío communities from Guajaray, Burapaco, and Los Bajíos. Topete claimed that the commando talked to one thousand families and that most of them became guerrilla sympathizers.[47] The CGOG then carried out several spectacular actions: It successfully kidnapped Hermenegildo Sáenz, the most prosperous merchant of San Bernardo, Sonora; it killed Agapito Enríquez and Agapito Enríquez, Jr., heads of the cacique family responsible for oppressing the Guarijío nation since the nineteenth century; and it burned the Enríquez's hacienda in Burapaco and the military barracks in the area. These displays of guerrilla power counterbalanced the effects of state terror on the communities and helped to explain why Guarijíos remained loyal to the CGOG.

The upper class of the Sierra Baja did not expect such political convulsion, while indigenous people longed for a change and were receptive to the message of the young men dubbed as Mechudos (long hairs), who promised that the revolution would put an end to divisions between the rich and the poor, and poverty itself.[48] In the Rarámuri and Guarijío languages, the word *yori* means both "white people" and "devil's children."[49] Guarijíos usually did not trust yoris and foreigners, but they crossed the racial line because they saw the Mechudos as allies against caciques.

The war polarized the region. Caciques teamed up with the military and the Judicial Police against the guerrillas but had little support from the population. While some Guarijíos sided with their *patrones* (bosses), the majority refused to cooperate with security forces, and several became guerrillas' support bases. The CGOG recruited the most politically advanced Guarijíos, among them Tío Celes (Celestino Ruelas), an eighty-four-year-old shaman and one of the most respected figures of the Guarijío nation, and his lover, Carmen Zazueta ("Juana"), a key supporter of the group.[50]

Guerrillas did not value the importance of having a woman in their group. They believed that Juana did not meet the fitness requirements to participate in the commando, and she was expelled three months after joining. Celes followed her, and the commando lost its most valuable allies. Topete and Angulo also removed the presence of women from their personal accounts even though women participated in the CPMAG as leaders, nurses, and messengers. The Liga was the armed organization with the highest female membership, yet women's rights were not part of its agenda. The erasure of women in this history has obscured our understanding of how female guerrillas dealt with clandestine life, patriarchy, and state terror.[51]

During 1974, the military raided the Guarijío communities to torture, kill, and imprison guerrillas' support bases. For its part, the CGOG proved incapable of protecting them, which Topete regarded as "politically unjustifiable."[52] On

November 24, 1974, after arresting and torturing a Guarijío rebel, the military located and ambushed the CGOG camp in La Ventanita. The leader, Gabriel Domínguez, and a Guarijío, Severo Zazueta, died in the assault, while the rest of the commando fled and found a haven with the Guarijíos' help.

In December 1974, when the state's extermination policy had decimated the Liga, Angulo visited Quiriego for the first time in nine months to explain to the CGOG that the Liga was in decline and that he had already split from the organization. Angulo convinced the urban cadres to continue the fight in the towns, and the CGOG abandoned the zone. On January 16, 1975, because Topete was injured and could not walk, the commando hijacked an airplane belonging to Roberto Sáenz—the son of the man that the CGOG had kidnaped exactly one year before—and flew to the Urique zone. The guerrillas burned the airplane and found a way to travel to Jalisco undetected.[53] They founded an armed group called the Organización Revolucionaria Profesional (Organization of Professional Revolutionaries, ORP), which remained active until 1981.[54]

THE "INDIAN QUESTION" AND THE GUARIJÍO VICTORY

In their testimonies, the urban cadres acknowledge the difficulties of working with an indigenous population they believed had "400 or 500 years of backwardness in their mode of production."[55] Guarijíos and Rarámuris practiced subsistence agriculture and were hardly related to the capitalist economy. They worked for the caciques or migrated to the valleys as seasonal workers. In his *Historia*, Angulo described the differences between Guarijíos and Rarámuris. In the Rarámuri case, Angulo maintained that the capitalist economy had undermined the original social indigenous organization with ejidos and factories, which had a major impact on the transformation of the communities' religion and culture.[56] With the indigenous people's insertion into the capitalist workforce and the prevalence of racial discrimination, Spanish was replacing Rarámuri. In contrast, Guarijíos were almost monolingual and were largely isolated; they never received land officially and had not participated in an armed conflict since the eighteenth century.

The Liga did not have a paternalistic approach to Indians, nor did it make any effort to learn about their worldview, culture, and demands—except for Indian survival strategies. As Topete confessed, before arriving in the Sierra urban cadres had never heard about the Guarijíos and saw peasants as a sort of raw material for their army.[57] Guerrillas were outraged by the living conditions of communities where deaths from starvation were prevalent, but that did not prevent the Liga from reinforcing a hierarchical political relationship. However, it would be inaccurate to argue that Indians were victims of student radicalism. Rarámuris and Guarijíos were political subjects before meeting the Liga, and their radicalization owed more to a combination of state negligence and repression than to guerrilla indoctrination. Regardless of their level of understanding of the Liga's ideology, Indians believed in the armed struggle as a last resort to win their land. Given their isolation, it is unlikely that they could have mobilized the resources to take up arms without external help. Thus, guerrillas and Indians provided mutual support for their political projects.

The Liga did not trigger a revolution but rather what Herbert H. Heines called the "radical flank effect." This refers to the phenomenon where the presence of extremists encourages support for other sectors' moderate demands as a way of undercutting the influence of radicals.[58] After security forces carried out gross human rights abuses, the state launched civic action programs to gain peasant support. Similar to what it did in Guerrero, the federal government built hospitals, shelters, schools, roads, and highways, and opened branches of the Instituto Nacional Indigenista (National Indigenous Institute, INI) in San Bernardo and San Rafael de Orivo.[59] Furthermore, between 1975 and 1976, President Echeverría expropriated roughly one hundred thousand hectares of land from landowners in both the Yaqui and Mayo Valleys and distributed it to eight thousand petitioners. There is no evidence that the armed struggle caused this initiative, but it was certainly a crucial factor, as it had been in the Madera case.[60]

On October 23, 1975, the Federal Judicial Police and the military, commanded by Arellano Noblecía, slaughtered a group of seven peasants who had invaded an estate demanding land reform in San Ignacio Río Muerto, in the Yaqui Valley. Although the order to dislodge the peasants probably came from the presidency, Echeverría blamed the governor, Carlos Biebrich, and forced him to resign.[61] San Ignacio Río Muerto was relatively close to Quiriego, but its agrarian movement was unrelated to guerrillas. Nevertheless, Guajaray—the main guerrilla support base, whose land petition dated back to 1963 and was authorized in 1973—was among the first to receive land that the government bought from local caciques in 1976. The official narrative about the granting of this ejido overlooks the Guarijío struggle. In 1975, the Mexican government credited Edmundo Faubert, a Canadian merchant who traded Indian handicrafts, as the man who found out that the Guarijío was a distinct tribe from the Mayo and the Yaqui, and accepted him as the mediator between Echeverría and Guarijío land petitioners.[62] Media outlets promoted the discovery of a "lost tribe," despite the fact that anthropological and linguistic research about Guarijíos began in the 1940s.[63] This propaganda strategy might have been intended to promote Echeverría's image as a champion of indigenismo while concealing the ravaging of Guarijío communities.

Guerrillas abandoned the region several months before the San Ignacio massacre, but according to Angulo, during 1975 the military continued searching for the commando that had burnt the plane.[64] Echeverría likely carried out land reform in the region to prevent an alliance between both the radicalized peasant movement and guerrillas, and gave land to Guarijíos to put an end to their support of the Liga.[65] By radicalizing the agrarian struggle, Guajaray became a source of inspiration to other Guarijío communities, which received land in a staggered manner from 1977 to 1982.[66]

If we explained land reform as a mere strategy to preserve the status quo, the experiences, sacrifices, and beliefs of indigenous peasants would be invalidated. In 2007, I had the opportunity to accompany a group of former Liga militants on a visit to the Golden Quadrilateral. In Makurawe, San Bernardo, we met with a Guarijío community. The indigenous governor expressed gratitude to the guerrillas because his people believed that the armed struggle brought about land reform in the 1970s. As soon as the meeting finished, Topete insisted that land reform was not a victory because it had not been the Liga's historical objective, and he was disappointed to see that peasants did not understand their message but rather interpreted the process through the lens of the "petite bourgeois reformism." The Liga never understood that for Indians land was not only property but also the basis of their identity. Although Guarijíos still live under extreme poverty and continue to deal with the long-lasting consequences of counterinsurgency, they do not regret their participation in the Liga.

CONCLUSIONS

The guerrilla foco in the Golden Quadrilateral is a useful case for refuting some of the generalizations about the Mexican Dirty War, a war that first intensified in the aftermath of the Madera attack of 1965 and experienced brutal proportions in the 1970s. Traditional interpretations maintain that the state defeated the socialist armed movement both politically and militarily, yet a nuanced analysis of organizations like the Liga proves that the radicalism of the 1960s and 1970s did make contributions to transform the balance of power between the state and society. The Liga was not a group of extremists detached from society, as some of the historiography has portrayed it, but a complex organization that mobilized different levels of popular support in the five regions where it was present.[67] Their activism was not exclusively framed in the shadow of the Mexican Revolution but was rather articulated in a complex language that paid attention to both local and global realities and symbols. Finally, the Liga incorporated Indian communities as a subordinate ally, but the latter also used the Liga to "win their war." Notwithstanding the sense of triumphalism among Guarijíos, the ejidos only bring them limited food security. Since the early 1980s highlanders have also dealt with a new wave of colonial violence: drug traffickers have encroached on their lands to use them for illegal crops or livestock, a front for money laundering.[68] Nevertheless, Guarijíos are aware of their agency and rights and feel proud of their victories.

NOTES

1.   Joseph and Buchenau, *Mexico's Once and Future Revolution*, 2.
2.   Bellingeri, *Del agrarismo armado a la guerra*; Castellanos, *México armado*; and Herrera Calderón and Cedillo, *Challenging Authoritarianism*.
3.   Padilla, *Rural Resistance*; and McCormick, *Logic of Compromise*.
4.   Cedillo and Calderón, "Análisis de la producción."
5.   Rangel Lozano and Sánchez, *México en los setenta*.
6.   Aguayo Quezada, "El impacto de la guerrilla"; Oikión Solano, "El impacto de la oposición."
7.   Aviña, "'We Have Returned to Porfirian Times'"; Montemayor, *La guerrilla recurrente*.
8.   Almada, *Breve historia de Sonora*, 47.
9.   Aguilar Camín, *La frontera nómada*.
10.   Bantjes, *As If Jesus Walked on Earth*, 135–46.
11.   Matson, *Seeds of Sustainability*.
12.   Henson, "The 1965 Agrarian Revolt."
13.   Astorga, *El siglo de las drogas*.
14.   Carlos Montemayor helped to reframe Madera as a symbol of the beginning of the Dirty War through his novels *Guerra en el Paraíso* (1997), *Las armas del alba* (2003), and *Las mujeres del alba* (2010).
15.   García Aguirre, *La revolución que llegaría*; Henson, "Madera 1965"; and Vargas Valdés, *Madera Rebelde*.
16.   Castañeda, *La utopía armada*.
17.   Keller, *Mexico's Cold War*.
18.   Hodges and Gandy, *Mexico, the End of the Revolution*, 108–109.
19.   Hernández, *El asalto al cuartel de Madera*; Ornelas, *Sueños de libertad*.

20. Oikión Solano and García Ugarte, *Movimientos armados*; Herrera Calderón and Cedillo, *Challenging Authoritarianism*; Alexander Aviña, *Specters of Revolution*.

21. See the chapters by Tanalís Padilla and Carla Villanueva in this volume.

22. Armendáriz, *Morir de sed*.

23. Delgado, "Recordando Madera," 14.

24. The MAR was an organization founded by students from Michoacán who received military training in North Korea. Pineda Ochoa, *En las profundidades del MAR*, 168.

25. For a detailed account of the formation process of the Liga, see López Limón, "Proceso de construcción," 184.

26. In 1971, Los Procesos lumped together a scission of the Mexican Communist Party and a dissident group of the Professional Student Movement (MEP). The MEP was the only faction that did not come from the Left, but from a group of Catholic students. Pensado, "El Movimiento Estudiantil Profesional," 156–92.

27. Salas Obregón summarized the Maderas and the discussion among the guerrilla groups in a document that became the official doctrine of the Liga: *Cuestiones fundamentales del Movimiento Revolucionario*.

28. Hirales Morán, *La Liga Comunista 23 de Septiembre*.

29. Angulo Luken, *Nos volveremos a encontrar*, 40, 75.

30. For an analysis of how the guerrilla students thought about themselves as the legitimate vanguard of the proletariat, see Tecla Jiménez, *Universidad, burguesía y proletariado*, 26; and the chapter by Fernando Herrera Calderón in this volume.

31. Topete, *Los ojos de la noche*, 21.

32. See Aguayo Quezada, *La charola*.

33. For a biography of Angulo Luken, see Alonso Vargas, *Los guerrilleros mexicalenses*.

34. Topete, interview with the author.

35. Topete, *Ayer en la mañana clara*.

36. Topete, *Los ojos*, 21. In 1968, the so-called Macías set a guerrilla foco in the Durango highlands, which lasted two months. The Liga unearthed the Macías' weapons, but why it did not plan on setting a foco in Durango is unclear. "Declaración de Elías Orozco Salazar," October 22, 1973, Archivo General de la Nación, Dirección Federal de Seguridad (AGN-DFS), Versión Pública de la Liga Comunista 23 de Septiembre, 107.

37. According to Angulo Luken, in media outlets the federal government announced that the military siege in the Sierra was due to an antidrug campaign but, in fact, the security forces only hunted down guerrillas. It seems that the government used the drug war as a smokescreen to hide the Dirty War. Angulo Luken, *Nos volveremos*, 37, 94.

38. Topete, *Los ojos*, 69.

39. The radical factions of the student movement of Sinaloa and Sonora became a Liga platform for recruitment and formation of urban brigades from 1973 to 1982. Duarte Rodríguez, *Días de fuego*, 81–93.

40. Lagarda, *El color de las amapas*, 69–73.

41. Topete, *Los ojos*, 203.
42. Topete, *Los ojos*, 3. For more on Gabriel Domínguez, see Domínguez, "Cuatro hermanos en la guerrilla."
43. Angulo Luken, *Nos volveremos*, 51.
44. Ibid., 46. Translation by the author.
45. Topete, *Los ojos*, 46.
46. Hirales Morán, *Memoria de la guerra*.
47. Topete, *Los ojos*, 131.
48. See the testimonies that Lagarda collected in *El color de las amapas*.
49. About the Guarijío cosmogony, see Aguilar Zeleny and Moctezuma, *Los pueblos indígenas del noroeste*.
50. Topete, *Los ojos*, 150.
51. Women survivors of the rural guerilla in the Golden Quadrilateral have not talked overtly about their role. Other Liga's female guerrillas have sustained that they saw their participation as a subversion of gender roles per se and shared the common socialist view that women's rights would be recognized after the triumph of the revolution. See Aguilar Terréz, *Guerrilleras*.
52. Topete, *Los ojos*, 52.
53. Lagarda, *El color*, 128.
54. Angulo Luken, *Apuntes para el desarrollo teórico del marxismo*.
55. Angulo Luken, *Nos volveremos*, 55.
56. Ibid., 64.
57. Topete, *Los ojos*, 36.
58. McAdam, McCarthy, and Zald, *Comparative Perspectives*, 14.
59. Angulo Luken, *Nos volveremos*, 128. For a discussion about the effects of indigenismo in the region, see Sariego Rodríguez, *El indigenismo en la Tarahumara*.
60. The dominant interpretation about land reform in Sonora focuses solely on elite divisions and fails to address the armed struggle. Almada, *Breve*, 161.
61. Angulo Albestrain, "Se cumplen 38 años."
62. Lagarda, "Crónica de un viaje a la nación guarijía."
63. See Hilton, *Palabras y frases*.
64. Angulo Luken, *Nos volveremos*, 44.
65. Jiménez, "Movimiento campesino en Sonora."
66. Valdivia Dounce, *Entre yoris y guarijíos*, 85–88.
67. Cedillo, "Violencia, memoria, historia y tabú."
68. Yetman, *Sonora*, 53; Alvarado, *La Tarahumara*.

BIBLIOGRAPHY

ARCHIVES

Archivo General de la Nación, Mexico City.
Library "Fernando Pesqueira" of the Universidad de Sonora, Hermosillo, Sonora.

INTERVIEWS

Miguel Topete. Author's interview. Guadalajara, Jalisco, July 21, 2011.

PUBLISHED SOURCES

Aguayo Quezada, Sergio. "El impacto de la guerrilla en la vida Mexicana: Algunas hipótesis." In *Movimientos armados en México, siglo XX*, edited by Verónica Oikión Solano and María Eugenia García Ugarte. Vol. 1, 91–98. Zamora, Mexico: COLMICH/CIESAS, 2006.

———. *La charola: Una historia de los servicios de inteligencia en México.* Mexico City: Grijalbo, 2001.

Aguilar Camín, Héctor. *La frontera nómada: Sonora y la Revolución Mexicana.* Mexico City: SEP, 1977.

Aguilar Terréz, Luz María, ed. *Guerrilleras: Antología de testimonios y textos sobre la participación de las mujeres en los movimientos armados socialistas en México.* Mexico City: n.p., 2014.

Aguilar Zeleny, Alejandro, and José Luis Moctezuma. *Los pueblos indígenas del noroeste: Atlas etnográfico.* Mexico City: INAH, 2013.

Almada, Ignacio. *Breve historia de Sonora.* Mexico City: COLMEX, 2000.

Alonso Vargas, José Luis. *Los guerrilleros mexicalenses.* Mexico City: Riva Ediciones, 2014.

Alvarado, Carlos. *La Tarahumara: Una tierra herida.* Chihuahua: Talleres Gráficos de Chihuahua, 1996.

Angulo Albestrain, Francisco. *Nos volveremos a encontrar.* Guadalajara: La Casa del Mago, 2011.

———. "Se cumplen 38 años de la masacre de San Ignacio Río Muerto." *Sur de Sonora,* October 22, 2013. Accessed September 5, 2016. http://www.surdesonora.com/article/se-cumplen-38-a%C3%B1os-de-la-matanza-de-san-ignacio-r%C3%ADo-muerto.

Angulo Luken, Leopoldo. *Apuntes para el desarrollo teórico del marxismo: Proyecto político de la Organización de Revolucionarios Profesionales (ORP).* Mexico City: 2015.

Armendáriz, Minerva. *Morir de sed junto a la fuente.* Mexico City: UOM, 2001.

Astorga, Luis. *El siglo de las drogas: El narcotráfico, del Porfiriato al nuevo milenio.* Mexico City: Plaza & Janés, 2005.

Aviña, Alexander. *Specters of Revolution: Peasant Guerrillas in the Cold War Mexican Countryside.* New York: Oxford University Press, 2014.

———. "'We Have Returned to Porfirian Times': Neopopulism, Counterinsurgency, and the Dirty War in Guerrero, Mexico 1969–1976." In *Populism in Twentieth Century Mexico: The Presidencies of Lázaro Cárdenas and Luis Echeverría,* edited by Amelia M. Kiddle and María L. O. Muñoz, 106–21. Tucson: University of Arizona Press, 2010.

Bantjes, Adrián. *As If Jesus Walked on Earth: Cardenismo, Sonora, and the Mexican Revolution.* Wilmington, Del.: Scholarly Resources, 1998.

Bellingeri, Marco. *Del agrarismo armado a la guerra de los pobres: Ensayos de guerrilla rural en el México contemporaneo, 1940–1974.* Mexico City: Casa Juan Pablos, 2003.

Castañeda, Jorge. *La utopía desarmada.* Mexico City: Joaquín Mortiz, 1994.

Castellanos, Laura. *México armado, 1943–1981*. Mexico City: Era, 2007.

Cedillo, Adela. "Violencia, memoria, historia y tabú en torno a la Liga Comunista 23 de Septiembre." In *La Liga Comunista 23 de Septiembre: Cuatro décadas a debate: Historia, memoria, testimonio y literatura*, edited by Rodolfo Gamiño, Yllich Escamilla, Rigoberto Reyes, and Fabián Campos, 343–73. Mexico City: UNAM, 2015.

Cedillo, Adela, and Fernando H. Calderón. "Análisis de la producción historiográfica en torno a la 'guerra sucia' Mexicana." In *El estudio de las luchas revolucionarias en América Latina (1959–1996): Estado de la cuestión*, edited by Verónica Oikión Solano, Eduardo Rey Tristán, and Martín López Ávalos, 263–88. Zamora, Mexico: El Colegio de Michoacán, 2014.

Delgado, Héctor. "Recordando Madera, orígenes de la Liga 23 de Septiembre." *Unomásuno*, September 21, 2011.

Domínguez, José. "Cuatro hermanos en la guerrilla." *Nexos*, July 1, 2004. Accessed September 2, 2016. http://www.nexos.com.mx/?p=11194.

Duarte Rodríguez, Rubén. *Días de fuego: El movimiento universitario sonorense de los años '70*. Hermosillo, Mexico: Universidad de Sonora, 2003.

García Aguirre, Aleida. *La revolución que llegaría: Experiencias de solidaridad y redes de maestros y normalistas en el movimiento campesino y la guerrilla moderna en Chihuahua, 1960–1968*. Mexico City: Self-published, 2015.

Gentry, Howard Scott. *The Warihío Indians of Sonora-Chihuahua: An Ethnographic Survey*. Anthropological Papers, No. 65. Bureau of American Ethnology Bulletin 186, 61–154. Washington, D.C.: Smithsonian Institution, 1963.

Henson, Elizabeth. "Madera 1965: Primeros Vientos." In *Challenging Authoritarianism in Mexico: Revolutionary Struggles and the "Dirty War," 1964–1982*, edited by Fernando H. Calderón and Adela Cedillo, 19–39. New York: Routledge, 2012.

———. "The 1965 Agrarian Revolt in Madera, Chihuahua." In *Oxford Research Encyclopedia of Latin American History*. Accessed April 30, 2017. http://latinamerican history.oxfordre.com/view/10.1093/acrefore/9780199366439.001.0001/acrefore -9780199366439-e-381?rskey=Vysfpf&result=14.

Hernández, Florencio. *El asalto al cuartel de Madera: Chihuahua, 23 de septiembre de 1965*. Mexico City: Centro de Derechos Humanos Yaxkin, 2003.

Herrera Calderón, Fernando, and Adela Cedillo, eds. *Challenging Authoritarianism in Mexico: Revolutionary Struggles and the "Dirty War," 1964–1982*. New York: Routledge, 2012.

Hirales Morán, Gustavo. *La Liga Comunista 23 de Septiembre: Orígenes y naufragio*. Mexico City: Ediciones de Cultura Popular, 1977.

———. *Memoria de la guerra de los justos*. Mexico City: Cal y Arena, 1996.

Hilton, Kenneth S. *Palabras y frases de las lenguas tarahumara y guarijío*. Mexico City: Instituto Nacional de Antropología e Historia, 1947.

Hodges, Donald, and Ross Gandy. *Mexico, the End of the Revolution*. Westport, Conn.: Praeger, 2002.

Jiménez, Rubén. "Movimiento campesino en Sonora." *Cuadernos Políticos*, no. 7 (January–March 1976): 67–78.

Joseph, Gilbert M., and Jürgen Buchenau. *Mexico's Once and Future Revolution*. Durham, N.C.: Duke University Press, 2013.

Keller, Renata. *Mexico's Cold War: Cuba, the United States, and the Legacy of the Mexican Revolution*. New York: Cambridge University Press, 2015.

Lagarda, Ignacio. "Crónica de un viaje a la nación guarijía." Unpublished manuscript.

———. *El color de las amapas: Crónica de la guerrilla en la sierra de Sonora*. Hermosillo, Mexico: UTS/ITESCA/LTS, 2007.

López Limón, Alberto. "Proceso de construcción de la Liga Comunista 23 de Septiembre (1973–1975)." *Cuadernos de Marte: Revista latinoamericana de sociología de la Guerra*, no.1 (April 2011): 177–207.

Matson, Pamela, ed. *Seeds of Sustainability: Lessons from the Birthplace of the Green Revolution in Agriculture*. Washington, D.C.: Island Press, 2012.

McAdam, Doug, John D. McCarthy, and Mayer N. Zald, eds. *Comparative Perspectives on Social Movements*. Cambridge: Cambridge University Press, 1996.

McCormick, Gladys I. *The Logic of Compromise in Mexico: How the Countryside Was Key to the Emergence of Authoritarianism*. Chapel Hill: University of North Carolina Press, 2016.

Montemayor, Carlos. *Guerra en el paraíso*. Mexico City: Seix Barral, 1997.

———. *La guerrilla recurrente*. Mexico City: Debate, 2007.

———. *Las armas del alba*. Mexico City: Joaquín Mortiz, 2003.

———. *Las mujeres del alba*. Mexico City: Random House Mondadori, 2010.

Oikión Solano, Verónica. "El impacto de la oposición armada en la Reforma Política del Estado: Las decisiones de 1977." In *Formas de gobierno en México: Poder político y actores sociales a través del tiempo*, edited by Víctor Gayol. Vol. II, 501–23. Zamora, Mexico: El Colegio de Michoacán, 2011.

Oikión Solano, Verónica, and María Eugenia García Ugarte, eds. *Movimientos armados en México, siglo XX*. Zamora, Mexico: COLMICH/CIESAS, 2006.

Ornelas, Francisco. *Sueños de libertad*. Chihuahua: Self-published, 2005.

Padilla, Tanalís. *Rural Resistance in the Land of Zapata: The Jaramillista Movement and the Myth of Pax Priísta, 1940–1962*. Durham, N.C.: Duke University Press, 2008.

Pensado, Jaime M. "El Movimiento Estudiantil Profesional (MEP): Una mirada a la radicalización de la juventud católica mexicana durante la Guerra Fría." *Mexican Studies/Estudios Mexicanos* 31, no. 1 (Winter 2015): 156–92.

Pineda Ochoa, Fernando. *En las profundidades del MAR: El oro no llegó de Moscú*. Mexico City: Plaza y Valdés Editores, 2003.

Rangel Lozano, Claudia, and Evangelina Sánchez, eds. *México en los setenta: Guerra sucia o terrorismo de Estado? Hacia una política de la memoria*. Chilpancingo: Universidad Autónoma de Guerrero/Itaca, 2015.

Salas Obregón, Ignacio. *Cuestiones fundamentales del movimiento revolucionario*. Mexico City: Huasipungo, 2003.

Sariego Rodríguez, Juan Luis. *El indigenismo en la Tarahumara*. Mexico City: CONACULTA, 2002.

Tecla Jiménez, Alfredo. *Universidad, burguesía y proletariado*. Mexico City: Fondo de Cultura Popular, 1978.

Topete, Miguel. *Los ojos de la noche: El comando guerrillero Oscar González*. Guadalajara: La Casa del Mago, 2009.

———, ed. *Ayer en la mañana clara: Salvador Gaytán y el 23 de septiembre de 1965*. Guadalajara: La Casa del Mago, 2012.

Valdivia Dounce, María Teresa. *Entre yoris y guarijíos: Crónicas sobre el quehacer antropológico*. Mexico City: UNAM, 2007.

Vargas Valdés, Jesús. *Madera Rebelde: Movimiento agrario y guerrilla (1959–1965)*. Chihuahua: Ediciones Nueva Vizcaya, 2015.

Yetman, David. *Sonora: An Intimate Geography*. Albuquerque: University of New Mexico Press, 2000.

6

MEXICO'S TURN TOWARD
THE THIRD WORLD

Rural Development Under President Luis Echeverría

A. S. DILLINGHAM

ON DECEMBER 2, 1972, Salvador Allende, the embattled president of Chile, spoke to a group of university students in Guadalajara, Mexico. To a packed auditorium, Allende thanked Mexican President Luis Echeverría for hosting him and then addressed issues of poverty, imperialism, and revolution. He emphasized the overwhelming youthfulness of Latin America, with half of its population under twenty-seven years of age, and noted that after 150 years of political independence, Latin America remained poor and dependent on external powers. Describing the lack of literacy, housing, and food in the Americas, Allende argued progressive governments such as those of Mexico and Chile must address the issues directly. He noted the differences between "la vía chilena," or Chilean road to socialism, and guerrilla struggle, associated with the Cuban Revolution, to emphasize the plurality of paths toward revolutionary change. University students, he contended, had a "patriotic obligation" to use their knowledge to improve the conditions of their countries, particularly in rural areas. Allende's presence in Mexico was highly controversial. The conservative press, much of the Catholic Church, and northern business interests viewed the state visit with suspicion. Coming just two years into Luis Echeverría's *sexenio* (1970–76), the visit of the avowedly socialist president of Chile heightened fears and rumors of a creeping socialism under Echeverría.[1] In addition to domestic opposition, the visit antagonized U.S. President Richard Nixon and his national security advisor, Henry Kissinger, who actively worked to sabotage Allende's ruling coalition. While the Mexican Right viewed the event as part of a worrying leftward trend, much of the Mexican Left and student movement were also skeptical, albeit for different reasons. For post-1968 dissidents, Echeverría's leftist rhetoric, his invocation of Third World solidarity, even the visit of the *compañero presidente* Allende, was nothing more than progressive rhetoric masking a violent and authoritarian regime. Allende's speech, in which he admonished students to focus on their studies and work hard, only seemed to confirm this interpretation of events.[2]

The debate over Allende's University of Guadalajara speech is reflective of broader debates surrounding how to understand post-1968 Mexico and President Echeverría's officially termed *apertura democratica* (democratic opening), a series of wide-ranging reforms that included increasing press freedoms, the expansion of the education system at all levels, and the release of political prisoners.[3] Scholars of mid-century Mexico have debated how to understand the nature of the state and the centrality of the 1968 student movement. While participant memoirs emphasize the student movement in the capital as a watershed moment in Mexican history, the beginning of the end of the authoritarian Institutional Revolutionary Party's (PRI) rule, historians have begun to point to broader processes at work before 1968.[4] Indeed, the nature of the Mexican state, dominated by the PRI after the violent phase of the Mexican Revolution (1910–20), has been disputed, with some emphasizing its repressive features and others its relative democratic responsiveness.[5] Gillingham and Smith have popularized for an English-speaking audience the term *dictablanda* (soft dictatorship) to capture these two elements of the regime.[6] Others have emphasized regional approaches to understanding how power operated.[7] Yet scholars have yet to come to a consensus on the nature of the democratic opening or reckon with Mexico's short-lived Third Worldist project.

This chapter examines how the post-1968 Mexican establishment reformulated its rule in response to a dissident politics that included not only a university student movement in Mexico City but also broader opposition forces in both rural and urban Mexico. The 1972 state visit of President Allende was part and parcel of a shift in Mexican foreign policy towards a Third Worldist discourse and posture. That shift is significant in its own right but also shaped domestic politics in fundamental ways. Scholars, including many in this volume, rightly highlight the repressive aspects of Echeverría's presidency, including counterinsurgent campaigns, the detention of political dissidents, and the use of torture, in effort to combat the trope of Mexican Cold War exceptionalism.[8] Yet Echeverría's political response to discontent in rural Mexico has received far too little attention. Indeed, the connection between Mexico's Third Worldist posture abroad and its domestic reform agenda was laid out by the president in his 1973 annual governmental address, in which he argued, "In the same way we fight for the rights of the Third World to be respected, we do it in our own country so that workers and peasants have justice."[9] The Echeverría administration went on to dramatically increase social spending, particularly for poor and rural regions, and exponentially expanded rural development programs. I argue the existence of Third World politics internationally shaped Mexican officials' response to domestic opposition and contributed to a dramatic reformulation of rural development policy in the post-1968 era.

Scholars have increasingly begun to employ a "Global Sixties" framing to understand the period in question. This framework has the advantage of foregrounding the transnational connections that shaped a truly global period of world history and emphasizes demographic growth, technological change, the expansion of higher education, and Cold War ideologies as central processes shaping the period.[10] Yet as with any analytical framework, it has limitations. For example, despite the best intentions of its practitioners, Global Sixties frameworks have struggled to decenter iconic events in the United States and Western Europe and often emphasize urban over rural experiences.[11] In the case of Mexico, the 1968 Mexico City student movement no doubt developed in dialogue with events in the United States and Europe, and Mexican youth followed U.S. protests against the Vietnam War and civil rights organizing on Mexican television.[12] These youths also welcomed activists from Europe in the capital's universities. Yet the Global Sixties' emphasis on these relationships has often implicitly excluded Mexico's engagement with the Global South. This emphasis has kept us from exploring the ways in which the Global Sixties were grounded in south-south connections. Indeed, the Mexican establishment's engagement with Third World politics was a direct response to the swelling opposition and crisis of legitimacy it faced domestically. Third World alternative political and economic projects, such as those of Cuba and Chile, as well as international formations such as the Non-Aligned Movement, shaped Mexican rural development policy as well as dissident politics.

"MEXICO, OPENLY WITH THE THIRD WORLD, COMES OUT OF ITS 'SPLENDID ISOLATION'"[13]

Mexico's engagement with and contribution to the Third World has received little scholarly attention. With its origins in post–World War II decolonization and the 1955 Bandung Congress in Indonesia, the Third World was "not a place," as Vijay Prashad has pointed out, but rather a political "project."[14] As a project of formerly colonized countries, particularly in Asia and Africa, Third World politics achieved one of its most significant moments in 1961 with the creation of the Non-Aligned Movement. Latin American nations, despite a shared colonial past, were late to join this movement. Nonetheless, postrevolutionary Cuba's hosting of the 1966 Tricontinental Congress in Havana marked a significant increase in Latin American participation. Perhaps because of these distinct chronologies of decolonization, scholars have yet to fully reckon with Latin America's, and particularly Mexico's, role in the Third World project.[15] Given a perceived weakness of the United States on the world stage, Mexico under Echeverría made significant efforts to strengthen Third World politics internationally, particularly through the United Nations, as evidenced by its successful proposal of the Charter of Economic Rights and Duties of States, adopted by the UN General Assembly in December 1974. The charter was a key document in support of the New International Economic Order, a declaration passed by the General Assembly in May of that same year. These efforts aimed at a legally binding framework to insure sovereignty over both economic and political spheres.[16] While Mexico's involvement and engagement with Third World politics and Global South alliances have only recently begun to receive attention, several scholars have observed how foreign relations have served as a salve for domestic problems.[17] Yet precisely how Third Worldism shaped domestic politics in Mexico remains to be analyzed.

President Allende's speech at the University of Guadalajara was part of a three-day state visit to Mexico. Many of the Mexico City daily newspapers carried wall-to-wall coverage of the Chilean president's arrival in Mexico City. Indeed, they noted the dramatic departure from the staid state visits and receptions of previous administrations, describing how the Mexican president and his wife met the Chilean delegation at the capital city's airport and proceeded to lead a sixteen-kilometer procession from the airport to the Chilean embassy downtown, with thousands lining the streets. Along the parade route supporters raised chants in favor of Allende and his stand against U.S. imperialism, along with renditions of "The Internationale."[18] *El Día*, a newspaper highly sympathetic to the president, chose to frame the visit with the headline "apertura al socialismo" (socialist aperture), deliberately connecting Allende's Chilean "road to socialism" with Echeverría's "apertura democrática." In anticipation of the visit, Pablo González Casanova, the Mexican intellectual and then director of the Universidad Nacional Autónoma de México (National Autonomous University of Mexico, UNAM), warned of potential conflicts within the student movement sparked by the visit. While his worries appear to not have materialized, students in Mexico City used the opportunity to confront Echeverría in front of Allende, demanding a "permanent dialogue" with the president.[19]

Mexico's support of and collaboration with the Chilean government was part of a much broader realignment of Latin American diplomatic relations. In response to the U.S. war in Vietnam, the emergence of détente between the United States and the Soviet Union, and the oil crisis of the 1970s, governments as diverse as Peru, Argentina, and Venezuela reoriented their diplomatic relations toward more independent positions.[20] As Hal Brands has noted, a "period of distress for the West was a time of opportunity for those developing nations unsatisfied with existing systems of world commerce and diplomacy."[21] Governments such as Mexico's, emboldened by both high oil prices and seemingly weaker U.S. power internationally, strove to reorient international diplomacy and economic policy on fundamentally more favorable terms for Latin America, Africa, and Asia.[22]

Mexico under President Echeverría went above and beyond adjusting to a new international order. Echeverría aimed to provide leadership to a renewed Third World project internationally. During this period, Mexico increased the number of countries it had diplomatic relations with; the president visited over forty countries during his six-year term, an impressive number for any head of state, and Echeverría started an international think tank based in Mexico City, the Centro de Estudios Económicos y Sociales del Tercer Mundo (Center for Third World Studies). To further promote this international agenda, Mexico hosted the World Conference for the International Women's Year in June 1975 in Mexico City.[23] Perhaps his most significant effort was the successful adoption in the UN of the Charter of Economic Rights and Duties of States, albeit without any legally binding measures for member states. The notions of economic sovereignty and the rights of nations to equitable development outlined in the charter reflected the ideals associated with the 1910 Mexican Revolution and applied them to the context of a rapidly decolonizing world.

Mexico's participation in the September 1973 Conference of Non-Aligned Nations, held in Algeria, demonstrates its fraught and complex engagement with Third World politics. President Echeverría had actively attempted to provide leadership to the Non-Aligned Movement in the lead-up to the meetings. He visited Santiago, Chile, in April 1972 where he first promoted his proposed charter at the Third UN Conference on Trade and Development (UNCTAD III). President Allende then encouraged him to personally attend the upcoming Non-Aligned meeting in Algiers the following fall. Yet Echeverría ultimately chose to send his foreign minister, Emilio Rabasa, in his place, perhaps concerned about overly antagonizing the U.S. government. When the Chilean administration became aware of Mexico's plan, Chilean officials were deeply disappointed.[24] Though given their own previously professed skepticism of Echeverría's political commitment, perhaps they were not entirely surprised.[25] Nor was Allende himself able to attend, as the meetings occurred during the final days of his government. This incident highlights the delicate balance involved in Mexico's turn to the Third World.

Mexico's balancing act was intimately tied to its own long-standing relationship with the United States government. This relationship partially suffered in 1971, as the United States imposed higher tariffs on imports, including Mexican products. Despite this, the Mexican government under the PRI had a long history of collaboration with the United States, with Mexico City hosting one of the largest offices of the U.S. Central Intelligence Agency in the world.[26] While President Echeverría publicly represented himself as a flag-bearer for the Third World, declaring in 1974, "We have a fundamental purpose: to strengthen our political independence and our economic autonomy, objectives for which we fight alongside the peoples of the Third World," he privately reassured U.S. President Richard Nixon of his continued allegiance to the United States.[27] In White House conversations with Nixon in June 1972, he had contended his Third Worldist leadership was necessary, "because if I don't take this flag in Latin America, Castro will. I am very conscious of this."[28] Yet U.S. officials observed Echeverría's increasing Third Worldist discourse with concern. A September 1973 State Department cable from Mexico City summarized its analysis of the Mexican administration with characteristic paternalism: "In conclusion, although the Echeverría government is less easy to handle than its predecessor, I do not believe that our essential interests have suffered."[29]

This turn toward the Third World cannot be understood without reckoning with its place in the broader history of postrevolutionary Mexico. While President Echeverría invoked Third World solidarity, he also explicitly portrayed his own policies as a dramatic break with the previous two decades of Mexican policy at home and abroad. He consciously contrasted his administration with previous policies of "stabilizing development," and newspaper headlines described the democratic opening as a return to the policies of President Lázaro Cárdenas, putting the social movement back into "the revolution."[30] The domestic and foreign policy reforms under Echeverría certainly constituted a reformulation of the PRI political project, but scholars debate the severity of the rupture in Mexican foreign relations. Gerardo Lézama, for example, makes the claim that foreign relations served to justify the regime domestically, but that Echeverría's foreign policy did not ultimately constitute a "rupture."[31] Likewise, others point to long-standing Mexican diplomatic advocacy of principles of economic self-determination and sovereignty, dating back to the 1910 Revolution.[32] In the history of Mexican foreign relations, its turn to the Third World appears as a window that briefly opened and precipitously closed.[33] Echeverría was unsuccessful in his bid to lead the United Nations, and Allende died in a U.S.-backed military coup on September 11, 1973, but the experience underscores the contingent possibilities of Third World politics in Latin America.[34]

RURAL CRISIS AND THE ESTABLISHMENT'S RESPONSE: THIRD WORLD POLITICS IN THE COUNTRYSIDE

The Mexican establishment's domestic policies underwent a dramatic reformulation as well in the post-1968 period. While President Echeverría sponsored a host of reforms, his policies toward rural Mexico and poverty generally constituted a substantive break with previous administrations. During the previous three decades, Mexico had experienced a period of impressive macroeconomic growth, dubbed the "Mexican Miracle." This economic boom was fueled by green revolution agricultural reforms, particularly in northern Mexico, and increasing industrial production in cities such as Monterrey and the nation's capital.[35] Accompanying this growth came substantial migration, rural to urban as well as south to north (for commercial agriculture).[36] This model of economic development, termed "stabilizing development," achieved average growth rates of over 7 percent annually into the late 1960s.[37] Indeed, Mexico's hosting of the Summer Olympics in 1968, the images of which have become central to 1968 globally, was designed to be the crowning achievement of the "Mexican Miracle." Policy makers and observers at the time were aware of the inherent contradictions in the model of stabilizing development.[38] To promote an urban and industrial economy, rural producers were sacrificed. The model of commercial agriculture disproportionally benefited northern Mexico, and food prices were deliberately kept low to feed growing urban areas.

By the early 1970s, this model of development, particularly in terms of agricultural production, achieved its limit. During the mid-twentieth century, Mexico had been a net exporter of foodstuffs, yet by the mid-1970s it had become a net importer.[39] As Sanderson has pointed out through case studies of the fruit and vegetable, beef, and grains industries, the internationalization of these markets both undermined Mexico's agricultural self-sufficiency and frequently produced few benefits for agricultural workers.[40] This had dire consequences for the rural poor, who struggled to access and purchase basic corn, as wheat was prioritized in this development model. In addition, while Mexico stood out in Latin America as one of the few countries to have successfully implemented land reform in the first half of the twentieth century, the crisis in rural Mexico in the 1970s was exacerbated by a growing illegal concentration of communal and ejidal lands.[41] Thus in the 1970s a growing population of rural Mexicans struggled both to access land for subsistence agriculture and to find decently remunerated agricultural work.

As Armando Bartra has noted, if the "stabilizing development" model ran out of steam in the 1970s, "so did the patience of the campesinos."[42] The Central Intelligence Agency recognized the threat of a radicalized countryside in Mexico, noting in 1974, "The unrest is partly a result of corruption and exploitation, but ignorance, population pressures, a shortage of good land, and the concentration on industry during the last 30 years also play a part."[43] Peasants drawing on long-standing *agrarista* traditions, as well as radicalized youth who joined them, engaged in everything from illegal land seizures to armed rebellions.[44] Rural struggles took various forms, from fights over agricultural pricing, wages for agricultural work, access to land, and opposition to authoritarianism. Rural teachers at times provided leadership in struggles over land seizures (Padilla and Villanueva in this volume). In the Sierra Juarez of Oaxaca, communities employed by two major lumber companies struck for higher lumber prices in the late 1960s. The struggle involved thousands of rural people and multiple indigenous communities. After multiple years of bitter fights with the timber companies, the communities won a victory in 1972, which resulted in increased prices and improved working conditions.[45] This was just one of many struggles responding to a development model that had favored industrialization, corporate interests, and commercial agricultural production.

Regardless of the Echeverría administration's progressive rhetoric, government officials initially did not hesitate to use the military against a mobilized peasantry, particularly in the first half of the sexenio. Conforming to long-standing PRI practices, those who could not be dealt with through PRI corporatist structures, such as the Confederación Nacional Campesina (National Peasant Confederation, CNC), were potential victims of state violence. The case of Ruben Jaramillo and his followers in the state of Morelos is a prime example of such practices in the decades before.[46] Indeed, Trevizo notes at least sixty-four cases in the early 1970s of state officials forcibly dislodging campesinos from seized land, with twenty-six of those cases involving the army.[47] Nor was the army solely employed against land seizures. In multiple instances in the state of Oaxaca, military force was deployed to support PRI-backed candidates in disputed municipal elections.[48] Particularly in the country's south, but also in the north, military repression of rural discontent went hand in glove with more robust development programs.

Particularly after the first few years of Echeverría's presidency, federal officials expanded their political response to rural discontent with a broad-based strengthening and reorientation of rural development programs. Existing institutions such as the Instituto Nacional Indigenista (National Indigenist Institute, INI), long considered the caboose of the developmentalist train with relatively few resources, saw its overall budget double during this period. New initiatives such as the Programa de Inversiones en el Desarrollo Rural (Rural Development Investment Program, PEDIR) received support from federal officials and the World Bank, which was briefly animated by the philosophy of "redistribution with growth." Federal officials sought to provide increased access to rural credit, and legal protections for such credit were strengthened. Finally, one of the central ways federal authorities chose to counter rural discontent was through a dramatic expansion and reformulation of a previously existing institution, Compañía Nacional de Subsistencias Populares (National Basic Foods Company, CONASUPO).[49]

CONASUPO had its origins in long-standing agricultural price controls and subsidies but in the early 1960s became its own agency with an independent budget. Previous presidents Adolfo López Mateos and Gustavo Díaz Ordaz had gradually expanded the program. Díaz Ordaz specifically expanded the program's rural reach, establishing *tiendas rurales* (rural stores) to alleviate rural poverty while maintaining relatively orthodox "stabilizing development" policies.

Yet President Echeverría transformed the program through both a quantitative expansion and a qualitative reframing of the politics of the development agency.

"SHARED DEVELOPMENT" AND THE RADICALIZATION OF CONASUPO

Shortly after taking office, President Echeverría challenged long-standing traditions in Mexican economic policy. During much of the mid-twentieth century, Hacienda (the Ministry of Finance) and the Banco de México (Bank of Mexico) handled economic policy rather than the office of the presidency. Indeed, the arrangement was understood as a key component of stabilizing development after the years of agricultural reform under President Lázaro Cárdenas (1934–40). While the Ministry of Finance functioned under the economic thinking of comparative advantage, Echeverría rejected such theories in favor of nationalist and state-centered policies aimed at combatting inequality, which he dubbed "shared development."[50] His fight with the ministry was key to his ability to transform CONASUPO into his central rural policy instrument.[51] Once Echeverría had wrested control from Hacienda, he began to expand the program, both its urban and rural components. While the sharp increase in state spending on CONASUPO came in 1973, by 1974 the "federal government transfers to the agency were augmented in real terms by 270 percent."[52] The key reform of CONASUPO under Echeverría was the creation of *bodegas rurales* (rural warehouses), which aimed to help small producers store and bring their products to market. In addition, the number of rural stores selling subsidized goods increased from 43 in 1970 to 899 by 1975.[53] The government also raised guaranteed grain prices, which had stalled under President Díaz Ordaz. Fueled by oil wealth and a desire to relegitimize the regime, federal authorities matched their advocacy for economic self-determination abroad with robust domestic reform.

Communities and individuals seized on the rhetoric of the democratic opening and shared development to make demands on federal agencies. Town authorities from Los Tejocotes, in the state of Oaxaca, complained of having neither the ability to produce sufficient corn for their own consumption nor the ability to purchase it through intermediaries. Describing their town as one of the "most forgotten" of the region, the town authorities wrote directly to the director of the INI, the indigenous development agency, describing their plight.[54]

Indeed, the operational logic of many INI and CONASUPO policies at the time was to replace "bad" local intermediaries, such as regional strongmen or political bosses, with "good" intermediaries, such as federal employees and trustworthy community members. This strategy framed indigenous poverty as stemming from unequal local exchange and had its roots in postrevolutionary agrarian reform of the 1930s as well as 1950s indigenous development policy, which aimed to break the control of provincial elites through federal intervention.[55]

Indeed, much of the scholarship on post-1968 reformism has frequently looked backward to the postrevolutionary reforms under President Lázaro Cárdenas as a point of reference.[56] In this comparison, the reformism or "populism" of President Echeverría is often cast as a failure in contrast to the success of the 1930s. Scholars have argued a comparatively better organized rural bourgeoisie, in alliance with industrialists such as the Monterrey Group, were able to block many of Echeverría's more radical rural reforms. In addition, Basurto and Sanderson have noted that by the 1970s, state institutions had become exponentially larger and more bureaucratic than those of the Cárdenas era.[57] These arguments are compelling in their emphasis on the structural and political limits of the post-1968 reform agenda. Nonetheless, there are other points of comparison for Echeverría's reforms beyond Mexican national history. La vía chilena and agrarian reform under President Allende is one such comparison, but so too is the Cultural Revolution in China, which like Echeverría's rhetoric involved a critique of established political leadership, an effort to reinvigorate revolutionary traditions, and an emphasis on the role of youth. Indeed, the Cultural Revolution served as inspiration for many 1968-era dissidents and various currents of Maoism thrived in Mexico (see the Soldatenko chapter in this volume). While domestic agrarista traditions shaped rural development policy in the 1970s, so too did Maoist and Third World discourses. One sees evidence of these currents in the way rural development policy shifted not only to meet basic needs but also to empower the rural poor through active participation in government programs.[58]

That participation was encouraged primarily in two ways: one, the use of community members themselves to staff stores and warehouses; and two, the development of a large-scale popular theater program. Local staffing of stores was meant to block against bureaucratization and to ensure fair prices. CONASUPO stores received support from INI coordinating centers nearby, which provided oversight to guarantee fair pricing. The pricing of basic goods, such as sugar and corn, was often highly contentious and local populations frequently petitioned the INI to investigate pricing practices. In Oaxaca in the early 1970s, there were clear cases of success at monitoring prices.[59]

The second way mass participation was encouraged was through the creation of popular theater brigades. The Teatro Conasupo de Orientación Campesina (CONASUPO Theater of Peasant Training) program lasted from 1972 to 1976. The CONASUPO theater brigades formed part of a long history of rural theater in Mexico dating back to the 1910 Revolution.[60] Yet the revival of rural theater in the early 1970s was part of a more generalized revival of political theater through New Left politics and a turn toward the countryside internationally. CONASUPO created the brigades, providing training for young actors in Mexico City, with the mission of transforming the agency's work with poor communities throughout the republic. In the early years the brigades staged classical works by Moliére and Chekhov, but as the program developed they engaged the Brazilian method of "theater of the oppressed," developed by Augusto Boal, to create plays based on the rural poor's own experiences.[61] These works involved local community members in the productions and drew from peasant traditions and indigenous mythology to politicize the rural poor and facilitate their engagement in CONASUPO programs.[62] Urban theater troops on the other hand promoted CONASUPO milk production and distribution and held early morning performances with housewives in poor neighborhoods in Mexico City.[63] With themes of inequality, corruption, and rural poverty, Third World politics were implicit in many of the performances.

One of the professional actors employed by CONASUPO was Amdéli Yaber. Just nineteen years old in 1972, Yaber took theater classes through the CONASUPO training offered in Mexico City and went on to perform throughout Mexico in the following years. Yaber recalled one of the most important plays as being a work that consciously mocked CONASUPO itself. This play took aim at corrupt CONASUPO officials aligned with a rural strongman. Indeed, CONASUPO was riven by internal divisions between those aligned with a more conservative view of the agency's role and those who viewed it as a way to provide material benefits for the poor and create a more politicized and organized social base.[64] The latter faction supported the work of the theater brigades as a way to challenge the more conservative sector.[65] The brigades performed throughout Mexico, with an estimated two to three million people viewing six thousand performances from 1972 through 1976.[66] Much like 1970s development policy, these rural theater troops drew on long-standing Mexican agrarista traditions as well as new Third Worldist discourses.

As Echeverría moved to radically reform rural development policy, CONA-SUPO became the "showcase" program in his efforts.[67] The exponential expansion of the program meant that at times Echeverría had biweekly meetings with CONASUPO administrators.[68] One such administrator was Gustavo Esteva (b. 1936), who came of age in Mexico City in the late 1950s and early 1960s. After working for corporations such as IBM and Proctor and Gamble, he found political inspiration in the 1959 Cuban Revolution and the writings of Karl Marx. By the early 1960s, Esteva was a Marxist and participated in several revolutionary organizations.[69] After one of the groups fell apart due to internal disputes, he and several comrades chose the path of what they termed "conquering the state from within" and took jobs in federal agencies. By the time Echeverría assumed office in 1970 and began his reformulation of CONASUPO, Esteva had risen in the ranks of the federal agency to the position of coordinating executive in the senior management office. In that capacity, he oversaw the creation of new programs, including the theater brigades. In Esteva's assessment, the theater brigades had a radicalizing potential, to "create an organized social base to produce profound transformations" and to develop a global view of social change.[70] It is here that one sees more radical versions of Third Worldist politics at play within federal agencies during the mid-1970s.

In addition to the rural theater brigades, Jorge de la Vega Domínguez, the director of CONASUPO, tapped Esteva to create a brigade for "special persons," a few of them former political prisoners and leaders of the 1968 student movement. Esteva therefore put together the brigade of youth, whose tasks, while ill-defined, generally aimed at promoting CONASUPO programs. The brigade included one of the most notable leaders of the 1968 student movement, Luis Tomas Cervantes Cabeza de Vaca, along with one of the president's own sons, Alvaro Echeverría. The strategy of providing former dissidents employment and other benefits was a key component of the PRI's political repertoire. In this case, the expansion of antipoverty programs also provided resources to incorporate 1960s dissidents and others into state agencies. Yet framing Esteva's experience as merely part of tried-and-true PRI political authoritarianism disallows us from understanding the broader dynamics at stake. As a high-level functionary, Esteva participated in key debates about rural development policy, such as those involving the Ministry of Finance referenced earlier. Esteva and others were staunch advocates of increasing guaranteed pricing for commodities such as corn. Indeed, after the debate among policy makers was won in favor of raising prices, Echeverría asked the agencies to delay the announcement to have peasant organizations demand it, part of a long history of PRI-orchestrated mobilization and negotiation.[71] In this case, Esteva's strategy of working inside the government but on his own terms ("adentro pero afuera") benefited both rural producers and Echeverría's goal of rehabilitating the political system.

What is evident is that PRI strategies for containment of rural discontent in the mid-1970s, and perhaps during much of its reign, were always partial and contingent. Echeverría and Esteva, for example, ultimately had far different political goals, yet they coincided with each other on specific issues, such as the theory of unequal exchange, and the president benefited from the fights Esteva waged within federal bureaucracies. Nor did Esteva have illusions about the nature of the reforms during the democratic opening, later recalling that "we weren't making the revolution with Echeverría." Esteva consciously chose to leave his career in federal administration in 1976 and went on to serve as an advisor to the Ejército Zapatista de Liberación Nacional (Zapatista National Liberation Army, EZLN), after their 1994 uprising in the state of Chiapas.[72] Nonetheless, the democratic opening and official Third Worldist rhetoric provided the political space and institutional support for Esteva and others to develop innovative rural development policy. Those policies provided substantive benefits for large swaths of rural Mexicans through improved agricultural pricing (however short-lived) as well as land reform, as government officials conceded to land seizures instigated by activists throughout the republic.

Ultimately, the reality of Allende's government in Chile, not merely his December 1972 University of Guadalajara speech, facilitated Echeverría's turn toward the Third World. The existence of leftist governments in Latin America, such as those of Chile and Cuba, provided Mexico the space to pursue a Third World posture and renewed economic nationalism. Echeverría engaged in a careful balancing act, privately reassuring the United States of his role as a safe alternative to Fidel Castro and Salvador Allende, while simultaneously marching through the streets of Mexico City arm and arm with the compañero presidente. This U.S.-friendly version of Third Worldism in turn created space for figures such as Esteva, who consciously aimed to radicalize Mexico's rural development programs, yet also allowed for deep contradictions, evidenced in the Mexican military's simultaneous violent campaigns of counterinsurgency in parts of the country's south.[73] Indeed, Mexico's turn toward the Third World was short-lived. Allende, who Echeverría envisioned as a collaborator in the New International Economic Order, would be dead just ten months after his visit to Mexico. The Mexican government made significant efforts to provide safety and support for Allende's immediate family and other Chilean dissidents in the aftermath of the 1973 coup. That U.S.-supported coup violently signaled the limits of Latin America's move toward an independent path. Echeverría himself would end his term embattled, facing opposition from business interests and an increasingly fraught economic situation. Yet the experience of rural development in post-1968 Mexico points to the power of global Third World politics to shape domestic policies as well as to the limits of the Mexican political system.

NOTES

I would like to thank Pedro Monaville, Radhika Natarajan, Jesse Zarley, and Enrique Ochoa for providing thoughtful comments and suggestions on this essay.

1.   Walker, *Waking from the Dream*, 45–72; Agustín, *Tragicomedia Mexicana 2*, 116.
2.   For a detailed account of the domestic context of Allende's remarks, see Harmer, *Allende's Chile and the Inter-American Cold War*.
3.   On the role of the press in politics, see Freije, "Exposing Scandals, Guarding Secrets."
4.   Walker, *Waking from the Dream*; Vaughan, *Portrait of a Young Painter*; Pensado, *Rebel Mexico*.
5.   For an unorthodox analysis of democratic possibilities during midcentury PRI rule, see Smith, "Who Governed?"
6.   Gillingham and Smith, *Dictablanda*.
7.   Rubin, "Contextualizing the Regime"; Aviña, *Specters of Revolution*, 14.
8.   On challenging Mexican Cold War exceptionalism, see McCormick, "Last Door," 58.
9.   "Tercer Informe de Gobierno."
10. Zolov, "Introduction: Latin America in the Global Sixties," 354.
11. For a notable exception to this trend, see Christiansen and Scarlett, *Third World*.
12. On the consumption of international events in Mexico, see Volpi, *La imaginación y el poder*.
13. Headline, *Excélsior*, November 29, 1972.
14. Prashad, *Darker Nations*, xv.
15. Lee, *Making a World After Empire*, 6.
16. Gilman, "New International Economic Order."
17. See Keller, *Mexico's Cold War*; Shapira, "Mexico's Foreign Policy Under Echeverría."
18. Manuel Mejido, "Recorrido Entre Disparidades," *Excélsior*, December 1, 1972. The original chants, "Allende, seguro a los yanquis dales duro!"
19. Mejido, "Recorrido Entre Disparidades."
20. Brands, "Third World Politics."
21. Ibid., 107.
22. See Dietrick, "Oil Power and Economic Theologies."
23. Burke, "Competing for the Last Utopia?"
24. "Travel Plans of President Echeverria," U.S. State Department Cable from Mexico City, August 25, 1973, "Plus D: Public Library of U.S. Diplomacy," *Wikileaks*,

accessed May 17, 2017, https://wikileaks.org/plusd/. The cable concludes, "Chileans had called to indicate their sharp disappointment that Echeverría would not be present."

25.   Harmer, *Allende's Chile and the Inter-American Cold War*, 169. "In Almeyda's opinion, expressed privately a year earlier, the Mexicans were acting under the 'guise of progress and an attachment to a revolutionary tradition,' but were in reality closely tied to U.S. interests. Or, to put it another way, Echeverría wanted to appear 'progressive' among his own people, which is why he was reaching out to Allende, but as far as Chile's foreign minister was concerned, this was merely a 'facade.'"

26.   See Agee, *Inside the Company*.

27.   "Cuarto Informe de Gobierno del presidente Luis Echeverría Álvarez," September 1, 1974, accessed May 17, 2017, http://www.biblioteca.tv/artman2/publish/1974_81/Cuarto_Informe_de_Gobierno_del_presidente_Luis_Ech_1212.shtml.

28.   Conversation between President Nixon and President Echeverría, June 15 and 16, 1972, Transcript 27, June 15, 1972, 10:31 a.m.–12:10 p.m., Conversation no. 735–1, cassette nos. 2246–48, Oval Office, National Security Archives, accessed May 17, 2017, http://nsarchive.gwu.edu/NSAEBB/NSAEBB105/.

29.   "State of U.S.-Mexican Relations at Midway Point in Echeverría Administration," U.S. State Department cable, September 5, 1973, "Plus D: Public Library of U.S. Diplomacy," *WikiLeaks*, accessed May 17, 2017, https://wikileaks.org/plusd/. The report goes on to note, "This multiplication of Mexican activities on the world scene is not necessarily harmful from our viewpoint though the fawning adulation of Allende is more than a little nauseating."

30.   "La Revolución, Movimiento Social Frenado, Afirma Echeverría," *Excélsior*, November 21, 1972.

31.   Gerardo Lezama Juárez, "La política exterior de Echeverría. Continuidad o ruptura?," accessed May 17, 2017, https://www.academia.edu/15866658/La_pol%C3%ADtica_exterior_de_Luis_Echeverr%C3%ADa._Continuidad_o_ruptura.

32.   Thornton, "A Mexican International Economic Order?"

33.   Gilman, "The New International Economic Order," 1. Gilman similarly describes the NIEO as an "apparition" and an "improbable political creature" that disappeared as quickly as it emerged.

34.   Lee, *Making a World After Empire*, 8.

35.   Cotter, "The Mexican Revolution and the Green Revolution, 1950–1970," in *Troubled Harvest*, 233–79.

36.   Wright, *Death of Ramón González*.

37.   Ochoa, *Feeding Mexico*, 178.

38.   Ibid. For how this development model deepened domestic income inequality, see Navarrete, *La distribución del ingreso*.

39.   Bartra, *Los nuevos herederos de Zapata*, 125–26; Trevizo, *Rural Protest and the Making of Democracy*, 100.

40.   Sanderson, *Transformation of Mexican Agriculture*.

41. Andrews, "Departures and Returns," 51; Trevizo, *Rural Protest*, 97.
42. Bartra, *Los nuevos herederos de Zapata*, 27.
43. Central Intelligence Agency, Directorate of Intelligence, Weekly Review, "Mexico: Rural Discontent," June 14, 1974, Freedom of Information Request No. 18961, National Security Archive, accessed May 17, 2017, http://nsarchive.gwu.edu /NSAEBB/NSAEBB105/.
44. Padilla, *Rural Resistance in the Land of Zapata*; Schryer, *Ethnicity and Class Conflict in Rural Mexico*; Aviña, *Specters of Revolution*.
45. Mathews, *Instituting Nature*, 130–31.
46. See Padilla, *Rural Resistance*; McCormick, *Logic of Compromise*.
47. Trevizo, *Rural Protest*, 103.
48. Bailón Corres, "Los avatares de la democracia (1970–2008)," 254.
49. For the most comprehensive analysis of CONASUPO, see Ochoa, *Feeding Mexico*.
50. Dietrich, "Oil Power and Economic Theologies," 515.
51. Esteva, author's interview. For struggles over Banco de México's role in development policy, see Sanderson, *Agrarian Populism and the Mexican State*, 170.
52. Ochoa, *Feeding Mexico*, 180–81.
53. Ibid., 184–85, 187.
54. "Agencia Municipal de los Tejocotes, Mixtecpec, Juxtlahuaca, Oaxaca, Oax. Asunto: Solicita Expendio de Maiz," Caja 107, Expediente 1570, Acervo Alfonso Caso, Ex-Convento, Yanhuitlán, Mexico.
55. On the legacy of agrarian radicalism, see Ochoa, "Lic. Moisés de la Peña," 165–79. On indigenous development, see Aguirre Beltrán, *Regiones de refugio*.
56. Kiddle and Muñoz, *Populism in Twentieth Century Mexico*.
57. See Basurto, "The Late Populism of Luis Echeverría"; Sanderson, *Agrarian Populism*.
58. Esteva, "La experiencia de la intervención estatal reguladora."
59. Felipe Sánchez Bautista, "Untitled Letter," February 21, 1972, Caja 88, Expediente 1290, Acervo Alfonso Caso, Ex-Convento, Yanhuitlán, Mexico.
60. Frischmann, "Misiones Culturales, Teatro CONASUPO, and Teatro Comunidad."
61. Ibid., 291.
62. Ibid., 292.
63. Yaber, personal communication with author.
64. Esteva, author's interview.
65. Ibid.
66. Frischmann, "Misiones Culturales," 296; Esteva, author's interview.
67. Ochoa, *Feeding Mexico*, 177.
68. Esteva, author's interview.
69. Esteva recalls purchasing a copy of Marx and Engels's *German Ideology*, which converted him to Marxism. He participated briefly in two organizations, the Alianza Revolucionaria Espartaco and the Partido Revolucionario del Proletariado.
70. Esteva, author's interview.

71.   Ibid.
72.   Esteva has since become a public intellectual and a proponent of postdevelopment theory.
73.   For an example of the complicity of rural development with counterinsurgency, see Aviña, *Specters of Revolution*, 151–53.

BIBLIOGRAPHY

ARCHIVES

Acervo Alfonso Caso, Ex-Convento, Yanhuitlán, Mexico.
National Security Archive, George Washington University.

INTERVIEWS

Esteva, Gustavo. Author's interview. Oaxaca City, Oaxaca, July 14, 2016.
Yaber, Amdéleli. Personal communication with author. August 2016.

ONLINE PRIMARY SOURCE COLLECTIONS

"Cuarto Informe de Gobierno del presidente Luis Echeverría Álvarez," September 1, 1974, accessed May 17, 2017, http://www.biblioteca.tv/artman2/publish/1974_81/Cuarto_Informe_de_Gobierno_del_presidente_Luis_Ech_1212.shtml.
Doyle, Kate. "The Dawn of Mexico's Dirty War: Lucio Cabañas and the Party of the Poor." December 5, 2003. National Security Archive. Accessed May 17, 2017. http://nsarchive.gwu.edu/NSAEBB/NSAEBB105/.
"Tercer Informe de Gobierno del presidente Luis Echeverría Álvarez." September 1, 1973. Accessed May 17, 2017. http://www.biblioteca.tv/artman2/publish/1973_82/Tercer_Informe_de_Gobierno_del_presidente_Luis_Ech_1211.shtml.
Wikileaks. "Plus D: Public Library of U.S. Diplomacy." Accessed May 17, 2017. https://wikileaks.org/plusd/.

NEWSPAPERS

Excélsior

PUBLISHED SOURCES

Agee, Philip. *Inside the Company: CIA Diary*. New York: Farrar Straus and Giroux, 1975.
Aguirre Beltrán, Gonzalo. *Regiones de refugio: El desarrollo de la comunidad y el proceso dominical en Mestizoamérica*. Mexico City: Instituto Nacional Indigenista, 1967.
Agustín, José. *Tragicomedia Mexicana 2: La vida México de 1970–1988*. Mexico City: Editorial Planeta Mexicana, 1998.
Andrews, Abigail. "Departures and Returns: Migration, Gender, and the Politics of Transnational Mexican Communities." PhD diss., University of California, Berkeley, 2014.
Aviña, Alexander. *Specters of Revolution: Peasant Guerrillas in the Cold War Mexican Countryside*. Oxford: Oxford University Press, 2014.

Bailón Corres, Jaime. "Los avatares de la democracia (1970–2008)." In *Oaxaca: Historia Breve*, edited by María de los Ángeles Romero Frizzi, Carlos Sánchez, Jesús Mendoza, Jaime Bailón, Francisco Ruiz, and Luis Arrioja. Mexico City: El Colegio de México/Fondo de Cultura Económica, 2010.

Bartra, Armando. *Los nuevos herederos de Zapata: Campesinos en movimiento 1920–2012*. Mexico City: Partido de la Revolución Democrática/Secretaría de Trabajadores de Campo, Desarrollo Rural y Pueblos Indios, 2012.

Basurto, Jorge. "The Late Populism of Luis Echeverría." In *Latin American Populism in Comparative Perspective*, edited by Michael L. Conniff, 93–111. Albuquerque: University of New Mexico Press, 1982.

Brands, Hal. "Third World Politics in an Age of Global Turmoil: The Latin American Challenge to U.S. and Western Hegemony, 1965–1975." *Diplomatic History* 32, no. 1 (January 2008): 105–38.

Burke, Roland. "Competing for the Last Utopia? The NIEO, Human Rights, and the World Conference for the International Women's Year, Mexico City, June 1975." *Humanity: An International Journal of Human Rights, Humanitarianism, and Development* 6, no. 1 (Spring 2015): 47–61.

Christiansen, Samantha, and Zachary Scarlett, eds. *The Third World in the Global Sixties*. New York: Berghahn Books, 2012.

Cotter, Joseph. *Troubled Harvest: Agronomy and Revolution in Mexico, 1880–2002*. Westport, Conn.: Praeger, 2003.

Dietrick, Christopher R. W. "Oil Power and Economic Theologies: The United States and the Third World in the Wake of the Energy Crisis." *Diplomatic History* 40, no. 3 (2016): 550–29.

Esteva, Gustavo. "La experiencia de la intervención estatal reguladora en la comercialización agropecuaria de 1970 a 1976." In *Mercado y dependencia*, edited by Ursula Oswald, 207–46. Mexico City: Nueva Imagen, 1979.

Freije, Vanessa. "Exposing Scandals, Guarding Secrets: Manuel Buendía, Columnismo, and the Unraveling of One-Party Rule in Mexico, 1965–1984." *The Americas* 72, no. 3 (July 2015): 377–409.

Frischmann, Donald. "Misiones Culturales, Teatro Conasupo, and Teatro Comunidad: The Evolution of Rural Theater." In *Rituals of Rule, Rituals of Resistance: Public Celebrations and Popular Culture in Mexico*, edited by William Beezley, Cheryl Martin, and William French, 285–306. Lanham, Md.: Rowman and Littlefield, 1994.

Gillingham, Paul, and Benjamin T. Smith, eds. *Dictablanda: Politics, Work and Culture in Mexico, 1938–1968*. Durham, N.C.: Duke University Press, 2014.

Gilman, Nils. "The New International Economic Order: A Reintroduction." *Humanity: An International Journal of Human Rights, Humanitarianism, and Development* 6, no. 1 (Spring 2015): 1–16.

Harmer, Tanya. *Allende's Chile and the Inter-American Cold War*. Chapel Hill: University of North Carolina Press, 2011.

Keller, Renata. *Mexico's Cold War: Cuba, the United States, and the Legacy of the Mexican Revolution*. Cambridge: Cambridge University Press, 2015.

Kiddle, Amelia, and Maria L. O. Muñoz, eds. *Populism in Twentieth Century Mexico: The Presidencies of Lázaro Cárdenas and Luis Echeverría.* Tucson: University of Arizona Press, 2010.

Lee, Christopher. *Making a World After Empire: The Bandung Moment and Its Political Afterlives.* Athens: Ohio University Press, 2010.

Lezama Juárez, Gerardo. "La política exterior de Echeverría: Continuidad o ruptura?" Accessed May 17, 2017. https://www.academia.edu/15866658/La_pol%C3%ADtica _exterior_de_Luis_Echeverr%C3%ADa._Continuidad_o_ruptura.

Mathews, Andrew S. *Instituting Nature: Authority, Expertise, and Power in Mexican Forests.* Cambridge, Mass.: MIT Press, 2011.

McCormick, Gladys I. "The Last Door: Political Prisoners and the Use of Torture in Mexico's Dirty War." *The Americas* 74, no. 1 (January 2017): 57–81.

———. *The Logic of Compromise in Mexico: How the Countryside Was Key to the Emergence of Authoritarianism.* Chapel Hill: University of North Carolina Press, 2016.

Navarrete, Ifigenia Martínez de. *La distribución del ingreso y el desarrollo económico de México.* Mexico City: Instituto de Investigaciones Económicas, 1960.

Ochoa, Enrique. *Feeding Mexico: The Political Uses of Food Since 1910.* Lanham, Md.: Rowman and Littlefield, 2001.

———. "Lic. Moisés de la Peña: The Economist on Horseback." In *The Human Tradition in Mexico*, edited by Jeffrey Pilcher, 165–79. Lanham, Md.: Rowman and Littlefield, 2003.

Padilla, Tanalís. *Rural Resistance in the Land of Zapata: The Jaramillista Movement and the Myth of the Pax Priísta, 1940–1962.* Durham, N.C.: Duke University Press, 2008.

Pensado, Jaime M. *Rebel Mexico: Student Unrest and Authoritarian Political Culture During the Long Sixties.* Stanford, Calif.: Stanford University Press, 2013.

Prashad, Vijay. *The Darker Nations: A People's History of the Third World.* New York: New Press, 2007.

Rubin, Jeffrey. "Contextualizing the Regime: What 1938–1968 Tells Us About Mexico, Power and Latin America's Twentieth Century." In *Dictablanda: Politics, Work and Culture in Mexico, 1938–1968*, edited by Paul Gillingham and Benjamin T. Smith, 379–96. Durham, N.C.: Duke University Press, 2014.

Sanderson, Steven. *Agrarian Populism and the Mexican State: The Struggle for Land in Sonora.* Berkeley: University of California Press, 1981.

———. *The Transformation of Mexican Agriculture: International Structure and the Politics of Rural Change.* Princeton, N.J.: Princeton University Press, 1986.

Schryer, Frans. *Ethnicity and Class Conflict in Rural Mexico.* Princeton, N.J.: Princeton University Press, 1990.

Shapira, Yoram. "Mexico's Foreign Policy Under Echeverría: A Retrospect." *Inter-American Economic Affairs* 31 (Spring 1978): 34–43.

Smith, Benjamin T. "Who Governed? Grassroots Politics in Mexico Under the Partido Revolucionario Institucional, 1958–1970." *Past and Present* 225, no. 1 (November 2014): 227–71.

Thornton, Christy. "A Mexican International Economic Order? Tracing the Hidden Roots of the Charter of Economic Rights and Duties of States." *Humanity: An International Journal of Human Rights, Humanitarianism, and Development* (forthcoming).

Trevizo, Dolores. *Rural Protest and the Making of Democracy in Mexico, 1968–2000.* University Park: Penn State University Press, 2011.

Vaughan, Mary Kay. *Portrait of a Young Painter: Pepe Zúñiga and Mexico City's Rebel Generation.* Durham, N.C.: Duke University Press, 2014.

Volpi, Jorge. *La imaginación y el poder: Una historia intelectual de 1968.* Mexico City: Ediciones Era, 1998.

Walker, Louise. *Waking from the Dream: Mexico's Middle Classes After 1968.* Stanford, Calif.: Stanford University Press, 2013.

Wright, Angus. *The Death of Ramón González: The Modern Agricultural Dilemma.* Austin: University of Texas Press, 2005.

Zolov, Eric. "Introduction: Latin America in the Global Sixties." *The Americas* 70, no. 3 (January 2014): 349–62.

7

A WAR AGAINST POOR PEOPLE

Dirty Wars and Drug Wars in 1970s Mexico

ALEXANDER AVIÑA

The war on drugs is no less than continuing to use military force to contain noncomformist, disruptive movements, groups in resistance, and collectives who raise their voices.

ABEL BARRERA, DIRECTOR OF TLACHINOLLAN

For the first time in modern Mexican history there is the total military occupation of an entire region of the country. . . . We can say that we are fighting against a bunch of students, or Indians, or communists, but the truth is that we are controlling and managing entire communities, municipalities, cities, mountains, communication systems, everything.

GENERAL ESCÁCEGA, *GUERRA EN EL PARAÍSO*,
CARLOS MONTEMAYOR

AYOTZINAPA FORETOLD

If the 1994 guerrilla uprising in Chiapas helped crack open a longer history of armed struggle and resistance against the long-ruling Partido Revolucionario Institucional (Institutional Revolutionary Party, PRI), then perhaps the recent 2014 forced disappearance of forty-three Ayotzinapa *normalista* students in the northern region of Guerrero could aid in the uncovering of a longer history of state-sponsored (or at the very least, state-enabled) terror in southwestern Mexico. An earlier moment, the 2000 electoral defeat of the PRI and subsequent efforts to investigate its sordid histories of state terror via the declassification of government documents and an official "truth commission" report, provided valuable resources and narratives while ultimately failing to obtain justice for the victims of state terror. But the Ayotzinapa case and the social protest mobilizations it inspired, as with the Ejército Zapatista de Liberación Nacional (Zapatista National Liberation Army, EZLN) uprising in Chiapas, both contributed to the critical questioning of state-produced narratives that stressed progress, the restoration of order, salvation, and neoliberal utopias. The neoliberal "status quo," to borrow a quote from Walter Benjamin, "threaten[ed] to be preserved" until these two interruptions forced an "arrest of happening."[1] Additionally, the disappearance of the students (and the killing of six additional students and innocent bystanders on the night of September 24, 2014) involved at some level different but enmeshed networks of people with an outsized political and social presence in Guerrero since the 1960s: narco-traffickers and the Mexican military. In the midst of a current decade-long War on Drugs or "War Against the Cartels," Ayotzinapa forcefully suggests a rethinking of how such groups—*narcos* (drug traffickers), *militares* (military men), *policías* (police-men), and collaborating *políticos* (politicians)—possess intimate, shared histo-ries linked to broader processes of state formation, economic dispossession, and authoritarian political rule in Mexico's recent past.

This chapter situates the structural transformation of Mexico's narcotics economy beginning in the 1960s and government responses that took the form of militarized interdiction as interlinked to the campaigns of violent politi-cal repression concomitantly unleashed by the PRI against "internal enemies." During the 1960s and '70s, such repression—termed the Dirty War, or Guerra Sucia—encompassed the state application of terror, violence, and surveillance against individuals, communities, and organizations deemed threats to domestic political and social stability by the PRI. It took its most extreme, violent form in Guerrero, where soldiers, state police officers, government spies, and caciques (local bosses) terrorized dissident political activity and economic justice efforts beginning in the late 1950s, culminating with counterinsurgency campaigns in the early 1970s in response to two peasant guerrilla organizations. At the same time, key changes in the global economy of narcotics spurred the pro-liferation of marijuana and opium poppy production in the mountains of the southern state. A boom in marijuana and heroin demand from the United States beginning in the mid-1960s, combined with the closing down of key transnational heroin networks, expanded Mexico's role as the key supplier of drugs to its northern neighbor.[2] By 1975, Mexican heroin and marijuana con-trolled roughly 90 percent of the U.S. market.[3] Facing pressure from the U.S. government and a domestic moral panic over alleged increased drug addiction rates played out in the national press, the PRI ordered a national interdiction campaign with the military as the spearhead. These militarized counternarcotics programs—including the novel use of dangerous defoliant herbicides sprayed from helicopters and airplanes[4]—resembled, in practice, what counterinsurgent military units had practiced in Guerrero since at least 1963 after a contentious electoral campaign: brutal attacks on rural highland peasant communities that left behind a trail of tortures, razed homes, disappeared campesinos, destroyed agricultural harvests, and environmental damage.

Two Mexican "wars," one "dirty" and the other against drugs, and the multiple ways in which they intimately intersect historically during the 1970s, reveal the central premise of this chapter: they were wars directed against poor people intended to reassert state control. For the PRI, the boundary between drug control and political control, between popular political protest and drug criminality, became usefully permeable. Indeed, government and military officials publicly described counterinsurgency efforts in Guerrero as counternarcotic, anticrime campaigns.[5] They accused guerrillas of working with narcos, the former protecting the latter in exchange for weapons and supplies.[6] A maximalist version of this narrative asserted that guerrillas simply did not exist; rather, "it was people who cultivated opium poppies and marijuana."[7] At the same time, covertly, military units in Guerrero (and in Sinaloa) collaborated with known local narco-traffickers to attack leftist movements and guerrilla groups.[8] Having killed or disappeared the most influential guerrilla leaders in Guerrero by early 1975, some of the military counterinsurgent officers who led those campaigns—like General Mario Acosta Chaparro—would allegedly become narco-traffickers themselves, as they remained in the region to work as politically appointed police agents given broad policing powers by state politicians. Guerrero prefigured the sort of Mexican narco "deep state," to use historian Adela Cedillo's terminology from her contribution to this volume, that exists today. Other counterinsurgent officers, like the Fort Benning–trained General Roberto Heine Rangel, would apply their anti-guerrilla lessons learned in Guerrero to antidrug campaigns launched in northern Mexico during the late 1970s and early 1980s.[9] There, too, poor people—peasant drug farmers in the highlands of Sinaloa—would suffer the brunt of state violence.

After a discussion that historicizes the links between counterinsurgency and counternarcotics in 1960s and '70s Guerrero, a section will follow that describes one particularly heinous event during the Dirty War: the April 24, 1973, massacre of six campesinos in the highland community of Los Piloncillos by members of the Mexican military. Los Piloncillos encapsulates the biopolitical core of the Dirty War, of the military counterinsurgency waged against the campesino communities that supported (or were perceived as supporting) armed struggle, subsequently applied to drug-producing peasant farmers: selective "killing and collective welfare."[10] What can Los Piloncillos teach us about the Dirty War at large? Can this historical constellation of dirty wars and drug wars teach us something about sovereignty and power in a contemporary Mexico undone by mass violence?

A final section focuses on the tumultuous governorship of Rubén Figueroa Figueroa (1975–81), an influential cacique and PRI politician tied into national elite circles, who took power after the military defeat of the guerrillas. A man described as a "cruel, sanguine assassin" by the first state attorney general he appointed in 1975, Figueroa oversaw a ruling tenure characterized by intense social conflict, political violence, and continued state terror.[11] At the same time, this moment also witnessed the configuration of military, police, politician, and narco-trafficking networks at the local/regional level as Guerrero transformed into a prime producer of narcotics. Even as national interdiction campaigns targeted drug production throughout different parts of the country during the late 1970s and early '80s, certain state agents at the local level helped form the foundations for the gradual emergence of a "narco-state."

"BEHAVE AND GO TO WORK"

They [the military] released me . . . gave me twenty pesos and told me, "Behave and go to work."
DON ASCENCIÓN ROSAS, CAMPESINO
GUERRERENSE, VICTIM OF TORTURE, FATHER
OF DISAPPEARED GUERRILLA

Since the emergence of a statewide civil disobedience movement in 1959 and 1960 that sought the removal of a corrupt and violent governor, Guerrero has served as a theater of popular political radicalization in the face of constant state and cacique terror and, alternately, a laboratory of counterinsurgency.[12] Campesino movements that sought to undermine caciques and *acaparadores* (loan sharks and market monopolists) by demanding social justice and economic democracy fused with electoral opposition groups that organized for "effective suffrage" and students and rural schoolteachers who kept alive the most radical legacies of

1910. The rural teacher training school in Ayotzinapa produced a large number of key social activists and future guerrillas, including Lucio Cabañas. "We were born [politically] in Ayotzinapa," Cabañas once remarked.[13]

After a military massacre of anti-governor activists in the capital city of Chilpancingo in December 1960 and a contentious state-level electoral season in 1962 that also ended with the killing of protestors, thousands of military soldiers entered the state in 1963 violently targeting political dissidents and social movements. A report published by the leftist independent journal *Política* in mid-1963 revealed practices and tactics of repression that later became systematic during the Dirty War in the 1970s: An estimated twenty thousand deployed soldiers targeted political opposition zones along the coasts and razed hundreds of homes belonging to dissident campesinos, tortured and killed campesino leaders, and illegally detained hundreds. Working with cacique allies, military units terrorized coastal highland campesino communities that defended legal ejido (communal land) control over forestry resources.[14] The assassination of campesino activists included the horrific murder of a coffee-producer leader nicknamed "El Tabaco"; after troops cut out his tongue and castrated him, they slit his body open.[15]

The use of the Mexican military to maintain and reassert state control over rural Guerrero represented the political rule, not the exception, throughout the Mexican countryside after 1940. Military policing, the "maintenance of internal order," to quote historian Thomas Rath, gradually became the primary function of the armed forces by the 1950s.[16] Indeed, the professionalization of the military (training, logistics, weaponry, counterinsurgency doctrine) occurred in reaction to the sort of popular political protests and social movements that took place in Guerrero—a process accelerated by the national labor strikes of the late 1950s, regional civic protests in the early 1960s, and the emergence of the first modern socialist guerrilla struggle in Chihuahua in 1965.[17] Conterminously, the military also began to participate in drug interdiction and eradication on a national scale, but the drug trade flourished due to the protection granted at local levels by certain military officials, police, and politicians. Beginning with "The Great Campaign" in 1948, a national "permanent" program that involved federal police and military units in the physical eradication of marijuana and opium poppy plants, such programs became more urgent as Mexico emerged as a key supplier of narcotics in the late 1960s and early 1970s.[18] In large part pushed by Operation Intercept, Richard Nixon's unilateral decision in September 1969 to essentially close the U.S.-Mexico border as a War on Drugs initiative, the militarized drug interdiction campaigns of the 1970s occurred in dialogue with counterinsurgency operations in the state of Guerrero that had "formally" begun in 1968 and 1969.[19] Operation Condor and the sending of thousands of troops and police to the Sinaloa, Chihuahua, and Durango highlands in the late 1970s to attack peasant drug cultivators displayed a counterinsurgent edge. Counternarcotics drew its practices, epistemic rationale, and practitioners from counterinsurgency.

Drug control thus functioned as a project of social control and political repression on both sides of the border. By the time the guerrilla Asociación Cívica Nacional Revolucionaria (National Revolutionary Civic Association, ACNR) and the Partido de los Pobres (Party of the Poor, PDLP), respectively led by Genaro Vázquez and Cabañas, emerged in the late 1960s, backed by dozens of rural communities radicalized after a decade of state terror, the Mexican military simultaneously conducted counterinsurgency and counternarcotics operations in the state. Government officials publicly lambasted the guerrillas as criminal, narco-trafficking bandits while the military launched violent, at times disparate, counterinsurgency campaigns that targeted suspected civilian supporters of the armed movements.[20] Available evidence, derived from state documents and oral testimonies, indicates at that least six hundred to seven hundred *guerrerenses* remain disappeared, with hundreds, perhaps thousands, more tortured and illegally detained by military forces from 1969 to 1980 in this Dirty War *à la guerrerense*. Other estimates range as high as fifteen hundred disappeared persons.[21]

Many guerrerenses like Ascención Rosas remain haunted by memories of the Dirty War. Tita Radilla, a courageous, indefatigable human rights activist, recounted to me how tortured, lifeless bodies appeared almost daily on the outskirts of Atoyac de Alvarez as we conversed in the town's former army base (now a city services center called, ironically, The City of Hope). For decades Tita has worked to uncover the whereabouts of her father, Rosendo Radilla, detained and disappeared by the military at a checkpoint in August 1974 after being pulled off a bus. A noted *corridista* (folk singer), campesino leader, and former municipal president in Atoyac, he loved composing corridos about the guerrillas and revolution. The military officials at the checkpoint told him his crime: composing corridos. "It's a crime?" queried Radilla. "No, but for now you're fucked [ya te chingaste] anyway," responded a soldier.[22] Working as a university professor in the state capital of Chilpancingo while also a member of the guerrilla PDLP, Alejandra Cárdenas recalled living in a militarized city never knowing when soldiers would arrive to disappear her.[23] Campesino leader Hilario Mesino will never forget that day in 1974 when soldiers brutally beat his father and detained his nineteen-year-old brother, Alberto. Alberto never returned.[24]

The personal anecdotes briefly described above provide a glimpse of tactics used en masse by the military, on orders from PRI officials, as early as 1969 when it became apparent that two separate armed campesino organizations operated in the state. A massacre of five campesinos in the sierra community of Los Piloncillos (Atoyac de Alvarez municipality) in April 1973 marked the beginning of the most violent phase of the counterinsurgency in the Costa Grande region of Guerrero. Yet the use of extreme violence by members of the Mexican military certainly occurred prior to 1973. PDLP communiqués and declassified spy reports denounced the military's use of gasoline during the torture of campesinos suspected of supporting the guerrillas as early as 1970. After forcing their captives to drink gasoline, soldiers then lit the campesinos on fire and threw their charred corpses into the streets of Acapulco. Other bodies dumped on the outskirts of rural communities bore the marks of torture and gunshots.[25]

The application of collective punishment on entire campesino communities also occurred prior to Los Piloncillos. From August 28 to September 5, 1972, soldiers entered the small town of El Quemado and detained over ninety inhabitants, sending them first to the 27th Military Zone base in Atoyac and subsequently to Acapulco. The community's crime? Its geographical location near the site of a guerrilla ambush of military forces that occurred on August 23, 1972. Accused of supporting and participating in the ambush, the detained suffered torture and faced thirty-year prison sentences. Unable to withstand the beatings and electrical shocks, seven died while imprisoned, including a seventy-year-old man named Ignacio Sánchez Gutiérrez.[26] In mid-September 1972, PDLP communiqués once again decried the military's practice of mass detentions, torture, disappearances, and even the use of napalm during aerial bombings. On September 24, soldiers razed the small village of Llanos de Santiago de la Unión—fifty houses and an evangelical church. The violence not only physically destroyed families and communities but was also economically devastating, because military repression disrupted the regional agricultural season. Coffee harvests in the Atoyac region were supposed to begin in late September.[27] Just four days after the scorching of Llanos de Santiago, President Luis Echeverría (1970–76) announced the aperture of Plan Guerrero, a massive public investment designed to ameliorate socioeconomic inequality and poverty and to improve the state's transportation infrastructure.[28]

Despite such public declarations and stated intentions, counterinsurgent and counternarcotic campaigns launched by the Mexican state during the 1960s and 70s systematically targeted and brutalized rural campesino communities. And while different security apparatuses—primarily the Mexican military, the Dirección Federal de Seguridad (Federal Security Directorate, DFS), and different federal and local police forces—did achieve some publicly stated goals like the violent extermination of Guerrero guerrillas (officially called "cattle thieves and bandits") and urban guerrillas ("terrorists") as well as the alleged physical destruction of tons of narcotics, such achieved goals fundamentally required the targeting of highland campesino communities in states like Guerrero and Sinaloa, communities that supported armed struggle or engaged in the cultivation of illicit drugs (or were perceived to do so).

As such, both the Dirty War and the War on Drugs represented state-sanctioned violence and terror against poor people whose political or economic decisions and/or actions symptomatically reflected deeper structural and historical maladies. Functionally, these wars proved one and the same despite differently stated targets and goals. They shared practices and an epistemology expressed most "colorfully" by Rubén Figueroa: "muerto el perro se acaba la rabia" (dead dogs don't bite).[29] The state agents involved in carrying out the Dirty War and the War on Drugs in Guerrero proved capable of identifying symptoms but offered no "cures." Indeed, that was not their charge; the cure was the practice of terror. Both wars killed and disappeared, but they also generated new relations between citizen and state. Counterinsurgent and counternarcotic operations demonstrated a core biopolitical component that involved the military's control and management of Guerrero's civilian population. The introduction of limited socioeconomic modernization programs, alongside violence, targeted for extermination both chronic underdevelopment and lives deemed subversive—for the sake of Guerrero's broader population and regime security.[30] The winning of hearts and minds necessitated the torture, disappearance, and/or extralegal killings of bodies to "save" the rest. Hence, the central concern of counterinsurgency and counternarcotics operations: the targeted population that was "made to live" and be productive, that was coercively made to "behave and go to work"—as military officials told Ascención Rosas in 1974 upon releasing him after a week of imprisonment and torture—amid a disciplining state terror.[31] In Foucauldian terms, counterinsurgency "is therefore the manifestation of both positive and negative types of power simultaneously," destructive and generative, with lasting consequences for contemporary Guerrero and the system of domination that afflicts Mexico today.[32]

Indeed, the war against the guerrilla groups led by Vázquez and Cabañas made limited rural modernization possible in Guerrero. Counterinsurgency, as a militarized reactive response to two separate guerrilla movements that incarnated decades of unredeemed peasant demands, provided some of the very hallmarks of modernity that the highland countryside had long demanded: (some) yearlong passable roads, potable water, electrification, communications infrastructure, schools, and medical care. These achieved demands constituted part of a broader reform program ordered by President Echeverría that intended to sap popular support from the Cabañas-led PDLP. This program, along with the guerrilla penchant for kidnapping and/or executing locally hated caciques, expelled a series of regional agricultural bosses who dominated the coffee and copra markets (and access to credit). An equitable and democratic campesino economy seemed possible. Such instances of collective well-being though, tied intimately to military efforts to rid the region of guerrillas and their socialist dreams, occurred within the context of an unconstitutional state of exception. As the epigraph quote from the fictionalized General Escáceaga suggests, the military occupied an entire region and managed civilian populations. The events that occurred in Los Piloncillos revealed the naked power of military sovereignty in 1970s Guerrero.

"AFTER KILLING US, THE MILITARY ARRIVED IN HELICOPTERS TO GIVE US PLASTIC SANDALS"

The smell of coffee must have filled the air of Los Piloncillos on April 24, 1973. Nestled in the slopes of the Sierra Madre del Sur on the road that leads to El Paraíso, the small village contained some fifteen dwellings. Don Cutberto Calderón got up early that morning. The hard-working *caficultor* (coffee grower) arrived at his coffee plot with his brother around 6 a.m. After working for a couple of hours, Don Cutberto waited for the arrival of his wife knowing she was on the way with his midmorning meal. She arrived around 8 a.m. carrying his food and their two-year-old daughter. A half-hour later, they heard automatic gunfire coming from the direction of their home:

> At first, we thought it was chickens because we knew that *guachos* liked to shoot and kill our animals when they entered towns like ours. But when we heard a long series of gunshots, my wife went ahead of me to find out what was happening . . .

she returned to tell me that she saw people on the ground, riddled with bullets in front of a wall. We waited some time before descending from our coffee plot down to Los Piloncillos but we saw the government [soldiers] and took another route. When we reached the town, we witnessed the scene . . . the image that remained with me the longest was that of some women picking up the bodies and others shooing away approaching dogs.[33]

The military had arrived looking for the village's men. Moving from house to house yelling at the inhabitants to come out, the soldiers—a small number dressed in civilian clothes with red handkerchiefs wrapped around their hands—ordered the few men who had not yet gone to work to congregate on the school's patio. The husband and father of young Herminia Reyes Gutiérrez joined three other campesinos on the patio. She painfully remembered hearing the sickening sounds made by the impact of bullets. On the patio floor, torn apart and dismembered, lay the bodies of five men including her sixty-year-old father, Crescencio Reyes, and Toribo Peralta, her nineteen-year-old husband. A pregnant mother of a one-year-old daughter, Gutiérrez lost her second baby in a miscarriage two days after the massacre.[34]

Doña Francisca Sánchez and Doña Tranquilina Álvarez Sánchez remembered seeing an estimated four hundred troops enter the small coffee-producing village while four tanks surrounded the outskirts. The troops dragged entire families from their homes and forced them to the village center where the school was located. A pregnant Susana Bernal had the temerity to ask the soldiers why they entered her home without permission or judicial orders. They promptly responded by striking her with the butt of a rifle. Five men stood on the school patio with their backs to the soldiers, their frightened faces facing the school wall. Doña Tranquilina's two young nephews stood among the five with their arms on their heads: Santos (twenty years old) and Eleazar Álvarez Ocampo (sixteen). The sudden volleys of automatic gunfire dismembered the campesino men. A single man, Margarito Valdez (sixty years old), somehow survived the initial volley. With several bullets lodged in his body, he tried to escape only to fall dead into a gulley. For the witnesses and family members of the murdered, they still cannot forget "the pieces of flesh—arms, legs, and innards—spread all over in front the wall where the men were executed."[35]

Saturnino Sánchez could not leave his home. A seventy-year-old man who nursed a recent bullet wound on his leg, he could not convince interrogating military officers that he did not support or know the location of PDLP guerrilla camps. He showed them the humble coffee plot that he worked with his sons along with his identification papers to no avail. Doña Francisca recalled that her father refused to die without a struggle. He ran throughout his home avoiding the gunshots, until several destroyed his elderly body. "The only things that remained of my father were pieces of flesh stuck to the walls of the home, his guts on the ground."[36]

Despite an overwhelming fear, the surviving campesinos from Los Piloncillos refused to remain silent in the face of murderous injustice. Don Cutberto made his way back down to the village after he saw the military retreat. Watching various women recovering the massacred pieces of human flesh as they prevented dogs from coming close produced an indelible memory for the now elderly campesino. After helping bury the bodies, Don Cutberto led a village commission down the sierra, traveling sixty kilometers to the municipal capital of Atoyac. After some initial doubts, the municipal president called Governor Israel Nogueda Otero, who met the village commission in Acapulco. Both the municipal president and the governor believed the campesinos actively supported Cabañas and the PDLP. They repeatedly asked Don Cutberto and the rest of the commission if they belonged to the PDLP. Nogueda refused to believe their story.[37]

Following Governor Nogueda's almost predictable refusal to help, the commission traveled to the Ministry of the Interior in Mexico City with the recently widowed women. At the same time, the military initiated an investigation. Don Cutberto recalled various ensuing meetings with military officers in Los Piloncillos during which the latter attempted to convince residents that the PDLP had carried out the massacre. "But we did not fear Lucio [Cabañas]," Doña Francisca reminisced, "the people sympathized with him because he told them it was just to defend the poorest." The military concluded their investigation by promising to provide compensation for a massacre they denied occurred at the hands of army soldiers.[38]

Don Cutberto still possesses the document. Signed by regional military commander General Salvador Rangel Medina, document number 06206 guaranteed the safety of Los Piloncillos's residents as soldiers subsequently continued to pass through the village in search of PDLP insurgents. The letter also promised to respect any necessities the village had, along with giving a vague pledge of "moral support." As the military tightened its hold around the civilian population of the Costa Grande by restricting foodstuffs and medicines, they allowed Los Piloncillos to obtain more than the standard ration of "one kilogram of sugar and one kilogram of dough [flour]." Don Cutberto asserted that "we were the only community that left Atoyac with a truck full of provisions . . .

of course bought with the money we managed to collect."[39] He also mentioned that the Mexican military arrived in helicopters to provide one other compensation for the murder of six campesinos: "After killing us, the military arrived in helicopters to give us plastic sandals."[40]

Spy reports from the Ministry of the Interior and Secretaría de la Defensa Nacional (Secretariat of National Defense, SDN) military records documented the veracity of assertions expressed by the Los Piloncillos survivors. The scale and method of the massacre warranted attention from General Cuenca Díaz who sent a letter to President Echeverría to personally inform him. Yet the general presented a version of events in dark contrast to the testimonies produced by the survivors who possessed the courage to denounce the massacre to municipal and state authorities. According to this letter, General Cuenca Díaz asserted that military forces stationed near Los Piloncillos engaged an armed "gang" led by Saturnino Sánchez—the seventy-year-old man with a bullet wound in his leg—that actively collaborated with PDLP guerrillas. Subsequent military telegrams continued to refer to the massacre as an encounter between soldiers and armed gangsters. A report that listed the quantity of military munitions spent during the supposed encounter even mentioned that Cabañas himself had led the so-called gang.[41] A memorandum from the Ministry of the Interior written three days after the massacre explained that the military killed the six men after allegedly receiving hostile gunfire—a jumpy military response attributed by the report to military fears of another PDLP ambush. National newspapers uncritically repeated "the prose of counterinsurgency" emitted by the Mexican state that discursively transformed campesino victims into criminal aggressors. An Acapulco newspaper posted the following headline: "Cuenca Díaz flew over Atoyac: The army did not fire; it was the bandits."[42]

A REVANCHIST IN THE GOVERNOR'S PALACE

The repression failed to end after the death of guerrilla leader Lucio Cabañas on December 2, 1974; rather, it became more localized. Rubén Figueroa, the influential PRI cacique and descendent of 1910 Constitutionalist revolutionaries kidnapped and held by PDLP guerrillas during the summer of 1974, assumed the governorship in 1975 promising honest, transparent rule. His prior experience with political rivals and guerrillas, he stated, would not shape his ruling style: "I enter this office without resentment or anger, with no thirst for revenge . . . my government will always be open to dialogue."[43] The promises of dialogue, though, existed only as rhetoric, for the governor ruled despotically and violently, exacting revenge on surviving guerrillas and guerrilla supporters and attacking a bourgeoning human rights social movement anchored in the state university. The torture and disappearance of activists, university students, professors, Acapulco taxi drivers, common delinquents, and even some small-scale narco-traffickers and drug pushers continued throughout Figueroa's governorship.[44] "Death flights," the use of military aircraft to dump prisoners into the Pacific Ocean, likely increased in frequency after the death of Cabañas in late 1974. Fishing communities located north of Acapulco told journalist Simón Hipólito in the early 1980s that the sea "vomited" human remains, clothes, sandals, and brassieres from the end of 1973 to 1975. Acapulco itself was, as reported by local journalists, "a place of terror."[45] Despite the limited democratic opening legislated by President José Luis Portillo (1976–82), with the 1977 legalization of leftist political parties and the 1978 amnesty for political prisoners, Guerrero continued to suffer the Dirty War.[46]

To rule, Figueroa fundamentally depended upon a nexus of key military officers and state police agents who had participated previously in the Dirty War against the ACNR and PDLP, led by Major Mario Acosta Chaparro and Lieutenant Colonel Francisco Quirós Hermosillo. Wilfrido Castro, police (*judicial*) commander in Acapulco, also played a key leadership role. The PDLP kidnapping of a wealthy cacique's son in March 1972—and the state response—reveals the foundation of this military and police collaboration. Acosta Chaparro served as the counterinsurgent specialist link between the military and DFS while also authoring many of the strategies used against PDLP guerrillas that brutally targeted civilian supporters. "In the case of any detentions," a DFS document directed in reference to the kidnapping, "the detained should be INTERROGATED [original emphasis] by Acosta Chaparro and Castro," a charge they continued under Figueroa.[47] At the behest of the governor, all three men remained in state and occupied important police positions. By 1977, after serving as head of police in Acapulco and the coastal regions, Acosta Chaparro became chief of all state police forces and personally counted on four police groups, fifty agents in total and many from his native state of Chihuahua, to do his bidding. Quirós Hermosillo served a more covert role as head of "Group Blood," a sanctioned death squad integrated by military and police personnel originally created during the anti-PDLP struggle.[48] "A repressive group," as described in a DFS report, it served "to avenge criticism voiced against the Governor, or target individuals who have had problems with the Army or narco-traffickers (in order to come to an agreement) . . . the majority of the detained are disappeared."[49] Quirós Hermosillo gave the operating orders while Captain Francisco Javier Barquín[50] personally commanded the thirty army soldiers and state police officers that comprised the death squad. Barquín Alonso had an additional duty: he allegedly coordinated the shipment of narcotics to the northern frontier using Mexican Air Force planes.[51]

Declassified spy reports testify to the brutality of this military police nexus that sustained Figueroa's political rule—and its corruption. Indeed, members of the governor's cabinet along the repressive apparatuses he employed allegedly worked with noted local narco-traffickers as early as 1976. An extensive DFS analysis dated May 14, 1976, reports on rumors that both the head of the Acapulco police, Lieutenant Colonel Luis Aguirre Ramírez, and the state attorney general, Carlos Ulises Acosta Víquez, collaborated with known narco-traffickers like Enrique Villalva. Aguirre Ramírez allegedly provided Villalva with an official police (*Policía Judicial*) badge. The same report describes how local muckraking journalists targeted Acosta Chaparro for "his shady operations that yield large sums of money."[52] Though more research is needed, it seems that the Figueroa administration helped cement the political, military, and police relationships that historically and currently form the foundation of the Mexican drug trade. Acosta Chaparro, Quirós Hermosillo, and Barquín Alonso were later arrested and charged in military court in 2002 for narco-trafficking charges related to their involvement with the Ciudad Juárez cartel.[53] Police agents who worked for these officers—Juventino Sánchez Gaytán, José Agustín Montiel López, and Isidoro Galeana Abarca—would occupy important state police commander posts during the 1980s as they collaborated with narco-traffickers and the first national drug cartels fueled by Colombian cocaine money.[54] Under the cover of the Dirty War in Guerrero, its practitioners helped create important segments of the Mexican narco-state.

CONCLUSION: "MUCH POLICE, LITTLE POLITICS"

There is, admittedly, a presentist impulse and urgency in this chapter, as the opening paragraph on the Ayotzinapa students reveals. In the attempt to formulate some sort of "diagnostic of the present,"[55] a contemporary War on Drugs that has claimed more than 150,000 lives and 30,000 disappearances since 2006, we must look back to rebellious, intransigent highland regions in states like Guerrero during the 1960s and '70s. The Dirty War involved not just the attempted physical and ideological elimination of two peasant guerrilla

movements by terrorizing their base of popular support. It also generated a
new form of militarized governance in which the military—allied with key
cacique networks, politicians, some narco-traffickers, and police—served as a
sort of shadow sovereign working to identify and eliminate potential "insurgent" threats: rural teachers and professors, university students, poor peasant
communities, indigenous movements, and guerrilla cells that managed to gradually regenerate after the killing of guerrilla leader Lucio Cabañas in late 1974.
Counterinsurgency became a method of political rule with an outsized role
for military officials and police in Guerrero. The case of the disappeared Ayotzinapa students revealed what many guerrerenses have known since at least
the mid-1960s: "The Mexican Army, according to many journalists and other
commentators is the real government authority in Guerrero state. 'The army
knows the state millimeter by millimeter,' a Mexican legislator pointed out in a
recent speech, 'and they know minute by minute what's happening there.'"[56] This
is, to quote journalist Juan Angulo, the land of "much police, little politics."[57]

NOTES

1.   Benjamin, "On the Theory of Knowledge"; and Benjamin, "On the Concept of History," 396.
2.   "White Paper on Drug Abuse, 1975: A Report to the President from the Domes-tic Council Drug Abuse Task Force," in Archivo General de la Nación [hereaf-ter AGN], Dirección General de Investigaciones Políticas y Sociales [hereafter DGIPS], c. 1675, ex. 3, 14.
3.   Smith, "The Rise and Fall of Narcopopulism."
4.   Weimer, *Seeing Drugs*, 172–214.
5.   For a similar argument that helped clarify my thinking on these connections, see Carey, *Women Drug Traffickers*, 158–93.
6.   "Lucio Cabañas Trafica con Drogas Para Adquirir Armas afirma Cuenca Díaz," *Sol de México*, October 24, 1974, in AGN, DGIPS, c. 1747B, ex. 7, 93.
7.   Ruben Figueroa, quoted in Alberto Cañas G., "Declaró un senador: No son guer-rilleros," *Ovaciones*, July 15, 1972, in AGN, DGIPS, c. 1003, ex. 3.
8.   Smith, "The Rise and Fall of Narcopopulism," 147–55.
9.   Camp, *Generals in the Palacio*, 91–93. Both Acosta Chaparro and Heine Rangel wrote influential texts (for internal circulation within military circles and acade-mies) on counterinsurgency and guerrilla warfare.
10.   Williams, *The Mexican Exception*, 178.
11.   Eduardo López Betancourt, quoted in Misael Habana de los Santos, "López Betancourt: Personas vivas fueron tiradas desde aviones en la guerra sucia," *La Jornada*, November 30, 2003.
12.   The epigraph at the beginning of this section is from Ascención Rosas Mesino's interview with the author, Atoyac de Alvarez, Guerrero, May 16, 2007.

13. Suárez, *Lucio Cabañas*, 53.

14. Aviña, *Specters of Revolution*, 93.

15. "Terror en Guerrero," *Política* 74, May 15, 1963, 28, quoted in Bartra, *Guerrero bronco*, 99–100.

16. Rath, *Myths of Demilitarization*, 116.

17. Sierra Guzmán, "Armed Forces and Counterinsurgency," 183–88.

18. Toro, *Mexico's War on Drugs*, 11–18.

19. For Operation Intercept, see Timmons, "Trump's Wall at Nixon's Border."

20. See, for instance, AGN, Secretaría de Defensa Nacional [hereafter SDN], box 101, file 301, 9–14, 37–39.

21. In 2002, government witness (and participant in the Dirty War) Gustavo Tarín Chávez testified and provided the number of fifteen hundred disappeared persons. Gustavo Castillo García, "Acosta y Quirós ordenaron matar a más de mil 500," *La Jornada*, November 18, 2002.

22. Radilla's eldest son was with him on the bus and witnessed the exchange. Tita Radilla Martínez, interview with the author; and Rosendo Radilla Betancourt, quoted in "Publica la Secretaría de Gobernación la semblanza de Rosendo Radilla, el campesino desaparecido por el Ejército en 1974," *El Sur de Acapulco*, February 24, 2013.

23. That day arrived on July 18, 1978, when DFS agents abducted and disappeared Cárdenas and her partner (and PDLP militant) Antonio Hernández in Mexico City. They spent several months in clandestine prisons, tortured and interrogated, only being released after students and colleagues from the Universidad Autónoma de Guerrero mobilized to demand their "re-appearance." Cárdenas, interview with the author.

24. Rosas Mesino, interview with the author; Radilla Martínez, interview with the author; Cárdenas, interview with the author; Mesino Acosta, interview with the author; and Bartra, "Sur Profundo," 67.

25. Radilla Martínez, interview with the author; AGN, DGIPS box 1067, file 3, 18–19; and "La Guerra Sucia en Guerrero," Special Prosecutor for Social and Political Movements of the Past (leaked version) [hereafter *FEMOSPP Filtrado*], 86–87.

26. AGN, Dirección Federal de Seguridad [hereafter DFS], 100-10-16-4, legajo 6, 153, 176, 188–89; and "La Guerra Sucia en Guerrero," *FEMOSPP Filtrado*, 56–59.

27. AGN, DFS, 11–4, legajo 190, 166–67; and "La Guerra Sucia en Guerrero," *FEMOSPP Filtrado*, 59.

28. AGN, DGIPS, box 674, folder 1; and Bartra, *Guerrero Bronco*, 117.

29. "Rubén Figueroa."

30. Aviña, "'We have Returned to Porfirian Times.'"

31. Foucault, *"Society Must Be Defended,"* 239–54; Rosas Mesino, author's interview.

32. Lazau-Ratz, "Foucauldian Counterinsurgency," 51.

33. Don Cutberto Calderón, interview with journalist Gloria Leticia Díaz, in Díaz, "A 27 años de una masacre, el recuerdo huele a pólvora." *Proceso*, September 30, 2000.

34. Fierro Santiago, *El último disparo*, 105–6.

35. Ibid., 105–7; Diaz, "A 27 años de una massacre."

36. Díaz, "A 27 años de una massacre."

37. AGN, DGIPS box 2610, folder 1, 40, 226.

38. Diaz, "A 27 años de una massacre."

39. Ibid.

40. Ibid.; and Fierro Santiago, *El último disparo*, 112–15.

41. AGN, SDN box 92, folder 277, 178; AGN, SDN box 97, folder 289, 59, 63–68; and AGN, DGIPS box 2610, folder 1, 40, 226.

42. AGN, DGIPS box 2610, folder 1, 226.

43. AGN, DFS, Versión Pública [hereafter VP], "Rubén Figueroa Figueroa," Legajo 2, 166 (100–10–1, L. 51).

44. Even local police officers could be kidnapped, as occurred in early November 1976. AGN, DFS, VP, "Mario Acosta Chaparro Escapite," Legajo 1, 4 (100–10–1, 306), 12, 13; AGN, DFS, VP, "Francisco Barquín Alonso," Legajo 1, 11, 13–14.

45. Hipólito, *Guerrero, Amnistía y Represión*, 161–63; "La Guerra Sucia en Guerrero," *FEMOSPP Filtrado*, 130–31; "Chiro Galeana, de los poco policías guerrerenses de la contrainsurgencia," *El Sur*, January 5, 2004.

46. Covertly, Portillo López authorized the paramilitary "White Brigade" to act, in effect, as an anti-urban guerrilla death squad that destroyed the 23rd of September Communist League.

47. AGN, DFS, VP, "Acosta Chaparro," Legajo 1, 1–3. Human rights officials in Mexico attribute at least 143 murders to Figueroa's main enforcer, General Mario Acosta Chaparro (then a major) and his pistol that he dubbed the "Avenging Sword." Juan Veledíaz, "Acosta Chaparro: Las deudas de una boina verde," *Animal Político*, April 21, 2012.

48. AGN, DGIPS box 1067, file 3, 18–19 (dated January 9, 1974); and "La Guerra Sucia en Guerrero," *FEMOSPP Filtrado*, 86–87 (FEMOSSP investigators obtained this information from DFS records).

49. AGN, DFS, VP, "Rubén Figueroa Figueroa," Legajo 2, 137 (100–10–1–76, L.63).

50. For a specific accusation against Barquín Alonso, see AGN, SDN box 41, file 116, 2.

51. Gustavo Tarín Chávez testified against all three officers. Jorge Alejandro Medellín, "Muere militar implicado en la guerra sucia," *El Universal*, July 8, 2005.

52. AGN, DFS, VP, "Acosta Chaparro," Legajo 1, 5–10.

53. Francisco Gómez and Jorge Ramos, "Desde los 70, Quirós y Acosta en el narco," *El Universal*, October 24, 2002.

54. Jesús Aranda, "Desde los 70s, la carrera delictiva de Montiel López," *La Jornada*, June 15, 2004; Padgett, "Guerrero, red de narcos, policías y politicos"; "Montiel, según el ex procurador de Morelos," *El Sur*, April 16, 2004; "Del expediente de Carrera Fuentes," *Proceso*, July 18, 1998.

55. Dean and Villadsen, "Introduction," 5.

56. Goldman, "Crisis in Mexico."

57. Juan Angulo, quoted in Preston and Dillon, *Opening Mexico*, 281.

BIBLIOGRAPHY

ARCHIVES

Archivo General de la Nación, Mexico City
  Ramo Dirección Federal de Seguridad
  Ramo Dirección General de Investigaciones Políticas y Sociales
  Ramo Secretaría de Defensa Nacional
Versiones Públicas, Archivo General de la Nación
  "Mario Acosta Chaparro Escapite," Dirección Federal de Seguridad
  "Francisco Barquín Alonso," Dirección Federal de Seguridad
  "Rubén Figueroa Figueroa," Dirección Federal de Seguridad

INTERVIEWS

Cárdenas, Alejandra. Author's interview. Chilpancingo, Guerrero, April 23, 2007.
Mesino Acosta, Hilario. Author's interview. Atoyac de Álvarez, Guerrero, May 17, 2007.
Mesino (Don Chon), Ascención Rosas. Author's interview. Atoyac de Álvarez, Guerrero, May 16, 2007.
Radilla Martínez, Tita. Author's interview. Atoyac de Álvarez, Guerrero, May 16, 2007.

NEWSPAPERS

Animal Político
El Sur de Acapulco
El Universal
La Jornada

PUBLISHED SOURCES

Aviña, Alexander. *Specters of Revolution: Peasant Guerrillas in the Cold War Mexican Countryside*. New York: Oxford University Press, 2014.
———. "'We Have Returned to Porfirian Times:' Neopopulism, Counterinsurgency, and the Dirty War in Guerrero, Mexico, 1969–1976." In *Populism in Twentieth Century Mexico: The Presidencies of Lázaro Cárdenas and Luis Echeverría*, edited by María L. O. Muñoz and Amie Kiddle, 106–21. Tucson: University of Arizona Press, 2010.
Bartra, Armando. *Guerrero bronco: Campesinos, cuidadanos y guerrilleros en la Costa Grande*. Mexico City: Ediciones Era, 2000.
———, ed. "Sur Profundo." In *Crónicas del sur: Utopías campesinas en Guerrero*, edited by Armando Bartra. Mexico, D.F.: Ediciones Era, 2000.
Benjamin, Walter. "Convolute N: On the Theory of Knowledge, Theory of Progress." In *The Arcades Project*. Translated by Howard Eiland and Kevin MacLaughlin. Cambridge, Mass.: Harvard University Press, 1999.
———. "On the Concept of History." In *Selected Writings: Volume 4, 1938–40*, edited by Howard Eiland and Michael W. Jenning, 389–400. Cambridge, Mass.: Harvard University Press, 2006.

Camp, Roderic Ai. *Generals in the Palacio: The Military in Modern Mexico*. Oxford: Oxford University Press, 1992.

Carey, Elaine. *Women Drug Traffickers: Mules, Bosses, and Organized Crime*. Albuquerque: University of New Mexico Press, 2014.

Dean, Mitchell, and Kaspar Villadsen. Introduction to *State Phobia and Civil Society: The Political Legacy of Michel Foucault*, edited by Mitchell Dean and Kaspar Villadsen, 1–8. Stanford, Calif.: Stanford University Press, 2016.

Fierro Santiago, Felipe. *El último disparo: Versiones de la guerrillas de los setentas*. Atoyac de Alvarez: Colección ATL, 2006.

FEMOSPP (Special Prosecutor for Social and Political Movements of the Past). "La Guerra Sucia en Guerrero." In *Borrador Filtrado* [Leaked Version], 2006.

Foucault, Michel. *"Society Must Be Defended": Lectures at the College de France*. New York: Picador, 2003.

Goldman, Francisco. "Crisis in Mexico: The Protests for the Missing Forty-Three." *New Yorker*, November 12, 2014.

Hipólito, Simón. *Guerrero, amnistía y represión*. Mexico City: Grijalbo, 1982.

Lazau-Ratz, Alexandra. "Foucauldian Counterinsurgency: A Poststructuralist Reading of 'Hearts and Minds' in Iraq." Master's thesis, Central European University, 2010.

Padgett, Humberto. "Guerrero, red de narcos, policías y politicos." *SinEmbargo*, October 12, 2014.

Paley, Dawn. *Drug War Capitalism*. Oakland, Calif.: AK Press, 2014.

Preston, Julia, and Samuel Dillon. *Opening Mexico: The Making of a Democracy*. New York: Farrar, Straus and Giroux, 2004.

Rath, Thomas. *Myths of Demilitarization in Postrevolutionary Mexico, 1920–1960*. Chapel Hill: University of North Carolina Press, 2013.

"Rubén Figueroa entrevistado por La Libération." *Proceso*, August 19, 1978.

Sierra Guzmán, José Luis. "Armed Forces and Counterinsurgency: Origins of Dirty War (1965–1982)." In *Challenging Authoritarianism in Mexico: Revolutionary Struggles and the Dirty War, 1964–1982*, edited by Adela Cedillo and Fernando Calderón, 182–97. London: Routledge, 2012.

Smith, Benjamin. "The Rise and Fall of Narcopopulism: Drugs, Politics, and Society in Sinaloa, 1930–1980." *Journal for the Study of Radicalism* 7, no. 2 (Fall 2013): 125–65.

Suárez, Luis. *Lucio Cabañas, el guerrillero sin esperanza*. Mexico City: Grijalbo, 1985.

Timmons, Patrick. "Trump's Wall at Nixon's Border." *NACLA Report on the Americas* 49, no. 1 (2017): 15–24.

Toro, María Celia. *Mexico's War on Drugs: Causes and Consequences*. Boulder, Colo.: Lynne Rienner, 1995.

Weimer, Daniel. *Seeing Drugs: Modernization, Counterinsurgency, and U.S. Narcotics Control in the Third World*. Kent, Ohio: Kent State University Press, 2011.

Williams, Gareth. *The Mexican Exception: Sovereignty, Police, and Democracy*. New York: Palgrave MacMillan, 2011.

PART III

YOUTH RADICALISMS
AND STATE VIOLENCE

8

WORKING-CLASS HEROES

Barrio Consciousness, Student Power,
and the Mexican Dirty War

FERNANDO HERRERA CALDERÓN

Donde hay represión hay resistencia *(Where there's repression, there's resistance)*.

FRENTE ESTUDIANTIL REVOLUCIONARIO

TWO REVOLUTIONARIES FROM GUADALAJARA, José María Carmona Chávez and José de Jesús Ramírez Meza, were picked up by the local police in December 1973. During their interrogation, they disclosed the whereabouts of the individuals responsible for the abduction of the Mexican industrialist Fernando Aranguren and the British honorary consul in Guadalajara, Anthony Duncan Williams. On December 12, agents assaulted a local safe house where other revolutionaries were hiding. After a brief shoot-out with its residents, they arrested Rodolfo Reyes Crespo and a group of women.[1] The police had been searching for Reyes Crespo from the time he joined the Frente Estudiantil Revolucionario (Student Revolutionary Front, FER) at the University of Guadalajara before ultimately joining the Liga Comunista 23 de Septiembre (23rd of September Communist League, LC23S), the nation's largest Marxist-Leninist guerrilla movement. While the kidnapping of Aranguren and Williams signified a national and international embarrassment for the Mexican government, for urban revolutionaries it symbolized the "vulnerability of the bourgeoisie" and "hurt the spirits of the enemy of the working-class."[2]

Reyes Crespo's detention, and the subsequent arrests of several other revolutionaries, produced a double effect. On the one hand, despite its long conservative and Catholic roots, Guadalajara was transformed into one of the primary centers of revolutionary activities during "the urban guerrilla experience" that came to characterize the 1970s.[3] On the other hand, the counterinsurgency that took place across Jalisco simultaneously transformed Guadalajara into one of the nation's most brutal epicenters of counterinsurgency during Mexico's Dirty War. Yet despite the vicious state repression launched against the FER during the 1970s, its members developed not only a new political line that profoundly benefited the LC23S's political and ideological development but also an unprecedented bridge of solidarity with working-class communities.

In the 1970s, a new generation of militant students abandoned what they saw as the reformist political projects of the past. Rejecting the "democratic bourgeois" politics of the Mexican New Left, they advocated for an armed insurrection to overthrow the Mexican state.[4] Based on conservative estimates, more than two thousand students organized across the nation in approximately thirty different groups "geared up for the urban insurrection."[5] The written work on these armed revolutionary movements has almost overwhelmingly condemned the socialist students who opted for armed struggle.[6] This view not only creates a monolithic picture of the various movements but also overlooks the distinct socioeconomic backgrounds that frequently influenced their unique forms of radicalization. In the case of the FER, barrio consciousness and its working-class origins led to the development of a new way of understanding radical politics in the 1970s and made a substantial contribution to the revolutionary ethos of the era. This chapter takes into consideration the distinctions that characterized the broad range of revolutionary movements that emerged during this period and particularly examines those led by students from poor working-class backgrounds in Guadalajara.

Students at the University of Guadalajara were instrumental in redefining student militancy after the 1968 student movement. During the early 1970s, the University of Guadalajara became the setting for vicious battles between two student groups. These included the revolutionary-leaning FER on the one hand and the long-lasting and hegemonic Federación Estudiantil de Guadalajara (Federation of Students from Guadalajara, FEG) on the other. Their commitment to destroy each other started in 1970 when the FER first announced its "expression of peaceful dissent"[7] and called its adversary "a politico-paramilitary unit."[8] According to the *feroces* (FER members), the FEG had aligned itself with the local government since it was founded in the late 1940s and had also evolved into a key ally of the central government. The feroces specifically accused the FEG of receiving funding from the "hardline members" of the Partido Revolucionario Institucional (Institutional Revolutionary Party, PRI).[9] Thus, for the FER, launching a revolutionary movement against the FEG represented the first step to violently overthrow the bourgeoisie state.

Composed of a broad range of individuals from an array of political back-grounds, the FER distinguished itself from other groups by nourishing its movement with members of one of Guadalajara's most influential local gangs, the Vikingos. This was a gang with long historical roots in the working-class neighborhood of San Andrés. The gang's integration into the movement and its direct link to its working-class barrio had a profound impact on the shaping of the FER and its revolutionary program. Based on oral histories, declassified secret police records, and revolutionary propaganda, this chapter examines the unique elements of this revolutionary program and pays particular attention to the different ways in which working-class youth shaped the goals, methods, and programs of the FER as well as its endorsement of a new barrio identity that, I argue, nurtured the revolutionary movement in Guadalajara against state authoritarianism and corruption. In paying close attention to the Vikingo-FER alliance and their endorsement of a new barrio and working-class conscious-ness, my larger goal is to make an intervention in the historiographies of urban guerrilla movements and state repression. In disputing the historical narratives that tend to gloss over the political turmoil of the 1970s, I examine the history of the FER and state repression in the local context of Guadalajara. Like the other contributors in this volume, I pay attention to the importance of local roots and frame these in the broader context of national politics during the Cold War era. This history of the FER allows us to see why so many young Mexicans decided to go underground during this period.

POST-REVOLUTIONARY GUADALAJARA AND STUDENT POLITICS

In Jalisco, the federal government sponsored the creation of several normal schools in rural areas, including new scientific and technical institutes in Guadalajara.[10] In 1925, the governor of Jalisco, José Guadalupe Zuno, further expanded educational opportunities by opening the Universidad de Guadalajara (University of Guadalajara, UG). His intention was to provide higher educa-tion opportunities for working-class and peasant students, and he envisioned UG as a key place to promote social justice capable of reproducing informed citizens.[11] In this context, students were essentially treated as social and polit-ical actors. They embraced this identity and saw themselves not as passive bookworms detached from real-life issues exclusively interested in defending their precious ivory tower, but rather as champions of Mexico's revolutionary progress. The educational goals promoted by the governor proved effective as they had a direct impact on the creation of a new revolutionary consciousness embraced by the students. The moral and social responsibility bestowed on the youth gave them a taste of political authority and empowerment never before experienced by students in Jalisco. Students were further radicalized when Zuno incorporated communists and socialists into his educational cabinet. Their job was to advise and oversee the various social programs that were incorporated into the university. Several of the most talented students were also invited to participate in these programs. Communists and socialists found fertile ground at UG and contributed to the creation of several student organizations with antigovernment, anticapitalist, and anti-imperialist tendencies.[12] In the 1940s these were further radicalized with the establishment of the Mexican Communist Youth faction at UG.

Nonetheless, the popularity that Zuno enjoyed among students and the popular classes was not always welcomed by competing political forces. His radical policies first came under fire during the administration of President Plutarco Elías Calles (1924–28). As the president started clamping down on populist and radical figures during his tenure, he set his mind to undermine the undisputed power of Zuno in Jalisco.[13] The unwillingness of the governor to take orders from Mexico City unleashed further tensions with Calles. In an inferior position, Zuno began losing control of Jalisco. The loss of his grip on power was further expedited by mass corruption scandals that Callista and other rising opponents helped to conspire. Against this backdrop, hundreds of university and preparatory students took to the streets to protest the federal government's assault on state's rights. But not until the presidential candidate of the Partido Nacional Revolucionario (National Revolutionary Party, PNR), Lázaro Cárdenas, won the election in 1934 did student activism experience a revitalization in Jalisco. This occurred in large part after Cárdenas and the Minister of Public Education, Narciso Bassols, modified Article 3 of the Mexican Constitution, which partially stated: "The education that the state delivers will be socialist . . . to create in young people a rational and exact concept of the Universe and social life."[14] The energy of student radicalism increased when influential Catholics criticized the state's imposition of socialist education. In this polarizing context, UG was immediately transformed into a hostile battleground where Catholic students and proponents of socialist education frequently and violently clashed with each other.

The socialist experiment on education did not last long, as President Cárdenas gradually weakened these programs toward the end of his term.[15] Yet radical tendencies remained a force to be reckoned with inside UG and other schools in Jalisco thereafter. The conservative shift of the central government under the administrations of Manuel Ávila Camacho (1940–46) and Miguel Alemán (1946–52) did little to decrease radical leftist students from engaging in political agitation. However, internal political factionalism caused several groups to disintegrate during this period, leaving the Frente de Estudiantes Socialistas de Occidente (Eastern Front of Socialist Students, FESO) and the FEG as the two primary organizations on campus.

The year 1948 saw the emergence of the FEG as the chief student representative on campus.[16] Its first president was Carlos Ramírez Ladewig, the son of former governor Margarito Ramírez who was Guadalupe Zuno's main political rival. Under his leadership, the FEG offered what its critics called its "faithful" endorsement to the "revolutionary ideology of the bourgeois state."[17] This strong relationship with the state was further strengthened by strategic connections that *fegistas* (FEG members) established with a local political elite loyal to the ruling party and its "revolutionary-nationalist ideology." This relationship not only yielded positive results for Ramírez Ladewig but also helped the FEG consolidate its power at UG and condemn the FESO to oblivion.

Ramírez Ladewig held a tight grip on the FEG throughout the 1950s and 1960s. While others held the office of the president, he remained its chief consigliere, ideologue, and primary link to the political class throughout these years. Another key leader was Enrique Alfaro Anguiano who, during his leadership of the FEG (1967–69), relied on a combination of both soft politics and authoritarian measures of control. For instance, like the central government, he frequently supported student campaigns that called for the country's self-determination. He also championed leaders who called for the support of national liberation movements and criticized U.S. imperialism. However, the FEG under the leadership of Anguiano simultaneously relied on mafia-style practices, and through censorship, intimidation, extortion, and violence, it frequently "emulated the corporate and patronage control mechanisms of the PRI."[18] Put differently, as the FEG exalted its "deep revolutionary roots and track record of fighting in popular causes"[19] during this period, it simultaneously became incredibly hostile toward students and organizations that challenged their hegemony.

During the 1968 student movement, Enrique Alfaro Anguiano and Ramírez Ladewig became some of the most loyal supporters of President Gustavo Díaz

Ordaz. As the movement expanded in Mexico City, they transformed the FEG into a powerful paramilitary organization. Organized in shock brigades, fegistas intercepted brigades arriving from the nation's capital and successfully cracked down on those students who expressed solidarity with the movement in Guadalajara.[20] After the massacre on October 2, the FEG pledged loyalty to Díaz Ordaz, and similar to other conservative sectors of society, it also congratulated him for "succeeding" in protecting Mexico from the so-called "communist agitators."[21]

For many leftist student activists in Guadalajara, the massacre in the nation's capital and the loyal support of the government that characterized the role of the FEG had a profound impact on their lives. Quoting Lenin, many felt compelled to ask, "What is to be done?" In answering this question some of the most radical students at UG reflected on the state of student activism in general and specifically called for the need to redefine their militancy. They identified the mistakes made by their comrades in the past. These voices grew louder in the following months. By 1970, two student groups opposing the FEG could no longer be ignored: one led by Pedro Orozco Guzmán and a second and more influential group led by Alfredo Campaña López, a member of the Mexican Communist Party's youth wing—the Confederación de Jóvenes Mexicanos (Confederation of Mexican Youth, JCM). Independently, they distributed political and satirical propaganda on campus that attacked the FEG and its connection to the local elite and the central government.[22]

But loyal supporters of the FEG did not hesitate to retaliate against leftist student activists. Fearing a local replica of 1968, influential members of Guadalajara's ruling class and loyal supporters of the PRI ordered the FEG to take the necessary measures to eliminate all forms of radical student dissent. In late 1970, fegistas complied by launching the first wave of several attacks against the student agitators. They expected the repression would wipe out dissent, but the attacks only further radicalized the opposition. Maoists, Bolsheviks, Trotskyites, and Guevarists joined the opposition to the FEG and so did members of the JCM, the Juventud Juaristas, and the Liga Comunista Espartaco (Spartacus Communist League, LCE). Independently, they joined the emerging resistance against fegistas and fought for the control of UG.[23]

The FER emerged as the primary organized leftist opposition on campus. Its first attack against the FEG took place in a dramatic fashion on September 23, 1970, when more than seventy feroces stormed the Casa del Estudiante (student housing complex) on the main UG campus, where several fegistas resided. From inside the Casa, Andrés Zuno, the youngest son of the political juggernaut and former governor Guadalupe Zuno, delivered a communiqué officially declaring the founding of the FER and stated, "the students decided to take over the residency to drive out the gangsters and vandals who [have illegally] occupied the building."[24] The FER called for the democratization of the university by demanding the immediate expulsion of the FEG from UG and the prosecution of all fegistas responsible for past crimes against the students. In addition, the communiqué stated that public education should be guaranteed to all young people, regardless of class status.[25]

Feroces remained in the Casa de Estudiante until September 30 when the military violently intervened and expelled them from the premises. Twenty-five members of the FER were subsequently incarcerated and interrogated. Six of them were charged with "gangsterism" and accused specifically of destruction of property.[26] Shortly after the military's assault on the Casa, the authorities demolished the building and the FEG inaugurated its new building with the presence of the newly elected president of Mexico, Luis Echeverría. According to José de Jesus Morales Hernández ("El Momia"), an ex-member of the FER, once officials tore down the complex, "they declared war on the FER."[27]

THE VIKINGOS AND BARRIO CONSCIOUSNESS

The FER and its war against the FEG not only attracted different factions of the student body at UG but also members of the neighborhood gang, the Vikingos.[28] Located in the working-class barrio of San Andrés, the Vikingos made a substantial contribution to the FER's militant line and revolutionary identity. Situated just east of downtown Guadalajara, San Andrés was a historic neighborhood where dozens of migrant families and residents "expelled from urban zones"[29] settled in and established roots. The small businesses, plazas, parks, and street food stalls that its residents built over the years celebrated the working-class character that distinguished their barrio. This frequently led to "discrimination and classism" from neighboring middle-class residents in Guadalajara who often associated the barrio of San Andrés with crime, violence, and youth delinquency.[30] For the same reason its young residents were also frequent subjects of police harassment, particularly members of the Vikingos, including those who attended UG and the local high schools.

Negative yet misguided attitudes toward the Vikingos were nothing new. Before joining forces with the FER, some proudly embraced their identity as *pandilleros* (gangsters) and frequently joined the *grupos de choque* (shock brigades) used by the FEG to crush their opponents. Others, however, rather saw themselves as *luchadores sociales* (social fighters). For them, the gang represented a space of sociability where they could continue to build their collective identity and share a unified political project. For these social fighters, the defense of their barrio identity depended on the adherence of the group to a series of values, norms, and shared social experiences that only individuals from working-class backgrounds could understand. In solidifying this shared identity, the Vikingos defended a set of moral codes that emphasized "solidarity" and "brotherhood." Those who swore to protect these two principles by joining the gang also vowed to protect one another.[31] While society believed gang activities were unlawful, the Vikingos viewed them as political expressions against bourgeois authority.

Conscious of their socioeconomic disadvantages, the Vikingos took pride in their working-class identity. According to Antonio Orozco Michel, "youngsters realized they shared the same aspirations, shortcomings, and lack of alternatives" with the working class. For him and other former feroces who have expressed similar attitudes, their shared identity "became the essence of camaraderie-building."[32] Combined with their overall rejection of hierarchy, this shared identity created a sense of equality in which, at least socially, no one was above the other.[33] This attitude proved effective as the Vikingos not only grew in numbers but also in power. By the end of the 1960s, their reach expanded across fourteen different barrios adjacent to San Andrés and comprised approximately two thousand active members.[34]

Growing up in the poor working-class community of San Andrés exposed the young members of the Vikingos to a politicized world frequently foreign to the more privileged world of UG students. They understood firsthand the day-to-day hardships of their parents. They appreciated what their parents endured to bring food to the table and sustain their families. These and similar memories of former feroces profoundly shaped their political consciousness and the community projects that they implemented to overcome their hardship.[35] Nonetheless, as noted earlier, the general public frequently overlooked their role as social and political activists and instead became fixated with their alleged "delinquent tendencies."[36] But criminalizing working-class youth did not end there. When the Vikingos first joined the struggle against the FEG in the early 1970s, both as student activists and gang members, their opponents systematically exploited the FER's link to the barrios by attributing their "violent behavior to class resentment."[37] By depoliticizing the movement, local and national authorities portrayed the political actions of the FER as illegitimate expressions of vigilantism. The FEG shared this attitude and launched "legitimate" acts of self-defense against them.[38]

The FER retaliated and, determined to broaden its support, created further links with the barrio of San Andrés. By the late 1960s, UG witnessed a new and larger wave of student agitation. But despite having the motivation and extending its numbers, "politically and ideologically," remembers a former Vikingo, they remained "quite behind." He elaborates, "we felt tremendous sympathy for Che Guevara, Ricardo Flores Magón, and for Zapata," but lacked a coherent plan or ideology.[39] Anxious to join a political movement, the Vikingos were helped by Héctor Zuno, the nephew of the former governor of Jalisco and a Vikingo himself. Zuno brought several working-class youth into the Juventudes Juaristas, an organization linked to the Zuno clan. Vikingos started nominating members of their gang to student government positions in the high schools. But like their counterparts at the UG, they also came under attack by fegistas.

To strengthen their movement at UG, Vikingos established closer relationships with members of the JCM and Andrés Zuno. Yet despite their participation in student politics, the Vikingos still lacked the ideological foundation that characterized other radical student activists at UG. Nonetheless, with these other groups, they shared a common hatred of the FEG. Influenced by these other groups, Vikingos started reading radical literature provided by the JCM. Moreover, their integration into the movement against the FEG prompted this increasingly radicalized barrio youth to think of themselves as instruments of social change capable of transforming not only the university setting but also other social spheres.[40] The most influential of these leading Vikingos in transforming members of the gang into "social fighters" included Arnulfo Prado Rosas ("El Compa"), Enrique Pérez Mora ("El Tenebras"), and René Delgado Becerra ("El Perico").[41] Collectively, they used their clout in the San Andrés barrio to lure working-class youth to take part in the struggle against the FEG and its allies.

THE UPRISING

The Vikingos assumed a greater role in the FER after the assault on the Casa de Estudiantes in September 1970. This time coincided with the departure of

Andrés Zuno who went underground in Mexico City in order to avoid the authorities. Moreover, thanks to his family's influence and his relationship to President Echeverría, Zuno remained untouched by the law. His departure left a political vacuum in the organization that leading Vikingos were eager to fill and use to further revise the political line of the FER.[42] The alliance of these two groups allowed feroces to evaluate their situation. Together they took a close look at the persecution of students in other parts of the country and watched, read, and discussed how repressive forces similar to the FEG further aligned themselves with the government. This new relationship presented them with an unprecedented opportunity to "fight back" and demonstrate that working-class students were no longer going to be victims of state-sponsored violence.[43] For the most radical of these rising leading figures, such as El Compa, the success of this alliance depended on its commitment to socialism. He commented on the new course for the FER as follows: "Our parents lost the revolution because [the government] killed their leaders. It's our duty to give [the revolution] continuity until we see its triumph and the creation of a new socialist state."[44] Adopting this position the FER urged its militants to "think in greater revolutionary terms and aspire to build a movement capable of toppling bourgeois power, eradicating capitalist exploitation, and establishing socialism."[45]

As the FER leaders became increasingly radicalized in the 1970s, they also reflected on previous student movements. They applauded the efforts and sacrifices of their 1968 *compañeros* but criticized them for failing to appeal to working-class youth and other popular sectors of society.[46] According to them, the 1968 movement had been primarily led by a privileged social group of students who did not understand what it meant having to worry about the day-to-day hardships of their parents. By contrast, they argued, the revolutionary success of the FER largely depended on representing the interests of the poor. For them, the social composition of their members made them more revolutionary and in tune with the needs of the working class.

The FER suffered its first major blow two months after having successfully taken the Casa de Estudiante. In November of 1970, a group of fegistas ambushed five members of the FER during one of its meeting. While the feroces managed to take out their pistols and fight off their attackers, the famous leader of the Vikingos, El Compa, perished in the assault.[47] The FER saw his assassination as payback for the death of Fernando Medina Lúa, the president of the FEG who had died in September during a skirmish with the feroces at the Polytechnic School in Guadalajara.[48] Hundreds of people from around the country attended the burial of El Compa and accompanied the Vikingos in their grief.[49] Law enforcement attended the burial, but with different intentions. They raided the funeral and arrested several Vikingos and feroces. El Compa's death and the disrespectful display orchestrated by law enforcement, which working-class youth equated to the elite's armed apparatus, further galvanized the FER. Vikingos and non-Vikingos alike expressed their solidarity with the movement against the FEG, and many more joined the feroces as active militants of the FER.

The death of El Compa affected the movement's morale, but few feroces refused to dwell on the past. First, they responded by appropriating a radio station in Guadalajara to announce their new set of objectives to the people. Specifically, they called on students to rise up against the injustices of the FEG and join the FER. Second, they identified Javier Agustín García Garibay, a leading figure of the FEG, as the assassin of El Compa. They subsequently shot him at point-blank range.[50] The killing of García Garibay transformed Guadalajara not only into a violent combat zone but also, for the regime, into a key place for its counterinsurgency campaigns against all armed revolutionary organizations. For their part, fegistas lashed out against a number of local authorities that, according to them, had not done enough to ensure the safety of their members. They also spoke directly with influential members of the government of Jalisco and provided them with the names and addresses of those involved in the alleged killing of their members. With little faith in the system, they also threatened that if local authorities failed to bring justice to the FEG, they would "personally locate" all Vikingos involved in the killing of their compañeros and "kill them."[51]

Within a year of El Compa's death, local authorities and the FEG launched a vicious witch hunt against the feroces. The governor of Jalisco, whom many labeled a "political puppet for the ruling class," also participated by taking a variety of measures to discredit and further tarnish the image of the FER. He frequently referred to its members as "criminals" and "gang members" and accused them of deliberately causing disorder on the various school campuses. But his calls for law and order only brought further violence to Guadalajara. Between 1971 and 1972, the repression reached new heights and ultimately forced several top-ranking feroces to go into hiding to avoid attacks from the FEG and the police authorities.[52] Those who remained politically active on the various campuses denounced the aggression launched against the FER and the Vikingos and called others to join their movement. They demanded the imprisonment of members of the FEG and accused them of "murder" and "gangsterism," asserting that it was the FEG members who were guilty of damaging "private property and carrying weapons" inside the schools.[53] Police authorities did not agree. Siding with the FEG, they sent an unprecedented number of units to the barrio of San Andrés. Police units combed the barrio for militants and frequently visited the families of well-known feroces demanding to know their whereabouts.[54] But the community refrained from disclosing any information that could compromise barrio solidarity and put in danger its youth.

The police raids in San Andrés and the FEG violence inside the various schools further radicalized the FER and its Vikingo alliance. But not everyone agreed on how to best organize a response. One camp, led by Campaña López, identified "taking power" of the schools as the central goal of the FER. Members of the JCM and the rising independent Left supported this position.[55] A second and more radical camp, which came to dominate the leadership of the FER, rather called for the destruction of the capitalist-bourgeoisie system. According to this group, the raising of the revolutionary consciousness of Guadalajara's barrio youth was a key to their success and so was drawing a clear linkage between the plights of the workers and the historical struggles of the peasants and the students. In this effort, the leaders of this camp divided the FER into two branches. One branch was responsible for organizing new FER chapters inside the university. The other was in charge of recruiting in proletarian neighborhoods.[56] Initially, only the most politically mature feroces were asked to facilitate the meetings with barrio youth. However, with time, Vikingos were also asked to lead the discussions that took place during these meetings. These discussions were framed on a wide range of topics pertaining to the social and political issues affecting the country in general and their barrios in particular. According to El Momia, in these meetings "there was a strong emphasis on [Marxist] readings." The goals included raising the militant's "level of awareness and political-ideological consciousness" and ensuring that they clearly understood the group's "project for a new society."[57] This tactic proved successful for the FER as more than eighty *comités de barrio* (barrio committees) actively worked together in the barrios by 1972.[58]

BARRIO CONSCIOUSNESS

Leaders representing several armed revolutionary organizations arrived in Guadalajara for a clandestine meeting in March 1973. Their primary objective was to create a broad national coalition representing the different organizations that had emerged across the nation in the late 1960s and early 1970s. After several days of deliberation, the attendees referred to the new coalition as the Liga

Comunista 23 de Septiembre (LC23S). The meeting also brought together some of Mexico's most prominent revolutionary leaders of the 1970s, including, among others, the LC23S's most iconic intellectuals, Ignacio Salas Obregón ("Oseas") and Ignacio Olivares Torres ("El Sebas"). Oseas was a former member of the Movimiento Estudiantil Profesional (Movement of Professional Students, MEP), a radical Catholic organization that, partly influenced by liberation theology, called for a dialogue between Christianity and Marxism.[59] El Sebas was a student of economics at the Monterrey Institute of Technology who, like Oseas, also became radicalized in the late 1960s and early 1970s. In their writings, both recognized the importance of the FER. Oseas studied its strategies and particularly recognized in his communiqués the achievements that the feroces had made, not only in the radicalization of youth in the barrios of Guadalajara but also in their spectacular victories fighting the FEG.[60] Similarly, El Sebas drew from the experiences of the FER as well as those from the movement in Sinaloa, where students had built a popular front, to write one of the most important pieces of radical literature produced in Mexico in relation to the urban guerrilla experience, "Acerca del Movimiento Revolucionario Estudiantil del Proletariado" (AMREP).

The AMREP, also popularly known as the "Tesis sobre la Universidad Fábrica" (1973–74), was widely disseminated across Mexico as a foundational piece of revolutionary literature, propelling its author into the pantheon of the nation's most celebrated radical social activists. In the document, Olivares Torres described students as the legitimate vanguard of the 1970s revolution. By contrast, in theorizing on the function of the university, he pointed to the historical role this institution had played in both the ideological reproduction of the capitalist system and the modernization projects of the state. Specifically, he argued, "the university today is a new industry, a product of capitalist development and response to the needs of its development." Olivares Torres further added, "the university is a bourgeois institution that 'produces' technicians, administrators, ideologies, etc., that help to support the exploitive system."[61] In making this argument, Olivares Torres applied historical, political, and economic evidence to draw parallels between student movements and class conflict, further positing, "the student movement has been participating as an integral part of the revolutionary process."[62] Within its pages, Olivares Torres "diversified" the meaning of the proletarian, arguing "students are a productive sector, which constitutes one of the branches of capitalist production." With that in mind, the university had been converted "into veritable knowledge factories [which] had as their overriding concern the reproduction of capitalist social relations. Moreover, radicalized youth realized they had a hand in helping to perpetuate the system" they so much loathed and that oppressed them for contesting the state.[63] In essence, whereas once the factory had been a "paradigmatic site of struggle between workers and capitalists," the university, as understood by Olivares Torres, "had become a key space of conflict, where the ownership of knowledge, the reproduction of the labor force, and the creation of social stratifications and culture were all at stake."[64] Put differently, the university was no longer exclusively a place of higher education, but a "universidad-fábrica" (university-factory).

Based on the AMREP's redefinition of the proletariat, a new political identity was born. The student-proletarian moniker became a popular neologism appropriated by nearly all urban guerrillas in Mexico, particularly those who joined the LC23S. The meteoric development of a student-proletarian identity reinvented the classic image of the student insurgent. It demanded students to correspond with their historical evaluation of class struggle and the correlations they made to draw parallels with the struggles of the working class. Clearly, the formation of the student-proletarian did not imply a physical metamorphosis. But students were expected to develop a student-proletarian mindset regardless of class origin. Purging oneself of bourgeois tendencies was fundamental to the survival of this revolutionary struggle. Militants had to learn how to fight temptations that compromised their revolutionary commitment.

CONCLUSION

Never losing touch with their working-class backgrounds, members of the FER built an armed revolutionary organization with the support of the Vikingos. Together, they dramatically influenced the revolutionary ethos of the 1970s. In Guadalajara, the decade of the 1970s represented a moment ripe for revolution. Like other militant organizations of this period, the FER-Vikingo alliance spoke of emancipation, utopias, and revolutionary change. Yet what set its members apart was the commitment they made with each other in building a strong collective identity, rooted, above all, in working-class consciousness. For them this was essential for the success of their revolutionary project and had precedent over any other politico-military maneuver.

While all revolutionary movements, including the FER, ultimately failed in their quest to forge a robust mass base, spark a revolution, and overthrow the regime, the urban guerrilla experience in Guadalajara not only marked an important chapter in the history of youth activism in Mexico but also in the memory of future revolutionary uprisings. Today the ideas developed by the FER continue to be expressed in Mexican student politics. Its legacy is manifested in both the militant discourse and visual propaganda employed by student activists. They juxtapose images of legendary Mexican revolutionary leaders, such as Emiliano Zapata and Ricardo Flores Magón, with those of iconic figures of the urban guerrilla movement of the 1970s. Similarly, in the working-class barrio of San Andrés, the spirit of rebellion that characterized the 1970s continues to live on. While the Vikingos no longer exist, they are memorialized through the oral testimonies of their former members. Murals continue to pay homage to El Compa and El Tenebras. They are remembered in these murals not simply as victims of the Dirty War but as revolutionary combatants who refused to stand idle as authoritarianism and exploitation plagued their communities in the 1970s. Today, many of them remain active in grassroots movements while others are involved in building truth and reconciliation committees.

The feroces and the Vikingos who joined them were swept up by the revolutionary ambiance that characterized Mexico in the early 1970s. They felt a moral obligation to take a radical stand against injustices. But because they opted for armed struggle, their revolution is typically and wrongly characterized in the historiography as "adventurist" at best and "ludicrous, at worst."[65] This couldn't be further from the truth. Their revolutionary movement not only exposed the violence of the FEG and the close relationship fegistas successfully established with local and national authorities, but it also influenced iconic thinkers such as Oseas and El Sebas, whose writings were widely read across Mexico and played a profound role in shaping the ideas and tactics of the nation's largest urban guerrilla movement, the LC23S.

NOTES

I want to thank María L. O. Muñoz for suggesting I use the term "barrio consciousness." The epigraph is from Rafael Sandoval Álvarez, "Prólogo," in Topete et al., *Memoria guerrillera*, 11.

1.   Archivo General de la Nación-Dirección Federal de Seguridad (hereafter AGN/DFS), Exp. 11-235-73 H 94 L 4.

2.   Miguel Topete, author's interview.

3.   Aguayo Quezada, *La Charola*, 57.

4.   Salas Obregón, *Cuestiones fundamentales*, 21–22.

5.   Liga Comunista 23 de Septiembre, "Manifiesto al estudiantado," 3. According to declassified spy documents from the Dirección Federal de Seguridad (Federal

Security Directorate, DFS), thirty-two urban guerrilla movements were active across Mexico during the 1970s and early 1980s. Similar estimates are provided in Sierra Guzmán, *El enemigo interno*, 19.

6. See Scherer García and Carlos Monsiváis, *Los patriotas*.
7. Martín, "La represión política en Jalisco," 147.
8. Gil Olivo, "Orígenes de la guerrilla en Guadalajara," 551.
9. Martín, "La represión política en Jalisco," 147.
10. Many of these institutes already existed before the Mexican Revolution, but since the 1920s they began receiving financial funding from the state primarily to improve instruction.
11. According to Pablo Yankelevich, more than 60 percent of Jalisco's population was illiterate before the implementation of education reforms in the 1920s. See Yankelevich, *La educación socialista en Jalisco*, 9.
12. For a general overview of early student activism at UG, see Mendoza Cornejo, *Organizaciones y movimientos*.
13. Buchenau, *Plutarco Elias Calles*.
14. Palacios Valdés, "La oposición a la educación socialista," 49; originally cited in Britton, *Educación y radicalismo en México*, 138–39. See also Secretaría de Educación Pública, *La educación pública en México*, 21–22.
15. Palacios Valdés, "La oposición a la educación socialista."
16. Mendoza Cornejo, *Organizaciones y movimientos*, 11–13.
17. FER, "La política de la FEG contra el proletariado estudiantil en Guadalajara," Mandeville Special Collections Library, Reel 3 Folder 2, 2. See also Hodges, *Mexican Anarchism*, 133; and Aguayo Quezada, *La Charola*, 51.
18. Gamiño, *El Frente Estudiantil Revolucionario*, 78.
19. Díaz Ordaz, *El movimiento estudiantil*, 121.
20. *La verdad negada*, 188–89.
21. Gutiérrez, author's interview. On conservative support of President Díaz Ordaz during the 1968 student movement, see Rodríguez Kuri, "El lado oscuro de la luna"; and Pensado, *Rebel Mexico*, 201–34.
22. *La verdad negada*, CIHMS, 189.
23. Ibid.
24. AGN, DFS, Exp. 100-12-1-70 H-149 L-17. See also Aguayo Quezada, *La Charola*, 161.
25. AGN, DFS, Exp. 100-12-1-70 H-149 L-17.
26. AGN, DFS, Exp. 100-12-1-70 H-168 L-17; and Exp. 100-12-1-70 H-253 L-17.
27. Morales Hernández, *Memorias de un guerrillero*, 71.
28. Many conflicting stories exist about the origins of the gang's name. See, for example, Zamora García and Gamiño, *Los Vikingos*, 27–29.
29. Ibid., 24.
30. Ibid.
31. Ibid., 18–19.

32. Orozco Michel, *La fuga de Oblatos*, 47; Topete, author's interview.

33. See Morales Hernández, *Memorias de un guerrillero*.

34. Castellanos, "Cuando los Vikingos se hicieron feroces."

35. Orozco Michel, author's interview; Morales Hernández, *Memorias de un guerrillero*; Zamora García and Gamiño, *Los Vikingos*.

36. Morales Hernández, *Memorias de un guerrillero*.

37. Topete, author's interview.

38. "Frente Estudiantil Revolucionario," AGN, public version, vol. 1, 135.

39. Morales Hernández, *Memorias de un guerrillero*, 18.

40. Zamora García and Gamiño, *Los Vikingos*, 32.

41. Topete, author's interview.

42. With the help of his family and his brother-in-law, President Luis Echeverría, Andrés escaped apprehension by leaving Jalisco and hiding out for a period of time.

43. Topete, author's interview.

44. Morales Hernández, *Memorias de un guerrillero*, 53.

45. Enrique Velázquez, author's interview, June 16, 2014, Guadalajara, Jalisco.

46. Topete, author's interview.

47. AGN, DFS, 100-12-1-70 H-113 L18; and AGN, DFS, 100-12-1-70 H-128 L-18.

48. Robles Garnica, *La guerrilla olvidada*, 142–43.

49. Many students around the country, especially in Sinaloa, expressed their solidarity with the FER and joined them to celebrate El Compa's life after his murder.

50. Robles Garnica, *La guerrilla olvidada*, 143–44.

51. AGN, DFS, 100-12-1-70 H-137 L18.

52. Topete, author's interview.

53. Archivo Memoria de la Resistencia en Jalisco, "El Vikingo," número 3, April 24, 1972, 4, 5.

54. Gutiérrez, author's interview.

55. Gil Olivo, "Orígenes de la guerrilla en Guadalajara," 556.

56. De Dios Corona, *La historia que no pudieron borrar*, 57; Gutiérrez, author's interview.

57. Morales Hernández, *Memorias de un guerrillero*, 33.

58. Many of these comités were entirely composed of female participants. See, for example, Castellanos, "Cuando los Vikingos se hicieron feroces."

59. See Pensado, "El Movimiento Estudiantil Profesional."

60. Marquéz, author's interview.

61. Tecla Jiménez, *Universidad, burguesía y proletariado*, 27.

62. Olivares Torres and Orozco Guzmán, "Acerca del movimiento revolucionario del proletariado estudiantil," 1.

63. Olivares Torres, *Movimiento Estudiantil Revolucionario*, 20, 21.

64. Ortega Olivares, "Movimiento estudiantil, clase y subjetividad."

65. See Scherer García and Monsiváis, *Los patriotas*; and Guevara Niebla, *La democracia en la calle*.

BIBLIOGRAPHY

ARCHIVES

Archivo General de la Nación, Frente Estudiantil Revolucionario, public version, vol. 1
Mandeville Special Collections Library, UC-San Diego
Archivo Memoria de la Resistencia en Jalisco

INTERVIEWS

Gutiérrez, Bertha Lilia. Author's interview. Guadalajara, Jalisco, July 17, 2008.
Marquéz, Francisco ("El Ful"). Author's interview. Guadalajara, Jalisco, June 8, 2014.
Orozco Michel, Antonio. Author's interview. Guadalajara, Jalisco, July 20, 2008.
Topete, Miguel. Author's interview. July 18, 2008.
Velázquez, Enrique. Author's interview. Guadalajara, Jalisco, June 16, 2014.

PERSONAL COLLECTIONS

Olivares Torres, Ignacio, and Pedro Orozco Guzmán. "Acerca del movimiento revolucionario del proletariado estudiantil." 1973. Personal collection of Fernando Herrera
Calderón.

PRIMARY PUBLISHED SOURCES

*La verdad negada: Informe Histórico sobre la Guerra Sucia del Estado Mexicano entre los años
60's a los 80's.* Mexico City: Centro de Investigaciones Históricas de los Movimientos
Sociales A.C. version, 2009.
Morales Hernández, José de Jesus "El Momia." *Memorias de un guerrillero: La guerra sucia
del México de los 70's.* Guadalajara: Self-published, 2006.
Olivares Torres, Ignacio "Sebas." *Movimiento Estudiantil Revolucionario: Tesis de la
Universidad-Fábrica.* Mexico City: Editorial Brigada Roja, 2014.
Orozco Michel, Antonio. *La fuga de Oblatos: Una historia de la LC 23-S.* Guadalajara:
Taller Editorial La Casa del Mago, 2007.
Salas Obregón, Ignacio. *Cuestiones fundamentales del Movimiento Revolucionario.* Mexico
City: Editorial Huasipungo, 2003.

SECONDARY PUBLISHED SOURCES

Aguayo Quezada, Sergio. *La charola: Una historia de los servicios de inteligencia en México.*
Mexico City: Grijalbo, 2001.
Britton, John A. *Educación y radicalismo en México.* Mexico City: Dirección General de
Divulgación, Secretaría Pública, 1976.
Buchenau, Jürgen. *Plutarco Elias Calles and the Mexican Revolution.* Lanham, Md.: Row-
man and Littlefield, 2006.
Castellanos, Laura. "Cuando los Vikingos se hicieron feroces." *La Jornada*, December 7,
2003.

De Dios Corona, Sergio René. *La historia que no pudieron borrar: La Guerra Sucia en Jalisco, 1970–1985*. Guadalajara: Casa del Mago, 2010.

Díaz Ordaz, Gustavo. *El movimiento estudiantil de 1968 y la U de G: Discursos en el Consejo General Universitario de la Universidad de Guadalajara el 30 de junio de 1966 y el día 5 de septiembre de 1968*. Guadalajara: Taller Editorial, La Casa del Mago, 2011.

Gamiño, Rodolfo. *El Frente Estudiantil Revolucionario: Antecedentes, nacimiento y represión*. Guadalajara: Taller Editorial La Casa del Mago, 2016.

Gil Olivo, Ramón. "Orígenes de la guerrilla en Guadalajara en la decada de los setenta." In *Movimientos armados en México, Siglo XX*, edited by Verónica Oikión Solano and Martha Eugenia Garcia Ugarte. Vol. 2, 549–66. Zamora, Mexico: El Colegio de Michoacán/CIESAS, 2008.

Guevara Niebla, Gilberto. *La democracia en la calle: Crónica del movimiento estudiantil mexicano*. Mexico City: Siglo Veintiuno Editores, 2009.

Hodges, Donald C. *Mexican Anarchism After the Revolution*. Austin: University of Texas Press, 1995.

Martín, Rubén. "La represión política en Jalisco, 1968–2011." In *Memoria guerrillera, represión y contrainsurgencia en Jalisco*, edited by Miguel Topete, Juan Antonio Castañeda, Rafael Sandoval, and Rubén Martín, 141–232. Guadalajara: Grietas Editores, 2012.

Mendoza Cornejo, Alfredo. *Organizaciones y movimientos estudiantiles en Jalisco de 1900 a 1937*. Guadalajara: Editorial Universidad de Guadalajara, 1989.

Organizaciones y movimientos estudiantiles en Jalisco de 1948 a 1954 la consolidación de la FEG. Guadalajara: Editorial Universidad de Guadalajara, 1992.

Ortega Olivares, Mario. "Movimiento estudiantil, clase y subjetividad." *Veredas* 21 (2011): 129–47.

Palacios Valdés, Mario. "La oposición a la educación socialista durante el cardenismo (1934–1940): El caso de Toluca." *Revista Mexicana de Investigación Educativa* 6, no. 48 (January–March 2011): 43–71.

Pensado, Jaime M. "El Movimiento Estudiantil Profesional (MEP): Una mirada a la radicalización de la juventud católica mexicana durante la Guerra Fría." *Mexican Studies/Estudios Mexicanos* 31, no. 1 (Winter 2015): 156–92.

———. *Rebel Mexico: Student Unrest and Authoritarian Political Culture During the Long Sixties*. Stanford, Calif.: Stanford University Press, 2013.

Robles Garnica, Héctor Guillermo. *La guerrilla olvidada: La historia de una página manchada con sangre de estudiantes de la Universidad de Guadalajara*. Guadalajara: Taller Editorial La Casa del Mago, 2013.

Rodríguez Kuri, Ariel. "El lado oscuro de la luna: El momento conservador en 1968." In *Conservadurismo y derechas en la historia de México*, edited by Erika Pani, 512–59. Mexico City: Fondo de Cultura Económica, 2009.

Sandoval Álvarez, Rafael. "Prólogo." In *Memoria guerrillera, represión y Contrainsurgencia en Jalisco*, edited by Miguel Topete, Juan Antonio Castañeda, Rafael Sandoval, and Rubén Martín, 11–19. Guadalajara: Grietas Editores, 2012.

Scherer García, Julio, and Carlos Monsiváis. *Los patriotas: De Tlatelolco a la guerra sucia.* Mexico City: Aguilar, 2004.

Secretaría de Educación Pública. *La educación pública en México: Desde el 1º de diciembre de 1934 hasta el 30 de noviembre de 1940.* Mexico City: Talleres Gráficos de la Nación, 1941.

Sierra Guzmán, Jorge Luis. *El enemigo interno: Contrainsurgencia y fuerzas armadas en Mexico.* Mexico City: Plaza y Valdés Editores, 2003.

Tecla Jiménez, Alfredo. *Universidad, burguesía y proletariado*: Mexico City: Ediciones de Cultura Popular, 1976.

Topete, Miguel, Juan Antonio Castañeda, Rafael Sandoval, and Rubén Martín, eds. *Memoria guerrillera, represión y contrainsurgencia en Jalisco.* Guadalajara: Grietas Editores, 2012.

Yankelevich, Pablo. *La educación socialista en Jalisco.* Guadalajara: Ediciones del D.E.P., 1985.

Zamora García, Jesús, and Rodolfo Gamiño Muñoz. *Los Vikingos: Una historia de lucha política social.* Guadalajara: Centro de Estudios Históricos del Colectivo Rodolfo Reyes Crespo, 2012.

9

THE VARIOUS LIVES OF MEXICAN MAOISM

Política Popular, a Mexican Social Maoist Praxis

MICHAEL SOLDATENKO

WITH THE COLLAPSE OF Soviet Marxism-Leninism, we are able again to engage Marxist thought and politics, now without a Eurocentric lens, and at the same time break the political stranglehold of looking at politics through the binary of reform or revolution.[1] The history of Mexican Marxism allows us to explore how a country of the Global South engaged Marxist politics by progressively adopting, adapting, and translating Marxism and then Maoism based on local conditions. Simultaneously, activists interrogated the simple dichotomy of reform or revolution by affirming an equivocal Marxist praxis, constructing a "social left."[2] Therefore, this chapter examines one particular expression of Maoism that emerged in Mexico in the aftermath of the 1968 student movement: Política Popular (Popular Politics, PP). PP activists sought a Marxist politics that was not constrained by a traditional reading of Marxism and Maoism but generated its principles from the contradictions of Mexican capitalism and a praxis to transform communities, improve the lives of participants, and construct an alternative subjectivity able to grasp and act beyond normative political behavior.[3]

Simultaneously, PP militants challenged a Marxist narrative with its two well-worn tracts: reform or revolution. After the repression of the student movement in 1968, many protestors found themselves faced, like many before them, with this Gordian knot: "What is to be done—reform or revolution?" PP activists believed they resolved this query by placing at the center class consciousness built by struggles for economic and social reforms driven by participatory democracy. They argued that when those subject to capital come to understand their subjectivity, reform becomes part of the strategy for the establishment of a socialist society. To evaluate whether this tactic was viable, we need to understand Maoism in Mexico and in particular the story of PP.

MAOISM AND THE MEXICAN LEFT

Mexican Maoism presents us with a particular construction and deployment of Mao Zedong's thought. Many Mexicans were introduced to at least two aspects of Mao's thought: his approach to economic development and his theory of revolution. The Chinese presented their approach to economic development as a solution to the "underdevelopment" experienced by Third World economies. For some Mexicans, Mao's economic idea offered a solution to their underdevelopment. When thinking about revolution, Mao presented several elements. Given the economic and social reality of China, Mao advanced a two-stage approach to revolution, first forming a democratic government based on a united front, then the turn to socialism. In order to achieve victory, Mao elaborated his conception of a people's protracted war that led him to explore the relationship among the revolutionary army, the vanguard party, and the masses, formulating his version of the "mass line." Mexican interpreters of Mao's thoughts on revolution only selected what they felt was necessary for the conditions in which they lived.

With the sharpening of the Sino-Soviet split (1960–64) and the start of the Great Proletarian Cultural Revolution (1966), many began to view Mao's positions through his philosophic reinterpretation of Marxism-Leninism, articulated in "On Practice" and "On Contradiction."[4] This articulation of Mao's thought as Maoism and its conversion into a theory of global revolution transfigured Marxism-Leninism into a non-Western knowledge and theory, underscoring its universal and global nature.[5] In this chapter I take this one step further and argue that some Mexicans articulated and at times transformed Maoism to accord with Mexican history and experience, giving us a Mexican Maoism.

Vicente Lombardo Toledano introduced Mao to the Mexican public in his *Diario de un viaje a la China nueva* (1950). Lombardo Toledano portrayed Mao as the socialist leader of a nationalist anti-imperialist movement reflecting

Lombardo's own political position. Lombardo's Partido Popular (Popular Party) then promoted the Chinese experience by establishing the Sociedad Mexicana de Amistad con China (Mexico-China Friendship Society) in 1957. Most of the Sociedad's activities focused on organizing presentations by activists who visited China and the distribution of Chinese publications. Through the Sociedad, Mexico was introduced to Mao's ideas and the Chinese revolutionary experience with particular emphasis on China's approach to economic development and its cultural traditions.

However, the Mexican political and social struggles of the 1950s, in particular the railroad workers' strike and its repression by the state (1958–59), together with the Cuban Revolution (1959) altered Mexico's relationship with Mao and China. Interest shifted away from applying China's model of development toward using Mao's revolutionary practice in Mexico. The policies of the Partido Revolucionario Institucional (Institutional Revolutionary Party, PRI) and the Mexican state throughout the 1950s increasingly made it difficult to see the PRI as a progressive institution trying to implement the aims of the Mexican Revolution. For example, Ester Chapa, a professor of microbiology, a feminist, and an activist with both the Partido Comunista Mexicano (Mexican Communist Party, PCM) and the Partido Popular, frustrated by continuous state repression, endorsed the Chinese approach to revolution as a model for Mexico. For Chapa, the study of Mao's revolutionary thought should provide Mexican revolutionaries with the initial step to a protracted Mexican people's war.[6]

For many activists the "errors" of the PCM and the Partido Popular, especially during the railroad workers' strike, led to conflicts within the organizations, resulting in expulsion or withdrawal from these and sister organizations. The Thirteenth (1960), Fourteenth (1962), and Fifteenth (1967) PCM Congresses reflected the growing frustration within the party. Members who were thrown out of the PCM were accused of a variety of heresies: revisionism, opportunism, infantile leftism, factionalism, sectarianism, or the more classical denunciations as social democrat, Menshevik, or liquidator, to name a few. Differences over the PCM's position on the character of the Mexican Revolution, the concept of the state and the nature of the state, the classification of the national bourgeoisie, the current nature of the class struggle, and the nature of private property, as well as the role of nationalism, imperialism, and the socialist block, appeared in multiple books, journals, and periodicals in this period.[7]

The Liga Leninista Espartaco (Spartacus Leninist League, LLE) was established by expelled members of the PCM as well as other organizations. The acclaimed writer José Revueltas was initially part of the organization and many of the ideological points of the LLE were present in his *Ensayo sobre un proletariado sin cabeza* (1962). The LLE prefigured many of the positions of later Mexican Maoist organizations as the LLE articulated itself as a Marxist-Leninist organization with its call to orthodoxy. Thus, for the LLE the central task was to create a real working-class party based on the principles of Leninism, to begin to help workers escape bourgeois ideology, and to sustain a Mexican road to socialism.[8] However, the LLE succumbed to infighting and factionalism and soon after its founding began to experience splits, expulsions, and restructured organizations. According to Fernández Christlieb, an activist and scholar of Mexican politics, the original base of the LLE allied itself with the original base of the Partido Revolucionario del Proletariado (Revolutionary Party of the Proletariat),[9] which together with the Unión Reivindicadora Obrero Campesina (Worker-Peasant Vindicating Union)[10] formed the Liga Comunista Espartaco (Spartacus Communist League, LCE).[11] The process continued in future years with new organizations formed by further rifts and realignments—ending in 1981 with a unification of the Movimiento Marxista-Leninista de México (Marxist-Leninist Movement of Mexico, MMLM).[12] All the new organizations shared a rejection of the PCM, a critical acceptance of the Chinese Communist Party line on the international communist movement, the need to create a working-class communist party, and the requirement of a proletarian revolution to take state power. The LCE came to "view . . . 'the masses' rather than 'the party' as the revolutionary subject," focusing attention on Mao's position of the "mass line."[13] The political scientist Rodríguez Araujo, who is a critic of the Spartacists, concludes: "In short, Mexican Spartacism was, in general, the hotbed of various organizations of revolutionary appeal, mostly very small (groupuscule) though belligerent and active."[14]

The proliferation of Spartacist organizations reflected different enunciations of Mao Zedong's thought. Some scholars who analyze these and other organizations in Mexico and elsewhere place them in the category of "International Maoism" and view them as bit players in the conflict between two ideologies and practices of Marxism-Leninism. Robert Alexander, a scholar of Latin America, writes that Maoism was the consequence of the conflict between the world's two dominant communist parties and their theory and practice. He therefore looks at Maoism's presence in the Third World with little autochthonous agency. Alexander construes Mexican Maoism as a continuation of the conflict between the Soviet Union and China and says that the central activity of Mexican

Maoism was the construction of a communist party that would accept the Chinese critique of the Soviet Union.[15] The view that Mexican Maoism was simply a continuation of the Sino-Soviet split reinforced a trope that local Third World communist parties were "controlled" by Moscow or Beijing.[16]

In contrast to Alexander's reading, I explore how Mexican thinkers and activists interpreted and then practiced Mao's ideas.[17] We can avoid reading the articulation of Marxism and Maoism through a Eurocentric lens by rooting our discussion in the particulars of Mexico. Only then are we free to investigate the cases of Lombardo, Revueltas, the PCM, the Partido Popular, the various Ligas, and other organizations as well as leading leftist thinkers who influenced the competing forms of student activism of the 1960s and 1970s, explored in this volume, without reducing them to preconceived conceptions drawn from the European experience.

With this caveat, we can understand how Mexicans differed over their engagement with Marxism, Marxism-Leninism, and Maoism. Therefore, we have the appearance of a variety of Mexican Maoist organizations. Some Mexican Maoist organizations follow the trajectory set by earlier expressions of Maoism like the LLE and its "anti-revisionist struggle" with the goal of building an authentic communist party. Others will see its role in connecting with local labor and peasant struggles—a social Maoism. Thus, even before the outbreak of '68, the Sección Ho Chi Minh (Ho Chi Minh Section, Ho) of the LCE "had greater willingness to work with the popular masses and to develop more contacts with real social movements of the moment."[18] The Ho's version of Maoism became dominant among Maoist activists after '68. Critics of Maoism like Rodríguez Araujo, who viewed these various expressions as "ultra," "radical," and "extreme," however, had to recognize that Maoism formed the core of Mexico's *nueva izquierda* (New Left) and part of a global New Left that was antiauthoritarian and broke with much of the traditional leftist thinking, accepting a humanist libertarian socialism.[19]

1968 AND THE RISE OF POLÍTICA POPULAR

As we have seen, Mexican Maoism had an extensive intellectual, organizational, and political history before the events of '68. The Ho had already suggested the need for militants to adopt the mass line. However, as other authors in this volume further point out, '68 was a transformative event for the individuals who were swept up in activism. In the 1960s, a generation of youth came to question normal political and civic behavior. Gunderson in his dissertation argues:

> A much larger fraction of the students radicalized in 1968 would, under the auspices of a number of radical left parties and organizations, join in a movement of "going to the people" in which former student activists poured into the poorest urban barrios, into industrial jobs, and into the countryside with the intention of assisting in building up mass democratic popular organizations with the power to challenge the system that they as students alone did not possess. . . . [T]he dominant ideological trend within it, and the one that encountered the greatest success in actually building popular democratic movements and organizations, was Maoism.[20]

Many Mexico City youth found a voice in '68 and acknowledged the possibility of a different world that did not succumb to the logic of the traditional Left or the PRI. Furthermore, the development of the mass line offered another political choice to youth who had decided that only radical change could remake Mexico. In the past the only alternatives were armed struggle or electoral politics; now there was the possibility offered by a Mexican interpretation of the mass line, a practice that brought reform together with revolution.[21]

Out of the repression of '68, two organizations came on the scene that built on the work of the Ho: La Organización Revolucionaria Compañero (Comrades Revolutionary Organization, Compañero)[22] and the less organized Política Popular (PP). In the years after 1968, both organizations turned to joining residents of working-class neighborhoods (*colonias)* to participate in their self-organization for social services and self-defense as well as developing forms of self-governance often through popular assemblies. "For a period . . . the Maoists facilitated the emergence of an impressive array of independent and radical popular movements across Mexico."[23] PP took its name from a pamphlet titled *Hacia una Política Popular* and began its move to the masses in 1969 with Adolfo Orive Bellinger as one of its leaders.[24]

The shadow of Orive stands over PP and Mexican social Maoism because of his intellectual acumen, political vision, and tactical imagination. At the same time, his personal story is often used to undercut what PP cadres achieved. Orive was born to the second generation of PRI leadership. His father, Adolfo Orive de Alba, was the first minister of Hydraulic Resources in the administration of Miguel Alemán, his grandfather was part of Carranza's faction during the 1910

Revolution, and his family was close to Lázaro Cárdenas. Orive therefore had a familial relationship with many of the leaders of the revolutionary family like Luis Echeverría Zuno and up-and-coming PRI activists like the Salinas de Gortari brothers whom he taught at UNAM. Orive grew up in the PRI family where one might draw a line of patronage from Cárdenas to Echeverría and then Salinas de Gortari's political crews.[25] While in high school, Orive became involved in campus politics. To remove him from this environment, his family sent him to France to study; there he dedicated himself to absorbing Marxism under the tutelage of Charles Bettleheim and Louis Althusser. After participating in the civil unrest in France in May 1968, he returned to Mexico in the midst of its '68.[26]

POLÍTICA POPULAR AND MEXICAN MAOISM

Mexico '68 borrowed much from prior protests, especially in reclaiming public spaces through the mass demonstration and informational brigades.[27] Many who have written about '68 have noted the role of the student brigades in bridging students with other communities in Mexico City. The testimony of student activist José Guillermo Palacios Suárez demonstrates how his *brigadista* experience shaped him into a lifetime militant.[28] After the massacre at Tlatelolco and what Palacios felt was the betrayal by PCM, the question for him, as well as other brigadistas and many other activists noted in the various chapters in this volume, was "¿qué hacer?" (what to do next?). While many did not fully comprehend the discussions among the leadership of the student movement after Tlatelolco, "what we acknowledged was the imperative of not to surrender, to continue to organize 'brigades to the people,' not only to express our readiness to continue the struggle, but to call the people to organize themselves, to fight against injustice."[29] While for a few this was the time to join the armed struggle, for others who had engaged with the writings of Mao it was the moment to integrate oneself with the people and their struggles. "It was at that moment that [the slogan] 'the people united!' was transformed into 'join the people!'"[30] Moreover this union with the people had to be based on direct democracy through their self-elected and self-managed organizations.

In his memoirs, Palacios recalled how the brigadistas coalesced into the Coalición de Brigadas Emiliano Zapata (Emiliano Zapata Coalition Brigade). Out of the conversations that took place within the Coalición emerged the pamphlet *Hacia una Política Popular* (1968). The main idea proposed in the document was for student activists to integrate into the popular struggles based on the Maoist mass line—in the process becoming PP. Their militancy was based on three principles: "(1) Trust the masses and obtain their support. (2) Ideas must come from the masses and then return to the masses for their discussion. (3) Be the student of the masses before being their teacher."[31] Because the PP centered its work on following the needs of the masses at the expense of party building, I refer to their activism as social Maoism. From Palacios's perspective, the brigadistas worked to formulate and implement the mass line of "¡Unifiqué-monos!" (Let us come together!).

The initial task was to engage student demands in order to prepare an effective response to popular struggles and to transform the brigadistas into future cadres. The aim was "to organize students around their specific demands, independently of the PRI controlled state, to be able to provide real and effective support to popular struggles" and in the process "to transform the student movement into a seedbed for activists."[32] Other Marxist organizations accused him, like other PP activists, of undermining the struggle by engaging in reformism and economism—as well as populism, empiricism, and spontaneism.[33] He recalled conversations with folks in the socialist armed movements who felt that this approach would take years, if ever, to succeed, and that what was needed now was armed revolution. For Palacios, these critics misunderstood the mass line of "¡Unifiquémonos!"

Palacios abandoned school and entered the working class following the Maoist mass line to "serve the people." He worked in many different places, trying to learn and participate with workers as they self-organized: "I saw that it was not a question of going to 'teach' anything to the workers, but to learn together and relearn those issues of the class struggle that we understood in theory, but now to comprehend them from the perspective of the productive process, enduring firsthand capitalist exploitation, to find, as a worker, the path to the proletarian struggle."[34]

He called this integration *proletarización física* (physical proletarianization). This entailed leaving his previous comfortable life with family and friends and living the life imposed by capital. But this was done with compañeros, fellow militants who choose this life; they would meet to study and coordinate with other comrades. Through the 1970s, from these early study groups "took shape a group of workers who saw possibilities to escape company unions [*charros sindicales*], to push aside authoritarian and anti-democratic practices at the local level, and transform union organizing into an instrument of workers' struggle and resistance."[35]

In Palacios's writings, it is clear that the theoretical development of "¡Unifiquémonos!" came from *Hacia una Política Popular*, and the continued engagement with the mass line evolved into a Mexican social Maoism. For those who followed *Hacia una Política Popular*, they believed that they had found a path to transform Mexico without turning to armed struggle. They forged forms of participation in which people came together to understand and then endeavored to resolve their problems.[36] In a 1974 follow-up pamphlet, *Sobre el desarrollo de Política Popular y sus cuadros medios*, they placed democratic practices at the center of any organization.[37]

In 2010, Orive provided his interpretation of PP, or what he called Poder Popular (Popular Power).[38] Orive contended that the revolutionary struggle in Mexico had to follow the protracted people's struggle. He and his colleagues were critical of the fact that in socialist countries, workers and peasants did not make the decisions; all decision-making was in the hands of party leaders and state functionaries. Therefore, they felt that Mao's mass line was a way to avoid this situation. As anticapitalists, they wanted a socialist revolution to transform the system, but they also aspired to make sure this was done as democratically as possible. From '68, they learned how to make collective decisions and use two types of struggle—brigades and demonstrations. Through the *brigadas*, they made the city their own; they entered all types of communities to talk with folks. For the brigadistas, "the people's emancipation can only be the work of the people themselves; no person or ethics can make that emancipation for [them]."[39]

So, PP members left their homes and work to integrate themselves with workers, the peasants, and the urban poor to serve the people in their process of self-empowerment that would lead to emancipation.[40] When it came to organization, they avoided the fetishism of the party and the cult of personality. They wanted people in their meetings to be able to share their opinions, to discuss issues, and to take responsibilities. At the same time, there were smaller group meetings to give those who felt intimidated at the larger assemblies an opportunity to participate. They judged that everyone is an essential part of decision-making. Orive concluded that it was through these general lines that people in different regions of Mexico were able to be empowered as citizens and community.[41] Torres and Orive's book explored five cases where social struggles greatly improved the quality of lives of thousands of Mexicans. In these struggles people became the authors of their own possibilities and histories.

The leadership of PP initially sent out cadres to work in the countryside—beginning with an attempt in San Sebastian Tecomaxtlahuaca/Santiago Juxtlahuaca, Oaxaca. After a discussion of the limitations of their first exercise, the PP cadres decided to integrate themselves with various communities in Nayarit, Durango, and Sonora followed by San Luis Potosí, Coahuila, Chihuahua, Zacatecas, Hidalgo, Michoacán, Querétaro, Chiapas, and Guerrero.[42] Building on earlier activism in these areas, youth from Mexico City linked up with activists in these communities who sympathized with the mass line. PP activists shifted their militancy to Mexico's northern slums in cities like Durango, Monterrey, Chihuahua, and Torreón, working with the urban poor and dispossessed, again building on the work of earlier militant organizations as well as radicalized youth ready to adopt this social Maoism.[43] From 1973 to 1976, PP, for instance, continued their work in Durango creating liberated and self-managed territories in urban settings, such as the Comité de Defensa Popular (Popular Defense Committee), and even shifted back to organizing in the countryside.[44] In Monterrey, building on earlier work of the PCM, PP repeated their success with urban communities creating liberated zones and organizing them into the Frente Popular Tierra y Libertad (Land and Liberty Popular Front).[45] By 1976, PP had expanded into the Comarca Lagunera and in particular Torreón.[46] These popular urban movements began to link up with other urban popular movements, leading to the formation of the Coordinadora Nacional de Movimientos Urbanos Populares (National Coordinator of the Urban Popular Movement, CONAMUP) in 1981.[47] Many of the groups were self-defense organizations struggling for land, housing, and services as well as democratic rights using the tactics of legal complaints, demonstrations and marches, negotiation, and popular education and ideological campaigns.[48] Juan Manuel Ramírez Saiz, a scholar on Mexican urban social movements, maintains that successful long-lasting popular urban movements were the result of a united ideology and single leadership.[49] Jorge Puma Crespo, an up-and-coming scholar of PP, stresses that linking local student activists with pastoral work helped PP develop an effective activist model.[50]

Tensions developed within the leadership of PP, however, over ideology, leadership, and interpretations of where the struggle should be located, leading to a rupture of PP in 1976 into Línea de Masas (Line of the Masses) and Línea Proletaria (Proletarian Line, LP). By 1978, Línea de Masas became the Coordinadora Línea de Masas (Coordinating Line of the Masses, COLIMA).[51] Members of Línea de Masas, led by Hugo Andrés Araujo, an activist close to Orive, argued to retain a decentralized structure, while those in LP, led by Orive, favored a more centralized approach. Orive felt the need to construct a centralizing organization given the growth of PP. For this reason, he pushed for a Comisión Permanente General de la Organización (Permanent Commission of the General Organization).[52] After the split, COLIMA, together with Compañero, continued to work in the colonias and became the major leaders of popular urban movements in the 1980s. PP's success, therefore, was the result of giving primacy to the organization of the masses and not the party.[53]

LÍNEA PROLETARIA

Following the rupture in PP, LP relocated to Coahuila and Durango joining workers in mining and metallurgy in the north, connecting with peasants in creating effective organizations in Durango, Sonora, Guerrero, and Chiapas, and assisting telephone workers and teachers nationwide. It was around this time that LP was invited by Bishop Samuel Ruíz to send cadres to work in the communities of eastern Chiapas to continue the work of Unión del Pueblo (The People's Union), which became part of LP in 1976.[54] One of the Maoists' most successful endeavors in Chiapas was their support for the Unión de Uniones Ejidales y Grupos Campesinos Solidarios de Chiapas (Union of Ejidal Unions and Peasant Groups of Chiapas). According to Montemayor, "The diocese pastoral action and the political action of the invited brigades converged for some years in strengthening peasant organizations, of training community activists with rapid action tactics that the EZLN would later use, such as the clandestine construction of premade housing structures overnight, or a village or camp on land disputed by communities or agrarian organizations."[55]

LP continued using the PP approaches in their work within the Sindicato Nacional de Trabajadores Minero-Metalúrgicos y Similares de la República Mexicana (National Mining Metallurgical and Similar Activities Union of the Mexican Republic, SNTMMSRM) in the 1970s.[56] Building on the immediately felt needs of workers, PL activists advanced working-class organization and consciousness in preparation for future struggles. As a result, in sections of the industry where LP was strong, there were widespread democratic practices, shop-floor meetings, elections held at the factory gate, and more. Workers, together with LP activists, formed small discussion groups to talk about their problems and solutions as well as examine the larger political realities.[57] LP activists endeavored to apply the method of *pretextos-objetivos* (pretexts-goals); activists used the struggle for better living conditions and against company unions in order to develop a proletarian consciousness among the workers. This activity was part of the protracted struggle progressively taking the terrain from the enemy.[58]

By 1979, for some of the cadres the attempt to establish an LP clearing house in a Comisión Permanente resulted in a leadership and ideology that was no longer grounded in the masses. Orive himself was criticized, and in order to resolve this crisis, he tendered his resignation. However, the crisis was not settled, and various factions followed their own courses, leading eventually to the demise of LP. Today many look at PP/LP/COLIMA with distrust because the authors and organizers behind *Hacia una Política Popular* (Orive, Alberto Anaya, and Andrés Araujo) participated within a corrupt and repressive political system by either taking on a government office or creating a political party that aligned itself with the PRI. Furthermore, they placed themselves in opposition to what many feel is the only political alternative—the Zapatistas and their allies.[59] However, we need to separate the leadership from the militants who under the banner of PP joined the masses and engaged in a struggle with capitalism. Many of these former PP/LP/COLIMA activists continue to form part of oppositional organizations like a variety of nongovernmental organizations as well as Zapatista solidarity committees.[60] While LP did not survive, cadres influenced by the mass line as a revolutionary project continue their commitment.

CONCLUSION

There are three types of criticism typically leveled at Mexican social Maoism as articulated by PP, LP, and COLIMA. The first was that the activism of PL and COLIMA was simply traditional reformist politics. Thus, these organizations could only end up repeating the errors of Lombardo Toledano or worse, Fidel Velázquez. For some, negotiation unfortunately invites integration with state elites.[61] At the same time the mass line strategy was weakened by the shift to a "protracted people's struggle" since it took the one weapon the organization could use off the table—socialist armed struggle.[62] Others have gone further (criticism two) and suggested that the very nature of the Mexican Maoist mass line was simply a populist, possibly nativist, reformist practice that intentionally supported capital.[63] In the Zapatista narrative, similar accusations are leveled against LP, Unión del Pueblo, and Compañero as reformists guilty of econom-ism and collaborators with the ruling party who misled the Indian communi-ties and their organizations.[64] Thus, many Zapatistas argued that the Mexican Maoist use of the mass line helped "facilitate their effective liquidation into the ruling party."[65]

The third criticism was that these Mexican Maoists were simply doing the work of the PRI and allowed the Mexican state to hijack their organizations. In Chiapas, Gunderson claims LP leadership redirected the peasant move-ment's demand for the redistribution of land to agricultural supports that "coin-cided with [the government's] national agricultural development objectives."[66] This third criticism took on greater relevance as the leadership of PP, LP, and COLIMA found themselves in various governmental positions, some even as elected politicians. The journalist Antonio Jáquez relates that from the start of PP, Orive was in close contact with President Echeverría and Secretary of the Interior Mario Moya Palencia, from whom he received money to support the brigadistas. The political scientist Paul Lawrence Haber suggests that the PP leadership was in cahoots with the Echeverría administration and its *apertura democrática* (democratic opening), therefore serving to legitimize an authori-tarian administration that was waging a Dirty War against the socialist armed struggle and their supporters. In Durango, for instance, "the government of Echeverría created a political space and gave financial support to activist youths who worked to construct new organizations and social movements in rural and urban areas."[67] For these critics, the initial success of PP was due to Orive's and other PP leaders' support of Echeverría's neopopulism due to their familial ties and shared political goals.[68] Thus, by the time the Salinas administration appears in 1988 with its "set of Machiavellian policies and reforms," the Maoist leader-ship was already a willing participant and ready to accept the Salinas reforms, especially the Programa Nacional de Solidaridad.[69] Haber suggests that this was not only an inevitable result of social Maoism, but the outcome of a planned usurpation of mass organizations.[70] For Roxborough and Bizberg, probably the most troubling aspect of LP's line in the metallurgy industry was that their focus on the local level avoided direct conflicts with the national leadership of the Miners' Union and reinforced an apolitical stance that permitted tempo-rary alliances with the PRI.[71] Bizberg concludes that LP agreed "to limit union struggles at the local level to purely economic or labor concerns."[72]

I cannot state whether Mexican social Maoism was bound to result in sim-ple reformism and even collaboration with the PRI and the Mexican state, especially after the neoliberal turn, nor can I state that the leadership was (or was not) made up of some type of Left-PRI infiltrators. Rather I share the frustration of Father Benigno Martínez, a Catholic catechist who had been active with PP in Coahuila and later in Chiapas: "I do not know if following this strategy, Orive and Araujo had to end up working together for the government, giving a turn that we still do not understand and that hurt many people who believed in them, especially in Araujo; he helped people find out how corrupt the system is and now is part of the system."[73]

What I can state is that the PP and later LP and COLIMA activists engaged in a profound Mexican Marxist political practice not seen since the 1930s. Hundreds of Mexican youth, radicalized by '68 and its aftermath, following the mass line, sought to achieve a socialist transformation with workers, peasants, and the urban poor by participating and living life under capital. Their praxis of using collective struggle to improve working and living conditions would highlight the limits of capital and prepare the ground for socialism, avoiding the dichotomy, so typical in Marxist activism, of reform or revolution. PP offered a creative albeit temporary reorientation of Marxist politics by articulating a Mexican social Maoism shunning dogmatism or accepting an outmoded revolutionary program.[74]

PP activists, like those who engaged in armed resistance, catechists who worked with community-based organizations, and anarchists and socialists who adopted the life of militants, constructed a loose community that rejected normal social and political behavior and visualized a society that was not enslaved by institutions that undermined self-determination, autonomy, and freedom. Puma Crespo argues that after LP's demise, "The bulk of the PP rank and file returned to civilian life and preserved their ideology to varying degrees. Most of them maintain their distaste for political parties and oligarchies."[75] While for a moment these activists resurrected a heterodox Marxism from the limitations of Marxism-Leninism, today many remain committed to the struggle for alternative and at times oppositional politics in Mexico.

NOTES

1.   As the nineteenth century came to an end, the German Social Democratic Party debated the role of trade unions and political parties in the construction of a socialist society. On one side was Eduard Bernstein and others who argued that capitalism had reached a stage that more social reforms and democratic freedoms would transform capitalism into socialism. On the other side was Rosa

Luxemburg and her allies who reasoned that socialism could only be realized by the working class through revolution. After the Russian Revolution and the formation of the Third International, the debate about strategy was reduced to a choice between capitulating to capital (reform) or pushing for a Leninist approach to revolution.

2. Puma Crespo, "Los maoístas del norte de México."

3. According to Puma Crespo, PP's "model of political action followed the rhythm of the formation of a 'social left' concerned with economic issues and popular mobilization outside the framework of a revolutionary vanguard and party building" (ibid., 202). For this reason, I call this version social Maoism.

4. Rothwell, *Transpacific Revolutionaries*, 18.

5. Dirlik, "Modernism and Antimodernism"; Dirlik, "Mao Zedong Thought."

6. Rothwell, *Transpacific*, 34–38.

7. Fernández Christlieb, *El espartaquismo en México*, 16–25.

8. Rodríguez Araujo, *Las izquierdas en México*, 37.

9. The Partido Revolucionario del Proletariado was founded in 1964. Its origins can be traced to the Liga Comunista por la Construcción del Partido Revolucionario del Proletariado. In turn, it was a split from Partido Comunista Bolshevique. The Partido Comunista Bolshevique seems to have been the first Mexican organization to align itself pointedly with the position of the Chinese Communist Party; the LLE soon followed. See Gunderson, "Provocative Cocktail," 279.

10. The Unión brought together elements of the Jaramillo movement, Partido Agrario-Obrero Morelense, Movimiento Revolucionario del Magisterio, Movimiento de Independencia Sindical, and Frente Obrero Comunista de México.

11. Fernández Christlieb, *El espartaquismo*, 67.

12. Other names used by the MMLM included the Asociación Revolucionaria Espartaco and the Asociación Revolucionaria Espartaco del Proletariado Mexicano.

13. Gunderson, "Provocative Cocktail," 280.

14. Rodríguez Araujo, *Las izquierdas*, 40.

15. Alexander, *International Maoism*, 1.

16. See Barbosa, "La izquierda radical en México," 123–25, who reduces Mexican Maoists to followers of Beijing.

17. Rothwell, *Transpacific*, 4, makes a similar argument.

18. Bennett, "Orígenes del Movimiento Urbano Popular Mexicano," 91.

19. Rodríguez Araujo, *Las izquierdas*, 93.

20. Gunderson, "Provocative Cocktail," 293.

21. There were, of course, socialist armed movements that articulated a specific Maoist position, albeit at times with Guevarist undertones. Examples of these include the Partido Popular Unido de América and the Unión del Pueblo. See, respectively, Gómez, *Revolutionary Imaginations of Greater Mexico*; and Bennett, "Orígenes del Movimiento," 98. Aviña also discusses how other socialist armed groups also tended toward a pro-Chinese Marxism-Leninism driven by their exasperation with the PCM and Partido Popular; see Aviña, *Specters of Revolution*,

94, 146. Similarly, Seward suggests that Fuerzas de Liberación Nacional (FLN) also embraced the Maoist tactic of the prolonged people's war; see Seward, "Fusing Identities and Mobilizing Resistance in Chiapas and Mexico, 1994–2009," 144.

22.   Compañero appeared at the same time as PP and followed the Maoist mass line. Like the later Línea de Masas, they believed that constructing bases in the colonias was the first step to organizing workers, the semi-employed, and the unemployed (Enzástiga Santiago, "La Unión de Colonias Populares.")

23.   Gunderson, "Provocative Cocktail," 302.

24.   There were always other expressions of Maoist militants in different parts of Mexico such as the Unión Popular de Vendedores Ambulantes who were influenced by the MMLM in Puebla. Mendiola-García, *Street Democracy*.

25.   Puma Crespo, "Small Groups Don't Win Revolutions," 3, 12.

26.   Jorge Iván Puma Crespo, "La lucha armada en la memoria de los maoístas de Política Popular" (unpublished manuscript), 2010, 4–5.

27.   Pensado, *Rebel Mexico*.

28.   Palacios Suárez, *Desde 1968 sigues siendo el mismo?*, 7.

29.   Ibid.

30.   Ibid., 44. In contrast, Joel Ortega Juárez argues that the brigadista experience was where the idea to resist through armed struggle was inculcated (Ruiz Mendoza, "El Movimiento Estudiantil de 1968," 366).

31.   Puma Crespo, "Small Groups," 3.

32.   Palacios Suárez, *Desde 1968*, 70, 66.

33.   Bracho, "La izquierda integrada al pueblo y la solidaridad: revisiones de Política Popular," 74.

34.   Palacios Suárez, *Desde 1968*, 121.

35.   Ibid., 158.

36.   Bracho, "La izquierda," 74. The activists of PP presented a momentary solution to the history of the Mexican Left that seemed stuck between two political and ideological poles, Lombardo or Revueltas, reform or revolution. Bartra, *El reto de la izquierda*.

37.   Bracho, "La izquierda," 78–79.

38.   Orive, "Construyendo Poder Popular, Ciudadanía y Comunidad, Una Introducción," 19–52.

39.   Ibid., 43.

40.   Bracho, "La izquierda," 73.

41.   Orive, "Construyendo," 41–43.

42.   Puma Crespo, "Los maoístas," 204; Montemayor, "La guerrilla en México hoy."

43.   Puma Crespo, "Los maoístas," 205; Bracho, "La izquierda," 73. There is a long history of the interchange of youth from Mexico City to the rest of the country and vice versa. The story of politicized students coming to study in Mexico City has been part of the long story of student activism. At times these students stayed and at times they moved back home or to other parts of Mexico. At the same time, politicized Mexico City students did not necessarily stay in Mexico City but found

themselves active in their adoptive homes. See Carla Villanueva's chapter in this volume, which explores the building of the Federación de Estudiantes Campesinos Socialistas de México (FECSM) in the *escuelas normales rurales* and the interaction of students from different parts of Mexico. Simultaneously, the PP benefited from radicalized youth in the many areas they went to.

44. Haber, *Power From Experience*, 123–171; Haber, "De revolucionarios a colaboradores."

45. Puma Crespo, "Los maoístas," 209; Ramírez Saiz, *El movimiento urbano popular en México*.

46. Puma Crespo notes that in Torreón, PP connected with local priests who were engaged in their pastoral work of helping the poor (Puma Crespo, "Los maoístas," 212). This experience of working with engaged clergy and the local dioceses would serve them well when they went to Chiapas. A key link was father José Batarse Charur.

47. Bautista González, *Movimiento urbano popular*.

48. Ramírez Saiz, *El movimiento*, 93–96.

49. For an alternative Reading, see Bouchier, "La paradoja de la unidad."

50. Puma Crespo, "Los maoístas," 212.

51. Bennett, "Orígenes," 97.

52. Initially, he proposed the Organización Ideología Dirigente. This organization would serve as a clearing house for political action and ideological consistency without breaking with the masses (Puma Crespo, "Los maoístas," 225).

53. Bennett, "Orígenes," 98. Bennett adds that COLIMA and Compañero eventually began the process to create revolutionary parties: Organización de Izquierda Revolucionaria-Línea de Masas (OIR-LM) and the Movimiento Revolucionario del Pueblo (MRP).

54. Unión del Pueblo was one of the many socialist armed groups of the 1960s and an early proponent of Mao's strategy of protracted people's war. By 1971, the group split between a guerilla organization and a segment that turned to the mass line in preparation for the protracted people's war. The guerrilla group survived, eventually becoming part of the Ejército Popular Revolucionario in 1996. As for the other faction, they began working with indigenous communities in Chiapas developing mass political consciousness, building ideological and political bases, and linking with progressive sections of the Catholic Church. Unión developed cadres that would continue to work with LP and become leading figures in various peasant struggles and organizations that would be critical to the evolution of the FLN into the Ejército Zapatista de Liberación Nacional (EZLN).

55. Montemayor, "La guerrilla," 28. For some, Unión de Uniones' tactic of taking advantage of the differences between federal and state government agencies to achieve their goals was found wanting. See Puma Crespo, "Los maoístas," 222.

56. Roxborough and Bizberg, "Union Locals in Mexico."

57. Esterbauer, "De la Línea Proletaria."

58. Puma Crespo, "Los maoístas," 217.

59. For examples of critical views of Orive and the others, see Cano, "Cuatro textos sobre los antecedentes 'políticos' de Adolfo Orive"; Jáquez, "Hablan tres fundadores

del movimiento Tierra y Libertad"; Cano, "La Larga Marcha de Adolfo Orive." Puma Crespo responds to the "black legend" articulated by these ex-PP activists and Subcomandante Marcos (Puma Crespo, "Small Groups").

60. Bracho, "La izquierda," 85.
61. Haber, *Power*, 126.
62. Puma Crespo, "La lucha," 21–23.
63. Barbosa, *La izquierda*, 129.
64. Gunderson, "Provocative Cocktail," 274.
65. Ibid., 302.
66. Ibid., 336.
67. Haber, "De revolucionarios," 9.
68. Haber, *Power*, 132.
69. Ibid, 31.
70. Ibid, 157.
71. Palacios's own experience with LP at the Sindicato de Telefonistas de la República Mexicana left much to be desired (Palacios Suárez, *Desde 1968*, 195).
72. Bizberg, "Política laboral y acción sindical en México (1976–1982)," 171. Orive responds that this and many other tactical moves were necessary in order to continue the advancement of the political and organizational capacities of the masses. The "policy of two faces" was to share one real and revolutionary face to the masses and a reformist face when making demands.
73. Puma Crespo, "Small Groups," 7.
74. Puma Crespo, "Los maoístas," 227.
75. Ibid., 8.

BIBLIOGRAPHY

PERSONAL COLLECTIONS

Hacia una Política Popular (1968). (Pamphlet.) Personal collection of Michael Soldatenko.
Sobre el desarrollo de Política Popular y sus cuadros medios (1974). (Pamphlet.) Personal collection of Michael Soldatenko.

PRIMARY SOURCES

Lombardo Toledano, Vicente. *Diario de un viaje a la China nueva*. Mexico: Ediciones Futuro, 1950.
Revueltas, José. *Ensayo sobre un proletariado sin cabeza*. Mexico, 1962.

SECONDARY SOURCES

Alexander, Robert J. *International Maoism in the Developing World*. Westport, Conn.: Praeger, 1999.
Aviña, Alexander. *Specters of Revolution: Peasant Guerrillas in the Cold War Mexican Countryside*. Oxford: Oxford University Press, 2014.
Barbosa, Fabio. "La izquierda radical en México." *Revista Mexicana de Sociología* 46, no. 2 (April–June 1984): 111–38.

Bartra, Roger. *El reto de la izquierdas*. Mexico City: Editorial Grijalbo, 1982.

Bautista González, Raúl. *Movimiento Urbano Popular: Bitácora de Lucha, 1968–2011*. Mexico City: Casa y Ciudad, 2015.

Bennett, Vivienne. "Orígenes del Movimiento Urbano Popular Mexicano: Pensamiento político y organizaciones políticas clandestinas, 1960–1980." *Revista Mexicana de Sociología* 15, no. 3 (July–September 1993): 89–102.

Bizberg, Ilán. "Política laboral y acción sindical en México (1976–1982)." *Foro Internacional* 25, no. 2 (October–December 1984): 166–89.

Bouchier, Josiane. "La paradoja de la unidad: El movimiento urbano popular y la coordinadora nacional del movimiento urbano popular (CONAMUP)." In *Movimientos sociales en México durante la década de los 80*, edited by Sergio Zermeño and Jesús Aurelio Cuevas Díaz, 203–20. Mexico City: UNAM, 1990.

Bracho, Julio. "La izquierda integrada al pueblo y la solidaridad: Revisiones de Política Popular." *Revista Mexicana de Sociología* 55, no. 3 (July–September 1993): 69–87.

Cano, Arturo. "La Larga Marcha de Adolfo Orive: Del Maoísmo a Gobernación." *Masiosare*, January 18, 1998.

———. "Cuatro textos sobre los antecedentes 'políticos' de Adolfo Orive." *Zapateando* 2 (July 2009).

Dirlik, Arif. "Mao Zedong Thought and the Third World/Global South." *Interventions: International Journal of Postcolonial Studies* 16, no. 2 (2013): 233–56.

———. "Modernism and Antimodernism in Mao Zedong's Marxism." In *Critical Perspectives on Mao Zedong's Thought*, edited by Arif Dirlik, Paul Healy, and Nick Knight, 59–83. Atlantic Highlands, N.J.: Humanities Press, 1997.

Enzástiga Santiago, Mario. "La Unión de Colonias Populares de cara al movimiento urbano popular: Recapitulación histórica." In *Los movimientos sociales en el Valle de México*, edited by Jorge Alonso. Vol. 1, 125–78. Mexico City: Centro de Investigaciones y Estudios Superiores en Antropología Social, 1986.

Esterbauer, Christine. "De la Línea Proletaria a una identidad competitiva: Los siderúrgicos en México; El caso de la sección 147." *El Cotidiano* 182 (November–December 2013): 7–16.

Fernández Christlieb, Paulina. *El espartaquismo en México*. Mexico City: Ediciones El Caballito, 1978.

Gómez, Alan Eladio. *The Revolutionary Imaginations of Greater Mexico: Chicana/o Radicalism, Solidarity Politics, and Latin American Social Movements*. Austin: University of Texas Press, 2016.

Gunderson, Christopher. "The Provocative Cocktail: Intellectual Origins of the Zapatista Uprising, 1960–1994." PhD diss., City University of New York, 2013.

Haber, Paul Lawrence. "De revolucionarios a colaboradores: un cuento aleccionador de la transformación del Comité de Defensa Popular de Durango, México." *Istor: Revista de Historia Internacional* 16, no. 64 (2016): 7–34.

———. *Power from Experience: Urban Popular Movements in Late Twentieth-Century Mexico*. University Park: Penn State University Press, 2006.

Jáquez, Antonio. "Hablan tres fundadores del movimiento Tierra y Libertad." *Proceso*, January 22, 1994.

Mendiola-García, Sandra C. *Street Democracy: Vendors, Violence, and Public Space in Late Twentieth-Century Mexico.* Lincoln: University of Nebraska Press, 2017.

Montemayor, Carlos. "La guerrilla en México hoy." *Fractal* 11 (October–December 1998): 11–44.

Orive, Adolfo. "Construyendo poder popular, ciudadanía y comunidad: Una introducción." In *Poder popular: construcción de ciudadanía y Comunidad,* by Jose Luis Torres, with Adolfo Orive, 19–52. Mexico City: Juan Pablos Editor, 2010.

Palacios Suárez, José Guillermo. *Desde 1968 sigues siendo el mismo? Testimonio de un activista.* Vol 2. Mexico City: Ediciones El Voz del Anahuac, Colectivo Azcapotzalco, 2015.

Pensado, Jaime M. *Rebel Mexico: Student Unrest and Authoritarian Political Culture During the Long Sixties.* Stanford, Calif.: Stanford University Press, 2013.

Puma Crespo, Jorge Iván. "Los maoístas del norte de México: Breve historia de Política Popular-Línea Proletaria, 1969–1979." *Revista Izquierdas* 27 (2016): 200–29.

———. "Small Groups Don't Win Revolutions: Armed Struggle in the Memory of Maoist Militants of Política Popular." *Latin American Perspectives* 44, no. 6 (November 2017): 140–55.

Ramírez Saiz, Juan Manuel. *El movimiento urbano popular en México.* Mexico City: Siglo Veintiuno, 1986.

Rodríguez Araujo, Octavio. *Las izquierdas en México.* Mexico City: Orfila, 2015.

Rothwell, Matthew D. *Transpacific Revolutionaries: The Chinese Revolution in Latin America.* New York: Routledge, 2013.

Roxborough, Ian, and Ilan Bizberg. "Union Locals in Mexico: The 'New Unionism' in Steel and Automobiles." *Journal of Latin American Studies* 15, no. 1 (May 1983): 117–35.

Ruiz Mendoza, Florencia. "El Movimiento Estudiantil de 1968 en el proceso de radicalización hacia la lucha armada en México: 1968–1971." *Revista del Programa de Investigaciones sobre Conflicto Social* 4, no. 5 (June 2011): 355–73.

Seward, Ruhiya Kristine. "Fusing Identities and Mobilizing Resistance in Chiapas and Mexico, 1994–2009." PhD diss., New School for Social Research, 2011.

10

THE OTHER "NEW MAN"

Conservative Nationalism and Right-Wing
Youth in 1970s Monterrey

LUIS HERRÁN AVILA

SINCE THE MID-1950S, right-wing students participated in the broader configuration of authoritarian political culture in Mexico. But they did so in contradictory ways. Emphasizing ideas of order and authority, some saw themselves
as part of a conservative body politic that needed protection from social and
moral subversion. Others embraced the spirit of political and cultural rebellion
of the time to forge new forms of dissident conservative subjectivity through
the refashioning of notions of tradition and nation. This chapter draws on this
apparent contradiction between conservatism and radicalism to examine the
case of Conciencia Joven (Young Conscience), a right-wing student group from
northern Mexico. In particular, the chapter explores the intersections of conservative nationalism, student activism, and entrepreneurial political culture in
Monterrey and locates the history of Conciencia Joven in relation to the local
and global genealogies of the Mexican Right.

Appearing in 1974 at the Instituto Tecnológico de Monterrey (Monterrey
Institute of Technology), Conciencia Joven embodied the anxieties of a sector
of the *regiomontano* (native of Monterrey) middle and entrepreneurial classes
who were historically socialized in a deep distrust of state intervention in the
spheres of labor, business, and education. Conciencia Joven was a local expression of the disaffections of the Mexican Right with the course of the postrevolutionary state. But from a broader perspective, they were also participants

in a transnational neofascist constellation that emerged in Europe and South America throughout the 1970s to propose "national-revolutionary" solutions to the alleged "global crisis" of the era.[1]

With its emphasis on actors and movements on the Left, the historiography of Cold War Mexico has overlooked the centrality of the Right in shaping the political landscape of the 1960s and 1970s.[2] Yet, with the same energy of their leftist counterparts, the Mexican *derechas* (right-wing forces) reacted to critical national and international moments of the Cold War (the Cuban Revolution, the rise and repression of the 1968 student movement, and the 1973 coup in Chile).[3] Seeing themselves as dissidents of the postrevolutionary state but also as interlocutors in the consolidation of its political, cultural, and economic project, the Mexican derechas responded to the radicalism of the New Left by reinforcing their anti-statism and antisecularism, and by proposing alternative conceptions of Mexican national identity. Like their leftist colleagues, moreover, they resorted to ideological repertoires rooted in national experience but that were also transnational in their making. In presenting this argument, I use the category of the "post-Cristero Right" as a way to analyze the crucial legacies of those disaffections with the postrevolutionary state and to examine Conciencia Joven in light of the historical trajectories of these derechas with respect to local and global interlocutors.

Representative of the post-Cristero conservative youth movements that sought to reshape and mobilize regiomontano middle-class values, Conciencia Joven was also a right-wing response to the neo-Cardenista and allegedly Third Worldist platform of the presidency of Luis Echeverría (1970–76), discussed at greater length by Dillingham and Oikión in this volume. Conciencia Joven articulated a specific rendering of contradictory middle-class sensibilities, which combined ideas of class harmony and national unity, championed conservative notions of gender and domesticity, and endorsed an anti-liberal "Third Position" between capitalism and socialism.[4] Similar to other contemporary right-wing movements around the world, its members saw youth as the agents of nationalist restoration and deployed neofascist notions of leadership, authenticity, and "action." These regiomontano students inhabited an unorthodox ideological space within the post-Cristero Right and inserted themselves in the spirit of youth revolt of the era through the idea of a nationalist-conservative "New Man" that could become the agent of transformation of Mexico's economy, politics, and society.

"MONTERREICH": THE POST-CRISTERO RIGHT AND REGIOMONTANO IDENTITY

As the last major conflict of the Mexican Revolution, the Cristero War (1926–29) pitted federal troops against Catholic peasant militias, predominantly in western Mexico, who reacted against the government's ban on political proselytizing by the Church, the closing of temples, and the expulsion of foreign priests.[5] The Cristero movement was a foundational moment for future generations of politically active Catholics who begrudged the limits on ecclesial participation in politics and the secular character of public education as attacks on religious freedom and as clear signs of the regime's authoritarianism. With the restructuring of Mexico's most important lay organization Acción Católica Mexicana (Mexican Catholic Action, ACM), the formation of the Unión Nacional Sinarquista (National Synarchist Union, UNS) in 1937, and the creation of the Partido Acción Nacional (National Action Party, PAN) in 1939, these conservative dissidents to the postrevolutionary state remained divided over the most effective method to reconstitute their social bases.[6] Throughout the twentieth century, these actors of the post-Cristero Right rebuked the legacies of postrevolutionary authoritarianism while seeking to resignify the revolution as a struggle of Mexico's Catholic popular classes and to place the Cristero War as an episode of martyrdom for Catholics in and beyond Mexico.[7] During the Cold War, post-Cristero Right organizations held a key and still understudied presence in the increasing politicization of Catholics, including anticommunist civic organizations and right-wing student groups that, like their leftist counterparts, shaped the cultural and political landscape of the 1960s and 1970s in Mexico.

In the northern city of Monterrey, the configuration of a local dissident conservative coalition relied on the social hegemony of powerful business groups that clashed with the federal government on matters beyond the religious question, making the memory of the Cristero War acquire different meanings. Historically, the regiomontano private sector resented what they perceived as the excessive interference of the central state in the economy, labor, education, and local elections. While the PRI regime attempted to subordinate local actors to its own corporatist project, the power and influence built by Grupo Monterrey (The Monterrey Group, a conglomerate of petrochemical, food, and mining companies) epitomized the quasi-autonomous status of the city as a regional anti-statist stronghold for Mexican capitalists.[8]

Since the 1930s, Grupo Monterrey effectively kept state unionism (the Confederación de Trabajadores Mexicano, or Confederation of Mexican Workers, CTM) at bay through its own corporatist, paternalistic system of company unions. These unions succeeded in rallying workers, often coercively, against outside labor organizers and against state mediation in labor disputes. The Grupo sponsored union demonstrations where regional identity and patriotism were seen as instruments to defend its workplaces and employers from communist influence.[9] For its defiant stance against these actors and agencies of the central state, the Grupo acquired the negative reputation, particularly among official and academic circles, as the quintessential national bourgeoisie with reactionary values. The regiomontano elites' sympathy for, and even militancy in, movements and organizations of the post-Cristero Right was consistent with a history of suspicion toward state intervention and the alleged hidden designs of communists infiltrated in the government. Playfully coined by a critical commentator of the Grupo's role in regiomontano society, the label of "Monterre-ich" invoked this convergence between anticommunism, social conservatism, corporate paternalism, and the concentration of economic power. This matrix of values permeated the forms of indoctrination and labor discipline enforced by company unions and reproduced a sense of exceptionality of the social and economic order of Monterrey.[10]

The conflicts between Grupo Monterrey and the federal government became the basis for the strong sense of self-sufficiency of regiomontano capitalism and its social and political isolation from Mexico City.[11] Historically, the Grupo had been defiant of state-sponsored business and industry organizations, which it saw as too nationalistic, anti-American, and excessively dependent on protectionism.[12] While leading the creation of a nationwide, independent business federation in 1929, Monterrey's entrepreneurial classes saw themselves as distinct from those of Chihuahua, Guadalajara, and Mexico City. They were, in the praising words of local historian José Fuentes Mares, "not a mere *association* of interests, but a *community* of principles," a "spiritual unity" linking two generations of entrepreneurs as active agents of the city's industrial prosperity.[13] Over the years, regiomontano entrepreneurs turned the city of Monterrey into a symbolic site of autonomous power with remarkable capacity to influence local politicians and place them in the structures of the official party.[14] Although federal labor laws, official socialist rhetoric, and state-sponsored unionism confronted them with the government of Lázaro Cárdenas (1934–40), by the 1940s the Grupo Monterrey ultimately reconciled with the policies and discourse of "national unity" of Presidents Manuel Ávila Camacho (1940–46) and Miguel Alemán (1946–52).[15]

As Mexico entered the Cold War period, the metropolitan area of Monterrey became an important epicenter of Catholic anticommunist activism. Like other states with a strong conservative presence, such as Jalisco and Puebla, business groups and the clergy in the state of Nuevo León collaborated against the power of the interventionist secular state in favor of building a Christian social order.[16] A trademark of lay Catholic movements, the project of re-creating "the Kingdom of Christ on Earth" was central to the alliance between actors who sought to defend and promote regiomontano social and cultural values against the alleged intrusion of "outsiders," be it federal authorities, radical students, labor organizers, or progressive priests. In Puebla, Jalisco, and Mexico City, these alliances mobilized civic and student organizations, in violent and non-violent ways, to counter the increasing leftist influence in public institutions, including the universities. In these cities, the emergence of right-wing student organizations, such as the Movimiento Universitario de Renovadora Orient-ación (University Movement for a Renewed Orientation, MURO) and the Frente Universitario Anticomunista (University Anticommunist Front, FUA), was the product of cross-sectorial and cross-class concerns. These and similar student organizations emerged to protect universities, churches, and businesses as important spaces of autonomy, crucial for the social reproduction of middle-class conservative sensibilities.[17] In Monterrey, these alliances were rooted in the history of collaboration between company unions and anticommunist Catholic civic groups to break or prevent strikes and promote notions of class cooperation and corporate loyalty among workers.[18]

In the 1960s, one of the most important movements backed by the Grupo Monterrey (aside from MURO) was the Cruzada Regional Anti-Comunista (Regional Anti-Communist Crusade, CRAC), the local protagonist of a nation-wide campaign of anticommunist propaganda and civic mobilization that emerged in the aftermath of the Cuban Revolution. CRAC's platform empha-sized notions of the common good, Christian social justice, and a rejection of communism for its atheism, its abolition of private property, and its tyrannical conception of the state.[19] Allied with local PAN politicians, the local press, the Unión Nacional de Padres de Familia (National Union of Parents, UNPF), the Movimiento Familiar Cristiano (Christian Family Movement, MFC), and the Knights of Columbus, CRAC rallied against secular education and the "impo-sition" of official textbooks, which, according to them, violated parents' rights to educate their children according to Christian and "Western" principles.[20] In April of 1963, CRAC and the Nuevo León Parents' Association mobilized to shut down a festival organized by leftist youth activists in the city of Sabinas Hidalgo, some sixty-five miles north of Monterrey. Known as "El Sabinazo," the ensuing violence resulted in several injured students, the burning of leftist literature, and the cancellation of the event.[21] Although we know of the presence of MURO in Nuevo León throughout the 1960s and of the participation of young people in El Sabinazo, we lack analyses of the regiomontano right-wing youth who also participated in this type of mobilization against local leftists. While the organic top-down linkages between groups like CRAC and the Grupo Monterrey are important, the existence of a young constituency within the local and national conservative body politic needs to be accounted for. As I will show in the following pages, this conservative youth was embedded in the social and cultural milieus of Monterreich, of the post-Cristero derechas, and of the global Right more broadly.

CONCIENCIA JOVEN AND THE CONSERVATIVE NEW MAN

A central piece in the efforts of the Grupo Monterrey to reassert its autonomy was the founding of the Instituto Tecnológico de Monterrey (hereafter, El Tec), an institution of higher education that specialized in business management, sciences, and technology. With industrialist Eugenio Garza Sada as its main benefactor, the central goal of El Tec was to train a new generation of *empresarios* (businessmen), well-versed in the values of capitalist entrepreneurship and capable of defending the "regiomontano faith," in a society "open to opportunity and trusting of the unlimited possibilities of individual action."[22]

Conciencia Joven (hereafter CJ) was, in many ways, a showcase for the type of youth conservatism that permeated the private universities founded by the managerial classes across Mexico. Similar to the extreme Right Los Tecos (The Owls) at the Autonomous University of Guadalajara, CJ was marked by the disaffections of the post-Cristero Right, namely the convergence of Catholic antisecularism and private sector distrust of government interference.[23] Operating in a more plural environment and in coexistence with leftist student organizations, its members did not embrace the intolerant Catholicism of Los Tecos.[24] Instead, they adopted a form of right-wing nationalism shaped by regiomontano conservatism and the global emergence of Third Position movements.

Created in 1974 by a small group of engineering and business management students, CJ published a monthly newsletter—*Conciencia Joven*—that put forward the idea of the youth as the leading agent in transforming the social and political reality of the country. Referring to the early 1970s as a period of agitation and "disruptive action," the leading voices of CJ aimed to contribute "con la pluma y la acción" (with the pen in action) to "purify" the young national consciousness. They saw journalism as a labor of political education aimed at their fellow students at El Tec, which they complemented by organizing public talks featuring noted figures of regiomontano entrepreneurial and academic circles.[25] Among others, these included Ricardo Margaín, head of the advisory council of Grupo Monterrey; Alejandro Junco, director of the influential newspaper *El Norte*; and Agustín Basave, a conservative philosopher who, like Junco, served as faculty at El Tec.[26] This convergence of business interests, the press, and conservative social thought channeled Grupo Monterrey's entrepreneurial, conservative, and oppositional ethos, which deeply shaped CJ's own political and cultural project.

During its brief existence (1974–76), *Conciencia Joven* put forward a platform that was reminiscent of early twentieth-century ideas of Mexico as an "unfinished" young nation that, like the rest of Latin America, would be the repository of the future of humanity.[27] The publication focused on the idea of the youth as "a social reality . . . a state of the soul, a spirit of sacrifice, responsibility, and capacity in labor"; it was "a strength of the will and a desire for self-improvement." The mission of its young readership, or "The Great War," as the journal called it, was to fight "our inner old man, to defeat him continuously and let the New Man be born." For CJ, "a New Man walks on Earth. In his right hand, he holds a sword, with the word Duty engraved in it. There is a glimmer in his eyes, caused by the discipline of his customs. His heart beats emboldened by Valour, Dedication, and Sacrifice. He is sure of himself because he loves, and he is not alone. He loves his family, his Homeland, his race, the fraternal races, the human species; he loves the Truth."[28]

To become this New Man it was necessary to "search within Man himself" and reach for the "arcane treasures of our civilization," which would provide the strength to "cleanse civilization of the dead weight and the dust of centuries, to reveal its hidden youth."[29] In this way, CJ posed the idea of a generational break to differentiate itself from the cultural nationalism of the past and to redefine the "arcane treasure" of tradition as a weapon against the decadence of modern liberal and socialist materialism.

Concerned with articulating a discourse of individual transcendence, the idea of the New Man championed by CJ revealed traces of the Catholic thought cultivated by prominent intellectuals of the post-Cristero Right, including Agustín Basave, the regiomontano writer Alfonso Junco, and the self-avowed Catholic "reactionary" Jesús Guisa y Azevedo. This New Man invoked the vitalist ideas of José Vasconcelos and the spiritual patriotism that Junco and Guisa had cultivated for decades: an insistence on the universality of Truth and Love, and the sense of duty, discipline, and sacrifice attributed to Mexico's essential connection with its Catholic Hispanic heritage.[30] These figures of conservative nationalism were deeply influenced by global conservative and fascist fellow travelers of the interwar period. CJ activists were, in fact, open admirers of Francoist Spain as the only true model for Mexico's rediscovery of its authentic Catholic and Hispanic *ser nacional*, the "national being" that had emerged from the violence of the Mexican Revolution and that was endangered by liberalism and communism. For them, the postrevolutionary state was an anti-Catholic and antinational tyranny that betrayed this ser nacional.

In its conception of the New Man, CJ looked to the transatlantic impact of fascism. He was akin to the Spanish Falangist ideal of a fascist "Hombre Nuevo," the "half-warrior, half-monk" whose sense of hierarchy and sacrifice would make him the agent of Spain's fascist "national-revolutionary" experiment.[31] Yet, while inspired by *falangismo*, CJ did not aim to become a mass movement, and, as noted above, it remained dedicated to a labor of nationalist edification for the future empresarios and limited to the sphere of student politics.

The post-1968 national and global context of youth radicalization placed CJ's quasi-falangista "New Man" in dialogue with a more proximate, even if counterintuitive interlocutor: Ernesto "Che" Guevara. The parallels are striking. In his famous formulation of a socialist New Man, Guevara posed the individual as an unfinished product that only becomes full by bringing "the vestiges of the past . . . into the present in one's consciousness; and a continual labor is necessary to eradicate them."[32] This process had to go "hand in hand with the development of new economic forms" as individuals acquired "more consciousness of the need for their incorporation into society."[33] Both CJ and Guevara stressed the importance of the youth as the seed of the New Man ("the malleable clay from which the new person can be built with none of the old defects," wrote Guevara) and resorted to tropes of heroism to articulate a communitarian vision of a utopian future.[34] Contrary to Guevara, for CJ, the New Man would not emerge from eradicating the past but from bringing the past into the present and by emphasizing individual abnegation. For CJ, abnegation was "a negation of the self," a "creative contradiction" that would integrate the New Man into a larger collectivity for the common good. Unlike Guevara's, CJ's New Man was not the product of liberation, but of self-repression in the name of a transcendental national community. In the particular regiomontano context of El Tec, the New Man endorsed by CJ was an invitation to its members and readership to rethink their place as future entrepreneurs by emphasizing notions of leadership and sacrifice, the glorification of the nation, and the scorn for the empty pursuit of material gain and purely technical knowledge.

CJ's notion of the New Man was rooted in a staunch moral conservatism that defended traditional ideas of the family as the central institution of society, the strict demarcation of gender roles, and a visceral rejection of feminism. For these young conservatives, gender equality—particularly in the workforce— undermined women's dignity, as it gave them more duties and obligations that clashed with "their authentic and natural inclinations" as mothers, lovers, and companions.

CJ found the "scientific" basis for this naturalization of sexual difference in the writings of Nobel Prize winner and Vichy collaborator Alexis Carrel, who in a famous eugenicist treatise published in 1935 proposed a hereditary biolog- ical aristocracy to correct the degeneracy of civilization.[35] Following Carrel, CJ activists scorned the disruptive presence of women in the workplace, claiming that women were to "develop their capacities according to their own nature" and without abandoning their "specific functions."[36] They blamed this disruption on both the unchecked demands for increased productivity in capitalism and on the spread of feminism that characterized the 1970s. They saw ideas related to gender parity as "traps of consumer society." In their view, gender parity translated into the masculinization of women and "the forced feminization of men," a subversion of gender and sexual roles exemplified by husbands who had relinquished their patriarchal authority and were too attached to the household (*los mariditos muy de su casa*, or "domesticated hubbies").[37] Feminism was thus also a threat to "natural" masculinity as it pushed men into domesticity and away from their role as breadwinners.

As imagined by CJ, women would be "virtuous mothers of heroes, thinkers, and saints," "responsibly free," dignified, selfless, brave, and willing to submit, with abnegation, to the task of "making history to build a new society."[38] While following the ideas of Carrel, CJ's antifeminism had roots in Mexican con- servatism, well represented by famed regiomontano Catholic writer Alfonso

Junco. In his writings, Junco referred to feminism as *hombrunismo*—that is, as a desire to turn women into an imitation, "a caricature" of men expressed in "licentious manners, careless drinking, and the triviality of smoking." For Junco, the basis of femininity was in women's otherness (*ser otra cosa*) vis-à-vis men: in their attention to detail; in the "intelligent and cultivated discretion" of their conversation; and in "the warm softness" of their hands, which "play the piano and display an exquisite ability for sewing, painting, or in the kitchen." Junco idealized the place of women in domestic life as one of leisure and companionship. He denied longing for the bygone era when women were absent from public life, but wished that they restrain their intellect and sexuality to avoid masculinization: "We don't want them to be ignorant, nor to be know-it-alls; we don't want them to be flirtatious, nor do we want marimachos [tomboys]."[39] CJ's exaltation of motherhood equally resonated with Junco's idea of the home as "a feminine miracle" and with his call to defend the sanctity of marriage from "the great conspiracy against the mother."[40]

According to CJ, these strict hierarchies of the household were the basis for a nonsocialist organization of the state and the economy. It proposed an organic social-corporatist state where municipalities, unions, and associations mirrored that "natural order" of the family while providing "equality of opportunities for all Mexicans to develop as individuals."[41] This order would guarantee that cooperatives worked as the basic unit of economic activity, as a solution to demands of social justice, and as a form of economic citizenship. Corporatism, CJ claimed, was the triumph of the true, natural, hierarchical "organic democracy" over electoral politics and Right and Left dictatorships.[42]

These ideas were part of a global and national milieu that, after the Mexican Revolution, made its way into the platforms of the post-Cristero Right. These ranged from the sinarquista ideal of an anti-liberal communitarian Catholic state and ACM's grassroots-oriented Christian social order to the PAN's platform based on charity, private property, and class cooperation.[43] CJ's corporatism was also an expression of regiomontano attempts to provide a concrete answer to the PRI's system of patronage, which its members saw as an illegitimate organicist model. The "liberal corporatism" of Grupo Monterrey, for instance, emphasized freedom of enterprise, the protection of property and profits from state-sponsored or independent unions, and the promotion of conservative values, class harmony, and social peace.[44] As critics of the bourgeois liberal ethos that prized material gain, individual effort, and business savvy, CJ was ambivalent toward this entrepreneurial liberal corporatism. For its activists,

liberalism's disregard for spirituality and its indifference toward moral degrada-
tion and exploitation bred selfless men, driven by individual or class interests,
and produced a disjointed society.[45] This anti-liberalism seemed to contradict
the aspirational middle-class entrepreneurial values promoted at El Tec. As I
will further explain below, this divergence was the product of the relative plurality of regiomontano conservatism and the post-Cristero Right more broadly,
and also of CJ's appeal to a global fascist repertoire and their attraction to Third
Position platforms.

For CJ, the alternative to the alienation caused by liberalism and socialism
was an "authentic nationalism" that could create a system based on social solidarity and equal opportunity, free of class struggle, and respectful of the proletarian's individuality.[46] Like their intellectual mentors, those who joined CJ
sought to recast Mexico as a people with one history and one destiny, marked
by "the triumph of mestizaje [miscegenation]" and the birth of a "collective
consciousness" at the hands of a minority of "true Mexicans" dispersed through
the social body.[47]

CJ's nationalism contained other elements that placed the group beyond the
context of regiomontano conservatism and in dialogue with the history of the
global Right. For instance, the front page of its newsletter displayed the group's
symbol, an arrow cross, which for its activists signified universality, with its four
arrows indicating the four cardinal points and a blank center representing "the
unity of consciousness, vision, and spirituality." This was also the symbol of the
Arrow Cross Party, a fascist organization formed in Hungary in the 1930s.[48]
Other similar elements appeared interspersed in the newsletter, often uncited
and disguised as generic nationalist messages. For example, the dictum, "a nation
is great when its spiritual force is transferred into reality," matched CJ's rhetoric
of national vitality.[49] The phrase actually stems from a famous speech delivered
by Benito Mussolini in 1922, when he rallied a multitude of fascist followers
in Napoli. Similarly, the phrase "action without thought is barbarism; thought
without action is delirium" was widely used by CJ to celebrate its members as
men of action and reason.[50] It belonged to the founder of the Spanish Falange,
José Antonio Primo de Rivera, and it is still used by falangistas around the
world. Following this parade of the fascist pantheon, CJ dedicated a full front-
page article to Corneliu Codreanu, the Catholic-fascist leader of the Romanian
Iron Guard, whom CJ admired for his "revolutionary attitude" and leadership
skills. These unambiguous gestures were indications of an operation of "concealment," which historian Reto Hoffman has associated with what he calls

"the fascist effect." In CJ's rhetoric, we see the unspoken presence of an articulation of fascism that was "nationally specific and structurally transnational,"
with notions of masculinity, leadership, and morality that its members sought
to adapt to the entrepreneurial world, while connecting their nationalism to
other fellow travelers across time and space.[51] This ideological repertoire reveals
the local impacts of the historical web of relations built by the constellation
of the global Right, which this group construed in more specific Mexican and
regiomontano terms.

As part of this operation of "concealment," CJ insistently defined its movement as neither Left nor Right. CJ members, in fact, disdained the regiomontano entrepreneurial derechas for being too fixated with order, for turning a
blind eye on injustice, and for dismissing solidarity. For them, these derechas had
betrayed spiritual beliefs to amass material wealth and "occupy themselves with
the vain frivolities of consumer society." In contrast, they claimed to belong to the
derechas fighting "the oppression of bourgeois chains," while also embracing the
revolutionary Left's "desire to change society from one day to another" but under
the banner of national unity.[52] They also embraced the Third Position, a term associated with a sector of the Global Right that, in the 1960s and 1970s, proposed
a nationalist, anticapitalist, and anticommunist alternative based on corporatism
and the revolutionary dimension of fascism. In Asia, Europe, and Latin America,
these Third Position groups combined nationalism, communitarianism, and anti-
Semitism together with various leftist elements discussed by other authors in
this volume, such as Trotskyism, Maoism, anti-imperialism, and tercermundismo
(Third-Worldism).[53] Rejecting clear-cut ideological distinctions, they revered
global "national-revolutionary" figures from Codreanu and Mussolini to Juan
Perón and Ché Guevara, for them a national revolutionary warrior and martyr.[54]

CJ carved out a space for its activists within the spectrum of the global Third
Position by way of Peronism. The justicialismo of Juan Perón was attractive for
them due to its platform of humanism and Christian values, its rejection of class
struggle, and its claim to harmony between individuality and community, and
between matter and spirit.[55] In the context of the 1970s (with Perón's return to
the presidency and the resurgence of the extreme Right within his party), the
attraction to Peronism was a return to CJ's own nationally specific and structurally transnational sources—that is, a return to the corporatist, syndicalist,
and nationalist core cherished by the Mexican derechas of the 1930s and 1940s,
and which its members shared, in many respects, with their counterparts in the
Americas and across the Atlantic.

The members of CJ did not limit themselves to esoteric discussions about man and nation, to ideological proselytism, nor to these implicit or explicit forms of neofascist affiliation. They also commented, with biting critique, about political events in Mexico and the world, often in accordance with the open defiance of regiomontano business organizations toward President Luis Echeverría. On the occasion of Echeverría's 1974 presidential address, for instance, an editorial in the CJ newsletter pointed to the president's failure to appeal to middle-class concerns. CJ did not mention the conflict caused by the introduction of sexual education in public school textbooks, which elicited protests by conservative organizations in Monterrey and across the country. Instead, CJ's critique addressed its idea of reorganizing the economy under a social corporatist system. In view of its members, the middle class was the sector most affected by Echeverría's erratic economic policies, by the legacies of statization and collectivization, and by the regime's refusal to conceive models of private property to substitute ejidos (communal lands). They rejected state intervention while retaining the notion that private property ought to have a social function (an important tenet of Catholic social doctrine). They also expressed concerns about Echeverría's foreign policy, particularly his openness to build bonds with the socialist world, which the organization feared would leave Mexico exposed to the interventionism of Cuba and China. They were equally discontent with the breaking of relations with Franco's Spain and Pinochet's Chile, nations with which, they claimed, Mexico had "shared values."[56] In contrast to groups like MURO, CJ seldom referred to the activities of the revolutionary Left as a problem. Yet when its leaders did so, their critiques focused on the chaotic policies of Echeverría and his alleged leniency toward the Left.[57]

Startlingly, CJ made no references to the failed kidnapping and killing of Eugenio Garza Sada, Grupo Monterrey's most emblematic figure. Attributed to the revolutionary leftist group Liga Comunista 23 de Septiembre (23rd of September Communist League, LC23S, which had Monterrey as one of its main centers of activity), the death of Garza Sada (in December 1973) sparked a large civic mobilization, including a work stoppage by thousands of workers affiliated with the Grupo's company unions who took to the streets to mourn the regiomontano magnate. Garza's coffin was taken to El Tec, where some five thousand students paid homage to the institution's founder and benefactor. During the burial at the cemetery of La Purísima, the head of Grupo Monterrey's advisory council, Ricardo Margaín, gave a public speech accusing the federal government of Echeverría for its infamous attacks on the private sector and alleged tolerance of Marxism.[58] Coinciding with a sharp economic downturn, and in the context of Echeverría's neopopulist redistributive policies, rumors of governmental complicity in the killing of Sada represented the highest point in the confrontation between Echeverría and the private sector. As Louise Walker notes, government anxieties about middle-class discontent and the spread of rumors about currency devaluations and capital flight were central to mutually reinforcing narratives of conspiracy: while regiomontano entrepreneurs insisted on Echeverría's complicity with Marxists home and abroad, government agents surveilled the political activities of Grupo Monterrey to back the official narrative of a "fascist" onslaught led by these elites.[59]

In 1975, Echeverría's breaking of relations with Spain in protest for the execution of five leftist and nationalist guerrilleros forced CJ to pose a critique of the contradictions between foreign and domestic policy, shedding light on the views that the group held with respect to political violence. Its leaders asked, "How can one defend the guerrilleros . . . [the so-called] paladins of liberty, when they have murdered police officers?" In that case, they noted, "Lucio Cabañas and all the members of the Liga Comunista 23 de Septiembre would be national heroes and we should let them continue killing police officers. In this light, how can we condemn the repression in Spain and not recall the repression of October of 68 and June of 1971 in Mexico?"[60]

Combined with their silence about the killing of Garza Sada at the hands of LC23S, CJ's invocation of such paradigmatic examples of state repression is particularly intriguing, as it seemed to run counter to mainstream conservative views that disdained protesters/victims while supporting the government's authoritarianism. However, I would argue, their observations on the contradictions of Mexico's foreign policy stances and the low tolerance for internal dissent were ultimately part of a broader critique of the government's loss of authority and of the perception that the country was being "dragged towards a dictatorship of the Castroist type."[61]

CONCLUSION: CONCIENCIA JOVEN AND MEXICO'S "OLD" NEW RIGHT

Despite its reduced membership and small sphere of action, CJ holds a much broader significance for the study of the Mexican derechas. Its rhetoric, intellectual genealogy, and symbols place the group on the wide spectrum of the Right, pushing us to reframe the historical constitution of the Mexican derechas as oppositional actors embedded in national and regional contexts and yet shaped by transnational trends. With its deceiving challenge to Left/Right distinctions, CJ is in fact quite revealing of the ways in which the global Right underwent a process of pluralization, spanning the rebirth of neofascist violence as terrorism, the revitalization of religious extremism, and the proliferation of Third Position national-revolutionary projects that allowed for otherwise unconventional "contact zones" between the two extremes of the ideological spectrum. Unlike the clandestine and violent models of other right-wing student organizations such as MURO or Los Tecos, CJ's Third Position sought to reconcile a deep-seated conservative nationalism with somewhat atypical claims for social justice. Its members appealed to "revolutionary" traditions within their own intellectual and political milieu, embracing social corporatist ideas, the cultural nationalism of right-wing critics of the postrevolutionary state, and a divergent mix of symbols and discursive tropes from a variety of right-wing, fascist, and neofascist ideologies, including the Peronist Right, Spanish falangismo, and European Catholic fascism.

Bearing the deadweight of these intellectual and political currents, CJ was the product of a specific matrix of regiomontano values and political culture that, under the shadow of Grupo Monterrey's social hegemony, grew increasingly confrontational with the PRI regime, particularly during the group's brief existence (1974–77). Inextricably linked to the political disaffections of the post-Cristero Right, this confrontation originated in the conflicts over secularism and in the perceived excessive interventionism of the federal government in labor disputes. By the 1960s, the state of Nuevo León became an important stage for leftist student and labor movements, and for conservative groups that reacted to both the radicalizing effects of the Cuban Revolution and to the transformations of certain notions of family, gender, and sexuality that characterized this period. Unlike other right-wing groups, CJ said little regarding the reforms that took place within the Church in the aftermath of the Second Vatican Council. Instead, it focused its attention on the regime's neopopulist turn but also spouted critiques against other derechas for their unfettered materialism and their renunciation of the common good. Here I have argued that the radical conservatism of these students from El Tec was a platform of right-wing dissidence that aligned CJ with other actors contesting the regime. However, CJ's anti-liberalism and its Third Position neofascist gestures located this regiomontano youth organization in an ideological fringe with respect to its context. And yet, as we research and learn more about other similar organizations elsewhere in Latin America and Europe, we can treat them as indications of a larger reconfiguration of right-wing politics with both local and global reverberations.

To the extent that the identity and political repertoire of the post-Cristero Right had a historical claim to "dissidence," and that this dissidence was not limited to the national scale, the experience of CJ sheds light on how right-wing youth understood "tradition" as the product of transnational currents, subject to adjustment and adaptation, and as an instrument to interpret and intervene in its own context. In rejecting Left and Right distinctions, these young regiomontano activists sought to redefine the boundaries of conservatism as a form of radicalism to persuade and transform the men and women of their generation.

NOTES

I would like to thank Jaime Pensado and Enrique Ochoa for their patient work as editors and for their mindful feedback on this chapter. Federico Finchelstein provided valuable comments on earlier drafts and invited me to discuss this text with students from his seminar on fascism and populism at The New School. I also thank the anonymous reviewers from the University of Arizona Press for their observations and suggestions, and all the contributors for the productive conversations that gave way to this volume.

1   See Mammone, *Transnational Neofascism in France and Italy*.
2.   See, among others, Keller, *Mexico's Cold War*; Aviña, *Specters of Revolution*; and Oikión Solano and García Ugarte, *Movimientos Armados en México*. For a recent exception, see Pensado, "'To Assault with the Truth.'"
3.   On the different derechas, see the collection of essays in Pani, *Conservadurismo y derechas en la historia de México*; and Collado Herrera, *Las derechas en el México contemporáneo*.
4.   See Walker, *Waking from the Dream*.
5.   See, among others, Meyer, *La Cristiada*; Fallaw, *Religion and State Formation in Post-Revolutionary Mexico*; and Dormady, *Primitive Revolution*.
6.   Meyer, *La Cristiada*, t. 1, 389–90.
7.   See, for example, Capistrán Garza, *La Iglesia Católica y la Revolución Mexicana*.
8.   Niblo, *Mexico in the 1940s*, 82–83.
9.   Snodgrass, *Deference and Defiance in Monterrey*, 202–28; Nuncio, *El Grupo Monterrey*, 71–74.
10.   Nuncio, *El Grupo Monterrey*, 83.
11.   Camp, *Entrepreneurs and Politics in Twentieth-Century Mexico*, 210–11.

12. Ibid., 163–64.

13. Fuentes Mares, *Monterrey, una ciudad creadora y sus capitanes*, 58–60. Emphasis is in the original.

14. On the limited capacity of the postrevolutionary state to curtail these challenges, see Hamilton, *Limits of State Autonomy*. On the conflicts between the regiomontano private sector and the postrevolutionary state, see Saragoza, *Monterrey Elite and the Mexican State, 1880–1940*. See also Camp, *Entrepreneurs and Politics*.

15. Nuncio, *El Grupo Monterrey*, 61–62, 102–106.

16. On the contested meanings of the idea of Christian social order, see Andes and Young, *Local Church, Global Church*.

17. On MURO and FUA, see González Ruiz, *MURO: Memorias y testimonios: 1961–2002*; Dávila Peralta, *Las Santas Batallas*; and Gema Santamaria's chapter in this volume.

18. Nuncio, *El Grupo Monterrey*, 83–92.

19. "Declaración de principios de la Cruzada Regional Anti-Comunista," *Cruzada Regional Anticomunista: Mensaje Quincenal*, no. 9 (February 20, 1962): 2–3.

20. Tirado, "Los empresarios y la derecha en México."

21. Treviño Villarreal, *El Sabinazo*, 109–18.

22. Fuentes Mares, *Monterrey*, 155.

23. On Los Tecos, see Romero, "El movimiento fascista en Guadalajara," 31–102.

24. Torres Martínez, "Monterrey Rebelde 1970–1973," 40–50.

25. "Personalidad," *Conciencia Joven*, no. 1 (September 1974): 1.

26. "Actividades de Conciencia Joven," *Conciencia Joven*, no. 1 (September 1974): 1.

27. These ideas seem to stem from Vasconcelos, *La raza cósmica*.

28. "Hombre nuevo," *Conciencia Joven*, no. 1 (September 1974): 2.

29. "Identidad," *Conciencia Joven*, no. 1 (September 1974): 1.

30. See Guisa y Azevedo, *Hispanidad y germanismo*; Alfonso Junco, *España en carne viva*.

31. Payne, *A History of Fascism, 1914–1945*, 261–62.

32. Guevara, "Socialism and Man in Cuba," 216.

33. Ibid., 218.

34. Ibid., 224.

35. Carrel, *Man, the Unknown*, 220–21.

36. Ibid., 75; "La mujer, segundo principio ideológico de Conciencia Joven," *Conciencia Joven*, no. 2 (December 1974): 2.

37. "¿Es el feminismo una trampa de la sociedad de consumo?" *Conciencia Joven*, no. 5 (October–November 1975): 3.

38. "La mujer," 1–2.

39. Junco, *Cuatro Puntos Cardinales*, 26.

40. Ibid., 12.

41. "La sociedad: Tercer principio ideológico de Conciencia Joven," *Conciencia Joven*, no. 4 (June 1975): 2.

42. "Algo nuevo y mejor," *Conciencia Joven*, no. 11 (January 1977): 2–3.
43. See Espinosa, "Restoring Christian Social Order"; Meyer, *El Sinarquismo, El Cardenismo y la Iglesia, 1937–1947*. On the global diffusion of corporatism, see Costa Pinto and Palomanes Martinho, *A onda corporativa corporativismo*.
44. On "liberal corporatism" in the Mexican private sector, see Luna, "¿Hacia un corporativismo liberal?"
45. "La persona, primer principio ideológico de Conciencia Joven," *Conciencia Joven*, no. 2 (December 1974): 1.
46. "Las derechas, las izquierdas, y nuestras aspiraciones," *Conciencia Joven*, no. 3 (March 1975): 3.
47. "Conciencia histórica" *Conciencia Joven*, no. 5 (October–November 1975): 4. Like Vasconcelos, Junco saw *mestizaje* as the essence of *mexicanidad* and as having "solved the indigenous question." Junco, *Cuatro Puntos Cardinales*, 57–59.
48. On the Arrow Cross Party, see Hanebrink, *In Defense of Christian Hungary*.
49. "La nación, cuarto principio ideológico de Conciencia Joven," *Conciencia Joven*, no. 6 (December 1975–January 1976): 1.
50. *Conciencia Joven*, no. 6 (December 1975–January 1976): 2.
51. Hoffman, *The Fascist Effect*, 2–5.
52. "Conociendo a Conciencia Joven," *Conciencia Joven*, no. 5 (October–November 1975): 3.
53. On the links between neofascism and leftist radicalism, see Panvini, *Ordine nero, guerriglia rossa*.
54. On the reception of Che Guevara by European neofascists, see La Ferla, *L'altro Che*.
55. "Justicialismo," *Conciencia Joven*, no. 5 (October–November 1975): 1. On the Peronist Right, see Finchelstein, *Ideological Origins of the Dirty War*. "Justicialismo" refers to the "Third Position" or "middle way" taken by Perón between communism and capitalism.
56. "Algunos comentarios al IV Informe," *Conciencia Joven*, no. 2 (December 1974): 2.
57. "Cuando el rio suena . . . agua lleva," *Conciencia Joven*, no. 10 (February 1977): 1.
58. Fuentes Mares, *Monterrey*, 200–202.
59. Walker, *Waking from the Dream*, 63–66.
60. "¿Franco y Echeverria, o España y México?", *Conciencia Joven*, no. 5 (October–November 1975): 2.
61. Córdova Olmedo, "El fuero de los españoles y los mexicanos sin fuero," *Conciencia Joven*, no. 6 (December 1975–January 1976): 6.

BIBLIOGRAPHY
PRIMARY SOURCES

Conciencia Joven
Cruzada Regional Anticomunista: Mensaje Quincenal

SECONDARY SOURCES

Andes, Stephen J. C., and Julia Young. *Local Church, Global Church: Catholic Activism in Latin America from Rerum Novarum To Vatican II.* Washington, D.C.: Catholic University of America, 2016.

Aviña, Alexander. *Specters of Revolution: Peasant Guerrillas in the Cold War Mexican Countryside.* New York: Oxford University Press, 2014.

Camp, Roderic Ai. *Entrepreneurs and Politics in Twentieth-Century Mexico.* Oxford: Oxford University Press, 1989.

Capistrán Garza, René. *La Iglesia Católica y la Revolución Mexicana: Prontuario de ideas políticas.* Mexico City: Editorial Atisbos, 1964.

Carrel, Alexis. *Man, the Unknown.* London: Wilco Publishing, 1959.

Collado Herrera, María del Carmen, ed. *Las derechas en el México contemporáneo.* Mexico City: Instituto de Investigaciones Dr. José María Luis Mora, 2015.

Costa Pinto, António, and Francisco Palomanes Martinho. *A onda corporativa corporativismo e ditaduras na Europa e na América Latina.* Rio de Janeiro: FGV, 2016.

Dávila Peralta, Nicolás. *Las Santas Batallas: La derecha anticomunista en Puebla.* Puebla, Mexico: BUAP, 2003.

Dormady, Jason. *Primitive Revolution: Restorationist Religion and the Idea of the Mexican Revolution, 1940–1968.* Albuquerque: University of New Mexico Press, 2011.

Espinosa, David. "Restoring Christian Social Order: The Mexican Catholic Youth Association," *The Americas* 59, no. 4 (2003): 451–74.

Fallaw, Ben. *Religion and State Formation in Postrevolutionary Mexico.* Durham, N.C.: Duke University Press, 2003.

Finchelstein, Federico. *The Ideological Origins of the Dirty War: Fascism, Populism, and Dictatorship in Twentieth Century Argentina.* Oxford: Oxford University Press, 2014.

Fuentes Mares, José. *Monterrey, una ciudad creadora y sus capitanes.* Mexico City: Editorial Jus, 1976.

González Ruiz, Edgar. *MURO: Memorias y testimonios: 1961–2002.* Puebla: BUAP, 2004.

Guevara, Ché. *Che Guevara Reader: Writings on Politics and Revolution.* Melbourne, Australia: Ocean Press, 2003.

Guisa y Azevedo, Jesús. *Hispanidad y germanismo.* Mexico City: Polis, 1945.

Hamilton, Nora. *The Limits of State Autonomy: Post-Revolutionary Mexico.* Princeton, N.J.: Princeton University Press, 1982.

Hanebrink, Paul A. *In Defense of Christian Hungary: Religion, Nationalism, and Antisemitism, 1890–1944.* Ithaca, N.Y.: Cornell University Press, 2006.

Hoffman, Reto. *The Fascist Effect: Japan and Italy, 1915–1952.* Ithaca, N.Y.: Cornell University Press, 2015.

Junco, Alfonso. *Cuatro puntos cardinales: La madre, la propiedad, la estirpe, la bandera.* Mexico City: Instituto Cultural Hispano-Mexicano, 1963.

———. *España en carne viva.* Mexico City: Ediciones Botas, 1946.

Keller, Renata. *Mexico's Cold War: Cuba, the United States, and the Legacy of the Mexican Revolution.* Cambridge: Cambridge University Press, 2015.

La Ferla, Mario. *L'altro Che.* Viterbo, Italy: Stampa Alternativa, 2009.

Luna, Matilde. "¿Hacia un corporativismo liberal? Los empresarios y el corporativismo." *Estudios Sociológicos* 15 (1987): 455–76.

Mammone, Andrea. *Transnational Neofascism in France and Italy.* Cambridge: Cambridge University Press, 2015.

Meyer, Jean. *El Sinarquismo, El Cardenismo y la Iglesia, 1937–1947.* Mexico City: Tusquets, 2003.

———. *La Cristiada.* Vol. 3. Mexico City: Siglo XXI, 1994.

Niblo, Stephen R. *Mexico in the 1940s: Modernity, Politics, and Corruption.* Wilmington, Del.: Scholarly Resources, 1999.

Nuncio, Abraham. *El Grupo Monterrey.* Mexico City: Nueva Imagen, 1982.

Oikión Solano, Verónica, and Marta Eugenia García Ugarte, eds. *Movimientos Armados en México, Siglo XX.* Vol. 2, *La Guerrilla en la Segunda Mitad del Siglo.* Zamora, Mexico: El Colegio de Michoacán; CIESAS; UNAM, 2006.

Pani, Erika, ed. *Conservadurismo y derechas en la historia de México.* Vols. 1 and 2. Mexico City: Fondo de Cultura Económica, 2009.

Panvini, Guido. *Ordine nero, guerriglia rossa: La violenza politica nell'italia degli anni Sessanta e Settanta (1966–1975).* Torino, Italy: G. Einaudi, 2009.

Payne, Stanley. *A History of Fascism, 1914–1945.* Madison: University of Wisconsin Press, 1996.

Pensado, Jaime M. "'To Assault with the Truth': The Revitalization of Conservative Militancy in Mexico During the Global Sixties." *The Americas* 70, no. 3 (January 2014): 489–521.

Romero, Laura. "El movimiento fascista en Guadalajara." In *Perspectivas de los Movimientos Sociales en la Región Centro-Occidente,* edited by Jaime Tamayo. Mexico City: Línea R, 1986.

Saragoza, Alex. *The Monterrey Elite and the Mexican State, 1880–1940.* Austin: University of Texas Press, 1988.

Snodgrass, Michael. *Deference and Defiance in Monterrey: Workers, Paternalism, and Revolution in Mexico, 1890–1950.* New York: Cambridge University Press, 2003.

Tirado, Ricardo. "Los empresarios y la derecha en México." *Revista Mexicana de Sociologia* 47, no. 1 (1985): 105–23.

Torres Martínez, Héctor Daniel. "Monterrey Rebelde 1970–1973. Un estudio sobre la guerrilla urbana, la sedición armada y sus representaciones colectivas." Master's thesis, El Colegio de San Luis, 2014.

Treviño Villarreal, Héctor Jaime. *El Sabinazo.* Monterrey, Mexico: Universidad Autónoma de Nuevo León, 2013.

Vasconcelos, José. *La raza cósmica: Misión de la raza iberoamericana.* Madrid: Agencia Mundial de Librería, 1925.

Walker, Louise. *Waking from the Dream: Mexico's Middle Classes After 1968.* Stanford, Calif.: Stanford University Press, 2013.

11

"THE DARKEST AND MOST SHAMEFUL PAGE IN THE UNIVERSITY'S HISTORY"

Mobs, Riots, and Student Violence in 1960s–1970s Puebla

GEMA SANTAMARÍA

A RIOT BROKE OUT ON July 10, 1968, in front of the house of Dr. Arturo Santillana, the *oficial mayor* (senior officer) of the Universidad Autónoma de Puebla (Autonomous University of Puebla, UAP). Lasting more than nine hours, this violent incident allegedly involved hundreds of students and more than forty pistoleros. The clashing groups were reportedly armed with stones, clubs, pistols, petrol bombs, and machine guns. The confrontation resulted in the assassination of a seventeen-year-old high school student, Marco Aurelio Aparicio, who was shot in the head. Dozens of students were also injured. According to local and national newspapers, the violent confrontation was primarily driven by the political differences that had come to characterize student elections at UAP during the 1960s. Violence escalated after high school and university students marched toward the university to protest the attacks perpetrated earlier that day by a group led by Ernesto Santillana, Arturo's brother. Ernesto had visited Benito Juárez High School to promote the faction he and his brother supported. However, Ernesto and his group were not welcomed by the high schoolers. Following this rejection, he and his followers responded with violence. It was after these attacks that high school and university students decided to organize a protest.

Newspaper accounts differ on the unfolding of the events. Some claim that on their way to the UAP a group of protesters stopped outside of Arturo Santillana's house and started throwing stones with the intention of lynching Ernesto and his allies.[1] Others explain that it was Ernesto and his more than forty gunmen who first fired at the crowd (reckoned to be in the thousands).[2] Violence went on for hours without the intervention of the police or local authorities. The unrest further escalated after protesters arrived at Santillana's house in one of the buses they had hijacked earlier that day. In retaliation, Santillana's gunmen threw petrol bombs at the protesters, setting the bus and, accidently, one of the neighboring houses on fire. Students representing both factions resisted police intervention. Protesters broke through the police security ring with a bus, while the Santillana gunmen resisted arrest after ignoring the promise made by the chief of the police, who reportedly told them that they would receive fair treatment. In the end, it took two hundred policemen and the use of tear gas to disperse the crowd and get Arturo, Ernesto, and their gunmen out of their house.

The two Santillana brothers were taken to the San Juan de Dios municipal prison. Interviewed there after the incident, Dr. Arturo Santillana denounced the attacks against his private property. He also stated that while his family had always sympathized with the Left, the group that attacked him and his house was clearly composed of "communists" whose aim was to "instigate terror."[3] The student protesters, for their part, marched behind the coffin carrying Marco Aurelio's body with signs demanding retribution. One of these signs read, "The university demands the maximum [penalty] for the Santillinista murderers." According to the protesters, "the guilty parties" included Santillana, his "apologists," and the government.[4]

In an article published on July 12 by the local newspaper, *La Prensa*, the university council called this incident "the darkest and most shameful page in the university's history."[5] However, as will become evident in this chapter, the episode was hardly the darkest page in the history of Puebla's university or its student movement. Many riots, assassinations, street brawls, and lynchings took place in Puebla during the 1960s and 1970s. Some of these violent episodes occurred in reaction to the different factions of the student movement that proliferated in Puebla. Other riots were also organized in support of the movement. A look at both of these antagonistic groups allows us to highlight a few elements regarding the relationship between violence and the student movement outside the nation's capital. First, it shows that in Puebla violence was used by students and against students, even if it involved the covert (and at times overt) participation of the state, including its security forces, professional gunmen, and agents provocateurs. Secondly, it illustrates that, despite the dominant narrative provided by Puebla's public opinion, student violence was not a byproduct of "external forces" or "foreign ideologies" operating in the state. Rather, this history of student violence was grounded in a local history.

Largely informed by the Tlatelolco massacre of October 2, 1968, and the profound impact this repression left on the memory and history of the student movement, scholarly accounts have tended to a privileged top-down and state-centered approach to our understanding of student violence.[6] In this chapter I question such an approach by bringing to the fore the many expressions of violence endorsed and perpetrated by students, be it against, or in conjunction with, other nonstate actors such as workers, farmers, and bus drivers. My purpose here is not to deny the importance of state-sponsored violence and the impact it had on students, particularly on those who sympathized with the Left or challenged the status quo. Rather, my aim is to pluralize our understanding of the broad range of competing actors that shaped the organization of violence during these decades. Furthermore, like the other contributors in this volume, I aim at "provincializing" Mexico's Cold War and the violence it precipitated in the country. I do so by highlighting the particular trajectory of anticommunism and conservatism in Puebla and its place within *poblano* (Pueblan) society in the 1960s and 1970s. It is against this regional context, I argue, that we need to analyze both students' inclinations to resort to violence and poblanos' apparent tolerance toward the potential repression of students.

Based mainly on a detailed reading of local newspapers and on the analysis of a series of events that marked Puebla's student movement, this chapter advances two arguments. First, that students' recourse to violence (kidnappings, the hijacking of buses, riots, and street fights) reflected a climate wherein violence constituted an effective means to press demands and advance political interests. Even when it was publicly condemned, the use of violence as a means to engage in politics was neither exceptional nor limited to the students. Furthermore, violence was at times condoned by public opinion so long as the situation was deemed appropriate (that is, to restore the peace, order, and morality of the state). Secondly, it argues that references to the Cold War provided a reductionist and easily graspable schema to understand student violence. These references were well reflected in newspaper allusions to communist "infiltration" or to "foreign" and "exotic" ideas aimed at destabilizing the nation. In the case of conservative groups and right-wing student organizations, these Cold War imaginaries provided a useful and effective means that helped them to assert themselves as "authentic" and "patriotic" actors that needed to resist a "deceitful" and "infiltrated" Left. For liberal and leftist students, the communist/anticommunist schema was actually detrimental inasmuch as it served to obscure, rather than advance, their interest to reform and democratize the university. As will be clear through the seven different yet emblematic vignettes that I present in this chapter, the Cold War was undoubtedly a reference point for student mobilizations, but its impact and reach was ultimately mediated by Puebla's own conflictive relationship between leftist and conservative ideologies.

The use of local newspapers to trace the dynamics of student violence deserves some clarification. Local newspapers such as *La Opinión* and *El Sol de Puebla* maintained a close relationship with Puebla's political and economic elites and served, oftentimes, as the government's mouthpiece. Furthermore, they promoted an anticommunist ideology combined with a strong sense of nationalism that echoed the official rhetoric and that was overall antagonistic toward leftist students. In this sense, the narrative offered by newspapers about the student movement was far from being impartial, and its "truthfulness" cannot be taken at face value. Nonetheless, when read alongside other sources—including secondary sources and interviews—newspapers offer an important window into the discourses, public imaginaries, and shared anxieties that informed Puebla's public opinion. These discourses and imaginaries, I argue, contributed in shaping the responses and attitudes articulated by different segments of poblano society toward students.

THE SPECTER OF COMMUNISM

On April 6, 1961, a student protest took place against the implementation of a "limited" telephone service (*servicio medido*) that, according to the protesters, would make customers pay an extra fee for additional phone calls. Despite its local nature, newspaper reports framed this protest in the broader context of the Cold War. For example, echoing what other newspapers reported, *El Sol de Puebla* stressed that the declarations against the servicio medido and its impact on Puebla's economy were followed by provocative speeches against the United States and in favor of Fidel Castro.[7] The article also reported damages against private property, including vandalized cars and coffee shops. It then lamented that the actual telephone issue had been hijacked by what the author referred to as "professional agitators." The author further stressed the alleged manipulation of "real" students as follows: "Unfortunately . . . the young students . . . were used as 'cannon fodder' by experienced agitators . . . who made students repeat their praises to Russia and their diatribes against the United States."[8]

According to the same article, a group of "authentic" students met with people from the newspaper after the incident. In the meeting, the students confirmed one more time that external elements to the student movement had provoked the damages. An editorial published the following day echoed this opinion by stating that external elements had taken advantage of the protest to instigate disorder in the city. The editorial referred to how "authentic" university students were busy at this time of the year preparing and performing theater plays, developing literacy campaigns, and training for the next pentathlon competitions.[9] In other words, the so-called "authentic students" were not involved in politics and less so in politics that ended up in vandalism. In reference to the telephone service demonstration, an op-ed published in the *Washington Post* referred to the "usually excitable and easy to mold" character of the student body in Latin American countries and described it as a fertile ground for skillful communist rabble-rousers.[10] As these contradicting accounts suggest, student protesters who engaged in provocative politics were either unauthentic or non-representative of the student body, or they were malleable and naïve. Moreover, because of both their "incendiary" behavior and alleged naïveté, students were considered easy prey for "the specter of communism" haunting Puebla.

MORAL ANXIETIES

Public opinion considered youth susceptible not only to communist ideas but also to "immoral" practices, ranging from vagrancy and the use of drugs to libertine behavior. For instance, newspapers condemned the use of drugs among youth and referred to it as a direct cause of violent and deviant behavior among youngsters.[11] They furthermore warned about the presence of so-called hippies in the state, who were supposedly responsible for spreading sexual diseases and vices.[12]

Newspapers furthermore encouraged, if not all-out lectured parents to supervise their children in order to secure their proper behavior inside and outside their homes. For example, exactly ten days after the telephone service protest, a newspaper article reported on a fight that took place among three students. According to the article, the skirmish ended with one of the students being shot.[13] The article attributed the incident to the irresponsibility of parents who had allegedly failed to supervise their children and prevent them from attending school armed with knives and pistols. The article served as a warning to all parents about the "imminent breakdown" of child and youth morality that had reportedly come to characterize Puebla during this period. Members of Puebla's private sector were particularly vocal when it came to urging parents to provide proper guidance for their children. In an interview with the press, representatives of the private sector expressed their concern about the future of Puebla's youth and called for the active involvement of parents in extirpating "the carcinogenic cells that endanger the vitality and unity of poblano society."[14]

The same month, the Moral Commission for the Improvement of the Municipality of Puebla announced that it would take firm actions to combat the growing problem of vagrancy among the poor. They argued that homeless youth were frequently recruited as agents provocateurs in student politics.[15] In short, public concern and rejection of communism coexisted with moral anxieties. In Puebla, as further evident in dozens of similar newspaper reports, many of these anxieties were often expressed with religious overtones and shared by conservative poblanos who often saw the counterculture and especially the Cuban Revolution as real threats to their society.

THE CUBAN "THREAT"

The moral and political anxieties related to the Cold War reached a boiling point during a student rally organized in support of the Cuban Revolution on the night of April 17, 1961. Specifically, the students joined the rally to condemn the involvement of the United States during the Bay of Pigs invasion. Approximately 250 students joined the protest, shouting "Cuba yes, Yanquis no."[16] By and large, most newspaper articles described these students as "professional agitators" who had incited violence and promoted acts of vandalism against private property.[17] The articles also cited attacks on a dozen policemen who, upon their arrival at the place of the rally, were allegedly received with stones, bottles, and petrol bombs. Students were accused of damaging private property, smashing cars, breaking windows, and vandalizing the central offices of *El Sol de Puebla*. By contrast, the commander of the military zone, General Ramón Rodríguez Familiar, was frequently presented in the press in a favorable light. A representative article, for example, reported that he arrived at the site with two other soldiers and successfully put an end to the riot. According to this interpretation, Rodríguez Familiar warned the crowd that he would not tolerate disorder, and if military force was necessary to guarantee public tranquility, he would not hesitate to use them.[18]

Influential members of the Catholic Church also voiced their concern. On April 22, 1961, Pedro Velázquez, the director of the Secretariado Social Mexicano (Social Secretariat of Mexico, SSM), commented on the student protest in an address given to the Church and a pro-family association, the Movimiento Familiar Cristiano (Christian Family Movement, MFC) of Puebla. Echoing the conservative reports in the newspapers, he also commented on the dangers of communism, as follows: "We should not close our eyes. Communism wants power in order to impose its dictatorship in Mexico and the world."[19] Like others, he praised the actions of General Rodríguez Familiar and regretted that "strange elements," many of them "foreign professors" and other "violators of the good conscience," had been allowed into the university to corrupt the youth. He reminded his audience that Catholics should unequivocally embrace the cry "Catholicism Yes, Communism No!" and urged poblanos to come in defense of the "liberty, dignity, and traditions" of the homeland.[20]

Velázquez's speech was just a prelude to the massive anticommunist rally planned for April 24. Announced with dozens of leaflets covering the walls of the university and other surrounding buildings, the rally was organized by the Frente Universitario Anticomunista (University Anticommunist Front, FUA).[21] It brought together hundreds of people—including university students and high school students from private high schools—who denounced not only the university's "communist infiltration" but also the "red invasion" of Cuba, Mexico, and other Latin American countries. During the rally, demonstrators uttered the "Viva Cristo Rey" ("Long Live Christ the King") cry in addition to the slogan "Catholicism Yes, Communism No!"[22] The former cry, with unequivocal Cristero undertones, appealed to a strand of anticommunism ideology that preceded the Cold War and that was rooted in Puebla's own trajectory of conservative and reactionary politics.[23]

After a group of university students opposing the demonstration arrived at the rally, a violent confrontation broke out between the two factions. According to the press, the fight involved the use of stones, bottles, clubs, and pieces of wood. This time, there was no mention of firearms. However, as in the past, the newspapers once again insisted that "exotic ideas" had infiltrated student politics in Puebla.[24]

A group of liberal students retaliated the next day by assaulting the private Catholic school, Colegio Benavente.[25] Once apprehended by the local authorities, students were held responsible for extensive damages to the school's building and were further accused before the public ministry of the crime of "social dissolution."[26] As stated in article 145 of the criminal code, this crime was directed toward any individual who "promoted ideas, programs, or actions of any foreign government disturbing the public order."[27] The Benavente incident was thus framed as an action allegedly driven by the interests or agendas of "foreign entities." Most importantly, as further emphasized in the various chapters in this volume, students were treated as "political enemies."

The attack to the Colegio Benavente provoked the outrage of conservative poblanos. Representative leaders of the Catholic Church as well as Puebla's most influential business associations further contributed to the criminalization of youth. The state's chamber of commerce announced the suspension of all commercial activities until authorities could guarantee the safety of private businesses.[28] Similarly, the Catholic Church strengthened its moral campaign and urged its people to resist all foreign ideologies that were irreconcilable with the Christian faith.[29] In this effort, the Church dedicated the year 1961 to the Sacred Heart of Jesus and invited its followers to honor the Holy Virgin Mary, whose sacredness had been allegedly defiled by the actions of communists.[30]

Student members of the FUA directorate, Manuel Antonio Díaz and Fernando Rodríguez Concha, sympathized with the anticommunist crusade of the Church. They explained to the press that the violent incidents that had unfolded in Puebla over the last days were provoked by well-known pro-Castro and pro-Soviet communist provocateurs.[31] Among these alleged provocateurs was Enrique Cabrera, a "militant of Soviet communism" who had just returned from Cuba with a group of "communist agitators" who had participated in the railway strikes of 1958. Similar accusations were made by the FUA during additional protests in 1961, particularly when liberal and leftist students joined forces with peasants, small farmers, and unionized workers.

CAROLINOS VS. FUAS

On May 1, 1961, a group of liberal students who demanded the democratization and modernization of the university took over the school and forced the conservative rector, Armando Guerra Fernández, to resign.[32] In his place, they named Jorge Ávila Parra as the new head of the university.[33] FUA students retaliated and came in support of Guerra Fernández, effectively dividing the student population into two factions: the "Carolinos" and the FUAs. The former defended the observance of Article 3 of the Constitution, which guaranteed the public and lay character of education, while the latter proclaimed that university curricula should reflect the values of Christian civilization.[34] Driven by political differences, the division between liberal and conservative students was also underpinned by class and educational background. Whereas most conservative students came from private and Catholic schools that served the privileged classes of Puebla, liberal students, by contrast, were overwhelmingly working- or middle-class students who had studied at public high schools either in Puebla City or its surrounding towns.[35]

Although ignored or overlooked by the conservative press, the demands to secularize and modernize the university were central to the student movement. It was these demands, not "communism," that gave cohesiveness to liberal and leftist students. As remembered by José de Jesús Romero, an Atlixco physician and mathematician who took part in the 1961 events, the possibility to democratize the highly conservative university (the only one in the state) was seen as a necessary step to bring about a more modern and scientifically oriented instruction.[36] In describing the university as a "convent," he recalls both the university and its authorities as follows: "The maximum authority was the Honor Council.[37] [They] were members of the Knights of Columbus [who] were extremely religious." They used to organize "a solemn mass next to the Carolino, the older building of the university." These and similar rituals made the university "a backward place, very, very, backward." He then goes on to say, "We wanted a university that was better, where there were graduate degrees, a greater number of scholarships, faculties, more things. That's what the students demanded. But no, they thought it was the communists who were infiltrating, who were getting in here." Indeed, as further evidenced in additional student testimonies, liberal students wanted to reform an institution that was controlled by Puebla's conservative factions. Furthermore, they wanted to transform an institution that was clearly limited in terms of its capacity to carry out scientific and humanistic research.[38]

For science students like Romero, admiration for the Soviet Union had nothing to do with politics. Rather, it had more to do with Soviet scientific achievements. Furthermore, for liberal students like Romero, the conservative, corrupt, and oppressive environment of the university appeared at odds with the liberating and youthful politics of the 1960s. Yet, as Puebla's own conservatism weighed upon the students' struggle, the FUA and other conservative actors in Puebla insisted on superimposing the communist/anticommunist schema.[39]

The conflicts surrounding the reform of the university would last several months. State governor Fausto Ortega was reluctant to intervene in the conflict, largely due to the different pressures he faced at both the local and federal level, which included a dominant conservative elite in Puebla and a relatively more open and progressive elite in the central government. By then, Julio Glockner had become the preferred candidate for liberal students, whereas Armando Guerra Fernández continued to enjoy the support of conservative factions.

On May 15, 1961, the archbishop of Puebla intervened in the student conflict by devoting an entire pastoral letter to the issue of communism. In the letter, which was meant to be read in all of Puebla's Catholic churches during the Sunday sermon, the archbishop warned his flock about the imminent threat posed by communism and asked them to stay alert. He further reminded them of the importance of defending Catholic values: "Let's raise our voice with all energy in defense of the Christian civilization and of the highest values it has. Let us defend the family, the human person . . . liberty, order, authority, religion, our motherland."[40]

That same day a riot broke out among more than a hundred liberal and conservative students. This time three policemen and two students were severely injured. Reportedly, the policemen had been instructed to dissolve and repress any disorder, even if it meant using force against the students. Still, a few policemen were injured. According to a police officer interviewed by the press, the students threw stones at them and then pushed them to the floor, where they started to kick them. Other students defended the policemen and were able to bring them inside the university to clean their wounds. Yet a second group of students also responded and allegedly shouted that they wanted the policemen killed and hanged. The Red Cross arrived just in time before the mob could take them back.[41] Only in August of that year, with the presence of the army and the arrival of liberal Arturo Fernández Aguirre as rector of the university, did Puebla experienced some months of relative peace.[42] A new wave of violence would return three years later.

FOREIGN INFILTRATION?

In August 1964, Puebla's governor, General Antonio Nava Castillo, announced a new law that would make the pasteurization of milk mandatory for all milk producers in the state. The government justified the law as a measure to improve the quality of milk and get rid of the disease and malnourishment produced by *leche bronca* (raw milk).[43] However, the urban poor resisted the law, claiming that it would increase milk prices. Small milk producers agreed and also opposed the law. They believed it would only benefit large producers, including the state's governor, who co-owned a pasteurization plant. The pressure exercised by the protesters was such that Nava Castillo was forced to resign by the end of October.[44]

The series of violent confrontations surrounding the pasteurization of milk offers important insights into the relationship between the student movement and the local demands articulated by the popular classes in Puebla. In particular, it shows how students became more engaged with social and popular demands in the state that went beyond the university and that had nothing to do with a foreign communist plot. The confrontation began on October 13, 1964, when more than two hundred people, including small producers, UAP students, and members of the independent peasants' union, the Central Campesina Independiente (Independent Peasant Center, CCI), organized a protest to prevent the pasteurization law from coming into effect.[45] As in the past, the local government responded with violence by repressing the demonstration and apprehending several of the protesters, including the well-known communist leader and founder of the CCI, Ramón Danzós Palomino.[46]

The next day, hundreds of students marched from the UAP building toward the municipal offices to demand that students, CCI members, and milk producers be released from prison. The government stepped up its repressive apparatus by sending more than 150 armed policemen, including members of the judicial and preventive police, to control the crowd. The rally turned violent when police riding motorbikes drove into the protesters. The students responded by throwing stones at them and setting their motorbikes on fire. The situation escalated further when the police responded by firing gunshots at the students, while the latter, in turn, retaliated using stones and petrol bombs.[47] The encounter ended with sixty-nine people imprisoned and forty-four injured, including two students with gunshot wounds.[48]

On October 15, the press reported the resignation of two high-ranking police officers, stating that many "neutral observers" had criticized the brutality used by the police against students.[49] The governor, however, did not acknowledge the potential abuse of force on behalf of the police. Instead, the governor insisted that it was CCI members and their leader, Ramón Danzós Palomino, who were responsible for the disturbances and the violence that impacted students. He stated furthermore that communists were the only ones to be blamed, as they had provoked peasants and students to use violence by distributing to them .22-caliber pistols.[50]

Conservative groups supported the official version of the events published in the press. The chambers of commerce, industry, and tourism, together with parents' associations, condemned communist activists for having "put into the students' hands petrol bombs and having incited them to violence."[51] Despite the participation of local milk producers, CCI members, and students, these conservative organizations emphasized that the destabilizing elements came from "outside."

But students rejected claims of the presence and influence of external elements. In a public statement, the president of the student federation declared, "students were not interested in agitation or public disorder." Instead, he insisted, "they are only concerned with defending the interests of the pueblo." He described "the movement [as] authentic" and assured its critics that "inside the movement" there were "no strange elements."[52] Similarly, other students rejected any connection with communists or with any other political party and insisted that their demands were rooted in local grievances.[53] Specifically, the demands students presented to the government included the resignation of Governor Nava Castillo, the reprimand of the abusive elements of the police, the creation of a strictly civilian government, and the support of small milk producers through the subvention of pasteurization.[54] None of these demands pointed at, or made reference to, external ideologies or to global tendencies. Rather, students demanded the democratization of the state, a more transparent use of police force, and the support of milk producers.

The protest demanding the resignation of Governor Nava Castillo evolved into a massive student rally on October 23, 1964. Railroad workers, peasants, telephone unionized workers, and thousands of people from different sectors of society joined the students. The protesters warned participants that the government was distributing communist propaganda to generate confusion.[55] Yet, despite false accusations printed in the press, Nava Castillo announced his resignation by the end of the month.

Liberal and leftist students collaborated with the CCI during the protest. This was an influential organization originally created by members of the Mexican Communist Party (PCM). Nonetheless, in their efforts to reaffirm the validity and autonomy of their claims, students went out of their way to deny any connection with communist ideology. Instead, they framed their collaboration with the Left in its local context. This became particularly relevant in the late 1960s, as poblano students became further involved in a homegrown version of communism.

CANOA AND HOMEGROWN COMMUNISM

The lynching of five university workers from UAP in the small town of San Miguel Canoa on September 14, 1968, brought the connections between the CCI and the student movement to the fore.[56] It further illuminated how students' exposure to communist ideas was grounded in the local context and in what can be seen as a homegrown version of communism—an expression of communist ideology that had more to do with Puebla's own social and political demands than with an international plot to advance the interests of Cuba, Russia, or the global working class.

As recalled by Eva Contreras, a former student of architecture at UAP and member of the Communist Party in Atlixco, university students connected to the PCM were indeed familiarized with Soviet politics and a few of them even travelled to Russia, yet their activism was ultimately directed at showing solidarity with workers and peasants from Puebla and at countering the state's repressive policies.[57] San Miguel Canoa, a small community just twenty-three kilometers away from the city of Puebla, was precisely one of the towns visited by students as well as by PCM members in order to raise political awareness among peasants.

Taking place only a few weeks before the Tlatelolco massacre, the violent lynching in San Miguel Canoa has come to epitomize one of the most political violent episodes of Mexico's Cold War era.[58] The lynching is further considered a defining episode in the regional history of Puebla's student movement as well as the collective memory that exists of it.[59]

The five university workers who were lynched were passing by the town of San Miguel Canoa on their way to go hiking at the mountain, La Malinche. The workers, who were all in their early or mid-twenties, were wrongfully accused of being "communist students" by the people of San Miguel Canoa. The accusation instigated a large group of villagers, thought to be in the hundreds, to capture and subsequently beat the workers.[60] Two of the victims died from lethal machete injuries, while three survived after undergoing a long process of physical and psychological recovery. Although literature has tended to emphasize the violence perpetrated against the "outside" university workers, one of the victims of this lynching was actually a local. His name was Lucas García, a villager who had agreed to provide shelter to the university workers even after others had rejected them.

A member of the CCI, Lucas García was a critical opponent of the town's Catholic priest, Enrique Meza Pérez. For his part, the priest had strong connections to the local PRI party and ruled the town of San Miguel Canoa with an authoritarian grip. In his sermons, the priest promoted an image of CCI members as communists and infidels, and referred to students as a threat for the material and spiritual integrity of the community.[61] The town was mostly dominated by the PRI, but at least 15 out of 120 families supported the CCI at the time.[62] By then, university students had developed stronger ties with the CCI, and many of them supported the CCI and militant actions, including street demonstrations, invasion of lands, and the hijacking of public transportation buses.[63] In fact, just a few days before the lynching, university students had been in San Miguel Canoa and held a meeting with local members of the CCI and other residents of the town.[64] The five university workers, who were neither students nor communists, would bear the consequences of the students' incursion into the town.

The presence of students in this small town confirms that the student movement in Puebla had transformed from an exclusively urban and university-based activism to a broader political movement with strong ties to popular, peasant, and workers' organizations. It further reaffirms the fact that students were indeed connected to communist organizations. But these leftist organizations were homegrown. They were not byproducts of Soviet or Cuban infiltration, as widely claimed in the press.

STUDENT VIOLENCE DURING THE 1970S

Homegrown communism would gain greater visibility as a legitimate political force within the university during the 1970s. But as remembered by José de Jesús Romero, violent student confrontations would also follow suit. He explains, "It was a scandal, political assassinations started. . . . The right would not allow it, it did not view favorably that the left dominated the university."[65] One of the most well-known episodes of violence during the 1970s was the assassination of teacher and high school director Joel Arriaga in July of 1972 by professional pistoleros.[66] But as Eva Contreras explained, there were many more episodes, including confrontations between students and bus drivers over the hijacking of buses, as well as violent encounters among students from both the Left and Right who were now armed with guns inside the university campus.[67] She reflected on the polarization of student politics during the 1970s as follows: "I learned afterwards that some of them [leftist students] were armed . . . [a compañero] told us about the time when they hijacked various buses and all that; in that time, they did things that had not been approved before."[68]

Despite the greater levels of violence characterizing this period, the participation of women such as Contreras in the student movement increased considerably during the 1970s.[69] The university remained a highly masculinized environment, and the press insisted on reproducing an image of women along traditional gender lines.[70] Still, the number of female students registered in the university grew during the 1970s, as did their participation as student activists.[71]

The greater momentum attained by leftist and progressive ideas within the university made the 1970s a particularly explosive decade. As remembered by both Romero and Contreras, right-wing and conservative groups saw student activism as a threat to Puebla in general and to their university in particular. A stronger left-wing student body, with greater connections to the PCM as well as to Puebla's popular movements, was also at the center of this contentious university politics. The arrival of a local and homegrown version of communism to the university expressed both the strength of social mobilizations in the city and the countryside, and the weakening of a regional and conservative political class that had controlled the state over the last forty years.[72]

CONCLUSION

In this chapter I have sought to analyze and document the politics of violence characterizing the student movement in 1960s and 1970s Puebla. Specifically, in briefly illustrating seven emblematic examples, I have aimed at both provincializing and pluralizing our understanding of Puebla's student violence during the height of the Cold War period. Despite an official rhetoric that tends to represent students—particularly from the Left—as prone to being manipulated by foreign and "exotic" elements, I have argued that student activism and recourse to violence were grounded on local demands and regional politics. Be it the need to reform and modernize the university, or the demand to attend issues of social justice among Puebla's popular sectors, the discourses and actions of leftist students were informed by regional conditions. Even if students were well aware of the international context that surrounded them, what drove both factions of the student movement was their firm conviction to either transform (in the case of liberal and communist students) or maintain (in the case of conservatives) Puebla's social and political order.

Furthermore, students' use of violence reflected a political climate wherein violence was seen as a legitimate means to advance political demands. Puebla's public opinion condemned student violence and countercultural practices, but at the same time, it condoned "immoral" behavior and called upon a greater presence of the police and the military in order to repress students. Through practices of covert and overt repression, Puebla's authorities and political elites added to the violence characterizing students' activism.

The politics of student violence in Puebla was influenced by Cold War imaginaries that were prevalent at the time. Examples include references to a national and "authentic" political project that had to counter a "communist plot" planned from abroad. In reality, however, it was Puebla's own trajectory of conservative politics, together with a more local strand of communism, that shaped the history of the student movement during these years.

NOTES

I would like to thank the editors of this volume, Jaime Pensado and Enrique Ochoa, for their valuable comments on previous versions of this chapter.

1. "Sangriento disturbio estudiantil en Puebla: 2 muertos y 9 heridos," *El Heraldo de México*, July 11, 1968; "Versiones de los sucesos ocurridos en la ciudad de Puebla el miércoles," *El Día*, July 13, 1968.
2. "Violencia en Puebla: Mueren 2 estudiantes," *Excélsior*, July 11, 1968. Although the first newspaper accounts refer to the killing of two students (Marco Aurelio Aparicio and Aurelio Núñez), later it is established that only one student died.
3. "Versiones de los sucesos."
4. "Cientos de personas en el sepelio de estudiante Marco Aurelio Paulín," *El Universal*, July 13, 1968; see also IPS-MSR, July 13, 1968, Dirección General de Investigaciones Políticas y Sociales (hereafter IPS), Archivo General de la Nación (hereafter AGN), Caja 760.
5. "Una página vergonzosa," *La Prensa*, July 12, 1968.
6. See, among others, Poniatowska, *La noche de Tlatelolco*; and Carey, *Plaza of Sacrifices*.
7. "Mitín estudiantil degeneró en vandalismo," *El Sol de Puebla*, April 7, 1961.
8. Ibid.

9.   Felipe Morales, "Universitarias," *El Sol de Puebla*, April 8, 1961.
10. Bert Quint, "New tinge to quiet Mexican town," *Washington Post*, August 20, 1961.
11. "Cinco mariguanos irán a la carcel: Estaban fumando la droga cuando fueron detenidos," *La Opinión*, November 4, 1969; "Un drogadicto golpeó a un menor para asaltarlo," *La Opinión*, November 4, 1969.
12. "¡Esa plaga! Se filtran los 'hippies': Pero se les expulsará," *El Sol de Puebla*, March 6, 1969; "Escalofriante cacería de hippies en todo el país," *La Opinión*, January 8, 1969; "¿Qué es un hippie?," *La Opinión*, January 8, 1969; "Cinco mariguanos irán a la cárcel," *La Opinión*, November 4, 1969.
13. "Mortal balazo le pegaron a un estudiante," *El Sol de Puebla*, April 16, 1961.
14. "Orden y garantías, objetivos del movimiento del sector privado," *El Sol de Puebla*, April 27, 1961.
15. "Combatirán la vagancia y delincuencia infantil," *El Sol de Puebla*, April 7, 1961.
16. "Escandaloso mitin se registró anoche," *El Sol de Puebla*, April 18, 1961.
17. "Protestan los directivos de Facultades por el atentado contra nuestro edificio," *La Voz de Puebla*, April 18, 1961.
18. "Escandaloso mitin."
19. "¡Cristianismo sí, Comunismo no! Es el grito de México," *El Sol de Puebla*, April 23, 1961.
20. Ibid.
21. The FUA was created in April of 1955 with the aim of "defending the growing aggressiveness of the communists and masons inside the University of Puebla." Dávila Peralta, *Las Santas Batallas*, 100–101.
22. Pansters, "Social Movement and Discourse," 90–91.
23. In the context of Puebla, the "Viva Cristo Rey" cry served to articulate Catholics' discontent toward the socialist and anticlerical policies promoted by the central government during the 1920s and 1930s. See, among others, Vaughan, *Cultural Politics in Revolution*.
24. "Zacapela en el mitín anti-comunista de ayer," *El Sol de Puebla*, April 25, 1961.
25. The Colegio Benavente, together with other private Catholic schools, such as the Instituto Oriente and the Instituto Carlos Pereyra of Puebla, were behind the organization of the anticommunist rally. See Torres Septién, "Un demonio con cola y cuernos: El comunismo."
26. "Consignarán a los autores del escándalo de ayer," *La Voz de Puebla*, April 26, 1961; "Acusan de disolución social a los dirigieron el ataque al Benavente," *La Voz de Puebla*, April 26, 1961.
27. Suprema Corte de Justicia. Primera Sala. Sexta Época. Semanario Judicial de la Federación. Volumen LXIII, Segunda Parte, p. 27, accessed February 19, 2017, http://sjf.scjn.gob.mx/sjfsist/Documentos/Tesis/260/260102.pdf.
28. "El comercio cierra mañana viernes," *La Voz de Puebla*, April 26, 1961.
29. "Church Fights Reds, Defies Mexican Law: Telegrams Financed," *Christian Science Monitor*, July 1, 1961.
30. Sánchez Gavi, "Cultos y devociones."

31. "Acusan de disolución social a los dirigieron el ataque al Benavente," *La Voz de Puebla*, April 26, 1961.

32. "Renunció el rector hoy," *El Sol de Puebla*, May 2, 1961.

33. "Ahora tiene dos rectores la universidad," *La Voz de Puebla*, May 3, 1961.

34. Dávila Peralta, *Las Santas Batallas*, 127–28.

35. Ibid., 87.

36. Romero, author's interview.

37. The Honor Council and the Patronato Universitario were two of the highest organizations within the university. The governor chose the seven members of the Honor Council, who would then name the directors of each of the faculties or institutes of the university. Members of the Catholic hierarchy and Puebla's economic elite integrated the Patronato Universitario, created to bring greater funds to the university. See Pansters, "Social Movement and Discourse," 89.

38. Vergara Ortega, "La relación universidad–Estado," 88–89; see also Pansters, "Social Movement and Discourse," 93.

39. Pansters, "Social Movement and Discourse," 96.

40. "XV Carta Pastoral del Arzobispo de Puebla sobre el Comunismo Ateo," May 15, 1961, quoted in Peralta, *Las santas batallas*, 135.

41. "Zafarrancho, policías contra estudiantes," *La Voz de Puebla*, May 16, 1968; "Lentamente se restablecen los policías heridos en el sangriento zafarrancho," *La Voz de Puebla*, May 17, 1968.

42. Fernández Aguirre would quit in March of 1962.

43. "¡A Pasteurizarnos, Pues! Pero poco a poco," *La Voz de Puebla*, August 21, 1964; "Se generalizó ayer la escazes de leche bronca," *El Sol de Puebla*, October 17, 1964.

44. "Nava Castillo solicitó licencia," *El Sol de Puebla*, October 31, 1964.

45. "Desautorizan la manifestación de lecheros," *La Voz de Puebla*, October 13, 1964.

46. Dávila Peralta, *Las Santas Batallas*, 151.

47. "Tiros, bombas molotv, gases y heridos frente a la Universidad," *La Voz de Puebla*, October 13, 1964.

48. "Nava Castillo hace un llamado a la cordura de los estudiantes," *El Sol de Puebla*, October 15, 1964.

49. "Culpan y censura a los 'cuerpos de seguridad,'" *La Voz de Puebla*, October 15, 1964.

50. "Agitaron a los campesinos y azuzaron a la juventud," *El Sol de Puebla*, October 16, 1964.

51. "Condenan la violencia e ilegalidad los principales organismos sociales de Puebla," *El Sol de Puebla*, October 17, 1964.

52. "La aprobación de las siete peticiones exigen los estudiantes," *El Sol de Puebla*, October 17, 1964.

53. "Los universitarios rechazan todo nexo con los comunistas," *El Sol de Puebla*, October 18, 1964.

54. "Refrendan sus demandas," *El Sol de Puebla*, October 19, 1964.

55. "Encendidas diatribas contra el gobierno local en el mitin de anoche," *El Sol de Puebla*, October 24, 1964.

56. I have analyzed elsewhere the impact that Catholic religion and conservative politics had in the organization of this and other lynchings in Puebla. Santamaría, "Lynching, Religion and Politics in Twentieth-Century Puebla."
57. Contreras, author's interview. For similar accounts on the relation between Puebla's student movement and communism, see Vergara Ortega, "La relación universidad–Estado," 93–94; Ortega Morales, "El movimiento estudiantil poblano en 1968 y sus enseñanzas," 38–39.
58. Carey, *Plaza of Sacrifices*; Meaney, *Canoa: El crimen impune*.
59. Chrisman, "Community, Power and Memory."
60. "San Miguel Canoa," Versión Pública, Dirección Federal de Seguridad (DFS), AGN.
61. Meaney, *Canoa: El crimen impune*, 23, 28, 47.
62. Romero Melgarejo and Pech Matamoros, "La violencia por la disputa de los recursos del bosque," 183–94.
63. See, for instance, "Información de Puebla," September 11, 1974. Caja 1083, Exp 2, fojas 166–69, IPS-AGN; Peralta, *Las santas batallas*, 151–53.
64. "San Miguel Canoa," Versión Pública, Dirección Federal de Seguridad (DFS), AGN.
65. Romero, author's interview.
66. An active member of the Communist Party, Joel Arriaga was the director of Benito Juárez High School affiliated with the UAP. "Surge la violencia gangsteril: Asesinan al director de la prepa nocturna," *El Sol de Puebla*, July 22, 1972.
67. Contreras, author's interview. See also "Sangriento choque entre universitarios en Puebla," *El Heraldo de México*, July 2, 1971; "Más de 200 estudiantes en la balacera," *Excélsior*, August 7, 1971; "Balacera en la universiad polbana, siete lesionados," *Periódico Avance*, April 30, 1976; "Amenazan matar rehenes: Denuncia de los que ya fueron liberados," *La Prensa*, May 3, 1976.
68. Contreras, author's interview.
69. Tirado Villegas, "Las universitarias en el contexto violento."
70. Tirado Villegas and Rivera Gómez, "A cuarenta años del movimiento estudiantil," 37–38.
71. Ibid., 31.
72. Márquez Carrillo and Diéguez Delgadillo, "Política, Universidad y Sociedad en Puebla."

BIBLIOGRAPHY
ARCHIVES

Archivo General de la Nación, Mexico (AGN)
Hemeroteca *El Sol de Puebla*, Puebla, Mexico
Hemerota Nacional de México, UNAM, Mexico
Hemeroteca Pública "Juan Nepomuceno Troncoso," Puebla, Mexico

INTERVIEWS

Romero, José de Jesús. Author's Interview. Atlixco, Puebla, July 2, 2016.
Contreras, Eva. Author's Interview. Atlixco, Puebla, August 6, 2016.

NEWSPAPERS

Christian Science Monitor
El Día
El Heraldo de México
El Sol de Puebla
El Universal
Excélsior
La Opinión
La Prensa
La Voz de Puebla
Periódico Avance
Washington Post

OTHER PUBLISHED SOURCES

Carey, Elaine. *Plaza of Sacrifices: Gender, Power and Terror in 1968 Mexico*. Albuquerque: University of New Mexico Press, 2005.

Chrisman, Kevin M. "Community, Power and Memory in Díaz Ordaz's Mexico: The 1968 Lynching in San Miguel Canoa, Puebla." PhD diss., University of Nebraska, Lincoln, 2013.

Dávila Peralta, Nicolás. *Las Santas Batallas: La derecha anticomunista en Puebla*. Puebla: Benemérita Universidad Autónoma de Puebla, 2008.

Márquez Carrillo, Jesús, and Paz Diéguez Delgadillo. "Política, Universidad y Sociedad en Puebla, El Ascenso del Partido Comunista Mexicano en la UAP, 1970–1972." *Rhela* 11 (2008): 111–30.

Meaney, Guillermina. *Canoa: El crimen impune*. Mexico: Editorial Posada, 1977.

Ortega Morales, Luis. "El movimiento estudiantil poblano en 1968 y sus enseñanzas." In *Entorno al 68 en Puebla: Memoria y encuentros*, edited by Enrique Agüera Ibáñez, 37–74. Puebla: Benemérita Universidad Autónoma de Puebla, 2008.

Pansters, Wil. "Social Movement and Discourse: The Case of the University Reform Movement in 1961 in Puebla." *Bulletin of Latin American Research* 9, no. 1 (1990): 79–101.

Paxman, Andrew. "William Jenkins, Business Elites, and the Evolution of the Mexican State: 1910–1960." PhD diss., University of Texas at Austin, 2008.

Poniatowska, Elena. *La noche de Tlatelolco: Testimonios de historia oral*. Mexico: Ediciones Era, 1971.

Romero Melgarejo, Osvaldo, and Alessa Pech Matamoros. "La violencia por la disputa de los recursos del bosque: Transformaciones agrarias en la región del volcán La

Malinche." In *Naturaleza-Sociedad: Reflexiones desde la complejidad*, edited by Alberto Conde Flores, 183–94. Tlaxcala: Universidad de Tlaxcala, 2013.

Sánchez Gavi, José Luis. "Cultos y devociones: Reforzamiento de la identidad católica; el caso de Puebla y Tlaxcala a mediados del siglo XX." Paper presented at the II Congreso Nacional de Estudios Regionales y la Multidisciplinariedad en la Historia, Universidad Autónoma de Tlaxcala, April 28–30, 2011. Accessed November 1, 2017. http://filosofia.uatx.mx/SanchezGavi.pdf.

Santamaría, Gema. "Lynching, Religion and Politics in Twentieth-Century Puebla." In *The Americas and Europe*. Volume 2 of *Global Lynching and Collective Violence*, edited by Michael J. Pfeifer, 85–114. Urbana: University of Illinois Press, 2017.

Suprema Corte de Justicia. Primera Sala. Sexta Época. Semanario Judicial de la Federación. Volumen LXIII, Segunda Parte. Accessed February 19, 2017. http://sjf.scjn.gob.mx/sjfsist/Documentos/Tesis/260/260102.pdf.

Tirado Villegas, Gloria. "Las universitarias en el contexto violento de la Universidad Autónoma de Puebla, UAP, 1972–1973 (Puebla-México)." *Ánfora* 23, no. 40 (2016): 51–73.

Tirado Villegas, Gloria, and Elva Rivera Gómez. "A cuarenta años del movimiento estudiantil: Universitarias de los años setenta en la Universidad Autónoma de Puebla, México." *Cuadernos Intercambio sobre Centroamérica y el Caribe* 11, no. 1 (2014): 27–44.

Torres Septién, Valentina. "Un demonio con cola y cuernos: El comunismo." *Tiempo Universitario: Gaceta histórica de la BUAP* 4, no. 12 (2001). Accessed May 16, 2017. http://www.archivohistorico.buap.mx/tiempo/2001/num12.htm.

Vaughan, Mary K. *Cultural Politics in Revolution: Teachers, Peasants, and Schools in Mexico, 1930–1940*. Tucson: University of Arizona Press, 1997.

Vergara Ortega, Blanca Edith. "La relación universidad–Estado: La Benemérita Universidad Autónoma de Puebla en los sesenta y setenta." In *Entorno al 68 en Puebla: Memoria y encuentros*, edited by Enrique Agüera Ibáñez, 87–104. Puebla: Benemérita Universidad Autónoma de Puebla, 2008.

12

STUDENT ORGANIZING IN POST-1968 MEXICO CITY

The Coordinating Commission of the Committees
of Struggle and State Violence

VERÓNICA OIKIÓN SOLANO

IN THIS CHAPTER, I analyze the reconfiguration of the student movement in Mexico City in the aftermath of the October 2, 1968, Tlatelolco massacre. After the dissolution of the Consejo Nacional de Huelga (National Strike Council, CNH) on December 6, a new, more democratic formula of student representation emerged, one that sought to combine students from the different schools and faculties of the Instituto Politécnico Nacional (National Polytechnic Institute, IPN), the Universidad Nacional Autónoma de México (National Autonomous University of Mexico, UNAM), the Escuela Nacional de Maestros (National Teacher's College, ENM), the Escuela Nacional de Agricultura de Chapingo (Chapingo National School of Agriculture, ENACH), and the Universidad Iberoamericana (Ibero-American University, UIA). In this effort, the Comisión Coordinadora de Comités de Lucha or Comité Coordinador de Comités de Lucha (Coordinating Commission of Committees of Struggle), better known as "COCO," gave the post-1968 student movement in the capital city its second wind of activism and a new opportunity for realignment.[1]

The COCO was reproduced in individual educational institutions through student representatives who set up local Committees of Struggle.[2] The most effective of these Committees, and the ones that achieved broader coverage on campus, were those at IPN and UNAM. In these and other institutions of higher education and their respective secondary schools, the COCO functioned like a conveyor belt, providing a fluid track for communications with the overarching Coordinating Commission. The raison d'être of the COCO was to discuss and transmit student agreements; execute specific plans, directives, strategies, and political postures; organize assemblies and acts of defiance; and exert political pressure on school and national authorities. Student assemblies, organized at each of the different schools where the COCO was present, played a fundamental role in the priorities of the COCO and its commitment to democratic consensus. The Committees in charge of holding the student assemblies were conceived as both the engines that propelled the student movement and as the space where the most highly conscious activists joined forces. Collectively, they developed a movement that opposed the repressive nature of the state that had come to characterize the rigid *priísta* regime (the Institutional Revolutionary Party, PRI), particularly during the final two years of the government of Gustavo Díaz Ordaz (1969–70) and the subsequent regime of Luis Echeverría Álvarez (1970–76).

The Committees were composed of various, and at times conflicting, student actors. Some represented the militant bases of the Partido Comunista Mexicano (Mexican Communist Party, PCM), specifically its youth branch, the Juventud Comunista Mexicana (Communist Youth of Mexico, JCM).[3] Others represented multiple and competing left-wing organizations, including the Liga Comunista Espartaco (Spartacus Communist League, LCE), the Grupo Comunista Internacionalista (Communist Internationalist Group, GCI), and the Partido Obrero Revolucionario Trotskista (Revolutionary Workers Party Trotskyist, PORT). Correspondingly, the Committees were often polarized by various ideological differences. These were broadly grouped between "reformers" and "revolutionaries." Representing the former were various Committees at IPN and UNAM, which became bastions of an antiestablishment student movement that questioned the system as a whole and sought to build alliances with popular sectors. Representing the latter were those that abandoned student politics and instead joined the various struggles of armed resistance that proliferated across Mexico in the early 1970s.

HISTORIOGRAPHY AND THE IMPORTANCE OF STUDYING THE COCO

The literature on the 1968 student movement is vast and diverse and represents multiple methodological approaches. These have ranged from chronological narratives and journalistic accounts to interpretations that are both panoramic and specific. There are also competing interpretations representing distinct analytical and ideological approaches. Examples of these include iconic testimonies of protagonists with diverse political postures and more recent studies that contain invaluable graphic and visual memory. By and large, this is a growing literature that exposes the authoritarianism of the regime and marks 1968 as a watershed in political life in Mexico. The most recent interpretations frame the movement in the global context of the Cold War and often highlight the transnational aspects of 1968.[4] Yet as researchers continue to gather new and competing testimonies of the movement, it becomes evident that much work remains to be done.

This chapter contributes to the historiography by incorporating the COCO in post-1968 Mexico City. But my goal in this chapter is not only to fill in the literature gap and to give the COCO its rightful place in historical memory but also to expose the repressive nature of the state, which, despite its so-called democratic opening during the Echeverría administration, relied on a web of mafia-like interests and old mechanisms of control to repress post-1968 leftist student politics in general and the COCO in particular.

The COCO has never been examined in detail.[5] My purpose here is to present and discuss the political and sociocultural elements of the COCO and, in so doing, reveal the complexity of the post-1968 student movement. Unfortunately, the testimonials of student activists who joined the Committees are scarce and brief.[6] However, they reveal important details of the COCO experience and suggest ways to understand how, and with what political and ideological weapons, student activists stood up to and resisted the obstinacy that marked the final months of the Díaz Ordaz regime and the repressive years of Luis Echeverría. In addition, these sources shed light on the nuances and challenges associated with the political tactics championed by the various Committees during these years. These testimonies further point to student activists' various efforts and achievements to create a broad social and political movement in solidarity with the working-class, peasant, and popular sectors. Specifically, they point to one of the long-term goals of the COCO, which consisted of developing a new form of political action, independent of the state, capable of generating a true and democratic front of popular struggle led by what members of the movement envisioned as "relentless worker-student revolutionary committees."[7] Finally, these testimonies point to the multiple challenges the COCO faced during the years of its existence, from 1969 to 1972, including the Corpus Christi massacre, when dozens of students were killed on June 10, 1971, at the hands of a group of agents provocateurs ("Los Halcones," or "the Hawks") during the Echeverría administration.

Over the years of writing about radical student politics, I have collected numerous documents on student politics. More recently, I was fortunate to obtain a voluminous archive on this topic thanks to an unexpected offer from a used books dealer, which allowed me to write not only the history of the COCO in this chapter but also a recent study that I published on the Central Nacional de Estudiantes Democráticos (National Organization of Democratic Students, CNED).[8] CNED was an organization of the mid-1960s with local communist roots that questioned and successfully ruptured the corporatist model that the state had established inside the schools since the 1930s for the control of student activism. After the Tlatelolco massacre, CNED found itself superseded by the COCO. The surviving leaders of '68 welcomed the founding of the new organization and saw it as a last opportunity to reignite student mobilization and rekindle the fervor of the 1960s. As noted by a student flyer at the time, failing to remain active in post-1968 Mexico implied complicity with the repressive state: "Comrade, do not be silenced: Returning to class means betraying our people, leaving our comrades-in-arms in prison, and allowing gorillas to continue occupying schools."[9]

IN THE DARK YEARS, THE STRUGGLE WENT ON

As Adela Cedillo and Ricardo Gamboa have affirmed, the flame lit in 1968 was revived months later despite government prognoses that smugly assumed that the massacre in the Plaza of the Three Cultures had extinguished all traces of youthful rebellion. That reactivation was expressed in various forms of direct action that included the continued use of brigades as well as "the adoption of nonbureaucratic forms of doing politics and a new appreciation of the value of reaching out to people through popular, union-oriented and communitarian actions."[10]

The COCO was a student-led organization whose purpose differed slightly from that of the National Strike Council (CNH) in 1968. Primarily, its operations were marked by greater flexibility. For example, unlike the more rigid chapters of the CNH, the committees established by the COCO did not expect their members to attend all of the different meetings and assemblies. Instead, what mattered most, regardless of the political or ideological position of their members, was their "real commitment" to their specific "bases" and respective objectives.[11]

At the level of the student base, local Committees of Struggle strove to perform organizational tasks capable of keeping "the Movement's [objectives] and forms of struggle alive." As the 1968 student leader, Raúl Álvarez Garín, accurately described the COCO years later, the students saw the Committees as a vanguard body with a shared structure and a common mechanism of recruitment. There were multiple political-ideological questions articulated during this period, but, according to Álvarez Garín, despite the various disagreements in ideology, the entry of new members in all the different Committees was voluntary and required the collective approval of each of the different militants that composed the group. Moreover, as with any other political organization, "the fundamental criteria" depended on "clarity, militancy [and] a willingness to fight."[12]

It is difficult to determine the total number of leaders and members that comprised the various Committees of the COCO. A 1971 report by the Dirección General de Investigaciones Políticas y Sociales (General Office of Political and Social Research, DGIPS) recorded the names of at least fifty-nine student leaders representing various institutions of higher education and different ideological leanings.[13] In all likelihood, however, the total number of COCO activists far exceeded those noted by the government. We know, for example, that at least fifty high schools and universities were represented by the COCO in Mexico City from 1969 to 1972, putting the total number of COCO activists likely in the hundreds, if we also take into consideration the older generation of activists who remained politically engaged inside the schools after 1968 as well as the brigade members and ex-directors of the CNH who were not in jail and were active in the Committees. Considering the heterogeneity of the student body, it is logical, then, to assume that both student participation and their level of combativeness varied widely in the Committees at each of the different schools and campuses. However, not all schools welcomed the COCO, especially in 1969, partly due to the fear of repression. Nonetheless, the Committees that were indeed active inside several institutions were militant, as reflected in the pronouncements they publicized exhorting student bodies to discuss the documents produced in their respective assemblies "and with their comrades-in-arms." The central shared idea for most of the Committees was to reanimate the earlier mobilization of 1968, reaffirm its principal demands, and succeed in challenging state authoritarianism. In addition, they hoped to create a lasting link of support with the popular classes. They argued, "Not only do we call upon the state to satisfy [our] democratic and popular demands but . . . [also recognize] the tactics of struggle, political brigades, popular meetings, [and] massive demonstrations . . . that [we have] employed [and that have] enabled [us to create] a close relationship between students and the people."[14]

Due to the ever-present repression that came to characterize the post-1968 period, the COCO was not able to convoke massive protests or attract more activists. Yet despite these hardships, it did manage to maintain democratic representation in most schools of the nation's capital and successfully legitimated the importance of student assemblies. In these assemblies, students discussed "essential . . . political issues" and established a "broad capacity of convocation and great combativeness."[15] The issues discussed ranged from national concerns, including repressive government actions and public policies, such as educational reform, and international issues, such as the Vietnam War, the U.S. bombing of Cambodia, Third World liberation struggles, and North American imperialism, to more specific matters related to their respective Committees (e.g., student elections, school violence).

The Committees of Struggle were organized largely under the leadership of activists affiliated with the JCM, though, as noted earlier, many also came from other independent left-wing groups, such as those affiliated with Trotskyists, Spartacists, and Maoists.[16] As mentioned above, this often created ideological conflicts and confrontations among different factions. It also made it impossible to create a cohesive and unified movement. The student bases that composed the COCO mirrored the consciousness and collective commitment of their respective schools. In this setting, "there was resistance that carried the Movement toward dispersion."[17] Nonetheless, despite these divisions, "the voluntary, isolated and tenacious activity of the [various] vanguards" achieved much. Moreover, the Committees shared a common "struggle . . . [of] carrying on the fighting spirit that had been set aflame among students in 1968."[18]

THE COCO ON THE CENTER STAGE:
PROPOSALS AND IDEAS

The COCO issued its "July 26 Manifesto" in 1969. Delivered "by students to the people of Mexico" and widely endorsed by many schools at IPN and

UNAM, the manifesto framed the COCO as the vanguard of the student politics movement rooted in 1968, "For the students and the people who marched with us on those historic days [commemorating the importance of the Cuban Revolution], the date of July 26 will always hold a profound significance. The principles that motivated us then are stronger than ever."[19] This statement reaffirmed that the right to democratic freedom was an aspiration of the whole society, and demanded the release from prison of their incarcerated comrades, detained "for the crime of FIGHTING FOR THE PEOPLE." Also, it expressed solidarity with the relatives of the hundreds of young people whose blood had been spilled during the fateful days of the summer of 1968.[20] In this and similar documents, the commission insisted upon the need to "honor the memory of our fallen comrades by fighting in real and effective ways." Likewise, it called for an end to the firings of teachers and expulsions of students who had participated in the movement.[21]

The combative discourse of the COCO and its insistence on democracy was also evident in its central publication, *La Hoguera*, which was first published in 1969. Here, students inserted the goals of the COCO in the broader context of Latin America. They framed their movement in relation to the multiple student uprisings that erupted across the continent in the aftermath of the Cuban Revolution:

> July 26, which marked the beginning of the liberation of Latin American peoples from Yankee oppression, has for us, as well, special significance. [I]t marks the beginning of our commitment to the people. We are not living a time of celebrations, but one of combative struggles; all across the continent, students are performing the task of definitively joining the people's struggles, shoulder-to-shoulder with them. [T]heir fate is our fate, their triumph our triumph. [A]s students, we are a sector of the people.[22]

Seeking to achieve its revolutionary objectives and employing a language shared by most students of the Left, the COCO hoped to project a united student front to advance the student movement's goals and to prevent it "from suffering a regression in its political and popular positions." Moreover, in adopting this language, it aimed at developing and deepening "its revolutionary essence so as to cement it in a line of action capable of continuing the battle at the level demanded by the situation created after October 2."[23] The COCO also sought to create close links between the student movements and popular sectors in working-class neighborhoods and factories. They hoped "to foster, develop, and multiply" the Committees of Struggle of workers and poor and working-class communities that had been created over the course of the student movement, as "a bridge of union between our movement, the working class and the people in general." The purpose, in short, was to extend political action to all the people.[24]

In *La Holguera* and in other manifestos, the leadership of the COCO aimed at forging a collective student identity, capable of "consolidating the movement." This largely depended "on the influence that the people [members] exert upon it." For the COCO, the success of this new political force depended on the trust that they built with each other and in the principles of democracy, and on "a profound spirit of loyalty to the people."[25] In essence, the various writings implicitly expressed the COCO's goal of constructing a counterforce capable of challenging the authoritarian regime, treading a thin line that at times blurred the student identity by overlapping it with revolutionary rebelliousness. At the same time, this goal reaffirmed the COCO's deeply felt obligation to "carry forth the struggle by taking the offensive in popular neighborhoods, factories and fields, side-by-side with working people, the true producers of social wealth and the principal protagonists of the history of our country."[26]

By making the people the central actor of Mexican history, the COCO revealed its utopian intention of organizing a cross-class coalition (a goal never realized). In this framework, it underscored a profound sense of history by interlacing its own student struggle with the grand moments of political opposition that, according to the COCO, had marked the two previous decades of national life. In particular, they pointed to the summer of 1968 as the most important year in the history of postwar Mexico. For them, there was one Mexico before 1968 and a different Mexico after 1968. Other important events included "the violent repression of the railroad workers [in 1958]; the killings of peasants [throughout the 1950s and 1960s]; the brutal assassination of Rubén Jaramillo [in 1962]; the struggles of teachers, doctors, and workers [throughout the 1960s]; [and the] popular and student struggles in Morelia, Sonora, Tabasco, [and] Durango [in 1966–1967]."[27] While unmasking "the true repressive and antidemocratic character of the Mexican State," these protests, the COCO argued, had both intensified long years "of popular struggle" and had provided the student movement with the necessary tools for their movement, including "political brigades and popular and student committees of struggle." For the COCO, the success of its "future actions" depended on the "effectiveness" of these local organizations.[28]

CHALLENGING THE REGIME
THROUGH ELECTORAL ABSTENTION

The 1970 presidential elections provided the COCO with an important opportunity to activate its bases and further spell out its political objectives. Specifically, it called on the people to abstain from participating in the presidential
campaign and the elections. The COCO argued that absolutely nothing would
change "with the transition of power." After all, everyone knew that "[t]he elections are a farce, a mockery, that try to induce [people] to believe that democracy
exists. The new president will be elected behind the people's back through a
pact by the wealthy minority that holds power. As of today, we, the students,
manifest our repudiation of the electoral farce, denounce its antidemocratic
character, and call upon the people to actively manifest their rejection of electoral maneuvering."[29]

As the COCO denounced the election, it placed special emphasis on unmasking Luis Echeverría Alvarez. As secretary of interior, the COCO argued, he
had "bloodily" repressed "the popular-student movement of 1968." In their writings, students characterized him as a "member of the bourgeoisie," exclusively
interested in defending the needs of "the rich,"—the same group of "owners
of factories and lands" that had been complicit in the "murder and imprisonment" of those who fought against "earlier presidents." The COCO also
exhorted "working people" to refuse to become accomplices of the electoral
farce and, instead, boycott and repudiate it by destroying "graffiti, posters, and
everything else that made reference to the campaign."[30] What mattered most
for the COCO was to raise people's consciousness so that they could see for
themselves the importance of joining "the independent struggle," and in so
doing "rupture" their historical dependence on the government and take charge
of their own lives.[31] Members of the COCO played a key role in making the
boycott more effective, not only in the nation's capital but outside Mexico City
as well. There, in the various hometowns of its members, they were encouraged
to "help orient and organize workers and peasants." The COCO further noted
the significance of this strategy: "We must consider the importance of public
opinion . . . begin to create it today, by handing out fliers, giving talks, organizing
roundtable discussions on the problem of the elections [and] holding popular
festivals and assemblies where we can disseminate our points of view and invite
the townsfolk to support us and participate."[32]

As election day approached, the government realized that it needed to intensify its actions to counteract the abstentionist strategy proposed by the COCO's

leaders. As documented in *La Holguera*, huge amounts of money were flowing from "the PRI's coffers" "in an attempt to impede the combative participation of citizens during the upcoming elections." Specifically, the students noted that the party had delivered resources to agents who had infiltrated schools and universities faculties to bribe and silence influential students and COCO leaders.[33]

THE COCO'S REPUDIATION OF EDUCATIONAL REFORM

Once in power, Echeverría responded differently to student activism than had his predecessor. While state repression continued, new, more elaborate forms of mediation and co-optation also emerged. These were largely designed to curtail the independent initiatives that were blooming inside the universities and high schools largely as a result of the COCO. But he also sought to greatly expand public education, and this created further ideological tensions within the various Committees of Struggle within the COCO.

With a reformist and nationalist discourse, Echeverría proclaimed himself as the second coming of Lázaro Cárdenas. He announced his presidential candidacy with "a great reform of Mexican education," for which, he argued:

> It is necessary that we find national strategies to improve all actions and policies by the Mexican revolutionary state on behalf of the Mexican people; but is also necessary that we plan toward the productive activities of the country because the younger generations long to contribute to the growth, with social justice, of the national economy. This can only be achieved by a restructuring of the educational structure and the basic premises—from their roots—of the systems in which the young generations of peasants, workers, [and] students are educated in cities and in all those new social springboards that so vigorously contribute to the growth of our country. . . . Without a profound educational reform, the Mexican Revolution will not be able to accelerate its march.[34]

In this and similar statements, Echeverría repeatedly justified the legitimacy of his regime, and he consistently linked his government to the most progressive elements of the Mexican Revolution. For instance, he framed the "ambitious goals" of his educational reform "in its totality" in order to link "the growing demand for education" to the nation's urgent need to "raise its productivity, reduce [its] technology gap [with the developed world], and satisfy [its] demands for competent men in all fields" of industry. In short, the educational reform program had to raise "the consciousness" of the nation and all of its citizens to expand economic development. "We seek to foster participation and the willingness to change teachers, heads of family, young people, and society," he further noted, with the goal of developing "firm foundations" and undertaking a concrete "renovation of structures, methods, and systems."[35]

These principles for educational reform sounded innovative, even revolutionary. But the leaders of the COCO understood that they concealed the underlying objectives of Echeverría's regime: namely, to contain and neutralize political dissent while simultaneously reestablishing the consensus that the government had lost during the student movement of 1968.[36] In the midst of Echeverría's educational reform, the COCO's socio-educational proposal was squashed by the president's fiery rhetoric and effectively relegated to the shadows of a few university halls.

The COCO originally hoped to repudiate Echeverría's reform and propose measures that would modify Mexico's rigid and anachronistic system of higher education. Its members emphasized that student learning had a social function and that public education should not be utilized by capital to extract surplus, but instead it should be used to positively transform the conditions of the people and raise the socioeconomic development of the entire society. It was with this perspective that the leadership of the COCO called for legitimate inclusiveness. For them, the antidemocratic nature of the Echeverrista regime could not be disguised with populist rhetoric or guayaberas instead of business suits.[37] They were certain that Echeverría's efforts to contain the "relatively weak worker, peasant . . . [and] student movement[s]" would be complemented with "rigid . . . structural changes." They further warned the students that "although . . . sector[s] of the bourgeoisie might seek to [capitalize on Echeverría's so-called] aperture . . . [they] would not hesitate to resort to repressive tactical resources,"[38] which is precisely what happened, as we will see later in this chapter.

For the COCO, significant changes could not come from above in the form of direct state intervention. Rather, any form of real democratic opening— including educational reform—should come from below, in the form of a "united strength" led by the student movement and linked to the needs of the masses: "There can be no educational reform that is not implemented by students and teachers through their own efforts. [There can be] no . . . scientific [or] technological development [unless it is led by] scientists and technicians . . . in close contact with the people."

Thus, the role of the student was to "support and spearhead the Mexican revolutionary movement," a movement that, according to the COCO, had to be solidified in all schools and had to include specific projects incisively designed toward the "exterior"—that is, for the benefit of the masses.[39] For this, students had to work for the reformulation of their study programs and critically evaluate their involvement as activists. This latter point required a more efficient communication with the people: "The knowledge we acquired—despite what we believe—in no way equips us to discuss the most important scientific problems or the most transcendent social developments, and when we speak in front of educated people, all we do is display ignorance and coarseness."[40]

These considerations led the COCO to present a proposal that would extend semesters and increase the number of classes. The idea was to curb the increase in the number of students who failed their studies, curb rising dropout rates, and improve the quality of their courses. This proposal reflected the COCO's goal of regularizing school periods, which its leaders had first proposed in 1969. The COCO at IPN, for example, refused to support the atypical school year that educational authorities sought to impose in August 1969–July 1970 by organizing three semesters, each lasting less than three months. The COCO objected that it would be impossible to effectively cover the study programs involved in such a short time and stated that "effectuating these 'bird' courses, [of 'inferior' quality] meant there will be insufficient time for regularization." What students needed, the COCO argued, was not "absurd regulations that plagued" their schools, but more efficient, rigorous, and relevant academic programs.[41] Moreover, it lamented that many teachers were simply irresponsible instructors or ill-trained to provide quality education. Willingly, or otherwise, these teachers impeded student participation "in the integral formation of future professionals."[42]

AGAINST GANGSTER-STYLE CONTROL AND THE VIOLENCE GENERATED IN SCHOOLS

Porrismo, or student gangsterism, was another major problem the COCO faced inside schools. Since at least the 1950s, agents provocateurs had been under the protection of politicians and corrupt university authorities, including teachers who frequently relied on *porros* (thugs for hire) to serve their needs or those of the authoritarian regime. This mechanism of control and mediation, which championed clientelistic networks that competing authorities used to co-opt and/or repress students, served the administration of Luis Echeverría well.[43] The COCO denounced the precarious school environment that evolved during his administration and specifically accused porros not only of stealing school materials and looting, as had been the case in previous years, but also of engaging in more aggressive acts of provocation and sabotage that included the trafficking and consumption of drugs and alcoholic drinks; selling protection to transportation entrepreneurs and merchants; and assaulting, beating, intimidating, and even kidnapping and executing students, professors, and school authorities. Frequently, the COCO pointed to Vicente Méndez Rostro, the general director of the Escuela Nacional Preparatoria (National High School), and explicitly accused him of hiring groups of goons or shock troops that ravaged the high schools affiliated with UNAM.[44] To protect their schools, the COCO set out to "lead the fight against the goons," but called its members to do it in an organized way. Specifically, they called for the creation of "vanguard cells" in the form of "cultural groups" and "Committees of Struggle" with "as many students as possible." Collectively, the COCO proposed, "We must denounce the goons not only as groups of gangsters but as [tools] of governmental political repression. [Our job is] to organize and fight . . . for all revolutionaries, only in this way can we eradicate the thugs."[45]

The remarks made by the COCO were not far from the truth. The constant presence of nonstudent elements inside the schools came to characterize the preferred mechanism of repression in post-1968 Mexico City. Porrismo served as an extralegal mechanism of control and mediation orchestrated from the domes of power—that is, instruments manipulated by the corporativist and clientelist system. This reality is evident in Jaime Pensado's research on the cases of UNAM and IPN, which underscores the government's gangsterlike policies that allowed those shock troops to infiltrate virtually every high school and university with instructions to discourage student activism and generate reigns of terror. According to Pensado, agents provocateurs had been present since the 1950s, but they played a greater role in the aftermath of the Tlatelolco massacre.[46] As understood by the COCO, "thuggery and goons" were the equivalent of "the lack of democracy in our schools." In response, the COCO urged students to not only denounce such acts but also to complement their cultural groups and Committees of Struggle with militant "self-defense groups," composed of at least twenty or thirty students capable of confronting "reactionary violence with the revolutionary violence."[47]

FINAL CONSIDERATIONS

The COCO, as the vanguard of the student movement in Mexico City, strove to pick up the pieces from the debacle of the summer of '68. The goal of the COCO was to convert the political praxis of the movement by exposing the "repressive and antidemocratic character of the Mexican State."[48]

The COCO that represented the various student bases in local Committees of Struggle aimed at motivating the larger student body with the slogan "Fight while you study," articulating it clearly and forcefully through diverse mobilizations and heartfelt demands. These demands included the release of comrades held as political prisoners, an end to political persecution, a complete crackdown of all porro groups, a true university reform from below, and a new and real democratic aperture at public universities. At the same time, the various groups that comprised the COCO developed and promoted ideological debates with the shared goal of counterpowering and confronting the Mexican State.

The COCO also welcomed self-criticism and acknowledged that it often fell short in achieving its objectives. For example, its support for the democratization of the Universidad Autónoma de Nuevo León (Autonomous University of Nuevo León, UANL) not only fell on deaf ears but the often-clandestine nature of its student bases also failed to expose the student repression that took place in Monterrey at the hands of local and national authorities.[49] The same was true on June 10, 1971, when the state unleashed its full force of repression in the nation's capital. Known as the *halconazo*, this second student massacre stopped the COCO in its tracks, impeding its capacity to convoke students and diluting its combativeness. In the aftermath of the massacre, the Committees of Struggle practically "disappeared at most schools and nothing emerged to replace them."[50]

The 1971 student massacre that effectively put an end to the COCO took place during Echeverría's "democratic opening." This was a time that coincided with both the escalation of porrismo and the co-optation of some of the COCO's central demands. Porros played an instrumental role for the control apparatus of the regime by disarticulating the collective action of the Committees of Struggle and implementing an unprecedented use of aggressive violence that, in turn, forced students to respond with violence. The numerous battles, widely reported in the newspapers, brought both tension and fear to the schools and outrage to the public. Thus, paradoxically, violence became the underlying layer that students utilized as they strove to construct a less unequal society, and one with democratic aspirations.

Government vigilance of schools and the everyday harassment of students were part and parcel of a well-planned tactic of the Echeverría administration that mediatized or annulled any initiatives that began to emerge in schools to carry out projects of collective action and political radicalization. Porros formed their own spurious "committees of struggle in which corruption and disorder discredited the [legitimate student] movement and caused confusion among students."[51] The COCO exposed the pseudo student committees and in the broader context of Latin America presented the administration of Echeverría not as a democratic champion of the Third World, but as an authoritarian and repressive regime akin to the military dictatorships in South America. Similarly, the COCO presented its movement as a continental struggle that fought for a "radical transformation of the existing economic and political structure."[52] Adopting the radical language of their Latin American counterparts, especially after the Corpus Cristi massacre, the few isolated voices that remained active in the COCO continued to call for destruction of "the exploitative regime that oppresses [its] people."[53] For many of them, there was only one option: the route of armed violence.[54]

NOTES

1. Throughout the text, I use the abbreviation COCO to refer to both the Coordinating Commission of Committees of Struggle and the Committees of Struggle at each educational institution (Committees, for short).

2. Grupo Zapata-Lenin, "El movimiento estudiantil y nuestras tareas políticas actuales," n.d., Archivo General de la Nación de México (hereinafter AGNM), Fondo de la Secretaría de Gobernación, Sección Dirección General de Investigaciones Políticas y Sociales (hereinafter FDGIPS), box 1604-B, 10–12.

3. "Nueva fase de la lucha," *Debate Ideológico, órgano de los comunistas de las escuelas superiores UNAM/IPN*, no. 3 (April 1, 1969), personal archives of Verónica Oikión Solano (hereinafter AVOS), El Colegio de Michoacán (Zamora, Michoacán, Mexico).

4. For a recent review of the literature, see Rivas Ontiveros, Sánchez Sáenz, and Tirado Villegas, *Historia y memoria*.

5. Some approximations can be seen in Cedillo and Gamboa, "Interpretaciones sobre los espacios"; and Rivas Ontiveros, *La izquierda estudiantil en la UNAM*.

6. Some exceptions can be found in Ortega Juárez, *El otro camino*; Ortega Juárez, *10 de junio*; Álvarez Garín, *La Estela de Tlatelolco*; and Jardón, *Travesía a Ítaca*.

7. Comités Revolucionarios Obrero-Estudiantiles, "Respuesta al V Informe Presidencial," in *Prensa Revolucionaria, órgano central de los Comités Revolucionarios Obrero-Estudiantiles*, no. 5 (September 1969), in AVOS.

8. Oikión Solano, "La Central Nacional de Estudiantes Democráticos."

9. E.S.F.M. I.P.N., Untitled flier, n.d., in AVOS.

10. Cedillo and Gamboa, "Interpretaciones sobre los espacios," 81.

11. Ibid., 83.

12. Álvarez Garín, *La Estela de Tlatelolco*, 216.

13. The most iconic of these leaders include Salvador Ruiz Villegas, Salvador Martínez Della Roca, Raúl Moreno Wonche, Raúl Jardón Guardiola, Benito Collantes, Jesús Vargas Valdez, Enrique Sevilla González, Alfonso Peralta, Germinal Pérez Plata, and Teódulo Trejo Osorio. See "Miembros de los distintos comités de lucha, integrantes del Comité Coordinador de Comités de Lucha UNAM-IPN-Chapingo-Normal Superior-Universidad Iberoamericana," (two dates appear in the document: May 31, 1971, and September 30, 1971), in AGNM/FDGIPS, box 2011-B, exp. 3.

14. Coordinating Commission, UNAM, "Compañeros estudiantes," n.d. [c. May 1, 1969], in AVOS.

15. Álvarez Garín, *La Estela de Tlatelolco*, 216–17.

16. "Nueva fase de la lucha," *Debate Ideológico*, no. 3 (April 1, 1969), in AVOS.

17. Álvarez Garín, *La Estela de Tlatelolco*, 216.

18. Guevara Niebla, *La democracia en la calle*, 55–56.

19. COCO, "Manifiesto 26 de Julio: De los estudiantes al Pueblo de México," *La Hoguera, órgano de información del Comité Coordinador Conjunto*, July 26, 1969, 3, in AVOS.

20. Coordinating Commission, UNAM, "Compañeros Estudiantes," n.d. [c. May 1, 1969], in AVOS (capital letters in the original).

21. COCO, "Compañeros" (September 23, 1969), in AVOS.

22. COCO, "Manifiesto 26 de Julio," 3.

23. Ibid., 16.

24. Ibid.

25. Ibid. See also "Respuesta al V Informe de Gobierno del Sr. Díaz Ordaz," *Prensa Revolucionaria*, no. 5 (September 1969), in AVOS.

26. COCO, "Manifiesto 26 de Julio," 16.

27. Ibid., 8.

28. Coordinating Commission, UNAM, "Compañeros estudiantes."

29. COCO, "Manifiesto 26 de Julio," 8.

30. Brigadas populares IPN, "No a la farsa electoral", n.d. (c. 1969–70), in AVOS.

31. COCO, "Compañeros" (September 23, 1969).

32. Ibid.

33. "La Línea del PRI y del Gobierno en la Universidad y el IPN," *La Hoguera*, July 26, 1969, 13–14, in AVOS.

34. "Tercera etapa: Candidato Luis Echeverría. Ideario."

35. Echeverría, "Documento 1," 27–29.

36. Rivas Ontiveros, *La izquierda estudiantil*, 647.

37. Grupo Zapata-Lenin, "El movimiento estudiantil," 2.

38. Ibid., 4.

39. Ibid.

40. "La rebelión de los enanos," *El Mortero, órgano del seminario de estudios de ingeniería bioquímica*, no. 3 (October 1970): 2, in AVOS.

41. Comité Coordinador de Comités de Lucha del I.P.N., "A los compañeros estudiantes del I.P.N.," August 18, 1969, in AVOS.

42. "Ingeniería . . . ¿Un problema de presupuesto?" *El Mortero*, no. 3 (October 1970): 3, in AVOS.

43. On porrismo, see Pensado, *Rebel Mexico*; Durón, *Yo, Porro*; Condés Lara, *Represión y rebelión en México*; Rivas Ontiveros, *La izquierda estudiantil*.

44. "Biografía de las Porras (7 años de gansterismo) (1962–1969)," *La Hoguera*, July 26, 1969, 9–12, 14, in AVOS.

45. "2 de Octubre 1968 Tlatelolco México: Dos años después," *La Internacional*, no. 12, n.d. (c. October 1970): 6, in AVOS.

46. Pensado, *Rebel Mexico*, 185–93, 197–99.

47. COCO, "Compañeros" (September 23, 1969).

48. Coordinating Commission, UNAM, "Compañeros Estudiantes."

49. Ortega Juárez, *10 de junio: ¡Ganamos la calle!*

50. Álvarez Garín, *La Estela de Tlatelolco*, 217.

51. Durón, *Yo, Porro*, 262–63.

52. Coordinating Commission, UNAM, "Compañeros Estudiantes."

53. Ibid.

54. COCO of UNAM, IPN, Normales, and the UIA, "Manifiesto 10 de junio" (July 1971), cited in both Rivas Ontiveros, *La izquierda estudiantil*, 822–25; and Ortega Juárez, *10 de junio: ¡Ganamos la calle!*, 135–42.

BIBLIOGRAPHY
ARCHIVES

AGNM: Archivo General de la Nación de México
  FDGIPS: Fondo de la Secretaría de Gobernación, Sección Dirección General de Investigaciones Políticas y Sociales
AVOS: Archivo Personal de Verónica Oikión Solano
El Colegio de Michoacán, Zamora, Michoacán, México

PUBLISHED SOURCES

Álvarez Garín, Raúl. *La Estela de Tlatelolco: Una reconstrucción histórica del movimiento estudiantil del 68*. Mexico City: Editorial Grijalbo, 1998.

Cedillo, Adela, and Ricardo Gamboa. "Interpretaciones sobre los espacios de participación política después del 10 de junio de 1971 en México." In *Violencia y sociedad. Un hito en la historia de las izquierdas en América Latina*, edited by Verónica Oikión Solano, 79–110. Morelia: Instituto de Investigaciones Históricas de la Universidad Michoacana de San Nicolás de Hidalgo and El Colegio de Michoacán, 2010.

Condés Lara, Enrique. *Represión y rebelión en México (1959–1985): Los años dorados del priato y los pilares ocultos del poder*. Vol. 2. Mexico City: Miguel Ángel Porrúa, 2007.

De Garay, Graciela, ed. *Para pensar el tiempo presente: Aproximaciones teórico-metodológicas y experiencias empíricas*. Mexico City: Instituto Mora, 2007.

Durón, Olga. *Yo, Porro (Retrato hablado)*. Mexico City: Editorial Posada, 1984.

Echeverría, Luis. "Documento 1." In *Informes de Gobierno 1971–1973*, 27–29. Mexico City: Complejo Editorial Mexicano, 1974.

Guevara Niebla, Gilberto. *La democracia en la calle: Crónica del movimiento estudiantil mexicano*. Mexico City: Siglo XXI, 1988.

Jardón, Raúl. *Travesía a Ítaca: Recuerdos de un militante de izquierda (del comunismo al zapatismo, 1965–2001)*. Mexico City: Grupo Editorial Cenzontle, 2008.

Oikión Solano, Verónica. "La Central Nacional de Estudiantes Democráticos, una historia de militancia juvenil." In *Historia y memoria de los movimientos estudiantiles: A 45 años del 68*, edited by José René Rivas Ontiveros, Ana María Sánchez Sáenz, and Gloria A. Tirado Villegas. Vol. 2, 109–37. Mexico City: UNAM/Editions Gernika, 2017.

Ortega Juárez, Joel. *El otro camino: Cuarenta y cinco años de trinchera en trinchera*. Mexico City: Fondo de Cultura Económica, 2006.

———. *10 de junio: ¡Ganamos la calle!* Mexico City: Ediciones de Educación y Cultura, 2011.

Pensado, Jaime M. *Rebel Mexico: Student Unrest and Authoritarian Political Culture During the Long Sixties*. Stanford, Calif.: Stanford University Press, 2013.

Ramírez, Ramón. *El movimiento estudiantil de México (julio/diciembre de 1968)*. Vol. 1. Mexico City: Ediciones Era, 2008. Page numbers in the notes refer to the second edition.

Rivas Ontiveros, José René. *La izquierda estudiantil en la UNAM: Organizaciones, movilizaciones y liderazgos (1958–1972)*. Mexico City: UNAM and Miguel Ángel Porrúa, 2007.

Rivas Ontiveros, José René, Ana María Sánchez Sáenz, and Gloria A. Tirado Villegas, eds. *Historia y memoria de los movimientos estudiantiles: A 45 años del 68*. Vols. 1 and 2. Mexico: UNAM/Editions Gernika, 2017.

"Tercera etapa: Candidato Luis Echeverría: Idario." *Polémica, órgano teórico doctrinario del PRI*, no. 4. Mexico (1970): 1038–39.

13

TORTURE AND THE MAKING OF A SUBVERSIVE DURING MEXICO'S DIRTY WAR

GLADYS I. MCCORMICK

"MY NAME IS SAÚL and I belonged to a guerrilla group the press referred to as the Lacandones. . . . We just referred to ourselves as the Organization."[1] Saúl was one of about twenty militants from an urban guerrilla group rounded up by state authorities in October 1972. They picked him up walking on a Mexico City university campus at 8 a.m. He was carrying a gun, and upon realizing plainclothes police officers followed him, he pulled out his weapon but did not discharge it. Afterward, he blamed it on the fact that this was a new gun and he did not know how to release the safety. The young officer following him most closely threw himself back on the ground to avoid being shot. Another officer shot Saúl in the leg and he fell to the ground. Four officers then dragged him into a waiting vehicle. They kicked and punched him. One took the butt of his gun and slammed it into the bridge of Saúl's nose, breaking it. "They didn't ask anything. Just threatened me and told me I was going to meet hell." Once Saúl arrived at the clandestine prison, "they brought in other comrades, all completely naked, dripping water, in terrible condition, holding them up because they couldn't stand on their own. They slapped them and at that moment I felt great tenderness for my comrades because they were torn to pieces."

For the past few years, my work has focused on how and why these young men, including Saúl, were torn to pieces. Elsewhere I have focused on mapping out the types of torture political prisoners endured as well as setting down a framework, what I term low-intensity Dirty War, to understand what took place in Mexico between the late 1940s and the early 1980s.[2] In this chapter, I take a closer look at the torture inflicted on political prisoners during the most violent stage of the Dirty War in the 1970s. It is during this period of Mexico's Dirty War, I argue, when government officials employed "enhanced" repressive techniques—some adapted from already existing techniques, and others imported from abroad—designed to destroy the emerging guerrilla threat in both urban and rural locales. These techniques ranged from the more precise use of psychological torture to setting up clandestine torture centers inside military installations to allow for coordination among agencies. They also included new forms of waterboarding, the use of electrical shocks, and the growing practice of "disappearing" dissidents by killing and disposing their remains in, for example, mass graves, instead of imprisoning them after the conclusion of their torture.

Most of the individuals at the heart of this chapter were members of different guerrilla groups in the 1970s. Other contributors to this volume, including Adela Cedillo, Tanalís Padilla, and Fernando Calderón, analyze who belonged to these groups and track their experiences across the decade. My interest here is to study why government officials targeted these so-called "insurgents" and what happened to them once they were arrested as part of counterinsurgency campaigns. Specifically, I follow these individuals into the torture chamber to understand what was done to them and for what purposes. Though some endured specific types of abuse, the testimonies have much in common and showcase the military's approach against political dissidents during this period. In other words, I seek to understand what made these individuals subjects of torture by studying how they were labeled "subversive" and what types of punishment they endured as a result. The final section grapples with questions of collaboration and what happened to torture victims when they chose to aid their torturers or, in one case, seek vengeance on them by employing the same tactics.

The individuals at the heart of this analysis are young men, and, as such, the paper employs a gendered and generational perspective of what drove them to their activism, why the government targeted them, and how they experienced torture. For government officials, especially those belonging to the security establishment, the identity of guerrilla and the countercultural *jipi* (hippie) were part of the same continuum. Alternative and countercultural lifestyles not only challenged authority, traditional notions of masculinity, and sexual and religious norms but also posed a threat to the established social order, thereby rendering these young men dangerous—even subversive—and therefore potential subjects of repression.[3] These qualities and the fact that they inhabited many of the same social circles on university campuses and frequently expressed similar ethos of rebellion often made it difficult for authorities to discern differences between so-called jipis and guerrilleros. For already anxious government officials, the threat posed by this ambiguous insurgency only worsened with the knowledge of transnational youth and guerrilla mobilizations gaining traction throughout the region.[4]

Mexico never had a truth commission to establish what human rights abuses took place or whom to hold accountable for atrocities sanctioned by the government. Neither did it have a transitional justice framework demarcating an institutional break ending the Dirty War. There was no withdrawal of the military or other government agencies entrusted with carrying out these abuses in the name of national security. The government also managed to deflect attention from the hemispheric human rights witnessing apparatus that emerged in the 1970s in response to other dirty wars. What we do know is primarily limited to testimonies and to what the government has allowed to filter out. For instance, even though the Fiscalía Especial para Movimientos Sociales y Políticos del Pasado (Special Prosecutors Office for Social and Political Movements of the Past, FEMOSPP) was unable to ascertain precise numbers of victims, we do have rough figures for the period between 1964 and 1982: approximately seven thousand people tortured, at least three thousand political prisoners, and more than three thousand disappeared or killed.[5] The role of scholars then is to provide a witnessing perspective on the events in question to focus on what happened to individuals during this period. For this reason and because of the dearth of documentary evidence in the public domain, this chapter draws on available published and unpublished testimonies and declassified intelligence reports from Mexico, specifically those of the secret police known as the Dirección Federal de Seguridad (Federal Security Directorate, DFS). It also includes reports by the Comisión Nacional para los Derechos Humanos de México (National Commission for Human Rights, CNDH) and the FEMOSPP.[6] Despite the debates surrounding these documents, I have chosen to mine them carefully for available information because they hold key evidence for a study of political prisoners.[7]

CLANDESTINE LIFE, A TORTURED LIFE

Similar to what happened to Saúl in the opening page, most political prisoners detained in the early 1970s were immediately sent to clandestine prisons after being picked up by the military or police, where they were tortured. Clandestine prisons included the Campo Militar-1 (Military Field, CM-1), the basement of the DFS offices, the barracks of Mexico City's mounted police squad in the Tlatelolco public housing project, an innocuous house in a suburb of Guadalajara, and the air force base at Pie de la Cuesta in Guerrero.[8] Yet the similarities in these accounts demonstrate a clear coordination of how torture was often carried out against guerrilla members. An individual was tortured anywhere between ten days to three months, until that point that officials deemed he no longer had viable intelligence. At this juncture, officials decided whether or not the individual should be killed, disappeared, or imprisoned. If the latter was decided, he was relocated to a formal penitentiary, such as the national penitentiary at Lecumberri or Reclusorio Oriente in Mexico City, Oblatos in Guadalajara, Topo Chico in Nuevo León, Islas Marias Federal Penal Colony off the coast of Nayarit, or Santa Martha Acatitla in the State of Mexico.

Upon entering prison, these activists were then processed and assigned a cellblock that segregated them from the rest of the prison population. A DFS report from 1969 gives a more precise breakdown: of the more than three thousand inmates at Lecumberri, 334 of them were political prisoners, most of whom were housed in the C and M blocks.[9] In prison, everyday routines of a clandestine life carried over and helped organize prison life. Upon arriving at the cellblock, as Saúl explains, longer serving political prisoners "interviewed" the new inmates. The job of the interviewer was to ascertain the political inclinations of the new prisoners. With this information, it was then decided where and with whom the new inmate would spend time. Each group had its own hierarchy, set of routines, and spectrum of strictness. Among the most regimented were those belonging to the Movimiento de Acción Revolucionaria (Revolutionary Action Movement, MAR), which had a fixed daily schedule to ensure obedience and cohesiveness among its members. The continuities between these two spaces—the clandestine and the imprisoned—thus lent a familiar inflection to being incarcerated, arguably rendering this life more tolerable. Both environments proved restrictive, hierarchical, and dependent on rules. Both involved constant surveillance, the absence of a divide between private and public, and fear of punishment. Even the number of individuals in both was similar: eight in the safe house and six to eight in the prison cell.

Yet a key difference cut across the two spaces: these men chose to enter a clandestine life, knowing prison could be a part of that. To understand the asymmetry, we need to take a closer look at the secret life of a guerrilla member in an urban environment. According to Saúl, "the fundamental objective of a safe house was to not draw attention and give the impression that its inhabitants have a normal life. We looked like students and we were students. We went to university. We were good young men. You ask what is a good young man? One who studies, focuses on his things, doesn't party, doesn't make a racket, doesn't get drunk. The owner of the house said, 'you are good young men.' She was only suspicious over our religious habits, 'I don't see you at mass, at the local church.'" The habits of these young men leading a clandestine life were reminiscent of those in a monastery because of the elements of sacrifice and abnegation. The religious comparison, however, extends only so far. Saúl continues:

> We were part of that generation of the sixties and the first to engage the counter-culture of that age. Some [used drugs] but it was a luxury that we criticized and challenged but not like a holy inquisition. . . . Alcohol was frowned upon because if you're in a struggle where your life and ideals are at risk—how would it look if you started talking because you were drunk? We considered it a great indiscretion. But we didn't completely reject it because we lived in a place where that was a part of being young. We would drink beer in front of the university halls. There was a lot of pot smoked at CU [Ciudad Universitaria, the main campus of the national university in Mexico City]. Some of us had our hippie girlfriend that taught us what we know. Pot was really common. After the student movement of 1966, the main distributors of drugs at CU were soldiers. Everybody knew that marijuana equaled soldiers and soldiers equaled marijuana.

Saúl's statement that guerrilla members did not reject the counterculture movement present on university campuses at the time is of critical importance to our analysis. For these young men, as well as the government officials wary of them, the line between hippie and alleged insurgent was indeed blurry. Perhaps Roger Bartra summed it best in his essay on counterculture in Mexico where he wrote that "marijuana was linked to Marxism; nonconventional forms of eroticism went the same way as guerrilla members."[10]

These young men, according to Saúl, adopted a clandestine life for reasons beyond the ideological. "Our primary motivation was tied to more than political convictions; it was also an ethical and moral conviction of building a new man—not a superman, but a new man influenced by Ernesto 'Ché' Guevara, influenced by the transformation of men and women into a new being free of prejudice, free of limitations." Guevara, and specifically the myths surrounding his life and death, as further examined by Luis Herrán in his chapter in this volume, provided the idealized archetype that these young men should aspire to be as guerrilla members living in hiding. Florencia Mallon describes how the legend of Ché Guevara galvanized gendered rebelliousness in her study of the Movimiento de la Izquierda Revolucionaria (Movement of the Revolutionary Left, MIR) in Chile in the late 1960s and 1970s.[11] As she explains, young guerrilla members "drew directly on the combination of the Cuban barbudo—the bearded and long-haired young romantic best symbolized by Ché Guevara—and the emerging 'hippie' rebels who preached free love, danced to rock music, and stormed the barricades of the bourgeois state."[12] Drawing on Ché's heroic attributes, many of which lay in the realm of the mythic given his untimely death in 1967, helped young men endure the deprivations of a clandestine life, give purpose to the guerrilla's mission, and recruit new members seduced by the romantic subjectivity of Ché's legend. This legend allowed them to set aside class and ethnic differences for the sake of being protagonists in bringing about social change, which for some took on a more countercultural bent and for others was about opting for armed revolution.

Romantic notions of being a guerrilla member and willingly opting to take on the deprivations of a clandestine life ran up against the reality of being targeted as an insurgent by government forces intent on destroying this threat. It is here that these young men encountered torture for the first time and experienced the ways in which it remade an individual. In a rare published memoir, José Arturo Gallegos Nájera discusses how a comrade released in 1973 described the torture he was subjected to while in captivity.[13] Nevertheless, Gallegos Nájera goes on to explain that the reality of being tortured was so much worse than anything described. "To know you're in the hands of the enemy, defenseless and without any chance of escape, makes one feel like the most vulnerable being in the universe."[14] The torture these young men experienced was intended to extract information as well as punish and transform the individual into a submissive subject. If released back into the population, instead of being killed and disappeared, the submissive subject acted as a deterrent to other possible insurgents.

The testimony of Francisco Juventino Campaña López, a leader of the Fuerzas Revolucionarias Armadas del Pueblo (People's Armed Revolutionary Forces, FRAP), captures the array of torture techniques commonly used as part of a counterinsurgent campaign.[15] He was detained on August 6, 1973, on the highway en route to Mazatlán. Once apprehended for allegedly transporting subversive literature in his car, he was then taken to Guadalajara's police headquarters. For two days, the officers interrogated him by having him kneel on a broomstick with his arms extended and high voltage lights shining on his face. In between sessions, they placed him in a cell with another individual who turned out to be an undercover informant entrusted with plying him for information.[16]

On August 8, he was transported to the DFS's headquarters in Mexico City where he first met Miguel Nazar Haro, who led the torture sessions of many of the individuals cited in this paper.[17] Nazar Haro had a long career inside Mexico's security establishment, primarily in the DFS, which he headed from 1979 to 1982. As part of his duties, he commanded tactical military units targeting guerrillas for elimination. These included the White Brigade in the first half of the 1970s, which decimated the Liga Comunista 23 de Septiembre (23rd of September Communist League, LC23S), an umbrella guerrilla group that was considered to pose the biggest threat to the government in the early 1970s. Nazar Haro oversaw the torture sessions of many of the activists in this chapter, including Saúl's and Campaña López's. The DFS officer began by commiserating with Campaña López over his brutal treatment at the hands of the Guadalajara officers, declaring that it was unnecessary if one just answered the questions.[18] When it became clear that Campaña López was not going to divulge information, Nazar Haro changed tactics and ordered that he be strapped to the parallel bars to begin his torture. Agents deliberately applied electric shocks to the bruised areas of his body and submerged Campaña López into water to the point of drowning. When it appeared he passed out, they threw Campaña López in a corner and Nazar Haro came over to stand on top of his body. Later, Nazar Haro told him that "[t]his is a war that you have lost."[19]

Campaña López's torture continued for approximately twelve days. Medical personnel briefly attended to him to little avail. He recalls the pain of having a tight blindfold on at all times pressing against his eyes and digging into the bridge of his nose. After begging for days, a guard finally loosened it enough for Campaña López to catch glimpses of his surroundings.[20] He grew to know his torturers and noted that "they were not all the same." According to him, some of them enjoyed inflicting pain and frequently boasted of raping women prisoners. Others appeared to not want to be there. Some talked about being students at the Universidad Nacional Autónoma de México (National Autonomous University of Mexico, UNAM) and others about their stints at training bases in the United States and Panama.[21] On August 19, his torture ended, and after receiving medical treatment, he was transferred to the Oblatos Penitentiary in Guadalajara.

What Campaña López endured is heard over and over again in testimonies with survivors. Armando Rentería remembers how the torture session always began with a combination of beatings and psychological threats, followed by electrical shocks and submersion in dirty water. Rentería affirms that the torturers "must have been trained to commit all sorts of irregularities."[22] Agents tied Mario Cartagena López down and put his head between two boards. They put a hose in his mouth and shot water in to simulate drowning.[23] "I knew they were going to destroy me with torture," he says. In his testimony, Cartagena López returns several times to the fact that "nobody can withstand torture" and that he managed to trick his torturers with incorrect information. Cartagena López stresses that "[he] felt [his] consciousness strong" because he had not given real information that led to the capture of other guerrilla members.[24] This is at odds with Saúl, who notes that there was an understanding that everyone broke down under torture. This meant that prisoners faced contradictory rules as the session began. On the one hand they had to try to survive what was coming, and on the other hand they had to protect their comrades. In the face of this contradiction, Saúl explains that survival was primordial. "All that psychological and physical aggression is documenting the total collapse of morality and consciousness. You have to remake yourself in every moment, assimilate, get a grip on your identity."

The marriage between psychological and physical pain takes on a deeper meaning when viewed through the lens of intimacy. Nowhere is this more apparent than in the sexual overtones of a torture session, such as the practice of castration. Elsewhere I discuss how Saúl had a testicle removed without anesthesia as part of his experience with torture.[25] This also happened to José Arturo Gallegos Nájera at the military base at Pie de la Cuesta, Guerrero.[26] He was strapped naked to a table and the torturer firmly held his testicles in his hands. "If you don't talk, I'm going to get rid of your balls to make you less macho [machín]."[27] The torturer wrapped a piece of string around one of his testicles and started pulling up. Gallegos Nájera arched his back as far as he could go before he passed out from the pain. Castration, as part of the arsenal of torture techniques employed against dissidents, is perhaps the most visceral of ways in which agents remade these young men. After all, state agents stripped them of their masculinity and punished their insubordination by making a farce of any pretensions to being a "new man" akin to Ché Guevara. Castration thus violated the romantic archetype of the barbudo.

Intimacy was also at play in the inclusion of family members in the experience of torture. The testimonies of brother and sister Raúl and Xóchitl

Mendoza Salgado on their time in CM-1 in 1977 are especially revealing of the familial overtones of torture in Mexico.[28] While it was too difficult for Raúl to describe, Xóchitl discusses how DFS officers tortured Raúl in front of her, including urinating on him and applying electrical prods to his genitals. DFS officers repeatedly raped her in front of Raúl and, after she tested positive for pregnancy, performed an abortion with her brother as witness.[29] As with others, Raúl and Xóchitl spent ten days being tortured at CM-1 before being relocated to a prison. This was also the case of Rodolfo Reyes Crespo from the LC23S, who was detained by the DFS on December 24, 1973, in Guadalajara and subsequently disappeared. After taking him to CM-1, DFS agents kidnapped his mother and tortured her in front of her son.[30] In another testimony, a mother of a guerrilla member described how agents took her, her husband, her other children, and her mother to a torture center in a residential area of Guadalajara. The family was kept in a small, darkened room for three days without access to food or water. The mother could tell that other family members were at the torture center as well and described the screams of the wife of another guerrilla member as they beat and raped her.[31]

THE AXIS OF TORTURE VICTIM AND COLLABORATOR

In his analysis of the legal foundations of torture, Mexican philosopher and lawyer Ignacio Carrillo Prieto details the history behind why perpetrators torture, the goals of torture, and the torturer's motives. His answers revolve around preserving and respecting political authority. The torturer follows orders, more often than not from a police or military commanding officer, to obtain information, extract a confession, intimidate a victim, and punish the offender.[32] While the act of torturing another human being may repulse most individuals, the torturer focuses on the end goals and overcomes any moral compulsion. The results of torture, according to Carrillo Prieto, are short- and long-term. While the short-term result enables coercion or punishment of an individual, the longer term can lead to a constellation of results.[33] These range from nurturing a culture of fear, where individuals live with a sense of insecurity, to forcing radical groups to adopt even more extreme responses. What Carrillo Prieto overlooks in discussing the results of torture is what happens when those tortured collaborate with the torturers not just for the short term, but for years to come.

Áyax Segura Garrido is one of the best-known informants because of his leadership profile in the 1968 student movement.[34] As a professor at the Instituto Politécnico Nacional (National Polytechnic Institute, IPN) and at the Escuela Normal Oral (Oral Normal School), he joined the national strike council in 1968, which went on to coordinate the student movement. He was imprisoned on October 2 and a week later was formally charged for his political activism. On October 7, he publicly declared that the students had incited the massacre by shooting weapons and went so far as to be photographed pointing to machine guns and identifying them as belonging to the students.[35] According to a DFS official, Segura Garrido approached the agency of his own volition and, in the agency's words, was a "collaborator" while imprisoned in Lecumberri.[36] His DFS file contains handwritten reports from throughout 1969 as he continued to inform on student activism.[37] One of the letters he wrote to the head of the DFS while in prison gives an inkling of his state of mind: he describes the intense isolation he felt, asking the director, "Give me a plan of action or I beg you to get me out of here."[38] In July 1969, the Mexican courts officially declared Segura Garrido not guilty of his involvement in the 1968 student movement.[39] The last document in his DFS file, dated July 1985, just before the agency was disbanded under accusations of involvement with drug cartels, contains a deposition explaining that he worked for the agency from 1968 to 1983.[40] In 1970, he changed his name to Benjamín Esquer Galicia and formally joined the DFS, going on to serve as an agent under the command of the DFS's Miguel Nazar Haro in his White Brigade, a joint police and military unit in charge of exterminating the guerrillas.

The case of Gustavo Hirales echoes what happened to Segura Garrido. Within just a few short months of helping found the LC23S in 1973, Hirales was detained by the DFS and subjected to brutal torture under Nazar Haro's supervision. He was subsequently imprisoned for seven years in Topo Chico for his political activities. Upon his release in 1980, he enlisted in the Partido Comunista Mexicano (Mexican Communist Party, PCM), which soon after became the Partido Socialista Unificado de México (Unified Socialist Party of Mexico, PSUM). He then joined the ranks of the ruling party, the Partido Revolucionario Institucional (Institutional Revolutionary Party, PRI), and as an influential figure of the Secretaría de Gobernación (Ministry of Interior) in the 1990s, he played a key role in leading the counterinsurgency efforts against the Ejército Zapatista de Liberación Nacional (Zapatista Army of National Liberation, EZLN) and other revolutionary groups.[41] In addition to collaborating with the very regime that had tortured him, Hirales wrote two books on his experiences with the LC23S and as a political prisoner. The first, published in 1978, details the history of the LC23S, and the second, released in 1996, describes his time as a political prisoner.[42] In both books, Hirales adopts a tone of disillusionment and regret for his role in LC23S and condemns the guerrilla group for its self-serving and idealistic agenda.[43]

Yet his recollections open a window into what took place inside and outside the torture chamber. Hirales writes vividly about his time as a political prisoner and the torture he and his comrades were subjected to in *Memoria de la guerra de los justos*. He describes the dozen steps between when he and a comrade were picked up and when he started his seven-year stint inside Topo Chico. As with Saúl, Hirales tells how he was first beaten up by common police officers with no knowledge of what questions to ask him. The second step has him meeting Nazar Haro for the first time, whom he describes as in his early forties, with green eyes and a prominent nose. Nazar Haro oversees the torture and begins by quoting Mao Zedong to dispense the advice that Hirales should know this is a "time to lose" and that he should "prepare to fight again."[44] After some preliminary questions, the torturers began by immersing Hirales's head in a sink to simulate drowning until he passed out. They then strung him up by his legs to two parallel metal poles and took turns hitting him until he again passed out. During this session, one of his torturers twisted one of his nipples as he asked questions.

During the second day, they sat him on the edge of a large tub. He had to hear as they first tortured his comrade by submersing him in water, kicking, thrashing, and screaming. They pushed Hirales back into the water and held him pinned to the bottom by his legs. Hirales describes the sensation of drowning, of fighting for air, of being allowed a half breath to recover before being submersed again. They forced him to drink liquor to revive him enough to continue with the torture session.[45] After five days of this routine, they took him to the DFS building in the Colonia Roma, where he recovered enough to meet the DFS director the following day. Hirales describes this meeting as more of a "sociopolitical interview than an interrogation."[46] This meeting ended with Nazar Haro transporting Hirales to Monterrey to deposit him at Topo Chico. Along the way, Nazar Haro kept a running political conversation with Hirales while referring to him as "mister nobody."[47]

Hirales's torture follows the same plot sequence as Saúl and others: The early stages of torture were brutal and intended to break down an individual. The later stages saw a more refined and deliberate approach to torture intended to extract information and reform an individual. Yet the process of extracting information and reforming took on a more profound psychological twist for Hirales when he described what happened to two of his comrades and leading members of the LC23S, Olivares Torres and Salvador Corral, in retaliation for the kidnapping of two businessmen.[48] Both Torres and Corral were apprehended in February 1974 and savagely tortured until they died. Not only did Torres's body have multiple fractures, his torturers drove hot nails into his kneecaps.[49] Their bodies were then thrown in front of their families' respective houses. Hirales, like Segura Garrido, proved the effectiveness of torture as a form of "cure." Not only did he go on to denounce both his comrades and LC23S, he used his formation in a guerrilla movement to help the government attack similar movements later on when he worked in the Secretaría de Gobernación.

The case of Zacarías Osorio Cruz, a first-class soldier and member of the First Battalion of Parachute Riflemen, stands out as an anomaly and stretches an analysis of collaboration as a result of torture. In seeking political exile from Canadian authorities in the late 1980s, Osorio Cruz discusses in detail his role in transporting and executing political prisoners in the period between 1970 and 1982.[50] His rationale for disclosing his participation lay in the claim that he would be killed if he returned to Mexico. Osorio Cruz describes approximately six occasions where he assisted in transporting hooded political prisoners from one detention facility to another.[51] As he advanced in his career, he was asked to partake in special operations that included accompanying a driver with two or three political prisoners to a nearby shooting range. Once there, Osorio Cruz and two other soldiers would lead the prisoners up a small hill, line them up, and shoot them with a high-caliber machine gun. Not only did the weapon obliterate the prisoners' bodies beyond recognition, the fact that it took place at a shooting range meant the sound of the shots did not draw attention.[52] Osorio Cruz stipulates that he never knew the identity of the twenty people he shot and the only identifying feature was the prisoner's number on the sealed order or the number above their prison cell. He repeatedly claims to the Canadian immigration court that he was only following orders from his superiors. He calls on the cases of two fellow soldiers who were found mysteriously murdered after, in one case, expressing discontent with the orders he had to follow and, in the second case, asking for a transfer to another unit.[53]

All of these cases tied together complicate the image of the passive victim. Yet the question of vengeance remains. Though singular, there is one case of retaliatory torture that challenges the narrative of collaboration. In January 1974, a guerrilla group known as "Los Enfermos" (The Sick Ones) from the Universidad Autónoma de Sinaloa (Autonomous University of Sinaloa, UAS) in Culiacán kidnapped, tortured, and killed a police officer.[54] The DFS agents reporting on the incident do not specify if the officer had been involved in the torture of political dissidents. They do, however, report on a phone call received from a student describing the torture inflicted on the officer and warning that others would be subjected to the same treatment. A follow-up phone call reported on the officer's death, after which his remains were located on the university campus. His body showed signs of brutal torture, including the stapling of his face, cuts on various body parts, and rape.[55] What happened to this officer at the hands of Los Enfermos muddies the image of the passive and broken victim. It also brings to the fore the parallels between the type of violence endorsed by this guerrilla group and that employed by government officials, such as Miguel Nazar Haro, against so-called insurgents. Cases such as that of Los Enfermos, Osorio Cruz, and Hirales show that the government did not have a complete monopoly on extreme forms of violence. Similar to the blurry line between the categories of hippie and guerrilla conflating them into subversives, these cases show a muddying between who is the enemy and who is the victim.

CONCLUSION

Governance in Mexico throughout the twentieth century was not a static system in which political violence played an occasional role. Instead, and as I have argued elsewhere, it was an integral part of the maintenance of the country's modernization that worked in tandem with the PRI-led state.[56] Nevertheless, cracks emerged in the governing regime's ability to control dissent beginning in the late 1940s and, most egregiously, in the 1970s. Those of us studying modern forms of political violence in Mexico, including all of the contributors in this volume, face the ongoing official silencing of government-sponsored atrocities, the absence of a truth commission, and the uncertain politics surrounding available sources, such as the restrictions on the use of the DFS files. Nevertheless, we persist in this important task. To this effort, I add the need to more fully understand the profile of who was deemed a subject of torture at the height of the Dirty War in the 1970s. The makeup of individuals targeted for torture—those considered so dangerous to national security interests that they were stripped of their basic human rights—sheds light on the official willed amnesia that denies them an identity by labeling them subversive. It also denies them an accounting of what the government did to them and, even more importantly, the promise of justice.

In this case, being rendered a subject of torture derived from blurring the line between hippie and insurgent—a blurring that happened both at the hands of government officials and guerrilla members. Louise Walker alludes to the conflation of these two identities when she discusses the fissures among urban middle-class youth between those who believed the government's commitment to reform, those concerned with counterculture, and those interested in the radical options for bringing about large-scale social change.[57] Nevertheless, "the lines dividing moderates, hippies, and radicals were not rigidly drawn: most of them came from the same middle-class world, and individuals often engaged in different kinds of protest."[58] In practice, this meant—and here she cites Eric Zolov's findings of Mexico's hippie culture—that Molotov cocktails and marijuana "were often found side by side at house parties in the 1960s and 1970s."[59] Roger Bartra echoes this in his recollections of gatherings at his house where "those in search of artificial paradises" joined "those seeking to overthrow oppressive systems."[60] The lack of a rigid line helped Saúl and other guerrilla members hide in plain sight as part of their clandestine life, but it also fed the government's paranoia that hippies and insurgents were one and the same. In official circles, young men sporting the trappings of a counterculture lifestyle, including Ché's iconic beard, rendered them as subversive and, as such, objects of imprisonment.[61]

Saúl and the many others like them deserve recognition as historical subjects worthy of remembering. Beyond being just victims of what was done to them in the torture chamber, these individuals sought to have a voice in the political process and represented a generational call to arms, both figuratively and, in some cases, literally. Their voices, their identities, and their histories—before, during, and after the Dirty War—are key to explaining the marriage between state formation and government-sanctioned terrorism. They were products of the governing regime: their parents were born near the start of PRI rule, they went to schools overseen by PRI officials, and they were expected to grow up to be obedient citizens. They also collectively expressed disillusionment with a political system premised on the promises of an institutionalized revolution and, instead, opted for other forms of revolution that challenged the status quo. They also, as in the cases of Segura Garrido, Hirales, and Osorio Cruz, bring into the conversation those who collaborated and even acted as agents provocateurs on behalf of the government. These individuals inhabit what Wil Pansters refers to as the "grey zone" of violence and coercion.[62]

Regime officials were emboldened to punish these young men and, in doing so, revealed yet again the government's authoritarian colors. Shedding light on these young men's experiences challenges Mexico's refusal to create a truth commission as well as the failure of the FEMOSPP to complete the official narrative of the Dirty War. This outright denial of the truth nurtures a culture of impunity and continues today with events surrounding the killings of the forty-three students in Ayotzinapa in 2014, among other massacres. The effects of this repression did not cease after 1982 or after the PRI was voted out of office in the 2000 presidential elections. In the same way that imprisoning, torturing, and disappearing dissidents were both historical and contemporary issues at the height of the Dirty War in the 1970s, they continue to be so today with the growing tally of victims at the hands of both the cartels and government agencies. While the causes and forms of forced disappearances today are different from those of a generation ago, both periods have seen the use of torture and other forms of human rights abuses by state institutions as well as resistance by the government to acknowledge its responsibility.

NOTES

1. The interviews with Saúl were conducted in May 2014 in Mexico City. Despite the fact that he is on record with his guerrilla activities, I conceal his identity because of the sensitivity of the information pertaining to his time as a political prisoner. Rather than footnote every instance I draw on his interview, I signal in the text itself if the information comes from him. Unless specified otherwise, all translations are my own.
2. McCormick, "The Last Door."
3. This point is also made in Jaime M. Pensado, *Rebel Mexico*, 169–70. See also Barr-Melej, *Psychedelic Chile*.
4. Though outside the scope of this chapter, young women also suffered for their guerrilla activity. See Herrera Calderón and Cedillo, *Challenging Authoritarianism*; Rayas Velasco, *Armadas*; and Aguilar Terrés, *Guerrilleras*.
5. Herrera Calderón and Cedillo, *Challenging Authoritarianism*, 8.
6. Comisión Nacional para los Derechos Humanos-Mexico, "Informe Especial sobre las Quejas"; Fiscalía Especial para Movimientos Sociales y Políticos del Pasado, "Borrador del Informe de la Guerra Sucia." The final report was heavily redacted, so researchers rely on the draft report as being the more reliable of the two versions.

7. The usefulness of these sources has been amply deliberated elsewhere. See, for example, Padilla and Walker, "In the Archives"; Piccato, "Comments: How to Build a Perspective."

8. Gallegos Nájera describes a torture center outside of Mexico City in his account of the military base at Pie de la Cuesta in *A merced del enemigo!*

9. Archivo General de la Nación, Fondo Dirección Federal de Seguridad (hereafter AGN-DFS), Exp 53-2 L 1 H 65–71 (September 30, 1969).

10. Bartra, "Memorias de la contracultura."

11. Mallon, "Barbudos, Warriors, and Rotos." See also Sorensen, *A Turbulent Decade Remembered.*

12. Mallon, "Barbudos, Warriors, and Rotos," 180.

13. Gallegos Nájera, *A merced del enemigo!*, 75–80.

14. Ibid., 80.

15. Oikión-Solano, "Represión y tortura en México."

16. Ibid., 126.

17. For more on Nazar Haro, see Aguayo Quezada, *La charola*, 125, 182–84.

18. Ibid., 127–28.

19. Ibid., 128.

20. Ibid., 129–30.

21. Ibid., 130.

22. Dios Corona, *La historia que no pudieron borrar*, 131–33.

23. Ibid., 170.

24. Ibid., 164–66.

25. McCormick, "The Last Door."

26. Gallegos Nájera, *A merced del enemigo!*, 87–93.

27. Ibid., 91.

28. Mendoza Salgado, *México, 1977*, 9–12, 96–100, 115–19.

29. Ibid., 115–19, 138–39.

30. Dios Corona, *La historia que no pudieron borrar*, 151–53.

31. Ibid., 188–189.

32. Carrillo Prieto, *Arcana Imperii*, 140–47.

33. Ibid., 145–47.

34. Carey, *Plaza of Sacrifices*, 145.

35. *El Día*, July 10, 1968. Note that others made similar claims, including Sócrates Lemus Campus, who was also accused of being an agent provocateur.

36. *La Jornada*, January 29, 2012; AGN-DFS, Exp 11-4 L 51, H 190 (October 31, 1968) and L 139, H 278–279 (July 15, 1971).

37. AGN-DFS, Exp 11-4 L 93, H 20–25 (April 2, 1969); Exp 63-3 L 2, H 227–229 (June 1, 1969); and Exp 63-55 L 1, H 8–17 (June 27, 1969).

38. AGN-DFS, Exp 11-4 L 58, H 278–279 (November 26, 1968).

39. AGN-DFS, Exp 11-7 L 86, H 152 (July 8, 1969).

40. AGN-DFS, Exp 009-046-025 L 1, H 154–160 (July 23, 1985).

41. For more on Hirales, see *Proceso*, January 8, 1994.

42.   Hirales Morán, *La Liga Comunista 23 de Septiembre* and *Memoria de la guerra de los justos*.

43.   Others have made similar "regrets," including Alberto Ulloa in Ulloa Bornemann and Schmidt, *Surviving Mexico's Dirty War*.

44.   Hirales Morán, *Memoria de la guerra*, 16–17.

45.   Ibid., 16–26.

46.   Ibid., 25.

47.   Ibid., 27–30.

48.   Ibid., 69–72.

49.   Their torture is also described in Dios Corona, *La historia que no pudieron borrar*, 135–38.

50.   Maza, *Obligado a matar*, 1–2. This document contains transcripts of the four sessions in which Zacarías Osorio Cruz testified in support of his application for political asylum.

51.   Ibid., 10–11.

52.   Ibid., 36, 101–102.

53.   Ibid., 13–14.

54.   AGN-DFS, "Los Enfermos," Exp 100-25-1 H 264–266 (January 24, 1974).

55.   In addition to the DFS, the officer's torture is detailed in Magdaleno Cárdenas, "Los otros muertos."

56.   I develop this argument in McCormick, *Logic of Compromise*.

57.   Walker, *Waking from the Dream*, 30–37.

58.   Ibid., 33.

59.   Ibid.

60.   Bartra, "Memorias de la contracultura."

61.   For the case of Brazil, see Cowan, *Securing Sex*; and Langland, *Speaking of Flowers*.

62.   Pansters, *Violence, Coercion, and State-Making*, 26–32.

BIBLIOGRAPHY

ARCHIVES

Archivo General de la Nación, Fondo Dirección Federal de Seguridad

National Security Archives, George Washington University. http://nsarchive.gwu.edu

PUBLISHED SOURCES

Aguayo Quezada, Sergio. *La charola: Una historia de los servicios de inteligencia en México.* Mexico City: Editorial Grijalbo, 2001.

Aguilar Terrés, Luz María. *Guerrilleras: Antología de testimonios y textos sobre la participación de las mujeres en los movimientos armados socialistas en México, segunda mitad del siglo XX.* Mexico City: 2014.

Barr-Melej, Patrick. *Psychedelic Chile: Youth, Counterculture, and Politics on the Road to Socialism and Dictatorship.* Chapel Hill: University of North Carolina Press, 2017.

Bartra, Roger. "Memorias de la contracultura." *Letras Libres*, no. 105 (September 2007).

Carey, Elaine. *Plaza of Sacrifices: Gender, Power, and Terror in 1968 Mexico.* Albuquerque: University of New Mexico Press, 2005.

Carrillo Prieto, Ignacio. *Arcana Imperii: Apuntes sobre la tortura.* Mexico City: Instituto Nacional de Ciencias Penales, 1987.

Comisión Nacional para los Derechos Humanos-Mexico (CNDH). "Informe Especial sobre las Quejas en Materia de Desapariciones Forzadas Ocurridas en la Década de los 70 y Principios de los 80," 2001. Accessed October 17, 2017. http://www.cndh.org .mx/sites/all/doc/Informes/Especiales/2001_Desapariciones70y80.pdf.

Cowan, Benjamin. *Securing Sex: Morality and Repression in the Making of Cold War Brazil.* Chapel Hill: University of North Carolina Press, 2016.

Dios Corona, Sergio René de. *La historia que no pudieron borrar: La guerra sucia en Jalisco, 1970–1985.* Guadalajara: La Casa del Mago, 2004.

Fiscalía Especial para Movimientos Sociales y Políticos del Pasado. "Borrador del Informe de la Guerra Sucia." 2006. Accessed October 17, 2017. http://nsarchive.gwu .edu/NSAEBB/NSAEBB180/index2.htm.

Gallegos Nájera, José Arturo. *A merced del enemigo! Detenciones, interrogatorios, torturas, mazmoras, y . . . algo más.* Guadalajara: Centro de Investigaciones Históricas de los Movimientos Sociales, Universidad de Guadalajara, 2009.

Herrera Calderón, Fernando, and Adela Cedillo. *Challenging Authoritarianism in Mexico: Revolutionary Struggles and the Dirty War, 1964–1982.* New York: Routledge, 2012.

Hirales Morán, Gustavo. *La Liga Comunista 23 de Septiembre: Orígenes y naufragio.* Mexico City: Cultura popular, 1977.

———. *Memoria de la guerra de los justos.* Mexico City: Cal y Arena, 1996.

Langland, Victoria. *Speaking of Flowers: Student Movements and the Making and Remembering of 1968 in Military Brazil.* Durham, N.C.: Duke University Press, 2013.

Magdaleno Cárdenas, María de los Ángeles. "Los otros muertos." *Históricas, Boletín del Instituto de Investigaciones Históricas*, UNAM, no. 99 (January–April 2014): 2–14.

Mallon, Florencia. "Barbudos, Warriors, and Rotos: The MIR, Masculinity, and Power in the Chilean Agrarian Reform, 1965–1974." In *Changing Men and Masculinities in Latin America*, edited by Matthew C. Gutmann, 179–215. Durham, N.C.: Duke University Press, 2003.

Maza, Enrique, ed. *Obligado a matar: Fusilamiento de civiles en México.* Mexico City: n.p., unknown year.

McCormick, Gladys I. "The Last Door: Political Prisoners and the Use of Torture in Mexico's Dirty War." *The Americas* 74, no. 1 (January 2017): 57–81.

———. *The Logic of Compromise in Mexico: How the Countryside Was Key to the Emergence of Authoritarianism.* Chapel Hill: University of North Carolina Press, 2016.

Mendoza Salgado, Victoria. *México, 1977: Testimonios de tortura.* Mexico City: Sigla Ediciones, 2008.

Oikión-Solano, Verónica. "Represión y tortura en México en la década de 1970: Un testimonio político." *Historia y Grafía*, no. 37 (July–December 2011): 115–48.

Padilla, Tanalís, and Louise Walker. "In the Archives: History and Politics." *Journal of Iberian and Latin American Research* 19, no. 1 (July 2013): 1–10.

Pansters, Wil G., ed. *Violence, Coercion, and State-Making in Twentieth-Century Mexico: The Other Half of the Centaur.* Stanford, Calif.: Stanford University Press, 2012.

Pensado, Jaime M. *Rebel Mexico: Student Unrest and Authoritarian Political Culture During the Long Sixties.* Stanford, Calif.: Stanford University Press, 2013.

Piccato, Pablo. "Comments: How to Build a Perspective on the Recent Past." *Journal of Iberian and Latin American Research* 19, no. 1 (July 2013): 91–102.

Rayas Velasco, Lucía. *Armadas: Un análisis de género desde el cuerpo de las mujeres combatientes.* Mexico City: Colegio de México, 2009.

Sorensen, Diana. *A Turbulent Decade Remembered: Scenes from the Latin American Sixties.* Stanford, Calif.: Stanford University Press, 2007.

Walker, Louise E. *Waking from the Dream: Mexico's Middle Classes After 1968.* Stanford, Calif.: Stanford University Press, 2013.

Ulloa Bornemann, Alberto, and Arthur Schmidt. *Surviving Mexico's Dirty War: A Political Prisoner's Memoir.* Philadelphia: Temple University Press, 2007.

FINAL REMARKS

TOWARD A PROVINCIALIZATION OF 1968

JAIME M. PENSADO AND ENRIQUE C. OCHOA

IN RECENT YEARS, a number of influential books on social movements have been published. In the work on democratic student uprisings, memoirs of ex-student leaders (*sesentaocheros*, or "sixty-eighters"), chronicles, and photographic testimonies are the most common. Rooted in groundbreaking studies of the 1968 movement published in the 1970s and 1980s, the most recent academic interpretations, while insightful, are often impressionistic and repetitive. Over time and with a few noted exceptions, this scholarship has helped to mythologize a particular interpretation of the 1968 student movement in Mexico City as the watershed moment in the second half of the twentieth century. The literature that ungirds this myth lacks a rigorous examination of the importance of other student uprisings that developed outside Mexico City during the broader period of the 1960s and 1970s. By comparison, the scholarship on the radicalism of the 1970s published in the last decade has taken a more revisionist approach. Published overwhelmingly in Spanish, this scholarship has been successfully correcting earlier interpretations of guerrilla movements that for too long had condemned and robbed its members of their agency.

In this concluding chapter, we examine the historiographic evolution of the 1960s and 1970s. We highlight recent studies that are working to provincialize the myth of 1968, including the work of many of the authors in *México Beyond 1968: Revolutionaries, Radicals, and Repression During the Global Sixties and Subversive Seventies*. This revisionist scholarship underscores how violence and state repression have been deeply rooted in Mexican history. It challenges the primacy of 1968 as a canonical date in Mexican history by contending that the myth of '68 has overshadowed, caricaturized, and ultimately devalued both the revolutionary movements that erupted in Mexico throughout the 1960s and 1970s and the multifaceted violence of state repression. By centering movements throughout Mexico, the various chapters underscore the deep-rooted histories of inequalities and the frustrations with a regime that tried to monopolize power and revolutionary rhetoric for decades. We conclude this essay by offering a few suggestions for future research.

THE HISTORIOGRAPHY OF THE MYTH OF '68

Stressing a language of martyrdom and sacrifice on the one hand and a vanguard democracy on the other, the articulation of the '68 myth began as early as the 1970s with the publication of three foundational books published by Ediciones Era.[1] Providing a detailed chronology of the movement and rich *testimonios* (collaborative oral memoirs) of activists and victims of state repression, these books included Carlos Monsiváis's *Días de guardar* (1970), Luis González de Alba's *Los días y los años* (1971), and Elena Poniatowska's *La noche de Tlatelolco* (1971).[2] In unison, this prominent body of work passionately refuted the negative press coverage, which wrongly depicted the student movement as a communist conspiracy hatched by Cuba and the Soviet Union. It also responded to the various publications that came to the defense of the government and the military, including the widely read books by Roberto Blanco Moheno (*Tlatelolco, historia de una infamia*, 1969), Manuel Urrutia Castro (*Trampa en Tlatelolco*, 1969), and Luis Spota (*La Plaza*, 1972).[3] These works of apologia stressed Mexico's "exceptionality" (frequently in relation to the "more violent" regimes of the Southern Cone) and depicted activists, including those who published their testimonios, as "traitors" of the Mexican Revolution. If Mexico already had Villa and Zapata, this literature alleged, there was no need to import Ché Guevera or support misguided revolts led by a handful of "opportunists" who cared more about Cuba than Mexico.[4] Monsiváis, González de Alba, and Poniatowska offered a counter response to what a student leader later convincingly identified as a Machiavellian operation of the state—that is, an organized government effort, in collaboration with the various means of communication, to minimize the importance of the movement, accentuate the violent nature of its base, vilify its leaders, and cast public doubt on both state repression and the Tlatelolco massacre.[5]

Seminal studies published in the late 1970s and 1980s by Sergio Zermeño and Raúl Álvarez Garín furthered our understanding of the 1968 student movement.[6] However, these and more recent influential studies have obscured the long and rich history of student uprisings before and after 1968 in both rural and urban Mexico.[7] More significantly, with a few exceptions, they have reduced the history of the movement to a largely homogenous one overwhelmingly represented by a handful of mostly male '68 activists, mainly from the Universidad Nacional Autónoma de México (National Autonomous University of Mexico, UNAM).[8] On the one hand, this literature has presented sesentaocheros as the leading vanguard of Mexico's democracy and has frequently stressed the "apoliticized" and "disorganized" nature of pre-1968 activists. In this scholarship, participatory democracy in general and *brigadismo*[9] in particular have been commonly (and inaccurately) presented as novel ideas established by the leading organization of the movement, the Consejo Nacional de Huelga (National Strike Council, CNH).[10] At the same time, as we argue further, these works have tended to scorn those who opted for armed struggle, or have often marked October 2 as the only detonating event that pushed young people to go underground and join the guerrilla movement.[11]

In stressing these views, many of the representative authors of this scholarship untenably suggest that there is a Mexico before 1968, and a different, more democratic nation after the student movement.[12] New interpretations of the student movement published in English have made important contributions to advance our understanding of the movement, but with some notable exceptions these have done little to challenge the myth.[13] While some have called for more attention to literature and cultural aesthetics and have introduced new analytical concepts of interpretation from memory and gender studies, by and large this literature all too frequently continues to rely on the same hegemonic voices of '68 and sees little interest in taking the narrative outside the nation's capital.[14] By contrast, those who have taken a longer and more global approach to student activism and radicalism, including some of the authors in this volume, have made important contributions that have forced us to think more transnationally, regionally, and comparatively about student politics and culture.[15]

Over time, the myth of '68 has contributed to an "official history" of "exceptionality" that was first solidified—with significant success—during the administration of Luis Echeverría Álvarez, when political prisoners were released, the

Law of Social Dissolution (used since the 1950s to imprison dissidents) was revoked, amnesty was granted to some of the political prisoners, a new and more independent press emerged, the voting age was lowered to eighteen, political exiles from other Latin American countries were welcomed, investment in public education increased, new spaces of democracy were created, and—as Dillingham examined in his chapter—a new populist rhetoric of *tercermundismo* (Third-Worldism) was employed.[16] In its effort to both distance itself from the presidency of Gustavo Díaz Ordaz and open a space of criticism from the Left, the Echeverría administration celebrated these changes and in so doing capitalized on the commercialization of the myth of '68 as did some of the leading activists who wrote about the movement during this period.[17]

As further emblematic of the myth, in this scholarship the October 2 massacre becomes synonymous with the student movement. But more significantly, the massacre is almost exclusively presented as an exception to an otherwise peaceful Mexico.[18] The authoritarianism of President Díaz Ordaz is portrayed as both anachronistic and, erroneously, not as ruthless as the military dictatorships that simultaneously emerged in South America.[19] In this broader Latin American context, as famously articulated by Carlos Fuentes and Fernando Benítez, two of the leading leftist intellectuals of the 1960s, the progressive forces of Mexico were left with two choices: "Echeverrismo or Fascismo."[20] By and large, most activists, including many influential voices of the sesentaocheros, iconic leftist intellectuals discussed in this book, and exiles who migrated to Mexico to escape persecution elsewhere, opted for the former.[21] Those who did not were forced to move underground or reorganized to create new organizations of dissent.[22] Many on the Left joined the guerrillas and, as McCormick and Aviña demonstrate with chilling detail in their chapters, lost their lives in clandestine prisons, were ruthlessly massacred, or joined the list of forced *desaparecidos* (disappeared persons) that swelled throughout Mexico and Latin America during this period.[23]

Other militants, frequently obscured by the myth, fought to revolutionize Mexico within the institutions of the state or in innovative movements they helped to create independently from the *priísta* apparatus. Similarly, as Santamaría alludes to in her chapter, many Catholic students, who have received little attention in the scholarship, also came together to question the hierarchy of the Church and what many saw as its complicit relationship with the repressive state.[24] In their respective movements, young men and women took advantage of Echeverría's populist programs, such as those discussed in the chapters by

Soldatenko and Dillingham, while many others, including the right-wing radicals and leftist militants examined by Herrán and Oikión in their respective
chapters, rejected the president's so-called "democratic opening" and instead
exposed the violent nature of his administration, including the apocryphal—yet
influential and overlooked—literature published by the government during this
period to discredit those who remained committed to challenging the authoritarian state.[25] As *México Beyond 1968* demonstrates, these various activists drew
public attention to and became critical of the creation of new paramilitary units,
the expansion of the government's agencies of espionage, the intensification
of *porrismo* (the use of *porros*, or agents provocateurs), and the blurring of the
lines between Mexico's Dirty War and the War on Drugs that characterized
the Echeverría administration, a period, as we note in the next section, that
was also overshadowed by the myth of '68 but has recently generated great
academic interest.

NARRATIVES OF RADICALISMS OF THE 1970S

Although much more marginalized in the academy and ferociously silenced by
the Mexican state, the scholarship on the Dirty Wars of the 1970s remarkably
parallels that of the 1968 student movement.[26] Influenced by the pioneering
works of José Santos Valdez's *Madera* (1968) and Jaime López's *Diez años de
guerrilla* (1974) in general and the articles published in the radical magazines
Sucesos para todos and *Por qué?* in particular, this first wave of scholarship made
extensive use of newspaper reports and political manifestos. They used these
sources to denounce the crimes of the state, humanize those who joined the
guerrilla movement, make preliminary efforts to understand the social and
political causes that led scores of people to launch a war of resistance against
the state, and define armed struggle as "inevitable." Similar to the first accounts
written of the 1968 student movement, these narratives employed a language
that emphasized the sacrifice and martyrdom of the guerrilleros.[27]

By the mid- to late 1970s, as Echeverría made conscious efforts to co-opt the
myth of '68, a number of books were published that condemned the "mistakes"
and "ill-fated" adventures of "misguided guerrilleros." Published with the support of the Partido Comunista Mexicano (Mexican Communist Party, PCM),
which disapproved of the use of violence, this literature is best represented
by Gustavo Hirales's *La Liga 23 de septiembre, orígenes y naufragio* (1977). The

disparaging tone that characterized this book is also present in the work of Mario Huachuca, José Woldenberg, Alfredo Tecla Jímenez, Jorge Castañeda, and Julio Scherer. This literature reacted to earlier interpretations of the guerrilla movement by prioritizing a condemnatory language and describing armed struggle as an "act of provocation" against Mexico led, if not by Cuba, then by the Central Intelligence Agency (CIA).[28] Specifically, this literature emphasized the internal disputes, crimes, desperate methods, and armed approach of radicals and in so doing created a homogenous portrait of all militants.[29] This view was shared and widely published by one of the most iconic leaders of the 1968 student movement, Gilberto Guevara Niebla, who frequently described political militancy and countercultural behavior (*jipismo*) as "salidas falsas," or "false solutions," to Mexico's problems.[30] This reproachful tone was also echoed by influential journalists who enjoyed the support of the government, such as Luis Suárez, a regular writer in the influential magazine *Siempre!* and author of *Luis Cabañas, el guerrillero sin esperanza* (1976). According to historians Cedillo and Herrera Calderón, by depicting armed struggle as a hopeless, erroneous, and dangerous adventure, Suárez perhaps made an effort to dissuade young people from joining the insurgent movements that erupted across Mexico during this period.[31] This cautionary approach contrasted with other, more inflammatory denunciations, such as those found in the apocryphal *El guerrillero* (1974) as well as those in Ramón Pimentel's *El secuestro: ¿Lucha política o provocación?* (1974) and Fernando Medina Ruiz's *El terror en México* (1974). Here, government-endorsed fabrications and rumors were presented as facts, and iconic guerrilleros, like Lucio Cabañas and Genaro Vásquez, were reduced to "terrorists."[32] Others who published influential studies of the guerrillas during this time attempted to provide a more balanced account of youthful militancy and offered pioneering interpretations of some of the nation's first urban guerilla movements.[33] An example of this is the short yet influential 1978 essay written by José Luis Rhi Sauri, "La parábola de la guerrilla mexicana," where he moved away from condemnatory descriptions and instead highlighted the difficulties radicals faced in a repressive country. In emphasizing the authoritarianism of the Mexican state, however, he simplified the diverse histories of the guerrilla experience and presented the 1968 and 1971 student massacres as the watershed moments that pushed young people to go underground and join armed struggle.[34]

A third and more academic wave of scholarship that emerged in the 1980s employed methodological tools from sociology, history, and anthropology to provide an analytical and causal interpretation of the radicalism of the 1960s and 1970s.[35] A trailblazing example is the work of Francisco Gomezjara who published two influential but different studies during this period, *Bonapartismo y lucha campesina en la Costa Grande de Guerrero* (1979) and *Las bandas en tiempos de crisis* (1987).[36] The former challenged monolithic and homogenous interpretations of the guerrilla experience by focusing on the communities of Guerrero and highlighting the local context of struggle.[37] The latter, similar to Enrique Marroquín's *La contracultura como protesta* (1978) and Sergio Zermeño's *Una democracia utópica* (1979), which respectively depicted jipismo (counterculture) and student activism as legitimate acts of protest, utilized sociological and cultural explanations to describe the youthful radicalisms of the era.[38] These studies coincided with the publication of pioneering studies of student movement, which made the first attempts to revise the myth of 1968 by providing a longer interpretation of the activism and taking the story outside of the nation's capital.[39] This period also saw the publication of Simón Hipólito's *Guerrero, amnistía y repression* (1982). As historians Cedillo and Herrera Calderón argue elsewhere, this study represents a seminal yet "silenced" work where Hipólito provided a voice to countless victims who directly suffered or witnessed the atrocities of the state, often in collaboration with the local authorities of the Sierra de Atoyac. Because of his work documenting state violence, Hipólito received numerous death threats, was imprisoned, and then driven into exile. Yet, as Cedillo and Herrera Calderón lament, the courageous effort by this author in denouncing with great detail the terrorist nature of the state has been overlooked by scholars.[40] But more significantly, ignored by the press, the horrific events of Atoyac described by Hipólito did not become part of Mexico's official history or generate public outrage.[41]

Three events gave rise to new and more rigorous and nuanced interpretations of the youthful radicalism of the 1960s and 1970s: the 1985 earthquake in Mexico City, the 1994 Zapatista uprising in Chiapas, and the 2000 opening of new state archives of espionage in the Archivo General de la Nación (National Archives, AGN—located at the former Lecumberri Prison).[42] Specifically, the social and political uprisings that developed in response to neoliberalism allowed for the opening of new research centers and pressure groups that both fought for the opening of the DFS and IPS archives and came together to create new memorial sites and human rights organizations. These included, among others, the Centro de Investigaciones Históricas de los Movimientos Armados (Center of Historical Research of Armed Movements, CIHMA), the Comité Eureka (founded in the late 1970s by Rosario Ibarra de Piedra), and the Comité del 68—Pro Libertades Democráticas (created in the 1990s by the resilient leader of 1968 and founder of the influential journal *Punto Crítico*, Raúl Álvarez Garín).[43]

The investigations that emerged from the new archives revised the earlier and often rudimentary interpretations of previous years. These provided further and more detailed evidence of state repression and exposed the diverse and at times divergent leftist and conservative radicalisms of the 1960s and 1970s. In particular, seven scholarly works influenced the innovative work published in *México Beyond 1968*: Montemayor's *Guerra en el Paraíso* (1991), Aguayo's *La Charola* (2001), González Ruiz's *MURO: Memorias y testimonios* (2004), Oikión Solano and García Ugarte's *Movimientos armados en México* (2006), Castellano's *México Armado*, Cedillo and Herrera Calderón's *Challenging Authoritarianism in Mexico* (2012), and Rangel Lozano and Sánchez Serrano's *México en los setenta: ¿Guerra sucia o terrorismo de estado?* (2015).[44] Written as a novel and complemented with the use of primary sources, Montemayor not only voiced those who followed the guerrilla of Lucio Cabañas in Guerrero during the 1960s, but he also offered a poignant critique of the brutality of the Mexican state and depicted the assault of the Madera barracks in Chihuahua as an overriding event of the era.[45] Based on government documents, Aguayo provided a groundbreaking study of Mexico's intelligence agencies as both agencies of espionage and repression.[46] The authors of *MURO* and *Movimientos armados* made extensive use of these archives, and like Castellano, who instead relied on extensive news coverage, they respectively provided a complex portrait of the ultraconservative and leftist militancy that developed across Mexico during the most violent years of the Cold War period.[47] Similarly, Cedillo and Herrera Calderón's *Challenging Authoritarianism in Mexico*, the first book on armed struggle published in English, and Rangel Lozano and Sánchez Serrano's *México en los setenta* called for further attention to the atrocities, magnitude, and consequences of Mexico's Dirty Wars. Like many of the original theses that have been recently published in Mexico, including Cedillo's own groundbreaking studies, the authors in these volumes relied on rich archival work and drew from both older and frequently obscured publications that were silenced in Mexico as well as from testimonios more recently published by independent publishers.[48] This latest body of literature, including the work published by many of the authors in *México Beyond 1968*, has demonstrated that state-sponsored terror further radicalized the nation's activists as many responded by joining the various armed organizations that tried to defeat the authoritarian apparatus of the state.[49]

In sum, over the last fifty years the Mexican student movement of 1968 and the guerrilla movements of the 1970s have been increasingly documented in the expanding scholarship of Mexico's Cold War. While attention to '68 has received more extensive coverage and has enjoyed a more celebratory endorsement in academia, the literature on the radicalism of the 1970s (overwhelmingly written in Spanish) has rather suffered from a more condemnatory tone. More significantly, it has been silenced in Mexico and largely neglected in the scholarship published in Europe and the United States.[50] Moreover, as Zolov alluded to in his essay in this volume, scholars writing on Mexico have made important contributions that have advanced our understanding of the 1960s and 1970s. Yet too frequently they continue to be pulled apart by two rich but divided bodies of literature. One, written under the framework of the Global Sixties, has largely called attention to cultural practices and transnational frameworks of activism and knowledge, while the other has prioritized the political and subversive aspects of the Guerra Sucia. Our hope is that by simultaneously featuring these two representative bodies of literature in the broader context of rural and urban Mexico with particular attention to the multilayered levels of state power and repression described in Pansters's essay and our chronology, we can expect greater dialogue in the scholarship and thus develop a more integrated periodization of the era and a more comprehensive understanding of the multiple and divergent actors that shaped it.

AVENUES FOR FUTURE RESEARCH

The authors featured here make important contributions to challenging the myth of '68 by contextualizing their case studies in the broader context of the nation's multiple Dirty Wars and the revolutionary, countercultural, and religious movements during the 1960s and 1970s. They denote this as a unique era in youth radicalism characterized by a new culture of democracy, more aggressive public protest, and various forms of political violence and state repression embedded in both global and local discourses and actions.

Yet no edited volume is ever comprehensive, and *México Beyond 1968* is no exception. While we know that there were numerous groups that reflected broad tendencies of revolutionary ideologies, there have been relatively few studies of these. Works like Soldatenko's analysis of the various Maoisms that proliferated across Mexico have yet to be carried out on other influential ideologies that informed student and revolutionary activism during the 1960s and 1970s, such as Trotskyism and anarchism.[51] How did the various leftist groups respond to the liberation movements in Africa and Asia? What role, as both Zolov and Dillingham point out, did "South-South"ideological relations and influences in general, and the Patrice Lumumba University and the Chinese Revolution in particular, have on the radicalization of the nation's youth?[52] How did Mexico's '68 compared to those in Latin America and elsewhere?[53]

Gendered analyses of the composition and actions of revolutionary and radical organizations during this period demand significant attention. Pioneering studies of the role of women in the guerrilla movements include the documentary *Mujer Guerrilla* (2008) and articles and collections of testimonies by Lucía Reyes, Adela Cedillo, and María Aguilar Terrés.[54] These social histories are significant correctives to the traditionally masculinist focus on the guerrilla. Few studies have yet to explore the construction of revolutionary and radical masculinity, female masculinity, and femininity among these movements. Luis Herrán's chapter in this volume begins to do this for Conciencia Joven and the radical right. Gladys McCormick's chapter suggests the importance of the gendered nature of torture. The common use of rape and sexual violence by security forces are areas in need of greater analysis as these are still widely employed in Mexican policing.

Like Soldatenko, Herrera Calderón and Oikión also shed light on some of the many efforts that took place during this period in which militant leftist students attempted to create alliances with the working class and the popular sectors. But historians have yet to examine the various perspectives of labor unions on youth radicalism, including from those who supported as well as those who challenged the authority of the state. For instance, what role did powerful *charro* (authoritarian union) leaders like Fidel Velázquez play in combatting student activism during this period?[55] What role did students play in shaping the radicalism of the 1970s that gave rise to independent labor unions?[56]

The complicated and at times contradictory alliances that students made with campesinos and indigenous people is also a theme that is extensively discussed by Cedillo, Padilla, and Villanueva. Specifically, they draw our attention to the particularities of the 1960s and 1970s in rural Mexico where issues related to the land and popular education were hotly debated. Many of these actors interacted with indigenous communities and/or urban students. Others also migrated to large cities, including to the nation's capital. But an explanation of how internal migration shaped radicalism is yet to be written. *Internados* (government-sponsored boarding houses) played a crucial role in this process, yet we know little about these institutions, about the relationships students living in this houses established with progressive authorities of the state, or about the various regional alliances that students from *la provincia* formed in urban centers during the 1960s and 1970s.[57] For example, scattered testimonies note that at UNAM and IPN students frequently formed regional clubs, led among others by *michoacanos* (citizens of Michoacán) and *sinaloenses* (citizens of Sinaloa).[58] But how did these and similar groups with rich histories of student activism in their town of origin shape the radicalism of both the '68 movement and the guerrilla uprisings of the 1970s?

As discussed in the Herrán and Oikión chapters, student journals and magazines, such as *Conciencia Joven* in Monterrey and *La Holguera* in Mexico City, played fundamental roles in radicalizing sectors of Mexico's youth. But what was the relationship between intellectuals and journalists with other radical organizations in both rural and urban Mexico?[59] What role did they play in other more widely distributed but distinct journals such as *Punto Crítico* and *Piedra Rodante*, among others?[60] Moreover, while we have some knowledge about the role youth wings of the PCM and artists played in the student movement, we know little to nothing about their roles in other oppositional parties.[61] Also, we know relatively little about the social history of the *granaderos* (members of the riot police), many of whom as young, or younger, as the student activists and most from poor backgrounds and/or indigenous communities.[62] Similarly, more work is needed on those who left Mexico to the United States and Europe to escape state repression or to participate in other movements.[63]

While several suggestive works have pointed out the linkages between the United States and Mexico during this period, we still know relatively little about hemispheric interactions during this period.[64] The crucial work of Kate Doyle and the National Security Archive has collected an important archive of declassified U.S. and Mexican documents that suggest significant collaboration and coordination between the two nations and their security and spy agencies during the 1960s and 1970s.[65] For example, President Nixon's oval office recordings captured his conversation with the Mexican president on June 16 and 17, 1971, in which Echeverría tells him,

> When I was about to leave from Mexico for this trip, Mr. President, I was
> informed by my various people that groups of Mexicans had been in touch with

friends of Angela Davis [a well-known Black activist at the University of California in Berkeley] in this country. And that we were aware of the plans of the organization that Angela Davis heads to mount a key demonstration in San Antonio protesting the existence of political prisoners in Mexico. All of this is connected to people in Chile, with people in Cuba, with the so-called "Chicano" groups in the United States, with certain groups in Berkeley, California—they're all working closely together.[66]

How accurate is this statement? How did Mexico's '68 and its Dirty Wars of the 1970s shape the radicalism of Chicanxs in the United States?[67]

Recently, scholars have also published valuable studies of this period that specifically look at literature, photography, film, journalism, television, architecture, and street theater.[68] However, attention remains to be given to the broader topic of the counterculture and those who shaped it.[69] To what extent did countercultural ideas mesh with those of the militant Left? How, if student rumors are true, and as Dillingham's study on the CONASUPO also suggests, did the administration of Luis Echeverría finance cultural events, such as the 1971 Avándaro Festival, to manipulate youth radicalism?[70] We know that porros played a key role in agitating and thus dividing secondary students during the Echeverría administration through the control of artistic events and the dissemination of drugs, but how did such a mechanism of control relate to the emergence of the War on Drugs that Aviña and Cedillo examine in their chapters?[71] Is it possible to further our understanding of these relationships, as McCormick does, by getting more direct access to those committing the crimes in general, and to those of agents provocateurs in particular,?[72]

Chapters by Herrán and Santamaría provide important windows into the different ways in which the business sector and the Catholic Church responded to the radicalism of the era, but in what other ways did the various and at times competing institutions and ideological wings of the Church simultaneously shape male and female radicalism during the 1960s and 1970s, particularly outside Mexico City?[73] Finally, there is also a pending gap in our understanding of the "silent majority," representing most people, including students of the 1960s and 1970s, who did not directly engage in political activism, but who nonetheless played a crucial yet understudied role in shaping this period.[74]

In short, the authors of *México Beyond 1968* provide us with new interpretations of the 1960s and 1970s in both rural and urban Mexico and, in so doing, challenge our understanding of '68. But in this fiftieth anniversary of the 1968 student movement, it is apparent that we continue to lack not only critical gaps in the literature but also additional and innovative revisionist approaches.

NOTES

1. Ediciones Era, which deserves a study of its own, was founded in 1960. It published some of the most influential books of the decade, including multiple literary, Marxist, and sociological studies that shaped the student radicalism of the era that ranged from the sociological studies of Pablo González Casanova to the first books by Gabriel García Márquez and eventually the militant manifestos of José Revueltas.

2. Monsiváis, *Días de guardar*; González de Alba, *Los días y los años*; and Poniatowska, *La noche de Tlatelolco*. Ramírez, *El movimiento estudiantil de México*, has also been very influential. His analytical arguments, however, are often overlooked, and instead most scholars simply reference his detailed chronology.

3. For a discussion of these and similar books, see Pensado, *Rebel Mexico*, 201–34.

4. Ibid.

5. Álvarez Garín, *La Estela de Tlatelolco*, 255–58.

6. Ibid.; and Zermeño, *México: Una democracia utópica*.

7. Revueltas, *México 68: Juventud y revolución*; and Volpi Escalante, *La imaginación y el poder*.

8. See, among others, Guevara Niebla, *1968: Largo camino a la democracia*. In comparison, little attention has been given to students from the Instituto Politécnico Nacional (National Polytechnic Institute, IPN) or the secondary schools. And although more attention has been given recently to the role of female participants in the movement, much work remains to be done. Some exceptions that examine IPN and secondary students include Álvarez Garín, *La Estela*; Rodriguez Kuri, "Los primeros días"; and Pensado, *Rebel Mexico*. On the role of female activists and studies that have employed a gender analysis, see, among others, Roberta Avendaño Martínez, *De la libertad y el encierro*; Cohen and Frazier, "Mexico '68"; and Carey, *Plaza of Sacrifices*.

9. *Brigadas* are mobile action brigades in support of a political organization. In the 1960s and 1970s, they helped organize rallies, produce propaganda, and protect organizing efforts. *Brigadismo* refers to the collective action of brigadas.

10. For an extensive and more careful study, see Rivas Ontiveros, *La izquierda en la UNAM*.

11. See, among many other numerous examples, Scherer and Monsiváis, *Los patriotas*; Guevara Niebla, *Libertad nunca se olvida*; and Pérez Arce, *El principio, 1968–1988*.

12. This is particularly evident in the work of Monsiváis. Besides *Días de guardar*, see also *El 68: La tradición de la resistencia*. But this argument is widely embraced in the literature. See, among others, Solana and Comesaña, *Evocación del*; Martínez Della Rocca, *Voces y ecos del* and *Otras voces y otros ecos del*.

13. This is also evident in some of the most common textbooks assigned to history courses of Mexico in the United States where '68 is almost unanimously used as the starting point of a new chapter of the nation's history. A contrasting example, which surprisingly makes no mention at all of the student movement of 1968, as recently noted by Juan Rojo, is Hernández Chávez, *Mexico: A Brief History*. Rojo, *Revisiting the Mexican Student Movement of 1968*, 5.

14. See, among other examples, Flaherty, *Hotel Mexico*; and Carey, *Plaza of Sacrifices*.

15. Particularly constructive is Gould, "Solidarity Under Siege."

16. Schmidt, *The Deterioration of the Mexican Presidency*; and Walker, *Waking from the Dream*.

17. On the commercialization of myths, see the collection of essays in Bilbija and Payne, *Accounting for Violence*.

18. See, for example, Pozas Horcasitas, *Los límites del presidencialismo en las sociedades complejas*.

19. This view is particularly evident in Krauze, *Mexico: Biography of Power*; and Pozas Horcasitas, *Los límites*.

20. But it is worth noting that many other influential intellectuals had also expressed harsh criticism of student activists in the 1960s, siding at times with the administration of Díaz Ordaz. These included, among others, Daniel Cosío Villegas, Agustín Yáñez, Rodolfo Usigli, Salvador Novo, Leopoldo Zea, Roberto Blanco Moheno, Martín Luis Guzmán, and even Lázaro Cárdenas. See Pensado, *Rebel Mexico*, 201–34; Gutiérrez, "Revolution Outside the Revolution"; "Cuando los intelectuales se fascinaron con Echeverría"; and Rodríguez Kuri, "El lado oscuro de la luna."

21. The role of South American exiles and their impact on the nation's Left during this period are themes that remain overlooked in the literature. One notable exception is Yankelevich, *Ráfagas de un exilio*.

22. Important yet limited exceptions that capture the leftist student activism of the early 1970s mainly in the nation's capital include Guevara Niebla, *La democracia en la calle*; Rivas Ontiveros, *La izquierda en la UNAM*; Jardón, *Travesía a Ítaca*; and Ibarra Chávez, *Juventud rebelde e insurgencia estudiantil*.

23. See also McCormick, "The Last Door."

24. The radicalization of Catholic students during Mexico's Cold War is a theme that remains largely overlooked in the historiography. Some recent exceptions include González, "Algunos grupos radicales de izquierdas"; Castillo Ramírez, "Jóvenes católicos de izquierda revolucionaria (1965–1975)"; and Pensado, "El Movimiento Estudiantil Profesional (MEP)."

25. Examples of these include *¡El Móndrigo* (1968); *¡Qué poca Mad . . . era la de José Santos Valdés!* (1969); *El Guerrillero* (1974); and *Jueves de Corpus Sangriento: Revelaciones de un Halcón* (1978). On these and similar books published by the far right to discredit political activism, see Pensado, *Rebel Mexico*, 201–34; and Cedillo and Calderón, "Análisis de la producción historiográfica en torno a la 'guerra sucia' mexicana."

26. For this brief historiographical discussion, we have consulted the books referenced in and expanded from three excellent reviews of the literature: Sánchez Parra, "La guerrilla en México"; Alonzo Padilla, "Revisión teórica sobre la historiografía de la guerrilla mexicana"; and Cedillo and Calderón, "Análisis de la producción historiográfica."

27. Cedillo and Calderón, "Análisis de la producción historiográfica."

28. Ibid.

29. Ibid.

30. See, among other examples by the same author, Guevara Niebla, *Libertad nunca se olvida.*

31. Cedillo and Calderón, "Análisis de la producción historiográfica," 267.

32. Ibid., 268–69.

33. Alonzo Padilla, "Revisión teórica."

34. Ibid., 270; and Sánchez Parra, "La guerrilla en México."

35. Alonzo Padilla, "Revisión teórica"; and Sánchez Parra, "La guerrilla en México."

36. Ibid.; Cedillo and Calderón, "Análisis de la producción historiográfica"; and Gomezjara, *Las bandas en tiempo de crisis.*

37. Sánchez Parra, "La guerrilla en México."

38. Marroquín, *La contracultura como protesta*; and Zermeño, *México: Una democracia utópica.*

39. See, for example, Mabry, *Mexican University and the State*; and de la Garza, Ejea León, and Macias, *El otro movimiento estudiantil.*

40. Cedillo and Calderón, "Análisis de la producción historiográfica," 271.

41. Ibid.

42. Sánchez Parra, "La guerrilla en México"; Alonzo Padilla, "Revisión teórica;" and Cedillo and Calderón, "Análisis de la producción historiográfica."

43. Cedillo and Calderón, "Análisis de la producción historiográfica"; Carey, "Transcending Violence: A Crisis of Memory and Documentation." On the late Álvarez Garín and his resilient commitment to bring justice to those killed during the 1968 movement, see Bacon, "A Hero of Tlatelolco."

44. Aguayo Quezada, *La Charola*; González Ruiz, *MURO: Memorias y testimonios, 1961–2002*; Oikión Solano and García Ugarte, *Movimientos armados en México, siglo XX*; Castellanos, *Mexico armado, 1943–1981*; Herrera Calderón and Cedillo, *Challenging Authoritarianism*; and Rangel Lozano and Sánchez Serrano, *México en los setenta.*

45. Montemayor, *Guerra en el Paraíso.* Other influential novels written by Montemayor include *Las armas del alba* (2003) and *Las mujeres del alba* (2010).

46. His work influenced, among others, Navarro, *Political Intelligence and the Creation of Modern Mexico*; and Rodríguez Munguía, *La otra guerra secreta.*

47. Other influential publications that have respectively influenced the studies of leftist and ultraconservative radicalism include Sierra Guzmán, *El enemigo interno*; and Delgado, *El yunque.*

48. Adela Cedillo's master's thesis was published as *El Fuego y el Silencio: Historia de las Fuerzas de Liberación Nacional.* For a partial list of some of the original research

that has been recently published as monographs and master's and PhD dissertations in Mexico, see Sánchez Parra, "La guerrilla en México."

49. In particular, see Padilla, *Rural Resistance in the Land of Zapata*; Aviña, *Specters of Revolution*; and McCormick, *Logic of Compromise in Mexico*.

50. Besides the work published by some of the authors in this volume, a notable yet translated exception includes Ulloa Bornemann, *Surviving Mexico's Dirty War: A Political Prisoner's Memoir*.

51. A useful starting point is Rivas Ontiveros, *La izquierda en la UNAM*.

52. See also Rothwell, *Transpacific Revolutionaries: The Chinese Revolution in Latin America*.

53. Gould, "Solidarity Under Siege"; and Carey, *Protests in the Streets: 1968 Across the Globe*.

54. Patitos, *Mujer Guerrilla*; Rayas, "Subjugating the Nation: Women and the Guerrilla Experience"; Cedillo, "Mujeres, guerrilla y terror de Estado en la época de la revoltura en México"; and Aguilar Terrés, *Guerrilleras*.

55. Two excellent points of departure include Fernández Christlieb and Rodríguez Araujo, *La clase obrera en la historia de México*; and Mendiola García, *Street Democracy*.

56. See the following two examples: Cook, *Organizing Dissent*; and Walker, *Waking from the Dream*.

57. For a study that gets at the daily life of the Internado, but with an emphasis on previous decades, see Civera Cerecedo, "El internado como familia."

58. Scattered references on this topic exist in the vast testimonial literature of 1968.

59. Cabrera López, *Una inquietud de amanecer*; Rodríguez Munguía, *La otra guerra secreta*; and Smith, *Stories from the Newsroom, Stories from the Street*. On intellectuals and the Left, see Volpi Escalante, *La imaginación y el poder*; Gutiérrez, "Revolution Outside the Revolution"; and Illades, *La inteligencia rebelde*.

60. Others have examined *Política* and *El Corno Emplumado*. See Reynaga Mejía, *La revolución cubana en México*; and Acevedes Sepúlveda, "Artists' Networks in the 1960s."

61. Some exceptions include Carr, *Marxism and Communism in Twentieth-Century Mexico*; Condés Lara, *Represión y rebelión en México*; Gómez, *La historia también está hecha por derrotas*; and Cárdenas and Librado, *La Academia de San Carlos en el movimiento estudiantil de 1968*. On the role of the Partido de Acción Nacional (PAN) during the '68 movement, see Medina Valdés, *Operación 10 de junio*; Medina Valdés, *El 68, Tlatelolco, y el PAN*; and Martínez Fischer, "La postura del Partido Acción Nacional ante el movimiento estudiantil de 1968."

62. Rath, *Myths of Demilitarization in Postrevolutionary Mexico, 1920–1960*, would be an excellent starting point. On indigenous youth during this period, see Dillingham, "Indigenismo Occupied: Indigenous Youth and Mexico's Democratic Opening (1968–1975)."

63. See, for instance, Marsh, "'Writing Our History in Songs': Judith Reyes, Popular Music and the Student Movement of 1968."

64. Morley, *Our Man in Mexico: Winston Scott and the Hidden History of the CIA*.
65. Kate Doyle, "Tlatelolco Massacre: Declassified U.S. Documents on Mexico and the Events of 1968," National Security Archive, last accessed October 15, 2017, http://nsarchive.gwu.edu/NSAEBB/NSAEBB10/intro.htm; and "Human Rights and the Dirty War in Mexico," National Security Archive, last accessed October 15, 2017, http://nsarchive.gwu.edu/NSAEBB/NSAEBB89/.
66. Kate Doyle, "The Nixon Tapes: Secret Recordings from the Nixon White House on Luis Echeverría and Much Much More," National Security Archive, last accessed October 15, 2017, http://nsarchive.gwu.edu/NSAEBB/NSAEBB95/.
67. This is a theme alluded to several years ago in Gómez Quiñonez, *Mexican Students por la Raza*, but it has received little attention. Notable exceptions include Soldatenko, "Mexican Student Movements in Los Angeles and Mexico"; Gómez, "'Por la reunificación de los pueblos libres de América en su lucha por el socialismo'"; and especially Gómez, *The Revolutionary Imaginations of Greater Mexico*.
68. See Castillo del Troncoso, *Ensayo sobre el movimiento estudiantil*; González de Bustamante, *Muy buenas noches*; Steinberg, *Photopoetics at Tlatelolco*; Flaherty, *Hotel Mexico*; and Rojo, *Revisting the Mexican Student Movement of 1968*.
69. Useful studies have been recently published since the influential writing of Zolov's, *Refried Elvis*. See, among other comparative cases from Latin America, Debroise, *La era de la discrepancia*; Eder, *Desafío de la estabilidad*; and Vaughan, *Portrait of a Young Painter*.
70. Rubli Kaiser, "Avándaro 1971."
71. See Oikión Solano's chapter in this volume and Pensado, *Rebel Mexico*.
72. Campos Lemus, starting with *El otoño de la revolución (octubre)*.
73. See, for example, Aspe Armella, "Jóvenes radicales y curas heterodoxos."
74. Carassai, *Argentine Silent Majority*.

BIBLIOGRAPHY

ARCHIVES

Doyle, Kate. "Tlatelolco Massacre: Declassified U.S. Documents on Mexico and the Events of 1968." The National Security Archive. Accessed October 15, 2017. http://nsarchive.gwu.edu/NSAEBB/NSAEBB10/intro.htm.

———. "Human Rights and the Dirty War in Mexico." National Security Archive. Accessed October 15, 2017. http://nsarchive.gwu.edu/NSAEBB/NSAEBB89/http://nsarchive.gwu.edu/NSAEBB/NSAEBB89/.

———. "The Nixon Tapes: Secret Recordings from the Nixon White House on Luis Echeverría and Much Much More." Accessed October 15, 2017. http://nsarchive.gwu.edu/NSAEBB/NSAEBB95/http://nsarchive.gwu.edu/NSAEBB/NSAEBB95/.

———. "Tlatelolco Massacre: Declassified U.S. Documents on Mexico and the Events of 1968." The National Security Archive. Accessed October 15, 2017. http://nsarchive.gwu.edu/NSAEBB/NSAEBB10/intro.htm.

PUBLISHED SOURCES

Acevedes Sepúlveda, Gabriela. "Artists' Networks in the 1960s: The Case of El Corno Emplumado / The Plummed Horn (Mexico City, 1962–1969)." In *The Global 1960s: Convention, Contest and Counterculture*, edited by Tamara Chaplin and Jadwiga E. Pieper Mooney, 196–216. New York: Routledge, 2017.

Aguayo Quezada, Sergio. *La Charola: Una historia de los servicios de inteligencia en México*. Mexico City: Grijalbo, 2001.

Aguilar Terrés, Luz María. *Guerrilleras: Antología de testimonios y textos sobre la participación de las mujeres en los movimientos armados socialistas en México, segunda mitad del siglo XX*. Mexico City: Unknown publisher, 2014.

Alonzo Padilla, Arturo Luis. "Revisión teórica sobre la historiografía de la guerrilla mexicana." In *Movimientos armados en México, siglo XX*, edited by Verónica Oikión Solano and Marta Eugenia García Ugarte. Vol. 1, 111–27. Zamora, Mexico: El Colegio de Michoacán, 2006.

Álvarez Garín, Raúl. *La Estela de Tlatelolco*. Mexico City: Grijalbo, 1998.

Aspe Armella, María Luisa. "Jóvenes radicales y curas heterodoxos: La incidencia de los jesuitas en el movimiento estudiantil de 1968." In *Historia y memoria de los movimientos estudiantiles: A 45 años del 68*, edited by José René Rivas Ontiveros, Ana María Sánchez Sáenz, and Gloria A. Tirado Villegas. Vol. 1, 325–49. Mexico City: UNAM/ Editions Gernika, 2017.

Avendaño Martínez, Roberta. *De la libertad y el encierro*. Mexico City: La Idea Dorada, 1998.

Aviña, Alexander. *Specters of Revolution: Peasant Guerrillas in the Cold War Mexican Countryside*. Oxford: Oxford University Press, 2014.

Bacon, David. "A Hero of Tlatelolco." *NACLA*, October 20, 2014.

Bilbija, Ksenija, and Leigh A. Payne, eds. *Accounting for Violence: Marketing Memory in Latin America*. Durham, N.C.: Duke University Press, 2011.

Cabrera López, Patricia. *Una inquietud de amanecer: Literatura y política en México, 1962–1987*. Mexico City: Plaza y Valdes, 2006.

Campos Lemus, Sócrates A. *El otoño de la revolución (octubre)*. Mexico City: Costa-Amic, 1974.

Carassai, Sebastián. *The Argentine Silent Majority: Middle Classes, Politics, Violence, and Memory in the Seventies*. Durham, N.C.: Duke University Press, 2014.

Cárdenas, Luna, and Daniel Librado, *La Academia de San Carlos en el movimiento estudiantil de 1968*. Mexico City: Facultad de Artes y Diseño, 2009.

Carey, Elaine. *Plaza of Sacrifices: Gender, Power, and Terror in 1968 Mexico*. Albuquerque: University of New Mexico Press, 2005.

———. "Transcending Violence: A Crisis of Memory and Documentation." In *Challenging Authoritarianism in Mexico: Revolutionary Struggles and the "Dirty War," 1964–1982*, edited by Fernando Herrera Calderón and Adela Cedillo, 198–210. New York: Routledge, 2012.

Carey, Elaine, ed. *Protests in the Streets: 1968 Across the Globe.* Indianapolis: Hackett Publishing Company, 2016.

Carr, Barry. *Marxism and Communism in Twentieth-Century Mexico.* Lincoln: University of Nebraska Press, 1992.

Castellanos, Laura. *México armado, 1943–1981.* Mexico City: Ediciones Era, 2007.

Castillo del Troncoso, Alberto. *Ensayo sobre el movimiento estudiantil: La fotografía y la construcción de un imaginario.* Mexico City: Instituto Mora, 2012.

Castillo Ramírez, María Gracia. "Jóvenes católicos de izquierda revolucionaria (1965–1975)." In *Violencia y sociedad, Un hito en la historia de las izquierdas en América Latina,* edited by Verónica Oikión Solano and Miguel Ángel Urrego Ardilla, 111–40. Zamora, Mexico: El Colegio de Michoacán, 2010.

Cedillo, Adela. *El Fuego y el Silencio. Historia de las Fuerzas de Liberación Nacional.* Mexico City: Comité 68 Pro Libertades Democráticas, 2008.

———. "Mujeres, guerrilla y terror de Estado en la época de la revoltura en México." Unpublished paper, n.d. Accessed October 2, 2017. https://wisc.academia.edu /AdelaCedillo.

Cedillo, Adela, and Fernando H. Calderón, "Análisis de la producción historiográfica en torno a la 'guerra sucia' Mexicana." In *El estudio de las luchas revolucionarias en América Latina (1959–1996): Estado de la cuestión,* edited by Verónica Oikión Solano, Eduardo Rey Tristán, and Martín López Ávalos, 263–288. Zamora, Mexico: El Colegio de Michoacán, 2014.

Civera Cerecedo, Alicia. "El internado como familia: Las escuelas noramales rurales en la década de 1920." *Revista Latinoamericana de Estudios Educativos* 36, nos. 3–4 (2006): 53–73.

Cohen, Deborah, and Lessie Jo Frazier. "Mexico '68: Defining the Space of the Movement, Heroic Masculinity in the Prison, and 'Women' in the Streets." *Hispanic American Historical Review* 84, no. 4 (November 2003): 617–60.

Condés Lara, Enrique. *Represión y rebelión en México.* 2 vols. Mexico City: Porrúa, 2007.

Cook, Maria Lorena. *Organizing Dissent: Unions, the State, and the Democratic Teachers' Movement in Mexico.* University Park: Penn State University Press, 1996.

"Cuando los intelectuales se fascinaron con Echeverría." *Proceso,* July 14, 2002.

Debroise, Oliver, ed. *La era de la discrepancia: Arte y cultura visual en México / The Age of Discrepancies: Art and Visual Culture in Mexico, 1968–1997.* Mexico City: UNAM, 2007.

Delgado, Alvaro. *El yunque: La ultraderecha en el poder.* Mexico City: Plaza y Janés, 2005.

Dillingham, A. S. "Indigenismo Occupied: Indigenous Youth and Mexico's Democratic Opening (1968–1975)." *The Americas* 72, no. 4 (October 2015): 549–82.

Eder, Rita, ed. *Desafío de la estabilidad: Procesos artísticos en México, 1952–1967 / Defying Stability: Artistic Processes in Mexico, 1952–1967.* Mexico City: Museo Universitario de Arte Contemporáneo, 2014.

Fernández Christlieb, Paulina, and Octavio Rodríguez Araujo. *La clase obrera en la historia de México en el sexenio de Tlatelolco.* Mexico City: Siglo XXI, 1985.

Flaherty, George F. *Hotel Mexico: Dwelling on the '68 Movement*. Berkeley: University of California Press, 2016.

Garza de la, Enrique, Tomás Ejea León, and Luis Fernando Macias. *El otro movimiento estudiantil*. Mexico City: Extemporáneos, 1986.

Gómez, Alan Eladio. "'Por la reunificación de los pueblos libres de América en su lucha por el socialismo': The Chicana/o Movement, the PPUA and the Dirty War in Mexico in the 1970s." In *Challenging Authoritarianism in Mexico: Revolutionary Struggles and the "Dirty War," 1964–1982*, edited by Fernando Herrera Calderón and Adela Cedillo, 81–104. New York: Routledge, 2012.

———. *The Revolutionary Imaginations of Greater Mexico: Chicana/o Radicalism, Solidarity Politics, and Latin American Social Movements*. Austin: University of Texas Press, 2016.

Gomezjara, Francisco A. *Las bandas en tiempo de crisis*. Mexico City: Ediciones Nueva Sociología, 1987.

Gómez, Pablo. *La historia también está hecha por derrotas*. Mexico City: Porrúa, 2008.

Gómez Quiñonez, Juan. *Mexican Students por la Raza: The Chicano Student Movement in Southern California, 1967–1977*. Santa Barbara, Calif.: Editorial La Causa, 1978.

González de Alba, Luis. *Los días y los años*. Mexico City: Ediciones Era, 1971.

González de Bustamante, Celeste. *Muy buenas noches: Mexico, Television, and the Cold War*. Lincoln: University of Nebraska Press, 2013.

González, Fernando M. "Algunos grupos radicales de izquierdas y de derecha con influencia católica en México (1965–1975)." *Historia y Grafía*, UIA, No. 29 (2007): 57–93.

González Ruiz, Edgar. *MURO: Memorias y testimonios, 1961–2002*. Puebla: Benemérita Universidad Autónoma de Puebla, 2004.

Gould, Jeffrey L. "Solidarity Under Siege: The Latin American Left, 1968." *American Historical Review* 114, no. 2 (2009): 348–75.

Guevara Niebla, Gilberto. *La democracia en la calle: Crónica del movimiento estudiantil Mexicano*. Mexico City: Siglo XXI, 1988.

———. *Libertad nunca se olvida: Memoria del 68*. Mexico City: Cal y Arena, 2010.

———. *1968: Largo camino a la democracia*. Mexico City: Cal y Arena, 2008.

Gutiérrez, Edgar Iván. "Revolution Outside the Revolution: 'Leftist' Intellectuals Face Mexico's Official 'Revolutionary' Party Since 1929." PhD diss., University of California, Los Angeles, 2000.

Hernández Chávez, Alicia. *Mexico: A Brief History*. Berkeley: University of California Press, 2006.

Herrera Calderón, Fernando, and Adela Cedillo, eds. *Challenging Authoritarianism in Mexico: Revolutionary Struggles and the "Dirty War," 1964–1982*. New York: Routledge, 2012.

Ibarra Chávez, Héctor. *Juventud rebelde e insurgencia estudiantil: Las otras voces del movimiento político-social mexicano en los años setenta*. Monterrey: Universidad Autónoma de Nuevo León, 2012.

Illades, Carlos. *La inteligencia rebelde: La izquierda en el debate público en México, 1968–1989*. Mexico City: Océano, 2012.

Jardón, Raúl. *Travesía a Ítaca: Recuerdos de un militante de izquirda (del comunismo al zapatismo), 1965–2001*. Mexico City: Grupo Editorial Cenzontle, 2008.

Krauze, Enrique. *Mexico: Biography of Power*. New York: Harper Perennial, 1998.

Mabry, Donald J. *The Mexican University and the State: Conflicts, 1910–1971*. College Station: Texas A&M Press, 1982.

Marroquín, Enrique. *La contracultura como protesta: Análisis de un fenómeno juvenil*. Mexico City: Editorial J. Mortiz, 1975.

Marsh, Hazel. "'Writing Our History in Songs': Judith Reyes, Popular Music and the Student Movement of 1968." In *Reflections on Mexico '68*, edited by Keith Brewster, 144–59. Hoboken, N.J.: Wiley-Blackwell, 2010.

Martínez Della Rocca, Salvador, ed. *Otras voces y otros ecos del 68*. Mexico City: Fondo de Cultura Económica, 2013.

———. *Voces y ecos del 68*. Mexico City: Porrúa, 2009.

Martínez Fischer, Margarita. "La postura del Partido Acción Nacional ante el movimiento estudiantil de 1968." In *Voces y ecos del 68*, edited by Salvador Martínez della Rocca, 233–53. Mexico City: Porrúa, 2009.

Martínez Nateras, Arturo. *El 68: Conspiración comunista*. Mexico City: Porrúa, 2011.

McCormick, Gladys I. "The Last Door: Political Prisoners and the Use of Torture in Mexico's Dirty War." *The Americas* 74, no. 1 (2017): 57–81.

———. *The Logic of Compromise in Mexico: How the Countryside Was Key to the Emergence of Authoritarianism*. Chapel Hill: University of North Carolina Press, 2016.

Medina Valdés, Gerardo. *El 68, Tlatelolco, y el PAN*. Mexico City: PAN, 1990.

———. *Operación 10 de junio*. Mexico City: Ediciones Universo, 1972.

Mendiola García, Sandra C. *Street Democracy: Vendors, Violence, and Public Space in Late Twentieth-Century Mexico*. Lincoln: University of Nebraska Press, 2017.

Monsiváis, Carlos. *Días de guardar*. Mexico City: Ediciones Era, 1970.

———. *El 68: La tradición de la Resistencia*. Mexico City: Ediciones Era, 2008.

Montemayor, Carlos. *Guerra en el Paraíso*. Mexico City: Editorial Diana, 1991.

Morley, Jefferson. *Our Man in Mexico: Winston Scott and the Hidden History of the CIA*. Lawrence: University of Kansas Press, 2008.

Navarro, Aaron W. *Political Intelligence and the Creation of Modern Mexico, 1938–1954*. University Park: Penn State University Press, 2010.

Oikión Solano, Verónica, and Marta Eugenia García Ugarte, eds. *Movimientos armados en México, siglo XX*. 3 vols. Zamora, Mexico: El Colegio de Michoacán, 2006–2008.

Padilla, Tanalís. *Rural Resistance in the Land of Zapata: The Jaramillista Movement and the Myth of the Pax Priísta, 1940–1962*. Durham, N.C.: Duke University Press, 2008.

Patitos, dir. *Mujer Guerrilla*. Documentary. Mexico: Producciones Patitos, April 9, 2008. Accessed October 2, 2017. https://www.youtube.com/watch?v=ywb9g25XxXQ.

Pensado, Jaime M. "El Movimiento Estudiantil Profesional (MEP): Una mirada a la radicalización de la juventud católica Mexicana durante la Guerra Fría." *Mexican Studies/Estudios Mexicanos* 31, no. 1 (Winter 2015): 156–92.

———. *Rebel Mexico: Student Unrest and Authoritarian Political Culture During the Long Sixties*. Stanford, Calif.: Stanford University Press, 2013.

Pérez Arce, Francisco. *El principio, 1968–1988: Años de rebeldía.* Mexico City: Itaca, 2007.

Poniatowska, Elena. *La noche de Tlatelolco.* Mexico City: Ediciones Era, 1971.

Pozas Horcasitas, Ricardo. *Los límites del presidencialismo en las sociedades complejas: México en los años sesenta.* Mexico City: Siglo XXI, 2014.

Ramírez, Ramón. *El movimiento estudiantil de México.* 2 vols. Mexico City: Ediciones Era, 1969.

Rangel Lozano, Claudia E. G., and Evangelina Sánchez Serrano, eds. *México en los setenta: ¿Guerra sucia o terrorismo de estado? Hacía una política de la memoria.* Chilpancingo: Universidad Autónoma de Guerrero, 2015.

Rath, Thomas. *Myths of Demilitarization in Postrevolutionary Mexico, 1920–1960.* Chapel Hill: University of North Carolina Press, 2013.

Rayas, Lucía. "Subjugating the Nation: Women and the Guerrilla Experience." In *Challenging Authoritarianism in Mexico: Revolutionary Struggles and the "Dirty War," 1964–1982*, edited by Fernando Herrera Calderón and Adela Cedillo, 167–81. New York: Routledge, 2012.

Revueltas, José. *México 68: Juventud y revolución.* Mexico City: Ediciones Era, 1978.

Reynaga Mejía, Juan Rafael. *La revolución cubana en México a través de la revista Política: Construcción imaginaria de un discurso para América Latina.* Mexico City: UNAM, 2007.

Rivas Ontiveros, Rene. *La izquierda en la UNAM: Organizaciones, movilizaciones y diderazgos (1958–1972).* Mexico City: Miguel Ángel Porrúa, 2007.

Rodriguez Kuri, Ariel. "El lado oscuro de la luna: El momento conservador en 1968." In *Conservadurismo y derechas en la historia de México*, edited by Erika Pani. Vol. 1, 512–59. Mexico City: Fondo de Cultura Económica, 2009.

———. "Los primeros días: Una explicación de los orígenes inmediatos del movimiento estudiantil de 1968." *Historia Mexicana* 53, no. 1 (July–September 2003): 179–228.

Rodríguez Munguía, Jacinto. *La otra guerra secreta: Los archivos prohibidos de la prensa y el poder.* Mexico City: DeBolsillo, 2007.

Rojo, Juan J. *Revisiting the Mexican Student Movement of 1968: Shifting Perspectives in Literature and Culture Since Tlatelolco.* New York: Palgrave Macmillan, 2016.

Rothwell, Matthew. *Transpacific Revolutionaries: The Chinese Revolution in Latin America.* New York: Routledge, 2013.

Rubli Kaiser, Federico. "Avándaro 1971: A 40 años de Woodstock en Valle de Bravo." *Nexos*, September 16, 2011.

Sánchez Parra, Sergio Arturo. "La guerrilla en México: Un intent de balance historiográfico." *Clío* 6, no. 35 (2006): 121–44.

Scherer, Julio, and Carlos Monsiváis, *Los patriotas: De Tlatelolco a la guerra sucia.* Mexico City: Aguilar, 2004.

Schmidt, Samuel. *The Deterioration of the Mexican Presidency: The Years of Luis Echeverría.* Tucson: University of Arizona Press, 1991.

Sierra Guzmán, Jorge Luis. *El enemigo interno: Contrainsurgencia y fuerzas armadas en México.* Mexico City: Plaza y Valdés, 2003.

Smith, Benjamin T. *Stories from the Newsroom, Stories from the Street: The Mexican Press, 1940–1976.* Chapel Hill: University of North Carolina Press, forthcoming.

Solana, Fernando, and Mariángeles Comesaña, eds., *Evocación del 68.* Mexico City: Siglo XXI, 2008.

Soldatenko, Michael. "Mexican Student Movements in Los Angeles and Mexico, 1968." *Latino Studies* 1, no. 2 (July 2003): 284–300.

Steinberg, Samuel. *Photopoetics at Tlatelolco: Afterimages of Mexico, 1968.* Austin: University of Texas Press, 2016.

Ulloa Bornemann, Alberto. *Surviving Mexico's Dirty War: A Political Prisoner's Memoir.* Translated by Arthur Schmidt. Philadelphia: Temple University Press, 2007.

Vaughan, Mary Kay. *Portrait of a Young Painter: Pepe Zúñiga and Mexico City's Rebel Generation.* Durham, N.C.: Duke University Press, 2014.

Volpi Escalante, Jorge. *La imaginación y el poder: Una historia intelectual de 1968.* Mexico City: Ediciones Era, 2008.

Walker, Louise E. *Waking from the Dream: Mexico's Middle Classes After 1968.* Stanford, Calif.: Stanford University Press, 2013.

Yankelevich, Pablo. *Ráfagas de un exilio: Argentinos en México, 1974–1983.* Mexico City: Fondo de Cultura Económica, 2010.

Zermeño, Sergio. *México: Una democracia utópica; El movimiento estudiantil de 68.* Mexico City: Siglo XXI, 1978.

Zolov, Eric. *Refried Elvis: The Rise of the Mexican Counterculture.* Berkeley: University of California Press, 1999.

CHRONOLOGY OF SELECTED EVENTS

Revolutionaries, Radicals, and
Repression (c. 1946–c. 1980)

JAIME M. PENSADO AND ENRIQUE C. OCHOA

NATIONAL	INTERNATIONAL
1946–1953	
1946: Miguel Alemán is elected president (1946–52). During this period, the Institutional Revolutionary Party (PRI) is founded, the first steps are taken to reverse popular education, *charrismo* emerges as a mechanism of control in the labor unions, and the Federal Security Directorate (DFS) and the *granaderos* (riot police) become key tools of surveillance and repression.	**1946–47**: The language of "national security" becomes emblematic of U.S. foreign policy with the founding of the National Security Council, the School of the Americas, and the Central Intelligence Agency (CIA).
1946–49: Students protest in defense of popular education at the National Teacher's College (ENM), the Rural Teaching Training Colleges (ENM), and San Nicolás de Hidalgo University in Michoacán.	The Mexican Agricultural Project, initiated by the Mexican government and the Ford Foundation in the previous administration, begins to aggressively expand and reverse campesino gains made under the Cárdenas presidency and undergirds the capitalist expansion in the countryside. Later dubbed the Green Revolution, it was an important weapon to contain communist expansion.
1948: The Federation of Students from Guadalajara (FEG) is created and soon transforms into a key institution of repression.	

NATIONAL   INTERNATIONAL

1946–1953 (*continued*)

July–December 1949: Student leaders Agustín Abarca and Armando Tavera are killed in Morelia; the leftist leaders and writers Manuel Terrazas, Gerardo Unzueta, and Valentín Campa are arrested.

1950: National Polytechnic Institute (IPN) students organize a protest against the government of Miguel Alemán, whose new Organic Law threatens popular education. The protests last more than forty days and make reference to the repression of 1942 when IPN students organized their first strike and witnessed their first martyrs.

1952: Adolfo Ruiz Cortines is elected president (1952–58). That same year, communist student leader and IPN activist Luis Morales is assassinated, a group of *henriquistas* (sympathizers of Manuel Henríquez Guzmán) is massacred in Mexico City, and ENRs are closed in Chihuahua and Jalisco.

1952: Rubén Jaramillo rises up in Morelos and coordinates with other movements throughout the state. He reissues his 1943 Plan de Cerro Prieto, updated to reflect his radicalization as a result of state repression.

1953: Women gain suffrage rights.

1951: The Bracero Program is extended with the signing of the Migrant Labor Agreement.

1951–53: The Soviet Union/China and the United States take opposing sides during the Korean War.

March 1953: Joseph Stalin dies and Nikita Khrushchev (1953–64) transforms the Soviet Union into a superpower.

NATIONAL	INTERNATIONAL
1954	

NATIONAL	INTERNATIONAL
May: A leading member of the Anti-communist Popular Front Jorge Prieto Laurens organizes the First American Congress against Soviet Intervention in Latin America. **1954–55**: The Anticommunist University Front (FUA) is founded in Puebla.	The CIA overthrows the government of Jacobo Árbenz in Guatemala. Adolfo Mexiac, a leading figure of the Taller de Gráfica Popular, illustrates *Libertad de expresión* (Freedom of Expression). The image (included on the cover of the book) of the man silenced with a metal chain was originally created in response to the 1954 CIA-sponsored intervention in Guatemala, and it was made famous worldwide during the 1968 student movement. The United States launches Operation Wetback and hundreds of thousands of people are deported to Mexico. Ernesto "Ché" Guevara arrives in Mexico City and a year later meets Fidel Castro.
1955	
	Ho Chi Minh initiates land reforms in Vietnam. The Latin American Episcopal Council (CELAM) is founded to study the problems facing the Church in Latin America and coordinate activities across the continent.
1956	
Miguel Dario Miranda y Gómez is appointed Archbishop of Mexico City (1956–71) and plays a key role in strengthening the relationship between the Church and the state. **June:** Students from IPN start organizing the nation's first massive student strike in Mexico City.	**1956–66**: The Sino-Soviet split marks the breaking of political relations between the People's Republic of China and the Soviet Union.

NATIONAL	INTERNATIONAL
1956 (*continued*)	

September 23: The government sends the federal army to occupy the dorms of IPN and put an end to the strike. Student leaders Nicandro Mendoza and Mariano Molina are accused of "social dissolution" and arrested.

In the aftermath of the movement, the National Front of Technical Students (FNET), which had played an important role in the 1942 and 1950 IPN strikes, starts collaborating with the government, and the DFS creates a special category of surveillance titled "student problems."

October: The Hungarian uprising is crushed by the Soviet Union.

| **1957** | |

The Mexico-China Friendship Society is established.

Jack Kerouac publishes *On the Road*.

| **1958** | |

Adolfo López Mateos (1958–64) is elected president, and women vote in their first presidential elections.

Colonel Manuel Rangel Escamilla is named the Director of the DFS (1958–64).

Carlos Fuentes publishes *Where the Air Is Clear*.

1958–59: Railroad workers, teachers, and university students organize massive strikes in Mexico City. The state responds with violence and employs the Law of Social Dissolution to imprison some of the main leaders responsible for the strikes, including Othón Salazar, Valentín Campa, and Demetrio Vallejo.

Mexican Archbishop Miguel Dario Miranda y Gómez is appointed president of CELAM (1958–63). He advocates social justice but emerges as a harsh critic of those who sympathized with the Cuban Revolution.

NATIONAL	INTERNATIONAL

1958 (*continued*)

The General Union of Mexican Workers and Peasants (UGOCM) steps up demands for land reform, and thousands of campesinos throughout the Northwest occupy lands.

Prieto Laurens hosts the World Anti-Communist Congress in Mexico City.

1959

The creation of free textbooks brings tensions between the most conservative wings of the Church and the state.	**January:** The Cuban Revolution, led by Fidel Castro and Ché Guevara, among others, triumphs and emerges as an anti-imperialist alternative to the Mexican Revolution.
	The Cuban news agency Prensa Latina is founded with headquarters in Havana.

1960

Cardinal José Garibi Rivera and various sectors of Mexico's conservative society initiate the civic campaign "¡Cristianismo si, comunismo no!"	Sit-ins and civil rights movements intensify in the U.S. South.
President López Mateos characterizes his administration as "extreme left within the Constitution."	The Pill is first made available for married women in the United States and soon becomes the contraceptive choice for other women across the world.
The PCM organizes its Twelfth Congress and redefines its struggle as "Democratic" and of "National Liberation."	
The publishing house Ediciones Era is founded.	
May: The magazine *Política* publishes its first issue.	
May–August: David Alfaro Siqueiros and Filomeno Mata are arrested.	**July:** Ché Guevara leads the Latin American Youth Congress in Havana under the banner "For the liberation of Latin America."

NATIONAL	INTERNATIONAL

1960 (*continued*)

September 4: The Spartacus Leninist League (LLE) is founded under the leadership of José Revueltas.

December 30: A massacre of more than a dozen people puts an end to the Student-Popular Movement in Chilpancingo, Guerrero.

1961

The National Liberation Movement (MLN) is founded as an effort to unite the various leftist movements; it emerges from the Latin American Conference for Political Sovereignty, Economic Independence, and Peace organized in March by Lázaro Cárdenas and remains active until 1966–67. Conservative sectors led by Miguel Alemán and Abelardo Rodríguez respond by creating their own unifying organization, the Mexican Civic Front of Revolutionary Affirmation (FCMAR).

Violent student protests are organized for and against the Cuban Revolution in San Luis Potosí, Mexico City, Puebla, Michoacán, and Chihuahua.

John F. Kennedy is elected U.S. president and soon after launches the Alliance for Progress (until 1969).

Oscar Lewis publishes *The Children of Sánchez.*

The Institute of Latin America of the Academy of Science is founded as the first Soviet institution to study Latin America.

April: The CIA-sponsored Bay of Pigs invasion fails to overthrow the government of Fidel Castro, yet in Mexico, it succeeds in recruiting high-ranking officials from the government, including López Mateos and future Mexican presidents Gustavo Díaz Ordaz and Luis Echeverría.

May: Pope John XXIII writes *Mater et Magistra* (Mother and Teacher), where he calls for social justice and aid to underdeveloped countries.

September 1–6: The founding conference of the Non-Aligned Movement (NAM) is held in Belgrade, Yugoslavia.

December: Fidel Castro declares that he is a "Marxist-Leninist."

NATIONAL	INTERNATIONAL

1962

José Revueltas publishes his 1958 *Ensayo sobre un proletariado sin cabeza*, where he criticizes the reformism and opportunism of the left.

Adolfo Christlieb is elected president of the PAN (1962–68) and develops a more conciliatory relationship with the PRI.

January: *El Corno Emplumado / The Plumed Horn* publishes its first issue (1962–69).

March: The right-wing University Movement for a Renewed Orientation Movement (MURO) is founded.

May 23: Campesino leader Rubén Jaramillo is killed.

June–July: John F. Kennedy visits Mexico.

August: The federal army occupies the ENM of Mactumatzá in Chiapas and arrests several activists.

December: Students in Guerrero commemorate the second anniversary of the Chilpancingo massacre and demand freedom for all political prisoners.

The United States launches its first combat missions against the Vietcong.

Algeria wins its independence from France.

Cuba is expelled from the Organization of the American States, and Mexico is the only country in the western hemisphere to maintain relations with the island.

March 26–April 8: President López Mateos travels to Europe (France, Yugoslavia, Poland, Holland, West Germany).

October: The Cuban Missile Crisis brings further tension to the Cold War.

October 3–24: President López Mateos travels to Asia (India, Indonesia, Japan, Philippines).

October 11, 1962–December 8, 1965: The Second Vatican Council addresses questions between the Church and the modern world and prioritizes the laity over the hierarchy.

NATIONAL	INTERNATIONAL
1963	

NATIONAL	INTERNATIONAL
The Independent Peasant Center (CCI) is founded by MLN and PCM members to unify dissident campesinos, challenge the official National Peasant Confederation (CNC), and demand land reform and social justice.	Frantz Fanon's *Wretched of the Earth* is translated into Spanish by the Fondo de Cultura Económica as *Los condenados de la tierra*.
Ramón Danzós Palomino and other leftist leaders create the People's Electoral Front (FEP).	Bishops Hélder Câmara and Manuel Larraín take the presidency of CELAM (1963–66) to a more conciliatory relationship with the left.
March: The army is sent to arrest student leaders in Morelia, student leader Manuel Oropeza García is killed, and Eli de Gortari is forced to resign as rector of Universidad Michoacana de San Nicolás Hidalgo.	Betty Friedan publishes *The Feminine Mystique*. **April**: Pope John XXIII issues *Pacem in Terris* (Peace on Earth). Addressing the broader theme of nuclear nonproliferation, the encyclical calls for the dignity of all individuals.
April 13: A violent confrontation between leftist students and anticommunist activists known as "El Sabinazo" takes place in Sabinas Hidalgo, Nuevo León.	
May 15–17: The National Organization of Democratic Students (CNED) organizes its first conference in Morelia.	
August: Special forces of the police raid the Student House of Baja California in Mexico City and beat up students.	**November:** John F. Kennedy is assassinated, and Lyndon B. Johnson becomes U.S. president (1963–69).

NATIONAL	INTERNATIONAL
1964	

NATIONAL	INTERNATIONAL
Gustavo Díaz Ordaz (1964–70) is elected president.	Military coups take place in Bolivia and Brazil.
Fernando Gutiérrez Barrios is named director of the DFS (1964–70).	The Christian Democrat Eduardo Frei Montalva is elected president of Chile.

NATIONAL	INTERNATIONAL

1964 (*continued*)

Land invasions and protests in Chihuahua lead to the arrests of dozens of students, *normalistas*, and teachers.	The Bracero Program ends.
	Herbert Marcuse publishes *One Dimensional Man*. It appears in Spanish the next year as *El hombre unidimensional*.
Rural and urban uprisings grow in Morelia, Puebla, Nuevo León, Durango, Tabasco, Sinaloa, Sonora, Chihuahua, and Guerrero.	The Beatles appear on television in the United States.
In Puebla, the reaction to the student protest is particularly violent.	Quino starts publishing *Mafalda*.
	The Palestine Liberation Organization is founded.
José Agustín publishes his first countercultural book, *La tumba*. Two years later he publishes *De perfil*.	**January:** Panamanian students riot in the Canal Zone and protest against U.S. imperialism.
1964–65: Thousands of medical students lead a massive student protest in Mexico City.	**March–June:** First meeting of the United Nations Conference on Trade and Development (UNCTAD) is held in Geneva, Switzerland.
	October 5–10: A second meeting of NAM is held in Cairo, Egypt.

1965

Iván Illich creates the International Documentation Center (CIDOC) in Cuernavaca.	United Farm Workers lead a national grape boycott in the United States.
Rius starts publishing *Los Supermachos*.	The term *hippie* starts to be used in San Francisco, California, and will be broadly employed across the world two years later.
Pablo González Casanova publishes *La democracia en México*.	
Gustavo Sainz publishes *Gazapo* and with José Agustín and Parménides García Saldaña begins the literature of "la Onda."	
The PCM starts publishing the journal *Historia y Sociedad*.	

NATIONAL	INTERNATIONAL

1965 (*continued*)

1965–66: The Mexican Federation of Campesino Socialist Students (FECSM) joins CNED.

February: Students protest in Guerrero against the reelection of the governor.

February 21: Malcolm X is assassinated.

March: Ché Guevara publishes "Socialism and Man in Cuba."

April: FECSM leads a five-week-long strike that includes the participation of all of the ENRs.

April: U.S. Marines land in the Dominican Republic, and Ché Guevara leaves Cuba, first going to the Congo and then to Bolivia.

April–August: Student protests are led in Mexico City against the U.S. invasions in the Dominican Republic and Vietnam.

August: The Voting Rights Act ends discrimination at the U.S. polls.

August: Students protest in Villahermosa and Xalapa.

August 11–16: The Watts Race Riots leave more than thirty people dead in Los Angeles.

September 23: A teacher-campesino alliance assaults the military barracks of Ciudad Madera in Chihuahua. Despite its failure, this event marks a watershed moment in the rise of militancy and state repression in Mexico.

October: Massive protests against the U.S. war in Vietnam strengthen the growing Free Speech Movement.

DFS agent Miguel Nazar Haro creates the Special Investigations Group C-047, a precursor to the infamous White Brigade, a repressive force largely responsible for the violence in rural Mexico during the 1970s.

December: The Second Vatican Council approves *Gaudium et spes* (joy and hope) as the Pastoral Constitution on the Church in the Modern World. The document expresses optimism about the possibilities for collaboration between the Catholic Church and non-Catholics in the common interest of humanity.

NATIONAL	INTERNATIONAL

1966

1966–67: The year 1966 marks a crucial year in the broader history of the student movement in Mexico. Student uprisings and state repression take place in various parts of the country.

Repression is particularly violent in Morelia, Sonora, and Chihuahua, but also in Mexico City, Chilpancingo, Yucatán, Durango, Guerrero, Tabasco, Monterrey, Tampico, Poza Rica, San Luis Potosí, Sinaloa, Puebla, and Chapingo.

The influential student strike in Michoacán is crushed with the military takeover of Universidad Nicolaíta. Military troops are also used to crush student activism in Sonora and Ciudad Juárez.

The Mexican Communist Youth (JCM) grows in numbers and in importance and so do new more independent leftist student organizations such as the Liga Obrero Estudiantil, the Alianza de Izquierda Revolucionaria de Economia, and many others.

Like its Latin American counterparts, Catholic student organizations start to adopt more progressive forms of activism including the "See, Judge, Act" method.

Members of the Revolutionary Action Movement (MAR) go to North Korea for military training.

Journalist Mario Menéndez travels to Guatemala, Cuba, Venezuela, and Colombia, and in *Sucesos para todos* starts writing about the shared experience of the Latin American guerrilla movements.

The Great Proletarian Cultural Revolution starts in China.

The "Argentine Revolution" marks the first wave of the military dictatorship.

Tensions grow in Brazil between students and the military government.

The film *Battle of Algiers* is released and is widely seen by the militant left, reactionary forces, and institutions of repression.

NATIONAL	INTERNATIONAL
1968 (*continued*)	

Rius publishes *Cuba para principiantes* and the book is soon translated into various languages.

The number of political prisoners grows, including activists of the medical student strike, journalist Víctor Rico Galán, and the Trotskyite leader Adolfo Gilly.

March: Thousands of students protest in Mexico City against the war in Vietnam.

April: Student take over the main building at UNAM and hold the rector, Ignacio Chávez, hostage until he is forced to resign.

May: The army intervenes in a student protest in Sonora.

June: Students decapitate the statue of Miguel Alemán inside UNAM with dynamite.

January: Havana hosts the Tricontinental Congress to organize a united front of liberation across Africa, Asia, and Latin America.

February 15: The Colombian priest Camilo Torres is killed after joining the National Liberation Army guerrilla organization.

July: The government of Juan Carlos Onganía sends the military to take over the universities in Argentina.

July–August: The Fourth Latin American Student Congress is held in Havana to promote the "anti-imperialist unity of all Latin American students." The meeting leads to the strengthening of the Continental Organization of Latin American Students.

September: The militant journal *Cristianismo y Revolución* publishes its first edition in Argentina.

October: The Black Panther Party is founded in the United States.

November: The campesino leader Genaro Vázquez Rojas is arrested in Mexico City.

NATIONAL	INTERNATIONAL
1967	

The Western Anticommunist Mexican Front is founded. Soon after it starts its far right-wing publication, *Réplica*.

Alejandro Jodorowsky starts publishing "Las fábulas pánicas" in *El Heraldo de México* and releases his first countercultural film, *Fando y Lis*; a year later, a riot takes place in response to the film during the Acapulco Film Festival.

February–May: Dozens of students are beaten and arrested in Hermosillo. Campesino leader Ramón Danzós Palomino is arrested.

May: A massacre in Atoyac further pushes Lucio Cabañas to armed struggle.

May–July: A student strike at the Agricultural School Hermanos Escobar in Ciudad Juárez, Chihuahua, receives wide support from the popular sectors and like the events in Morelia becomes a key point of influential reference to the larger Mexican student movement.

June: The PCM organizes its Fifteenth Congress, calls for a "popular-democratic and anti-imperialist struggle," and articulates many of the demands that would be included in the 1968 *pliego petitorio*, including freedom for all political prisoners, the disbanding of the riot police, and the repeal of social dissolution.

The World Anticommunist League (WACL) is created.

Gabriel García Márquez publishes *One Hundred Years of Solitude*.

André Gunder Frank publishes *Capitalism and Underdevelopment*, where he criticizes the reformist dependency theories hitherto championed by the Economic Commission for Latin America and the Caribbean and initiates a more revolutionary-oriented dependency analysis.

Régis Debray publishes *Révolution dans la révolution? et autres essais* and it is soon translated into various languages.

Brazilian students organize various anti-American protests and further strengthen their movement.

March 26: Pope Paul VI announces *Populorum progressio* ("on the development of peoples"). The encyclical starts carrying out the vision of Vatican II by stressing the importance of human dignity, dialogue, and solidarity.

April: Ché Guevara's "Message to the Tricontinental," where he calls for "one, two, many Vietnams," is widely circulated.

The "Summer of Love" marks the peak of the countercultural movement in the United States.

NATIONAL	INTERNATIONAL
1967 (*continued*)	

NATIONAL	INTERNATIONAL
September–October: Student strikes recur in Sinaloa and Morelia.	**August**: The "Mensaje de 18 Obispos del Tercer Mundo" (message of eighteen bishops of the Third World) gives rise to the Movement of Priests for the Third World in Argentina and calls for dialogue between Catholics and Marxists.
December: *Política* publishes its last edition.	**October 9**: Ernesto "Ché" Guevara is killed in action in Bolivia with the help of the CIA.

1968	
The Maoist pamphlet *Hacia una política popular* (towards a popular policy) is published.	Carlos Castañeda publishes *The Teachings of Don Juan: A Yaqui Way of Knowledge*. It is translated to Spanish in 1974 as *Las enseñanzas de Don Juan*.
Mario Menéndez starts publishing *Por qué?*	
University students rename the auditorium of UNAM from "Justo Sierra" to "Ché Guevara."	**January–April**: Violent student clashes with the police take place in Belgium, Italy, England, Spain, Germany, Venezuela, and Colombia. Newspapers and magazines across the world publish articles on the rising phenomenon of "Youth Power."
Parménides García Saldaña publishes the countercultural book *Pasto Verde*.	
February: Through their role in the CNED, *normalistas rurales* participate in the Marcha por la Ruta de la Libertad, members of the JCM are arrested, and the Batallón Olimpia is created.	**March**: Brazilian and Uruguayan students initiate massive protest movements.
	March: Chicanx high school students in five East Los Angeles schools walk out to protest racism.
April: A guerrilla commando breaks into a prison in Iguala and liberates Genaro Vázquez Rojas.	
	April 4: Martin Luther King, Jr., is assassinated.

NATIONAL	INTERNATIONAL

1968 (*continued*)

April: A musical festival is held in Mexico City in solidarity with the people of Vietnam.

May: Students join forces with workers in France and launch the world's largest student protest.

June: State repression escalates in Uruguay after President Jorge Pacheco Areco announces his "Prompt Security Measures."

July: The police occupies the offices of the PCM, CNED, and the leftist newspaper *La Voz de México*. The student movement grows in Mexico City with the increasing presence of the military, and clashes between students and the police take place in Villahermosa. In Mexico City, the first student killings are reported in the school newspapers.

August: Massive protests are organized in defense of the autonomy of the university as the student movement reaches its most successful phase in Mexico City.

August: The Soviet Union invades Czechoslovakia and further legitimizes the Prague Spring.

August 26–September 8: The Conference of Latin American Bishops takes place in Medellín, Colombia, where the preferential option for the poor is emphasized.

September 14: Five young people are lynched in San Miguel Canoa, Puebla.

September 18–23: Diáz Ordaz orders the military occupation of UNAM and IPN in Mexico City.

October 2: An undetermined number of people are killed during the Tlatelolco massacre.

October 12: Mexico City hosts the Olympics.

November–December: Violent clashes take place between students and the police in Berlin, Tokyo, Brussels, and San Francisco.

December: A new wave of student uprisings takes place in San Luis Potosí and Sinaloa. In Mexico City, the National Strike Council (CNH) is dissolved and the Coordinating Commission of Committees of Struggle (COCO) is formed.

NATIONAL	INTERNATIONAL

1969

January: The cartoonist Rius is kidnapped and taken to a military base where he was told he would be executed.

June 4: Reformist PRI candidate Carlos Madrazo is killed.

July: The government announces the closure of fourteen ENRs, students are beaten and arrested, and the FECSM loses half of its membership. Students protest until September and many start taking a more radical path.

October 30: Octavio Paz, who a year earlier had stepped down as ambassador to India to protest the Tlatelolco massacre, delivers a lecture at the University of Texas at Austin where he denounces the brutality of the state during the 1968 massacre. The lecture is published a year later as "postdata" in his *Labyrinth of Solitude*.

December: The Bishop Sergio Méndez Arceo of Cuernavaca visits political prisoners in Lecumberri who had declared a hunger strike.

Carlos Marighella publishes the *Minimanual of the Urban Guerrilla*.

February: Violent student protests begin to spread across the United States.

May: Students and workers join forces to protest the administration of Ongonía during the Cordobazo in Argentina.

July: Apollo 11 lands on the moon.

August 15–17: The Woodstock festival is organized in New York.

September: President Richard Nixon orders "Operation Intercept," the opening phase of the modern U.S.-Mexico War on Drugs.

1970

Luis Echeverría Álvarez (1970–76) is elected president.

Luis de la Barreda Moreno is named the director of the DFS (1970–77).

The socialist Salvador Allende is elected president of Chile.

U.S. President Nixon extends the Vietnam War to Cambodia.

NATIONAL	INTERNATIONAL
1970 (*continued*)	

Unarmed peasant mobilizations for land and justice occur in nearly all states in Mexico from 1970–75.	Paulo Freire's *Pedagogy of the Oppressed* is published.
Mexico hosts the FIFA World Cup and Díaz Ordaz is booed during the inauguration.	The Tupamaros grow in numbers in Uruguay and emerge as one of the most influential urban guerrilla movements in Latin America.
January: Political prisoners are beaten in Lecumberri, and José Revueltas sends a letter to Arthur Miller documenting the repression of political prisoners.	A group of approximately 200 Chicanxs travel to Mexico City and meet with young Mexican activists.
April: Students are arrested in Torreón.	
September 23: Students take over the Casa del Estudiante in Guadalajara.	**August 29**: Chicano Moratorium March Against the War in Vietnam occurs in Los Angeles.
October 19: Lázaro Cárdenas dies.	
October: The PCM organizes its Sixteenth Congress and redefines its struggle as "Democratic" and "Socialist."	
November 23: Iconic leader of the Vikingos Arnulfo Prado Rosas ("El Compa") is murdered.	

1971	
Los Tecos (the right-wing organization from Guadalajara) plays a leading role in the creation of the Latin American Anticommunist Confederation (CAL).	Gustavo Gutiérrez publishes *A Theology of Liberation*.
José Porfirio Miranda de la Parra publishes *Marx y la Biblia: Crítica a la filosofía de la opresión*.	With the support of the CIA, the Belgian Roger Vekemans starts publishing *Tierra Nueva* in reaction to the rise of Liberation Theology.
Elena Poniatowska publishes *La noche de Tlatelolco*.	The Pentagon Papers are published in the *New York Times*.

NATIONAL	INTERNATIONAL

1971 (*continued*)

Women in Solidarity Action (MAS) is founded as one of the leading organizations representing the second wave of Mexico's feminist movement.

The Front of Homosexual Liberation (FLH) is founded by Nancy Cárdenas. Two years later she appears as an openly lesbian woman on national television.

May: Heberto Castillo and José Revueltas are released from prison.

May 15: *Piedra Rodante* publishes its first issue and the government shuts it down the next year.

June 10: Dozens of students are killed during the Corpus Christi massacre.

September 11–12: The Avándaro Rock Festival is organized in the Valle de Bravo del Estado de México.

March 8: Antiwar activists break into an FBI office in Pennsylvania, steal classified documents, and publicly expose the FBI's counterintelligence program (COINTELPRO).

April–May: The Third Meeting of United Nations Conference on Trade and Development (UNCTAD-III) is held in Santiago, Chile, at which President Luis Echeverría calls for the creation of a "New International Economic Order."

June: The Turkish government implements a ban on the legal growing of opium, thereby cutting off the raw source of heroin for European traffickers who had dominated the drug market in the United States.

November: Fidel Castro visits Cuba and meets with Salvador Allende and members of the Christians for Socialism movement.

1972

Mexico City hosts the annual assembly of the WACL.

A group of MURO members create the Ibero-American Unified Guard (GUIA).

January: The leftist magazine *Punto Crítico* publishes its first issue.

April: A national student forum is organized in Mexico City to debate the option of armed struggle. Criticizing the reformist politics of many on the left, the most radical students argued, "We do not want a democratic opening. What we demand is Revolution."

April 23–30: The First Encounter of Christians for Socialism is held in Santiago, Chile. Sergio Méndez Arceo is one of the leading participants.

June 15: U.S. President Richard Nixon meets with Luis Echeverría. Days later the Mexican president meets with Chicanx activists in San Antonio, Texas, where he denies the existence of political prisoners.

July: A group of young Chicanxs travels to Mexico City to visit political prisoners. A few days later they publish the Carta de Lecumberri as a gesture of solidarity.

NATIONAL	INTERNATIONAL

1972 (*continued*)

1972–74: Large student protests are violently repressed in Mexico City, Sinaloa, Puebla, Colima, Guerrero, Chihuahua, Oaxaca, Zacatecas, Morelos, and Yucatán.

November: Adolfo López Trujillo is elected general secretary of CELAM (until 1984), and with Vekemans, he launches a counteroffensive against liberation theology.

December 2: Allende delivers speech at the University of Guadalajara.

1973

March 15: The 23rd of September Communist League (LC23S) is officially founded in Guadalajara. The founding members publish various influential documents that are read widely across Mexico, including the *Madera* pamphlets and the *Tésis sobre la Universidad Fábrica*.

April 24: The military massacres six campesinos in Los Piloncillos, Guerrero, inaugurating the most violent phase of the Mexican Dirty War.

September 17: Industrialist Eugenio Garza Sada is killed by members of the LC23S.

The Worker-Peasant Coalition of the Isthmus in Juchitán, Oaxaca, is established and attracts a large cross-class following.

1973–75: Echeverría significantly expands social and economic programs under his "Shared Development" strategy. Public spending increases, new universities and public housing programs are created, and IMSS, CONASUPO, and land reforms programs are expanded

The Argentina Anticommunist Alliance is founded.

March 29: The U.S. war officially ends in Vietnam.

September 11: The CIA orchestrates a military coup in Chile and overthrows Allende.

October: The economic crisis begins when key members of the Organization of Arab Petroleum Exporting Countries proclaim an oil embargo.

NATIONAL	INTERNATIONAL
1974	
The First Indigenous Congress is held in San Cristóbal de las Casas, Chiapas.	Juan Domingo Perón returns to the presidency in Argentina.
The Left starts publishing the journal *Cuadernos Políticos* (1974–90).	U.S. President Richard Nixon resigns.
The economy starts plummeting. By 1976, the nation reports 27 percent inflation.	
January 16: The "Oscar González" Guerrilla Commando kidnaps prominent Sonoran cattleman Hermenegildo Sáenz Cano.	
January 16: Los Enfermos carry out the operation "Assault to Heaven" in which they mobilize hundreds of peasants, workers, and students in Culiacán, Sinaloa.	
February: President Echeverría meets with Pope Paul VI at the Vatican.	
December 2: Lucio Cabañas is killed in a shootout with the army and state repression further intensifies in Guerrero.	**December**: The United Nations General Assembly adopts the Charter of Economic Rights and Duties of States, successfully proposed by Mexican officials.
1975	
Vast oil reserves are discovered in southern Mexico.	Right-wing leaders in Argentina, Bolivia, Chile, Paraguay, and Uruguay establish Operation Condor. Brazil, Ecuador, and Peru join soon after.
Nancy Cárdenas, leading founder of the FLH, publishes the First Homosexual Manifesto in *Siempre!* with Carlos Monsiváis and Luis Gonzáles de Alba.	Philip Agee publishes *Inside the Company: CIA Diary*, documenting his work inside the CIA and revealing the CIA's extensive network in Latin American including with the LITEMPO program in Mexico where high level government figures, including Díaz Ordaz and Echeverría, collaborated with the CIA.

NATIONAL	INTERNATIONAL

1975 (*continued*)

March: President Echeverría visits UNAM, but students throw stones at him, force him to leave the campus, and identify him as the main person responsible for the 1968 and 1971 student massacres.

April: Jesús Piedra Ibarra, son of Rosario Ibarra de Piedra, is arrested and disappears in Monterrey.

June 19–July 2: Mexico City hosts the World Conference on Women.

October 23: The Federal Judicial Police and the military slaughter a group of peasants in Sonora. The climate of confrontation prompts the Echeverría administration to expropriate large estates in the Yaqui and Mayo Valleys and distribute land.

1975–76: The military junta takes over Argentina and the Dirty War officially begins (and lasts until 1983).

November 20: Fascist dictator Francisco Franco, who had ruled Spain since 1939, dies.

1976

José López Portillo is elected president (1976–82) and moves away from the populist policies of Echeverría.

Lecumberri Prison is closed.

The government cracks down on *Excélsior*. In response, Julio Scherer and others create the influential magazine *Proceso* the following year.

October: The Nueva Cultura Feminista starts publishing the journal *Fem*.

1976–1978: Family members of *desaparecidos* (disappeared persons) start organizing and reach out to human rights organizations for support.

NATIONAL	INTERNATIONAL
1977	

Javier García Paniagua is named the director of the DFS (1977–78).

The military takes over the Autonomous University of Benito Juarez of Oaxaca (UABJO).

Díaz Ordaz is named the Mexican ambassador to Spain. Students and intellectuals protest across the nation and demand the demilitarization of the UABJO.

The General Coordination of the Plan for Depressed Zones and Marginal Groups is established as a large umbrella for coordinating all social programs aimed and rural and marginalized communities.

The Trotskyite magazine *Coyoacán* is founded.

1978	

Miguel Nazar Haro is named the director of the DFS (1978–82).

The magazine *Nexos* is founded.

An amnesty law is passed that legalizes left-wing political parties and grants liberty to political prisoners, including many who joined the guerrilla movements.

Mexico City hosts one of the first gay pride parades in Latin America.

Arturo Ripstein releases the film *El lugar sin límites*, in which homophobia is a central theme.

John Paul II becomes the pope and the Vatican clamps down on the Marxist influence on the Latin American church.

NATIONAL	INTERNATIONAL

1979

John Paul II gives the opening speech at the Third CELAM Conference in Puebla where he criticizes the radical elements of liberation theology.

The Nicaraguan Revolution triumphs.

The Shah is overthrown in Iran.

Luis Zapata publishes *Las aventuras, desventuras, y sueños de Adonis García, el vampiro de la Colonia Roma*, where the author draws inspiration from the literature of la Onda to describe Mexico's homoerotic culture.

July 15: Gustavo Díaz Ordaz dies.

1980

The National Archives (AGN) opens in what used to be the Lecumberri prison.

The Mexican Food System (SAM) is created to reestablish Mexico's food self-sufficiency and to stimulate peasant agriculture.

ABBREVIATIONS

ACM	Acción Católica Mexicana (Mexican Catholic Action)
ACG	Asociación Cívica Guerrerense (Civic Association of Guerrero)
ACNR	Asociación Cívica Nacional Revolucionaria (National Revolutionary Civic Association)
AGN	Archivo General de la Nación (National Archives)
CCI	Central Campesina Independiente (Independent Peasant Organization)
CCI	Centro Coordinador Indigenista (Indigenist Coordinating Center)
CELAM	Latin American Episcopal Council
CGOG	Comando Guerrillero "Oscar González" ("Oscar González" Guerrilla Commando)
CIDOC	Centro Intercultural de Documentación (International Documentation Center)
CIHMA	Centro de Investigaciones Históricas de los Movimientos Armados (Center of Historical Research of Armed Movements)
CJ	Conciencia Joven (Youth Conscience)
CJM	Confederación de Jóvenes Mexicanos (Confederation of Mexican Youth)

CNC	Confederación Nacional Campesina (National Peasant Confederation)
CNDH	Comisión Nacional para los Derechos Humanos de México (National Commission for Human Rights)
CNED	Central Nacional de Estudiantes Democráticos (National Organization of Democratic Students)
CNH	Consejo Nacional de Huelga (National Strike Council)
CNP	Consejo Nacional Permanente (Permanent National Council)
COCO	Comisión Coordinadora de Comités de Lucha or Comité Coordinador de Comités de Lucha (Coordinating Commission of Committees of Struggle)
COLIMA	Coordinadora Línea de Masas (Coordinating Line of the Masses)
CONAMUP	Coordinadora Nacional de Movimientos Urbanos Populares (National Coordinator of the Urban Popular Movement)
CONASUPO	Compañía Nacional de Subsistencias Populares (National Basic Foods Company)
CPMAG	Comité Politico-Militar "Arturo Gámiz" ("Arturo Gámiz" Political-Military Committee)
CRAC	Cruzada Regional Anti-Comunista (Regional Anti-Communist Crusade)
CTM	Confederación de Trabajadores Mexicanos (Confederation of Mexican Workers)
CU	Ciudad Universitaria (University City)
DFS	Dirección Federal de Seguridad (Federal Security Directorate)
DGIPS	Dirección General de Investigaciones Políticas y Sociales (General Directorate of Political and Social Investigations)
ENACH	Escuela Nacional de Agricultura de Chapingo (Chapingo National School of Agriculture)
ENM	Escuela Nacional de Maestros (National Teacher's College)
ENR	Escuelas Normales Rurales (Rural Teacher-Training Colleges)

EZLN	Ejército Zapatista de Liberación Nacional (Zapatista National Liberation Army)
FECSM	Federación de Estudiantes Campesinos Socialistas de México (Mexican Federation of Campesino Socialist Students)
FEG	Federación Estudiantil de Guadalajara (Federation of Students from Guadalajara)
FEMOSPP	Fiscalía Especial para Movimientos Sociales y Políticos del Pasado (Special Prosecutors Office for Social and Political Movements of the Past)
FEP	Frente Electoral del Pueblo (People's Electoral Front)
FER	Frente Estudiantil Revolucionario (Student Revolutionary Front)
FESO	Frente de Estudiantes Socialistas de Occidente (Eastern Front of Socialist Students)
FLH	Frente de Liberación Homosexual (Front of Homosexual Liberation)
FNET	Frente Nacional de Estudiantes Técnicos (National Front of Technical Students)
FRAP	Fuerzas Revolucionarias Armadas del Pueblo (People's Armed Revolutionary Forces)
FUA	Frente Universitario Anticomunista (University Anticommunist Front)
G23S	Grupo 23 de Septiembre (23rd of September Group)
GCI	Grupo Comunista Internacionalista (Communist Internationalist Group)
GPG	Grupo Popular Guerrillero (Popular Guerrilla Group)
GPGAG	Grupo Popular Guerrillero "Arturo Gámiz" (Popular Guerrilla Group "Arturo Gámiz")
INI	Instituto Nacional Indigenista (National Indigenous Institute)
IPN	Instituto Politécnico Nacional (National Polytechnic Institute)
JCM	Juventud Comunista de México (Communist Youth of Mexico)

LC23S	Liga Comunista 23 de Septiembre (23rd of September Communist League)
LCE	Liga Comunista Espartaco (Spartacus Communist League)
LLE	Liga Leninista Espartaco (Spartacus Leninist League)
M23S	Movimiento 23 de Septiembre (23rd of September Movement)
MAR	Movimiento Armado Revolucionario (Revolutionary Action Movement)
MAS	Mujeres de Acción Solidaria (Women in Solidarity Action)
MEP	Movimiento Estudiantil Profesional (Professional Student Movement)
MFC	Movimiento Familiar Cristiano (Christian Family Movement)
MLN	Movimiento de Liberación Nacional (National Liberation Movement)
MMLM	Movimiento Marxista-Leninista de México (Marxist Leninist Movement of Mexico)
MURO	Movimiento Universitario de Renovadora Orientación (University Movement for a Renewed Orientation)
OP	Organización Partidaria (Pro-Party Organization)
PAN	Partido de Acción Nacional (National Action Party)
PCM	Partido Comunista Mexicano (Mexican Communist Party)
PDLP	Partido de los Pobres (Party of the Poor)
PEDIR	Programa de Inversiones en el Desarrollo Rural (Rural Development Investment Program)
PNR	Partido Nacional Revolucionario (National Revolutionary Party)
PORT	Partido Obrero Revolucionario Trotskista (Revolutionary Workers Party Trotskyist)
PP	Partido Popular (Popular Party)
PP	Política Popular (Popular Politics)
PPS	Partido Popular Socialista (Popular Socialist Party)
PRI	Partido Revolucionario Institucional (Institutional Revolutionary Party)
PSUM	Partido Socialista Unificado de México (Unified Socialist Party of Mexico)

SAM	Sistema Alimentario Mexicano (Mexican Food System)
SDN	Secretaría de la Defensa Nacional (Secretariat of National Defense)
SEP	Secretaría de Educación Pública (Ministry of Public Education)
SNTMMSRM	Sindicato Nacional de Trabajadores Minero-Metalúrgicos y Similares de la República Mexicana (National Mining Metallurgical and Similar Activities Union of the Mexican Republic)
SSM	Secretariado Social Mexicano (Social Secretariat of Mexico)
Tec, El	Instituto Tecnológico de Monterrey (Monterrey Techno-logical Institute)
UABJO	Universidad Autónoma Benito Juárez de Oaxaca (Autono-mous University Benito Juárez of Oaxaca)
UANL	Universidad Autónoma de Nuevo León (Autonomous University of Nuevo León)
UAP	Universidad Autónoma de Puebla (Autonomous University of Puebla)
UAS	Universidad Autónoma de Sinaloa (Autonomous University of Sinaloa)
UG	Universidad de Guadalajara (University of Guadalajara)
UGOCM	Unión General de Obreros y Campesinos de México (Gen-eral Union of Mexican Workers and Peasants)
UIA	Universidad Iberoamericana (Ibero-American University)
UNAM	Universidad Nacional Autónoma de México (National Autonomous University of Mexico)
UNPF	Unión Nacional de Padres de Familia (National Union of Parents)
UNS	Unión Nacional Sinarquista (National Synarchist Union)

CONTRIBUTORS

Alexander Aviña is a historian of modern Mexico and Latin America in the School of Historical, Philosophical, and Religious Studies at Arizona State University. He is the author of *Specters of Revolution: Peasant Guerrillas in the Cold War Mexican Countryside* (2014).

Adela Cedillo is a PhD candidate in Latin American history at the University of Wisconsin-Madison. She received her BA in history and MA in Latin American studies at the National Autonomous University of Mexico (UNAM). She has published book chapters and articles on twentieth-century revolutionary movements and the Dirty War in Mexico. She is the co-editor of *Challenging Authoritarianism in Mexico: Revolutionary Struggles and the Dirty War, 1964–1982* (2012).

A. S. Dillingham is an assistant professor of history at Spring Hill College, in Mobile, Alabama. He is the author of "Indigenismo Occupied: Indigenous Youth and Mexico's Democratic Opening (1968–1975)," awarded the Antonine Tibesar Prize for Most Distinguished Article Published in *The Americas* (2016).

Luis Herrán Avila is a visiting assistant professor of history at Carleton College. He holds a PhD in politics and historical studies from The New School for Social Research. His work focuses on the intellectual and political history of the extreme right in Cold War Latin America. His book manuscript examines the national and transnational dimensions of Latin American anticommunism, particularly of neofascist and conservative Catholic movements during the "Long Sixties."

Fernando Herrera Calderón is an assistant professor of history at the University of Northern Iowa and specializes in modern Mexican history, political violence, student radicalism, memory, and human rights. He is the co-editor with Adela Cedillo of *Challenging Authoritarianism in Mexico: Revolutionary Struggles and the Dirty War, 1964–1982* (2011) and is currently working on his book manuscript titled "Laboratories of Dissent: The University, Student Power, and the Urban Guerrilla Experience in Mexico During the Dirty War, 1970–1982."

Gladys I. McCormick is an associate professor of history and the Jay and Debe Moskowitz Chair in Mexico-U.S. Relations at the Maxwell School of Citizenship and Public Affairs of Syracuse University. Her research interests include corruption, drug trafficking, and political violence in Latin America and especially Mexico. She is the author of *The Logic of Compromise in Post-Revolutionary Mexico: How the Countryside Was Key to the Emergence of Authoritarianism* (2016).

Enrique C. Ochoa is a professor of Latin American studies and history at California State University, Los Angeles. His publications include *Feeding Mexico: The Political Uses of Food Since 1910* (2000), *Latino Los Angeles: Transformations, Communities, and Activism* (2005), and special journal editions on Mexican political economy, history and critical pedagogies, and migration.

Verónica Oikión Solano is professor and researcher at the Centro de Estudios Históricos of El Colegio de Michoacán. She is the author of numerous articles and is co-editor of various volumes, including *Movimientos armados en México, siglo XX*, Vol. 3 (2006–2008) and *El estudio de las luchas revolucionarias en América Latina (1959–1996): Estado de la cuestión* (2014).

Tanalís Padilla is an associate professor of history at the Massachusetts Institute of Technology. She is the author of *Rural Resistance in the Land of Zapata: The Jaramillista Movement and the Myth of the Pax-priísta, 1940–1962* (2008) and is completing a book manuscript entitled "The Unintended Lessons of Revolution: Teachers and the Mexican Countryside, 1940–1980" on the history of Mexico's normales rurales.

Wil G. Pansters is a professor at the Department of Cultural Anthropology at Utrecht University, as well as professor of Latin American studies at the University of Groningen, where he also directs the Centro de Estudios Mexicanos. He is the author of *Política y poder en Puebla: Formación y ocaso del cacicazgo avilacamachista, 1937–1987* (1998), editor of *Violence, Coercion, and State-Making in Twentieth Century Mexico: The Other Half of the Centaur* (2012), and co-editor of *Caciquismo in Twentieth Century Mexico* (2006) and *Beyond the Drug War in Mexico, Human Rights, the Public Sphere and Justice* (2017).

Jaime M. Pensado is an associate professor of history at the University of Notre Dame. He is the author of *Rebel Mexico: Student Unrest and Authoritarian Political Culture During the Long Sixties* (2013) and is currently writing a book manuscript titled "Catholic Youth in Cold War Mexico."

Gema Santamaría is an assistant professor of Latin American history at Loyola University Chicago and a visiting fellow at the Kellogg Institute for International Studies at the University of Notre Dame (2017–2018). She is the co-editor with David Carey, Jr., of *Violence and Crime in Latin America: Representations and Politics* (2017). Her research focuses on violence and vigilante justice in twentieth-century Mexico.

Michael Soldatenko is professor of Chicana(o) and Latina(o) Studies at California State University, Los Angeles. He is the author of *Chicano Studies: The Genesis of a Discipline* (2009).

Carla Irina Villanueva is a doctoral candidate in history at the University of Notre Dame. She is currently working on her dissertation, "Normalistas Rurales and the Politics of Education in Peripheral Mexico During the Global Sixties."

Eric Zolov is an associate professor at Stony Brook University and former senior editor of *The Americas*. He is the author of *Refried Elvis: The Rise of the Mexican Counterculture* (1999) and has edited numerous collections, most recently *Iconic Mexico: An Encyclopedia from Acapulco to Zócalo* (2015). His forthcoming book, *The Last Good Neighbor: Mexico in the Global Sixties*, will be published by Duke University Press.

INDEX

Unión del Pueblo (The People's Union), 185, 186–87, 189n21, 191n54

Unión de Uniones Ejidales y Grupos Campesinos Solidarios de Chiapas (Union of Ejidal Unions and Peasant Groups of Chiapas), 185, 191n55

Unión General de Obreros y Campesinos de México (General Union of Mexican Workers and Peasants). *See* UGOCM

Unión Nacional de Padres de Familia (National Union of Parents, UNPF), 199–200

Unión Nacional Sinarquista (National Synarchist Union, UNS), 197

Unión Reivindicadora Obrero Campesina (Worker-Peasant Vindicating Union), 178, 189n10

unions. *See* company unions; labor unions; *and individual unions by name*

United Nations Charter of Economic Rights and Duties of States, 116, 316

Universidad Autónoma de Guadalajara (Autonomous University of Guadalajara, UAG), 200

Universidad Autónoma de Nuevo León (Autonomous University of Nuevo León, UANL), 249

Universidad Autónoma de Puebla (Autonomous University of Puebla). *See* UAP

Universidad Autónoma de Sinaloa (Autonomous University of Sinaloa, UAS), 266

Universidad Autónoma de Tamaulipas (Autonomous University of Tamaulipas, UAT), xi

Universidad de Guadalajara (University of Guadalajara). *See* UG

Universidad Iberoamericana (Ibero-American University, UIA), 236

Universidad Michoacana de San Nicolás de Hidalgo (Michoacan University of St. Nicholas of Hidalgo), 79, 297

Universidad Nacional Autónoma de México (National Autonomous University of Mexico). *See* UNAM

urban guerrilla movement, 141, 155–57, 167, 168–69, 169–70n5, 254, 313. *See also* FER; Guadalajara; LC23S

Vallejo, Demetrio, 59, 79, 300

Vasconcelos, José, 12–13, 202, 212n47

Vázquez, Genaro, 57, 59, 139, 142, 308, 310

Velázquez, Fidel, 186, 282

Velázquez, Pedro, 221

Vietnam, 7, 97, 99, 309

Vietnam War, 80, 115, 117, 241, 303, 306, 308, 312, 313, 315

Vikingos, 157, 161–66, 168, 169, 170n28, 313

Villa, Francisco, 92, 274

Villalva, Enrique, 147

Villanueva García, Héctor Alejandro, xi

"War on Drugs." *See* Drug War

"White Brigade," DFS, 150n46, 260, 263, 306

Williams, Anthony Duncan, 155

women activists, 7, 63, 108n51, 229, 240n8, 314. *See also* gender

World Anti-Communist League (WACL), 27, 309, 314

Yaber, Amdéli, 124

Yáñez, Agustín, 85, 286n20

Yaqui Valley, 95, 99, 104, 317

Yucatán, 13n6, 307, 315

Zacatecas, 65, 184, 315

Zapata, Emiliano, 4, 92, 163, 169, 181–82, 274

Zapatistas, x, 126, 134–35, 186–87, 279. *See also* EZLN

Zuno, Andrés, 160–61, 163

Zuno, José Guadalupe, 157–58, 159, 161, 164